The Therapeutic Relationship

The therapeutic relationship has been recognized by psychotherapy researchers and clinicians alike as playing a central role in the process and outcome of psychotherapy. This book presents innovative investigations of the therapeutic relationship focusing on various relationship mechanisms as they relate to changing processes and outcomes. A variety of perspectives on the therapeutic relationship are provided through different research methods, including quantitative and qualitative methods, and divergence in psychotherapy orientations, including psychodynamic, interpersonal, cognitive-behavioural therapy, emotion-focused process experiential therapy, narrative therapy, and attachment-based family therapy.

The chapters, written by leading psychotherapy researchers, present cutting-edge empirical studies that apply innovative methods in order to: study process-outcome links; explore in session processes that address the question of how the therapeutic relationship heals; examine the contributions of clients and therapists to the therapeutic relationship; and suggest practical implications for training therapists in psychotherapy relationships that work. Research on the therapeutic relationship has been identified as a natural arena for bridging the gap between research and clinical practice. Thus, this book will be of particular interest to practicing clinicians.

This book was originally published as a special issue of *Psychotherapy Research.*

Hadas Wiseman is Associate Professor in Counseling and Human Development at the University of Haifa, Israel. Her research interests include therapeutic relationships and attachments and the development of psychotherapists. She is a clinical psychologist and Past President of the Society for Psychotherapy Research.

Orya Tishby is Senior Lecturer in Clinical psychology and clinical social work at Hebrew University, Jerusalem, Israel. Her research interests include therapeutic relationships, countertransference, and psychotherapy with adolescents. She is a clinical psychologist and supervisor.

The Therapeutic Relationship

Innovative investigations

Edited by
Hadas Wiseman and Orya Tishby

Routledge
Taylor & Francis Group
LONDON AND NEW YORK

First published 2015 by Routledge

2 Park Square, Milton Park, Abingdon, Oxon OX14 4RN
711 Third Avenue, New York, NY 10017, USA

Routledge is an imprint of the Taylor & Francis Group, an informa business

First issued in paperback 2017

British Library Cataloguing in Publication Data
A catalogue record for this book is available from the British Library

ISBN 13: 978-1-138-85750-6 (hbk)
ISBN 13: 978-1-138-06044-9 (pbk)

Typeset in Plantin
by RefineCatch Limited, Bungay, Suffolk

Publisher's Note
The publisher accepts responsibility for any inconsistencies that may have arisen during the conversion of this book from journal articles to book chapters, namely the possible inclusion of journal terminology.

To the *Society for Psychotherapy Research* for inspiring and advancing research on the therapeutic relationship and for facilitating and nurturing collaboration

Contents

Citation Information

The chapters in this book were originally published in *Psychotherapy Research*, volume 24, issue 3 (May 2014). When citing this material, please use the original page numbering for each article, as follows:

Chapter 1: Introduction
The therapeutic relationship: Multiple lenses and innovations
Hadas Wiseman & Orya Tishby
Psychotherapy Research, volume 24, issue 3 (May 2014) pp. 251–256

Chapter 2
Understanding processes of change: How some patients reveal more than others—and some groups of therapists less—about what matters in psychotherapy
Robert J. Derubeis, Lois A. Gelfand, Ramaris E. German, Jay C. Fournier, & Nicholas R. Forand
Psychotherapy Research, volume 24, issue 3 (May 2014) pp. 419–428

Chapter 3
The associations among improvement and alliance expectations, alliance during treatment, and treatment outcome for major depressive disorder
Jacques P. Barber, Sigal Zilcha-Mano, Robert Gallop, Marna Barrett, Kevin S. McCarthy, & Ulrike Dinger
Psychotherapy Research, volume 24, issue 3 (May 2014) pp. 257–268

Chapter 4
How does the therapeutic alliance develop throughout cognitive behavioral therapy for panic disorder? Sawtooth patterns, sudden gains, and stabilization
Michal Weiss, Yogev Kivity, & Jonathan D. Huppert
Psychotherapy Research, volume 24, issue 3 (May 2014) pp. 407–418

Chapter 5
The therapeutic relationship in action: How therapists and clients co-manage relational disaffiliation
Peter Muntigl & Adam O. Horvath
Psychotherapy Research, volume 24, issue 3 (May 2014) pp. 327–345

Chapter 6
Therapeutic collaboration and resistance: Describing the nature and quality of the therapeutic relationship within ambivalence events using the Therapeutic Collaboration Coding System
António P. Ribeiro, Eugenia Ribeiro, Joana Loura, Miguel M. Gonçalves, William B. Stiles, Adam O. Horvath, & Inês Sousa
Psychotherapy Research, volume 24, issue 3 (May 2014) pp. 346–359

Chapter 7
Investigating the impact of alliance-focused training on interpersonal process and therapists' capacity for experiential reflection
Jeremy Safran, J. Christopher Muran, Anthony Demaria, Catherine Boutwell, Catherine Eubanks-Carter, & Arnold Winston
Psychotherapy Research, volume 24, issue 3 (May 2014) pp. 269–285

Chapter 8
To be or not to be immediate with clients: The use and perceived effects of immediacy in psychodynamic/interpersonal psychotherapy
Clara E. Hill, Charles J. Gelso, Harold Chui, Patricia T. Spangler, Ann Hummel, Teresa Huang, John Jackson, Russell A. Jones, Beatriz Palma, Avantika Bhatia, Shudarshana Gupta, Stacie C. Ain, Beth Klingaman, Robert H. Lim, Jingqing Liu, Kayi Hui, Matthew M. Jezzi, & Joseph R. Miles
Psychotherapy Research, volume 24, issue 3 (May 2014) pp. 299–315

Chapter 9
The role of empathy in promoting change
Jeanne C. Watson, Patricia L. Steckley, & Evelyn J. McMullen
Psychotherapy Research, volume 24, issue 3 (May 2014) pp. 286–298

Chapter 10
Client attachment, attachment to the therapist and client-therapist attachment match: How do they relate to change in psychodynamic psychotherapy?
Hadas Wiseman & Orya Tishby
Psychotherapy Research, volume 24, issue 3 (May 2014) pp. 392–406

Chapter 11
Types of countertransference dynamics: An exploration of their impact on the client-therapist relationship
Orya Tishby & Hadas Wiseman
Psychotherapy Research, volume 24, issue 3 (May 2014) pp. 360–375

Chapter 12
Client disclosure and therapist response in psychotherapy with women with a history of childhood sexual abuse
Barry A. Farber, Sarah Feldman, & A. Jordan Wright
Psychotherapy Research, volume 24, issue 3 (May 2014) pp. 316–326

Chapter 13
Good versus poor therapeutic alliances with non-accepting parents of same-sex oriented adolescents and young adults: A qualitative study
Maya S. Shpigel & Gary M. Diamond
Psychotherapy Research, volume 24, issue 3 (May 2014) pp. 376–391

Please direct any queries you may have about the citations to
clsuk.permissions@cengage.com

Notes on Contributors

Stacie C. Ain is currently at the George Washington University Counseling Center, DC, USA.

Jacques P. Barber is Professor at the Derner Institute of Advanced Psychological Studies, Adelphi University, Garden City, NY, USA.

Marna Barrett is an Adjunct Associate Professor in the Department of Psychiatry at the University of Pennsylvania, Philadelphia, PA, USA.

Avantika Bhatia is based in the Psychology Department at the University of Maryland, College Park, MD, USA.

Catherine Boutwell is based at the Clinical Psychology Program, New School for Social Research, New York City, USA.

Harold Chui is currently at the Gordon F. Derner Institute of Advanced Psychological Studies, Adelphi University, Garden City, NY, USA

Anthony DeMaria is based at the Clinical Psychology Program, New School for Social Research, New York City, USA.

Robert J. DeRubeis is Professor in the Department of Psychology, University of Pennsylvania, Philadelphia, PA, USA.

Gary M. Diamond is a Professor in the Department of Psychology at Ben-Gurion University of the Negev, Beer-Sheva, Israel.

Ulrike Dinger is MD, PhD Researcher at the Clinic for General Internal Medicine and Psychosomatics at the University of Heidelberg, Germany.

Catherine Eubanks-Carter is Assistant Professor of Clinical Psychology, Ferkauf Graduate School of Psychology, Yeshiva University, New York City, USA.

Barry A. Farber is Professor in Counseling & Clinical Psychology at Teachers College, Columbia University, New York City, USA.

Sarah Feldman is a Psychologist at the Center for Motivation and Change, Berkshires, New Marlborough, MA, USA.

Nicholas R. Forand is Assistant Professor of Psychiatry and Behavioral Health in the Department of Psychiatry, Ohio State University, Wexner Medical Center, Columbus, OH, USA.

Jay C. Fournier is Assistant Professor of Psychiatry at the University of Pittsburgh, PA, USA.

Robert Gallop is Professor of Mathematics at West Chester University, West Chester, PA, USA.

Lois A. Gelfand is a Post-Doctoral Fellow in the Department of Psychology, University of Pennsylvania, Philadelphia, PA, USA.

Charles J. Gelso is Professor Emeritus in the Psychology Department at the University of Maryland, College Park, MD, USA.

Ramaris E. German is a Research Associate for the Aaron T. Beck Psychopathology Research Centre, Department of Psychiatry, University of Pennsylvania, Philadelphia, PA, USA.

Miguel M. Gonçalves is Professor of Psychology at the School of Psychology at the University of Minho, Braga, Portugal.

Shudarshana Gupta is based in the Psychology Department at the University of Maryland, College Park, MD, USA.

Clara E. Hill is a Professor in the Psychology Department at the University of Maryland, College Park, MD, USA.

Adam O. Horvath is Professor Emeritus in the Faculty of Education at Simon Fraser University, Burnaby, BC, Canada.

Teresa Huang is based in the Psychology Department at the University of Maryland, College Park, MD, USA.

Kayi Hui is currently at the Counseling and Consultation Service, Ohio State University, Columbus, OH, USA.

Ann Hummel is currently at the Naval Medical Center, San Diego, CA, USA.

Jonathan D. Huppert is Associate Professor in the Department of Psychology at the Hebrew University of Jerusalem, Israel.

John Jackson is based in the Psychology Department at the University of Maryland, College Park, MD, USA.

Matthew M. Jezzi is currently at the Trauma Services Program, Washington, D.C. Veterans Affairs Medical Center, Washington, DC, USA.

Russell A. Jones is currently at the Trauma Services Program, Washington, D.C. Veterans Affairs Medical Center, Washington, DC, USA.

Yogev Kivity is a Doctoral Student in the Department of Psychology at the Hebrew University of Jerusalem, Israel.

Beth Klingaman is currently at the Mental Illness Research, Education, and Clinical Center (MIRECC), VA Capitol Health Care Network (VISN 5), Baltimore, Maryland and Department of Psychiatry, University of Maryland School of Medicine, MD, USA.

Robert H. Lim is based in the College of Education at the University of Maryland, College Park, MD, USA.

Jingqing Liu is currently at University Counseling and Testing Center, University of Oregon, Eugene, OR, USA.

Joana Loura is a Master's student at the School of Psychology, at the University of Minho, Braga, Portugal.

Kevin S. McCarthy is Associate Professor of Psychology at Chestnut Hill College, Philadelphia, PA, USA.

Evelyn J. McMullan is a Post-Doctoral Fellow at the Department of Applied Psychology and Human Development, University of Toronto, Canada.

Joseph R. Miles is currently in the Department of Psychology at the University of Tennessee, Knoxville, TN, USA.

Peter Muntigl is Assistant Professor in Linguistics at the University of Ghent, Belgium, and is Adjunct Professor in the Faculty of Education at Simon Fraser University, Burnaby, BC, Canada.

J. Christopher Muran is a Professor at the Derner Institute of Advanced Psychological Studies, Adelphi University, Garden City, NY, USA.

Beatriz Palma is based in the Psychology Department at the University of Maryland, College Park, MD, USA.

António P. Ribeiro is Post-doctoral Researcher in the School of Psychology at the University of Minho, Braga, Portugal.

Eugenia Ribeiro is Assistant Professor in the School of Psychology at the University of Minho, Braga, Portugal.

Jeremy Safran is Professor of Psychology at the New School for Social Research, New York City, USA, and Clinical Professor at the Postdoctoral Program in Psychotherapy & Psychoanalysis, NYU, New York City, USA.

Maya S. Shpigel is a Graduate Student in the Department of Psychology, Ben-Gurion University of the Negev, Beer-Sheva, Israel.

Inês Sousa is Assistant Professor in Mathematics and Applications at University of Minho, Guimarães, Portugal.

Patricia T. Spangler is currently at the Center for the Study of Traumatic Stress, Department of Psychiatry, Uniformed Services University of the Health Sciences, Bethesda, MD, USA.

Patricia L. Steckley is a registered Psychologist in Private Practice in Toronto, Canada.

William B. Stiles is Professor Emeritus in the Department of Psychology, Miami Univeristy, Oxford, OH, USA, and Adjunct Professor in the Department of Psychology, Appalachian State University, Boone, NC, USA.

Orya Tishby is a Senior Lecturer in Clinical Psychology and Clinical Social Work at Hebrew University, Jerusalem, Israel.

Jeanne C. Watson is Professor in the Department of Applied Psychology and Human Development at the University of Toronto, Canada.

Michal Weiss is a Doctoral Student in the Department of Psychology at the Hebrew University of Jerusalem, Israel.

Arnold Winston is Chair Emeritus, Department of Psychiatry, Mount Senai Beth Israel and Professor Emeritus, Mount Sinai School of Medicine, New York City, USA.

Hadas Wiseman is Associate Professor in Counseling and Human Development at the University of Haifa, Israel.

A. Jordan Wright is faculty and Academic Coordinator of Psychology at Empire State College, SUNY, New York, NY, USA.

Sigal Zilcha-Mano is Senior Lecturer in the Department of Psychology at the University of Haifa, Israel.

The therapeutic relationship: Multiple lenses and innovations

HADAS WISEMAN & ORYA TISHBY

In 2005, *Psychotherapy Research* marked 15 years of publication with a special issue, "The Therapeutic Relationship" (Volume 15, Issues 1–2). The challenges lying ahead were outlined in Horvath's (2005) introduction to the issue, and these and other challenges have been put forward during the last decade in other joint efforts published in special sections of other journals and in edited books devoted to the therapeutic relationship. They include prominent publications such as the special section of *Psychotherapy: Research, Theory, Practice, Training* that was devoted to the working alliance (Samstag, 2006), Muran and Barber's (2010) *The Therapeutic Alliance: An Evidence-Based Guide to Practice*, and Norcross's (2002, 2011) *Psychotherapy Relationships that Work* (which appeared both in book form and in a special issue of *Psychotherapy*). The latter presents the work of the contributors of the APA Interdivision Task Force on Evidence-Based Relationships and their conclusions and recommendations for research and practice (Norcross & Lambert, 2011; Norcross & Wampold, 2011). Research on the therapeutic relationship continues to develop and this special section is devoted to providing "multiple lenses" on some of the important and exciting new directions in research on the therapeutic relationship. The articles present an array of empirical studies in which the contributors offer innovative ways of studying various relationship mechanisms as they relate to change processes and outcomes.

The joint initiative for this special section originated during the course of a research workshop held in Jerusalem in the summer of 2010. As an extension of our collaboration in a psychotherapy research project (University of Haifa and the Hebrew University of Jerusalem), we had received support to gather leading psychotherapy researchers and clinicians to take part in a research workshop on a topic related to our ongoing research project (Wiseman & Tishby, 2011). We entitled the workshop *Multiple Lenses on the Therapeutic Relationship*. Its aims were to focus on research and clinical practice on the therapeutic relationship—past, present, and future—to paraphrase Castonguay, Constantino, and Holtforth (2006), where we were, where we are, and where should we go. The key speakers addressed theoretical underpinnings, client-therapist relationship processes and experiences, client and therapist variables, techniques versus the relationship and outcome, and implications for training therapists. The original work presented at this workshop by the key speakers formed the basis for the papers in this special section. Given our intention to bring together researchers from a variety of psychotherapy orientations and research methodologies, we have added two additional research groups to the contributors of the special section.[1] Thus, we set out to provide a panorama of cutting-edge studies on the therapeutic relationship that are intended to demonstrate and suggest promising pathways for future research.

Going back to the challenges for the next generation of research on the therapeutic relationship, we wish to highlight five: First, the *theoretical-conceptual* challenge of clarifying the construct of the therapeutic relationship and defining and refining new constructs and various specific components of the relationship; second, the *methodological* challenge of how best to measure the relationship and study process-outcome questions such as whether the therapeutic relationship is curative in itself; third, the *change process* challenge, entailing understanding the function of the relationship in the change process and its development over time at different phases of therapy; four, the *client and therapist contributions* challenge, concerning how the participants influence the kind of relationship that is formed between them; and five, the *training* challenge, consisting of the development of successful training programs for therapists regarding the development and management of their relationships with their clients (Castonguay et al., 2006; Crits-Christoph, Crits-Christoph, & Connolly, 2010; Horvath, 2006; Sharpless, Muran, & Barber, 2010).

Multiple Lenses and Innovations

The studies in this special section offer multiple lenses on how to tackle the above challenges by addressing one or more of these key issues, which are, to some extent, naturally intertwined. For example, suggesting new constructs is embedded in the development of new measures and methods for studying them. Similarly, efforts directed at understanding change mechanisms involve client and therapist contributions and training therapists to facilitate processes of change in the therapeutic relationship. Although the studies by no means encompass all the landscape or even most of it, each suggests new ways of studying the therapeutic relationship and the alliance. We found that the studies can be broadly divided into three groups according to the key issues they each tackle in their unique way: (a) methodological innovations, with an emphasis on process-outcome questions; (b) change processes and micro-processes, focusing on the question of how the therapeutic relationship heals; and (c) client and therapist contributions to the therapeutic relationship and the study of special populations of clients. All the articles offer (to a greater or lesser extent) implications for training therapists in psychotherapy relationships that work.

Process-Outcome Questions

The first group of studies includes methodological innovations, with an emphasis on process-outcome questions, especially the predictive validity of the alliance. These include questions about the causal role of the alliance and about variability in alliance patterns and their impact on change.

DeRubeis and colleagues (DeRubeis, Gelfand, German, Fournier, & Forand, 2014) set out to investigate an almost "truism" in the psychotherapy research literature, which they refer to as the "variance accounted for" approach to characterizing the sources of change in psychotherapy. They re-examine the pie chart that summarizes the percentage of explained variance in psychotherapy outcome as a function of therapeutic factors: 30% attributed to common factors, including the therapeutic alliance; 15% attributed to techniques; 40% attributed to patient extra-therapeutic change; and 15% attributed to expectancy (Lambert, 1992; Lambert & Barely, 2002). They suggest an alternative conceptualization for research based on the elements of psychotherapeutic processes, taking into account variability in patients and therapists. Using a set of sophisticated simulations, the authors show that in the typical psychotherapy study we cannot really expect process-outcome correlations beyond .25 or .30. They propose the concept of patient "response patterns" and therapy "quality" to test these ideas and suggest that we need to consider the "variability among patients in the degree to which the quality of therapy provided to them will affect their outcomes". They offer some implications of these new ideas in order to facilitate progress in process-outcome research.

The Barber and colleagues study (Barber et al., 2014) addresses the alliance-outcome correlation question by directly testing whether the alliance has a causal role in change or whether the alliance itself is merely a reflection of prior symptom change (for recent reviews of the equivocal evidence, see Barber, Muran, McCarthy, & Keefe, 2013, and Crits-Christoph, Connolly Gibson, & Mukherjee, 2013). In order to disentangle early alliance from early symptom improvement, they examine the predictive value of alliance both with and without accounting for early change in depressive symptoms. Using sophisticated statistical analysis of the temporal sequence of alliance and symptoms, they show that after controlling for prior symptom improvement, early alliance predicted subsequent depression change. As we will indicate later in their article, Barber et al. also address a client variable, namely, client expectations as they relate to symptom change.

Another related alliance-outcome question that goes beyond previous studies asks how the alliance develops over time in different phases of psychotherapy (e.g., Stiles, 2004). It has been shown that the alliance is particularly predictive of outcome when assessed early in treatment (usually once in the third or fifth session), but that in order to understand patterns of alliance development, there is a need to measure alliance throughout treatment. Weiss, Kivity, and Huppert (2014) therefore examine in their preliminary study of CBT for panic disorders, session-by-session alliance client ratings taken before and after each session in relation to session-by-session change in anxiety sensitivity and treatment outcome. This led them to the identification of three types of alliance patterns: "sawtooth," sudden gains, and stabilization. They found the sawtooth pattern, defined as "within-session improvements followed by decline between sessions" (identified in 63% of 19 patients), to be related to less symptom reduction between sessions.

In-Session Process and "How" Questions

The second group of studies focuses on specifying in-session therapeutic relationship processes exploring the "how" questions, such as how the therapeutic relationship heals. To advance our understanding of these processes, we need to develop concepts and new ways to measure diverse aspects of the relationship. Each article in this group offers a different lens for looking at in-session processes using different units of analysis, ranging from micro-processes to events.

Muntigl and Horvath (2014) suggest a new set of questions about client-therapist relational processes, such as how therapists gain clients' enthusiastic participation in the tasks of treatment; how the actual deterioration or breakdown (rupture) of the close alignment between therapist and client dynamically unfolds in the session; and how therapists interact with their clients to effectively re-negotiate their affiliation and re-align themselves with the client, re-build a sense of joint purpose, and resume productive work. To address these questions in their article, Muntigl and Horvath present an innovative application of conversational analysis to track at a micro-level the turn-by-turn therapist-patient dialogical interactions (verbal and nonverbal) in which relational disaffiliation occurs and, subsequently, successful re-affiliation (repair) is or is not achieved. In their study, the intensive conversational analysis is demonstrated using cases drawn from the York I Depression Study identified as less successful, in which two severely depressed female clients were seen by two therapists in Emotion-Focused Process Experiential Therapy.

Another innovative method for studying moment-to-moment client-therapist collaboration applied to session transcripts is the Therapeutic Collaboration Coding System (TCCS.) In Ribeiro and colleagues' article (Ribeiro et al., 2014), they apply the TCCS in the context of *ambivalence events* in the analysis of client-therapist interaction in a relatively poor-outcome case of narrative psychotherapy. The ambivalence events are conceptualized using the identification of Innovative Moments (IM) and Return to the Problem (RPM) markers. The authors shed light on client resistance in terms of ambivalence; their theory-based case study of poor outcomes offers a way to integrate the study of resistance with that of therapeutic collaboration.

Safran et al. (2014) take their ongoing programmatic research on alliance ruptures and resolution and Alliance Focused Training (AFT) a step further in a research design aimed at evaluating the additive effect of AFT to CBT for personality disorders (cluster C). In this multiple baseline design, all therapists began treating a case with CBT while receiving CBT supervision, and then at session 8 or session 16 they switched from CBT supervision to an AFT protocol designed to enhance therapists' abilities to detect and work constructively with alliance ruptures and negative therapeutic process. The rationale for this methodology is that "every therapeutic dyad is unique, and their style of mutual responsiveness will vary at different points in time", thus, rather than testing differences between patient-therapist dyads, within-dyads differences were tested, allowing the researcher to control for patient and therapist individual differences as well as differences specific to each dyad. The impact of AFT was tested in relation to theory-driven hypotheses on shifts in patient and therapist interpersonal process using SASB and therapists' awareness of internal experience on the Experiencing scale. The findings support the value of training therapists to improve their ability to work constructively with weakened alliances and negative therapeutic processes.

Hill and colleagues' (Hill et al., 2014) article focuses on *immediacy events*, a specific type of event in the client-therapist relational work, and how they affect client and therapist evaluations of process and outcome. Immediacy is defined as "a discussion of the therapeutic relationship, by both the therapist and client in the here-and-now, involving more than social chitchat". The frequency and consequences of immediacy events were studied in 16 cases of psychodynamic-interpersonal psychotherapy, applying a mixed quantitative-qualitative method. The associations between the use of immediacy and self-reports of session process and outcome, as well as judges' consensus qualitative ratings of the events (depth, appropriateness, resolution, and quality) and clients' post-therapy interviews about their experiences with immediacy were all applied to shed light on this relational event. The use of immediacy calls for specificity in its use with different types of clients, as demonstrated in two cases that differed in their attachment style, which we also refer to below in relation to client-contribution questions.

Watson, Steckley, and McMullen's (2014) article focuses on therapist empathy, which is considered a specific element of the relationship that has been found to have an effect size for empathy-outcome similar to that found for alliance-outcome (Elliott, Bohart, Watson, & Greenberg, 2011). How empathy facilitates client change in psychotherapy is investigated in Watson et al.'s study through data derived from a RCT comparing EFT-PE and CBT in the treatment of depression. The client's perceived therapist empathy was found to have a direct effect on client outcome and indirect effects as a mediator of changes in interpersonal (improvement of attachment insecurity) and intrapersonal (decreases in negative self-treatment) functioning at the end of therapy. This study makes use of comprehensive assessment in its reliance on clients' self-report of attachment, an observer process measure of clients' treatment of self applied to transcripts of therapy sessions (SASB-Introject) and an extensive battery of outcome measures. The mediation analysis provides evidence that clients' attachment styles, as well as their ways of treating their inner experience, mediate the relationship between empathy and outcome, demonstrating the role of empathy as a mechanism of change. The conceptualization and the mediation effects tested in this study provide a model for testing "how" questions through mediation effects that can be applied to other treatment orientations and other elements of the therapeutic relationship.

Clients' and Therapists' Contributions to the Relationship Questions

The third group of studies focuses on clients' and therapists' contributions to the therapeutic relationship and the study of special populations of clients. Studying client contributions to the relationship addresses what works when we adapt the relationship to patient characteristics. In the APA Task Force on Evidence-Based Relationships, this was referred to as "tailoring the therapy relationship to the individual patient: what works in particular" (Norcross, 2011). Two patient characteristics (beyond diagnosis and presenting problems) addressed in this group of articles that had been included in the Task Force are patient expectations and client attachment.

Patients' expectations about the outcome and process of treatment before they enter therapy have long been considered a key ingredient and common factor of successful psychotherapy (see Constantino, Glass, Arnkoff, Ametrano, & Smith, 2011). As part of their study, indicated above, Barber et al. tested both expectations about the alliance (the relationship prior to the first patient-therapist encounter) as a predictor of the alliance during the course of therapy, as well as pre-treatment expectations of outcome (symptomatic improvement) as potentially influencing both the alliance and symptom improvement. Interestingly, the alliance during the course of treatment was influenced both by expectations about the alliance and by expectations of good outcome. Unlike previous studies, however, pre-treatment expectations did not predict treatment outcome.

Research on client attachment style, originating from Bowlby's (1969/1982; 1988) attachment theory, has received growing attention in the last decade as a predictor of both the relationship that the client develops with the therapist and the final treatment outcome. Through the lenses of attachment theory, Wiseman and Tishby's (2014) article focuses on client attachment as a personality factor the client brings to psychotherapy and on the specific attachment the client forms with the therapist as an element of the therapy relationship. In a naturalistic study of psychodynamic psychotherapy, the association of these attachment aspects to outcome shows that clients characterized by avoidant attachment and by avoidant attachment to their therapist show the least improvement. This study also includes the therapist attachment with a focus on examining the benefits for outcome of match versus mismatch in client-therapist attachment styles (i.e., similar versus dissimilar). The findings point to the benefits of similarity in attachment for change in symptom distress, but only when therapists and their clients are both low in avoidance.

In Hill et al.'s (2014) study, indicated above, client attachment style is considered in relation to therapist's use of immediacy and the way the client experiences immediacy as a function of attachment style. The clinical examples further demonstrate how therapists respond differently in the case of a securely attached client as compared to a fearful/insecure client. In Watson et al.'s (2014) study, also discussed above, client attachment is considered to change as a result of therapy from insecure to more secure through the mediation of empathy.

Tishby and Wiseman's (2014) article grapples with the construct of countertransference (CT) and its impact on process. Applying the Core Conflictual Relationship Themes (CCRT) method (Luborsky & Crits-Christoph, 1998). To rate relationship episodes from therapists' narratives about their parents and about their clients, they identify countertransference patterns that are unique to each therapist (in a sample of 12 cases). The paper introduces an initial conceptualization of *CT types*, which depict therapists' internal responses triggered by their clients. These responses, such as "transferring the wish from parent to client" and "projecting the parent response of other on the client," generate different countertransference behaviors or manifestations (on managing countertransference, see Hayes, Gelso, & Hummel, 2011). The conceptualization of CT types helps us understand how clients actually trigger CT behaviors in their therapists and how CT is a product of an interaction between a particular client and a specific therapist. The study demonstrates possible links between CT types in different phases of therapy, the working alliance, session depth and smoothness, and rupture/repair over time, in a strong alliance and successful outcome case as compared to a weaker alliance and less successful case.

Special client populations are addressed in the last two papers in this group, one referring to the experience of trauma, specifically women with a history of childhood sexual abuse (CSA), and the second to the special case of non-accepting parents of lesbian, gay, and bisexual (LGB) adolescents or young adults.

Farber, Feldman, and Wright's (2014) article addresses a key process in psychotherapy with clients who have experienced trauma, namely, client disclosure to the therapist of the traumatic events. The study explores the debate over the benefits versus the costs of disclosure of CSA clients during psychotherapy by investigating the perceptions of subjective disclosure experiences of the clients themselves. The findings, based on an online survey of female self-reported survivors of sexual abuse who were currently in psychotherapy, indicate that disclosure has both benefits and costs. In addition, it was found that important client characteristics (demographic variables, time in therapy, extent of CSA, and mental health severity) impact positive consequences, as well as anxious feelings.

Shpigel and Diamond (2014) article focuses on the unique challenges faced by family therapists in engaging non-accepting parents of LGB adolescents and young adults in therapy, with a special focus on overcoming the obstacles to developing a strong alliance with the parents' family subsystem. In the context of Attachment-Based Family Therapy (ABFT) (Diamond, Siqueland, & Diamond, 2003) adapted for working with LGB individuals and their non-accepting parents, this hypothesis-generating study explores therapeutic themes and processes in good versus poor therapist-parent alliances. Observer-rated alliance was measured on a version of the Vanderbilt Therapeutic Alliance Scales (VTAS) (Hartley & Strupp, 1983); therapists' session notes and post-treatment follow-up interviews with the parents were subjected to a consensual CQR qualitative analysis. The picture that emerged showed that parents who developed stronger alliances with the therapist were those who were able to shift from anger, guilt, and shame regarding their child's sexual orientation to loss and longing to reconnect with their child.

Methodological Pluralism, Divergence and Convergence, and Implications for Clinical Practice and Training

We believe that the studies collected in this special section on innovations in studying the therapeutic relationship provide a panorama picture whereby the whole is more than the sum of its parts. Multiple lenses are provided through methodological pluralism in terms of measures, research designs, and quantitative and qualitative studies ranging from studies conducted in the context of RCTs (Barber; Watson), data simulations of "variance accounted" (DeRubeis), naturalistic medium samples (Wiseman & Tishby), medium to small samples (Safran et al.), intensive micro-analysis of single cases (Muntigl & Horvath; Ribeiro et al.), event analysis (Hill; Ribeiro), Consensual Qualitative Research (CQR) (Hill et al.; Tishby & Wiseman; Shpigel & Diamond), and an on-line survey (Farber). Divergence in therapy orientations included Psychodynamic/Interpersonal (Barber; Hill; Wiseman & Tishby; Safran & Muran; Tishby & Wiseman), CBT (DeRubies; Huppert; Watson), PET/EFT (Muntigl & Horvath; Watson), Narrative Therapy (Ribeiro), and Attachment-Based Family Therapy (Shpigel & Diamond).

Implications for clinical practice and training can be drawn from all the contributions. While training is directly addressed in Safran et al.'s article on Alliance Focused Training (AFT), it is also indirectly addressed by means of implications in the other articles, especially those dealing with micro-processes (Muntigl & Horvath; Ribeiro), rupture and repair and immediacy events (Hill et al.), and the study of countertranference (Tishby & Wiseman).

The clinical cases and excerpts in the second group of studies shed light on the investigated processes and illustrate their clinical meanings. Finally, the therapeutic relationship has been identified as a natural arena that attracts clinicians to research and for bridging the gap between research and clinical practice (Castonguay, 2011; Goldfried, 2013). In light of this, all of the authors have made an effort to present their sophisticated analyses in a manner that is as reader-friendly as possible, making their research accessible and relevant to clinicians.

Note

[1] Obviously, we were limited in the number of researchers we could invite to attend the workshop and to contribute to the special section. Of the workshop participants, two key speakers (Messer, 2010; Castonguay, 2010) are not included in the special section, but their writings and research appear in the articles of other contributors.

References

Barber, J. P., Muran, C. J., McCarthy, K. S., & Keefe, J. R. (2013). Research on dynamic therapies. In M. J. Lambert (Ed.), *Bergin and Garfield's handbook of psychotherapy and behavior change* (6th ed., pp. 443–494). New York: Wiley.

Barber, J. P., Zilcha-Mano, S., Gallop, R., Barrett, M., McCarthy, K. S., & Dinger, U. (2014). The associations among improvement and alliance expectations, alliance during treatment, and treatment outcome for major depressive disorder. *Psychotherapy Research, 24*, 257–268. doi:10.1080/10503307.2013.871080

Bowlby, J. (1969/1982). *Attachment and loss: Vol 1. Attachment.* London: Hogarth Press and the Institute of Psycho-Analysis.

Bowlby, J. (1988). *A secure base.* London: Tavistock Routledge.

Castonguay, L. G. (2010). *Bonding with Piaget: Integrating data and observations about the therapeutic relationship in CBT.* Paper presented at the international workshop on multiple lenses on the therapeutic relationship, Jerusalem, Israel, July.

Castonguay, L. G. (2011). Psychotherapy, psychopathology, research and practice: Pathways of connections and integration. *Psychotherapy Research, 21*, 125–140. doi:10.1080/10503307.2011.563250.

Castonguay, L. G., Constantino, M. J., & Holtforth, M. G. (2006). The working alliance: Where are we and where should we go? *Psychotherapy: Theory, Research, Practice, Training, 43*(3), 271–279. doi:10.1037/0033-3204.43.3.271

Constantino, M. J., Glass, C. R., Arnkoff, D. B., Ametrano, R. M., & Smith, J. Z. (2011). Expectations. In J. C. Norcross (Ed.), *Psychotherapy relationships that work: Evidence-based responsiveness* (2nd ed., pp. 354–376). New York: Oxford University Press.

Crits-Christoph, P., Connolly Gibson, M. B., & Mukherjee, D. (2013). Psychotherapy process-outcome research. In M. J. Lambert (Ed.), *Bergin and Garfield's handbook of psychotherapy and behavior change* (6th ed., pp. 298–340). New York: Wiley.

Crits-Christoph, P., Crits-Christoph, K., & Connolly Gibbons, M. B. (2010). Training in alliance-fostering techniques. In J. C. Muran & J. P. Barber (Eds.), *The therapeutic alliance: An evidence-based guide to practice* (pp. 304–319). New York: Guilford Press.

DeRubeis, R. J., Gelfand, L. A., German, R. E., Fournier, J. C., & Forand, N. R. (2014). Understanding processes of change: How some patients reveal more than others—and some groups of therapists less—about what matters in psychotherapy. *Psychotherapy Research, 24*, 419–428. doi:10.1080/10503307.2013.838654

Diamond, G. S., Siqueland, L., & Diamond, G. M. (2003). Attachment-based family therapy: A program of treatment development research. *Clinical Child and Family Psychology Review, 6*, 107–128. doi:10.1023/A:1023782510786

Elliott, R., Bohart, A. C., Watson, J. C., & Greenberg, L. S. (2011). Empathy. In J. C. Norcross (Ed.), *Psychotherapy relationships that work: Evidence-based responsiveness* (2nd ed., pp. 132–152). New York: Oxford University Press.

Farber, B. A., Feldman, S., & Wright, A. J. (2014). Client disclosure and therapist response in psychotherapy with women with a history of childhood sexual abuse. *Psychotherapy Research, 24*, 316–326. doi:10.1080/10503307.2013.817695.

Goldfried, M. R. (2013). What should we expect from psychotherapy? *Clinical Psychology Review, 33*, 862–869. http://dx.doi.org/10.1016/j.cpr.2012.09.006

Hartley, D. E., & Strupp, H. H. (1983). The therapeutic alliance: Its relationship to outcome in brief psychotherapy. In J. Masling (Ed.), *Empirical studies of psychoanalytic theories* (Vol. 1, pp. 1–37). Hillsdale, N.J.: Analytical Press.

Hayes, J. A., Gelso, C. G., & Hummel, A. M. (2011). Managing countertransference. *Psychotherapy, 48*(1), 88–97. doi:10.1037/a0022182

Hill, C. E., Gelso, C. J., Chui, H., Spangler, P. T., Hummel, A., Huang, T., … Miles, J. R. (2014). To be or not to be immediate with clients: The use and perceived effects of immediacy in psychodynamic/interpersonal psychotherapy. *Psychotherapy Research, 24*, 299–315. doi:10.1080/10503307.2013.812262

Horvath, A. O. (2005). The therapeutic relationship: Research and theory. An introduction to the Special Issue. *Psychotherapy Research, 15*, 3–7. doi:10.1080/10503300512331339143

Horvath, A. O. (2006). The alliance in context: Accomplishments, challenges and future directions. *Psychotherapy: Theory, Research, Practice, Training, 43*, 258–263. doi:10.1037/0033-3204.43.3.258

Lambert, M. J. (1992). Psychotherapy outcome research: Implication for integrative and eclectic therapists. In J. C. Norcross & M. R. Goldfried (Eds.), *Handbook of psychotherapy integration* (pp. 94–129). New York: Basic Books.

Lambert, M. J., & Barley, D. E. (2002). Research summary on the therapeutic relationship and psychotherapy outcome. In J. C. Norcross (Ed.), *Psychotherapy relationships that work* (pp. 17–32). New York: Oxford University Press.

Luborsky, L. A., & Crits-Christoph, P. (1998). *Understanding transference: The CCRT method.* Washington, DC: American Psychological Association.

Messer, S. B. (2010). *Psychodynamic perspectives on the therapeutic alliance.* Paper presented at the international workshop on multiple lenses on the therapeutic relationship, Jerusalem, Israel, July.

Muran, J. C., & Barber, J. P. (Eds.). (2010). *The therapeutic alliance: An evidence-based guide to practice.* New York: Guilford Press.

Muntigl, P., & Horvath, A. O. (2014). The therapeutic relationship in action: How therapists and clients co-manage relational disaffiliation. *Psychotherapy Research, 24*, 327–345. doi:10.1080/10503307.2013.807525

Norcross, J. (Ed.). (2011). *Psychotherapy relationships that work: Evidence-based responsiveness* (2nd ed.). New York: Oxford University Press.

Norcross, J. C., & Lambert, M. J. (2011). Psychotherapy relationships that work II. *Psychotherapy, 48*, 4–8. doi:10.1037/a0022180

Norcross, J. C., & Wampold, B. E. (2011). Evidence-based therapy relationships: Research conclusions and clinical practices. *Psychotherapy, 48*, 98–102. doi:10.1037/a0022161

Ribeiro, A. P., Ribeiro, E., Loura, J., Gonçalves, M. M., Stiles, W. B., Horvath, A. O., & Sousa, I. (2014). Therapeutic collaboration and resistance: Describing the nature and quality of the therapeutic relationship within ambivalence events using the Therapeutic Collaboration Coding System. *Psychotherapy Research, 24*, 346–359. doi:10.1080/10503307.2013.856042

Safran, J., Muran, J. C., DeMaria, A., Boutwell, C., Eubanks-Carter, C., & Winston, A. (2014). Investigating the impact of alliance-focused training on interpersonal process and therapists' capacity for experiential reflection. *Psychotherapy Research, 24*, 269–285. doi:10.1080/10503307.2013.874054

Samstag, L. W. (2006). The working alliance in psychotherapy: An overview of the invited papers in the special section. *Psychotherapy: Theory, Research, Practice, Training, 43*, 300–307. doi:10.1037/0033-3204.43.3.300

Sharpless, B. A., Muran, J. C., & Barber, J. P. (2010). Coda: Recommendations for practice and training. In J. C. Muran & J. P. Barber (Eds), *The therapeutic alliance: An evidence-based guide to practice* (pp. 341–354). New York: Guilford Press.

Shpigel, M. S., & Diamond, G. M. (2014). Good versus poor therapeutic alliances with non-accepting parents of same-sex oriented adolescents and young adults: A qualitative study. *Psychotherapy Research, 24*, 376–391. doi:10.1080/10503307.2013.856043

Stiles, W. B., Glick, M. J., Osatuke, K., Hardy, G. E., Shapiro, D. A., Agnew-Davies, R., et al. (2004). Patterns of alliance development and the rupture-repair hypothesis: Are productive relationships U-shaped or V-shaped? *Journal of Counseling Psychology, 51*, 81–92. doi:10.1037/0022-0167.51.1.81

Tishby, O., & Wiseman, H. (2014). Types of countertransference dynamics: An exploration of their impact on the client-therapist relationship. *Psychotherapy Research, 24*, 360–375. doi:10.1080/10503307.2014.893068.

Watson, J. C., Steckley, P. L., & McMullen, E. J. (2014). The role of empathy in promoting change. *Psychotherapy Research, 24*, 286–289. doi:10.1080/10503307.2013.802823

Weiss, M., Kivity, Y., & Huppert, J. D. (2014). How does the therapeutic alliance develop throughout cognitive behavioral therapy for panic disorder? Sawtooth patterns, sudden gains, and stabilization. *Psychotherapy Research, 24*, 407–418. doi:10.1080/10503307.2013.868947

Wiseman, H., & Tishby, O. (2011). The Client-therapist 'dance': Interplay of client and therapist interpersonal patterns, working alliance and psychothearpy outcome. *Final Scientific Research Report: Israel Science Foundation (ISF)*. [Grant No. 187/07, 2007–2011].

Wiseman, H., & Tishby, O. (2014). Client attachment, attachment to the therapist and client-therapist attachment match: How do they relate to change in psychodynamic psychotherapy? *Psychotherapy Research, 24*, 392–406. doi:10.1080/10503307.2014.892646.

Understanding processes of change: How some patients reveal more than others—and some groups of therapists less—about what matters in psychotherapy

ROBERT J. DERUBEIS[1], LOIS A. GELFAND[1], RAMARIS E. GERMAN[1], JAY C. FOURNIER[2], & NICHOLAS R. FORAND[3]

[1]*Department of Psychology, University of Pennsylvania, Philadelphia, PA, USA;* [2]*Department of Psychiatry, University of Pittsburgh School of Medicine, Pittsburgh, PA, USA &* [3]*Department of Psychiatry, The Ohio State University Wexner Medical Center, Columbus, OH, USA*

Abstract

Objective: We identify difficulties researchers encounter in psychotherapy process-outcome investigations, and we describe several limitations of the popular "variance accounted for" approach to understanding the effects of psychotherapy. **Methods & Results:** Using data simulations, we show how the expected correlation between an excellent measure of therapy quality and outcome would be surprisingly small (approximately .25) under conditions likely to be common in psychotherapy research. Even when we modeled conditions designed to increase the likelihood that strong process-outcome relationships would be observed, we found that the expected correlations were still only in the modest range (.38–.51). **Conclusions:** We discuss the implications of our analysis for the interpretation of process-outcome findings as well as for design considerations in future investigations.

Although most readers of the psychotherapy research literature will agree with the broad claim that "psychotherapy works," there is little agreement concerning the relative importance of the elements that constitute effective psychotherapy. Some of the obstacles to resolving these disagreements are well known; these include the difficulty of defining and operationalizing the elements of therapy, as well as measuring or manipulating them. However, we believe there are additional issues that have thus far received little attention, but nevertheless might have a substantial impact on estimates of the relationships between processes and outcomes.

The "Variance Accounted For" Approach to Characterizing the Sources of Change in Psychotherapy

We begin by offering a critical assessment of the dominant method used to illustrate these relationships. Lambert and colleagues have published a series of influential papers in which they attempt to characterize in quantitative terms the effects of various psychotherapy factors on patient outcomes. Their approach is to divide overall variance in psychotherapy outcomes into the percentages attributable to various therapeutic factors (Asay & Lambert, 1999; Lambert, 1992, 2013; Lambert & Barley, 2001, 2002). In their framework, typically represented in a pie chart, "Common Factors" and (specific) "Techniques" constitute the factors that vary across psychotherapy cases and are presumed to be under the control of the therapist. Also included in the pie chart are two other factors, "Expectancy" and "Extratherapeutic Change" (or "Client/Life"). Collectively, these four factors are said to account for the total variation in outcome that results from psychotherapy. The authors attribute 30% of outcome variance to common factors. (The therapeutic alliance is considered to be one of the common factors.) Techniques are said to account for 15%, and the remaining variance is attributed to extratherapeutic change (40%) and expectancy (15%).

The simplicity and seeming comprehensiveness of this way of understanding change has evidently held great appeal among those who publish on process and outcome research in psychotherapy; according to a "Google Scholar" search, the publications in which the pie charts appear have been cited over 1,500 times. Commonly, those citing the papers refer to the pie charts as if they represented quantitative reviews (meta-analyses) of the psychotherapy outcome literatures. However, as Lambert and Barley (2002) state, the charts are "not derived directly from meta-analytic techniques, (but instead) characterize the research findings of a wide range of treatments, disorders, and ways of measuring client and therapist characteristics" (p. 18). There is, therefore, no obvious way to replicate or verify the conclusions summarized in the pie charts. Moreover, as Lambert (2013) states, "It is really difficult to partition and compare sources of variability in psychotherapy because no single study encapsulates all the variables of interest" (p. 200).

Another, perhaps less well understood limitation of Lambert's (1992) approach concerns the use of the "percent variance accounted for" concept to indicate the relative contribution to psychotherapeutic change of a given factor. This metric is informative only insofar as there is substantial variability in each of the factors in each of the constituent studies. To illustrate, imagine that in a given population of therapist-patient dyads, a high level of technical skill is required if positive outcomes are to result from the therapy. If in a study of dyads from that population all therapists possess a high level of technical skill, the variance accounted for by technical skill will be very small, even though technical skill is critical for treatment success. Therefore, any factor on which the therapists did vary could appear to be important and, crucially, more important than skill. Although Lambert and Barley (2002) point to the fact that the studies they summarized "span extremes in research designs, and are especially representative of studies that allow the greatest divergence in the variables that determine outcome" (p. 18), this is a statement about the heterogeneity of the studies, and not about the variability of the factors represented within the individual studies. Thus, when they "average(d) the size of the contribution each predictor made to final outcome" (p.18) they were doing so across studies that, collectively, may have represented a wide range on all of the factors, even if many or most of these studies, individually, represented rather narrow ranges. If the ranges were in fact limited within the studies, averaging the findings across the studies, no matter how different they are from one another, would do nothing to address this problem.

An Alternative Approach to Understanding the Effects of Therapeutic Factors on Outcomes

With these and other issues in mind, we developed an alternative conceptualization that we hope will lead to refinements in thinking and research concerning the elements of psychotherapeutic processes. In our framework we explicitly incorporate two phenomena that are inadequately addressed in the "variance explained" approach. The first involves a hidden moderator variable in the outcome and process-outcome literatures: variability among patients in the degree to which the quality of therapy provided to them will affect their outcomes. The second addresses the likelihood that few, if any, studies of psychotherapeutic processes include sufficient variation in potentially relevant factors (e.g., adherence to the treatment; engagement in relationship-enhancing behaviors) to allow for meaningful examinations of the causal links between therapeutic factors and outcomes. In addition, we will briefly touch upon a few other phenomena that may be useful to consider when designing psychotherapy studies and interpreting results. In the process, we hope to stimulate ideas for future endeavors that can provide more informative tests of hypotheses embedded in the question: "How does psychotherapy work?"

As psychotherapy researchers, we are interested in the relationships between various therapeutic processes and outcome. In our framework, we use the summary term *quality* to represent all therapeutic influences on improvement in therapy. It is therefore an idealized construct in that it comprises all and only those elements, variability in which accounts maximally for variability in outcomes. It includes the therapist's use of interpersonal skills to engage the patient, to avoid or address unhelpful tensions in the service of promoting a mutual commitment to therapeutic growth. In most discussions of therapy processes these elements are subsumed in the "relationship" rubric. Also included under *quality* would be the skill with which the therapist assesses the patient's needs and then determines a course of action to address those needs. The extent to which a therapist succeeds in these aims might be referred to as the "fit" of the therapist's plan with what would most help the patient. Finally, *quality* also includes the skill with which the therapist employs appropriate "techniques." This would incorporate the intensity and frequency of the therapeutic procedures (similar to the concept of adherence) as well as the competence with which they are provided. It is beyond the scope of this paper to address the ways in which relationship, fit, and technique factors might interact with each other, or how they might each contribute in unique ways to therapeutic change. The conclusions we derive using the *quality* construct could, in future research, be applied to these or other factors.

A second causal influence, which we will assume is independent of therapy *quality*, concerns the variability in the potential for patients to improve with the passage of time, irrespective of the quality of therapy provided to them. Hereafter we will refer to the influence of the passage of time on a given patient's outcome as that patient's *time-effect*. The *time-effect* construct is similar to Lambert's Expectancy factor.

In the following, *quality* and the *time-effect* are the only influences on therapy outcome that we model. We will not include random extratherapeutic events as, by definition, these random events are not attributable to the therapist, his or her therapeutic methods, or the patient; these would present as random error or unexplained variance in any model. We note that insofar as positive (or negative) life events result directly from the therapeutic process and go on to affect outcome (such as when problem-solving results in changes in the patient's environment), they would be accounted for by the therapist-generated factors and thus captured by the *quality* variable in statistical models.

Taking into Account Variability in Patients and Therapists

Correlational analyses assess the degree of linear relation between two variables. The theoretical maximum positive correlation is 1.0, but the maximum correlation attainable in any study is usually less than 1.0. It is well understood that the unreliability of measures as well as the occurrence of events outside the explanatory system (such as random events) constrain the magnitude of the relationships that will be observed in process-outcome research. However, two other phenomena that can limit the magnitude of observed relations between process and outcome variables have tended to be overlooked; these are the focus of our analysis. One of these concerns the variability in *quality* within individual process-outcome studies. The other concerns variability across patients in how, and to what degree, they would respond to variation in therapy *quality*. In the following we illustrate how large a role these phenomena can play in the determination of estimates of process-outcome relationships in typical psychotherapy studies.

Figure 1 depicts a variety of relationships that might exist between percent improvement (hereafter *improvement*) and *quality*, where *improvement* can range from 0% (none) to 100% (complete resolution of relevant problems). For simplicity, we do not consider negative values, which would represent deterioration. *Quality* is scaled to vary from 0%, reflecting the absence of any therapeutic elements (as in, for example, a wait-list condition), to 100%, in which therapeutic factors are optimal. For ease of discussion, we refer to the 0%, 25%, 50%, 75%, and 100% points as Absent, Modest, Good, Excellent, and Highest *quality*. A linear relationship with a slope of 1.0 is what would be observed, assuming perfectly valid and reliable measurement of both *quality* and *improvement*, if all patients were to improve as a direct one-to-one function of the level of therapy *quality* provided to them. We will refer to a patient or set of patients who exhibit this "Response Pattern" as "Pliant," in that their response to therapy will be excellent if excellent therapy is provided, poor if the therapy is poor, etc. These concepts are instantiated in the framework we employ throughout the paper, such that when *quality* is Highest, the Pliant patient will improve to the fullest extent possible (i.e., 100% *improvement*), and gradations of *quality* between Absent and Highest engender *improvement* proportional to the degree of *quality*. For Pliant patients, then, assuming perfect measurement, the correlation between *quality* and *improvement* would be 1.0.

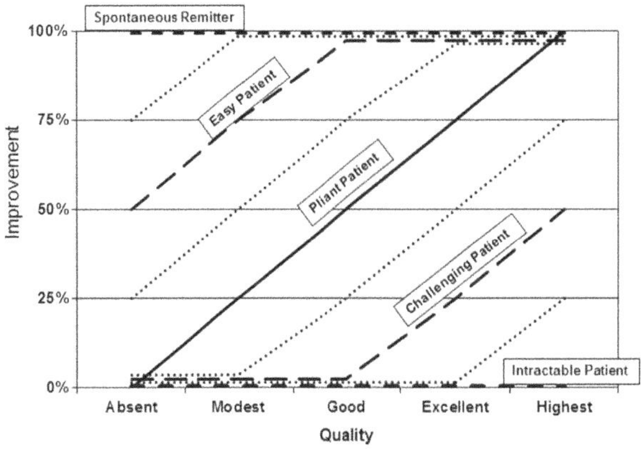

Figure 1. Relationship between therapy quality and improvement for five named Response Patterns, with four intermediate patterns.

While it is theoretically possible that all patients are Pliant, it is more in line with our clinical impressions to represent patients as differing in their patterns of response to variations in *quality*. Figure 1 includes depictions of the relationship between *quality* and *improvement* for eight types of patients who are not Pliant. We name four of these Response Patterns: the "Spontaneous Remitter," who experiences maximum improvement irrespective of *quality*; the "Easy" patient, who would experience considerable improvement even without therapy, and would evidence maximal improvement if *quality* is at least Good; the "Challenging" patient, who would experience no improvement unless *quality* is at least Good, and would achieve less than maximal improvement even if optimal therapy were provided; and the "Intractable" patient, who would experience no improvement no matter how low or high the *quality* of therapy provided to him or her.

The patients in this conceptualization are represented on a continuum such that the relationship between *quality* and *improvement* is always nonlinear (with the exception of the Pliant patients, Intractable patients, and Spontaneous Remitters) in the following way. Each relationship has a "hockey stick" shape composed of a horizontal piece, such that there is no relationship between *quality* and *improvement* over that range of *quality*, and a diagonal piece, where there is a linear relationship between *quality* and *improvement* (slope = 1.0) through that part of the range. Response Patterns are created by applying floor and ceiling effects to the diagonal lines such that a Response Pattern is uniquely identified by the Y-intercept of the line before any floor or ceiling effect is applied. These intercepts range from −100% ("Intractable") to +100% ("Spontaneous Remitter"). (Note: Figure 1 depicts the five named Response Patterns, plus four intermediate Response Patterns that are not associated with specific labels.) The horizontal piece may occur only at either 100% improvement (a ceiling effect, as is true for the Easy patient) or 0% improvement (a floor effect, as for the Challenging patient). The juncture between the horizontal and diagonal piece may occur at any value of *quality*. An example, from Figure 1, is the Easy patient, whose diagonal piece begins at 50% improvement, showing that even with the lowest quality of therapy (therapy *quality* is Absent), he or she will improve substantially, but not maximally. For the Easy patient, the diagonal piece reaches 100% when *quality* is Good. The horizontal piece, which runs from Good to Highest, represents the idea that at any level of *quality* Good or higher, the Easy patient will experience full (100%) improvement.

Figure 2 presents a different view of the model introduced in Figure 1, focusing on five of the patient Response Patterns and showing how the *time-effect* and *quality* influence *improvement* in different patients. When *quality* is Absent (0%), any *improvement* is attributed only to a patient's *time-effect*. As *quality* increases, the magnitude of the *time-effect* remains constant; at higher levels of *quality*, all and only the *improvement* beyond that attributable to the *time-effect* is due to *quality*. Note especially how *quality* can play either a crucial role (Pliant Patient), no role at all (Intractable Patient or Spontaneous Remitter), or degrees in between (Challenging Patient and Easy Patient).

This model is only one example of how patients might vary in their response to therapy quality, but two of its features would likely be represented in any realistic depiction of the relationships between

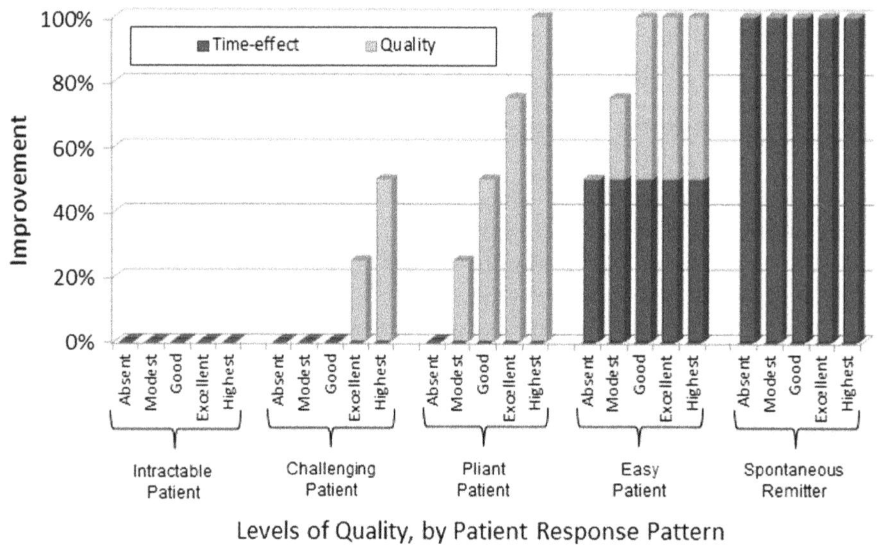

Figure 2. Example of the effects of time and quality on improvement in five hypothetical patients.

quality and *improvement*. First, for some patients (e.g., Spontaneous Remitters and Intractable patients), there is little or no relationship between *quality* and *improvement*. Second, the relationship between *quality* and *improvement* is not linear for most patients. These two features will serve to constrain estimates of the linear relationship between *quality* and *improvement* in any process-outcome study, because no process-outcome study would ever contain only Pliant patients.

We performed a set of simulations in order to estimate the correlation between *quality* and *improvement* under a variety of conditions. In each simulation, we took 1000 random draws from a distribution of the Response Patterns and crossed them with random draws from a distribution of *quality* values. Each pairing of a level of *quality* with a Response Pattern resulted in a percentage value reflecting the level of *improvement* that would be expected for that particular therapy case. We then calculated estimates of the correlation between *quality* and *improvement*, using all 1000 cases in the simulation. The value of the dependent variable, *improvement*, was determined by *quality* and Response Pattern, as described above and exemplified in the following three cases (see Figure 1 or Figure 2). If Response Pattern is Spontaneous Remitter and *quality* is Excellent (75), *improvement* is 100%. If Response Pattern is Easy and *quality* is Modest (25), *improvement* is 75%. If Response Pattern is Pliant and *quality* is Good (50), *improvement* is 50%. In this set of three cases, the correlation between *quality* and *improvement* is .50.

In the base simulation, we drew *quality* levels and Response Patterns from uniform distributions, representing a situation in which each of the levels of *quality*, and each of the Response Patterns, was equally likely. In this simulation, the correlation between *quality* and *improvement*, assuming perfect measurement, was .33 (Case 1, Table I). Recall that *quality* is an idealized construct. As such, its validity coefficient is 1.0.

Distribution of Therapy Quality and Patient Response Patterns in Studies

In many process studies it is the intention of the investigator and the therapists to provide high-quality treatment. Thus, we assume it is unrealistic to represent variation in *quality* with a uniform distribution. In our next simulation, we therefore drew *quality* from a left-skewed distribution,[1] depicted in Figure 3, in which the bins that contain Good and Excellent *quality* were over-represented, compared to those that contain Absent, Modest, and Highest. In this simulation we retained a uniform distribution for Response Pattern. The resulting correlation between *quality* and *improvement*, assuming perfect measurement, was .18 (Case 2, Table I).

In each of the two simulations we have described thus far we have represented the different Response Patterns equally across the range. Since it is possible or even likely that a uniform distribution does not represent samples or populations of patients who participate in process studies, we conducted a simulation that reflected a more realistic distribution of Response Patterns. The distribution we chose was like that of the left-skewed *quality* distribution, such that the extreme patterns (Spontaneous Remitter and Intractable) were represented less frequently than were the less extreme patterns. Likewise, Response Patterns between Intractable and Challenging were

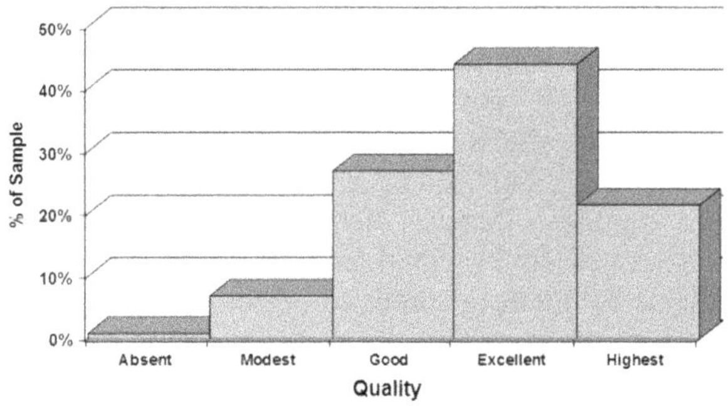

Figure 3. A skewed distribution of therapy quality in a study relating quality to improvement.

Table I. Correlations between quality and improvement from simulations that represent quality and response patterns with a variety of distributions

Case	Distribution of therapy quality	Distribution of response patterns	Assumes perfect measurement validity for both *quality* and *improvement*	Assumes that the measurement validity of both *quality* and *improvement* = .80
1	Uniform	Uniform	.33	.21
2	Skewed	Uniform	.18	.12
3	Skewed	Skewed	.39	.25
4	Skewed	Predominantly Pliant	.59	.38
5	Uniform	Predominantly Pliant	.79	.51

relatively rare. The correlation we obtained with this simulation, .39 (Case 3, Table I), represents an optimistic estimate of the correlation a researcher would obtain, with perfect measurement, under what is arguably the most realistic pair of distributions among those we tested.

As can be seen from Table I, for a given distribution of *quality* the correlation between *quality* and *improvement* increases as the proportion of Pliant or near-Pliant cases increases. Note that in an idealized case in which the sample is composed entirely of Pliant patients and the validity coefficient of *quality* and *improvement* is 1.0, the correlation will be 1.0. We considered a case in which the Response Patterns represented are predominantly in the middle of the range, centered on Pliant (hereafter referred to as Predominantly Pliant; see Figure 4[2]) in order to demonstrate how correlation estimates can be increased by focusing on such patients in process-outcome studies. The Predominantly Pliant distribution was represented in a simulation that used a skewed distribution of *quality*; the resulting correlation was .59 (Case 4, Table I), assuming perfect measurement. When we substituted a uniform *quality* distribution for the skewed distribution, we obtained the highest correlation of any of the five simulations, .79 (Case 5, Table I). This shows how important it is to understand and—to the degree possible and ethically justifiable—influence the distributions of both *quality* and Response Patterns in studies relating therapy processes to outcomes. Across the simulations, correlations ranged from .18 (Case 2), when the *quality* distribution was skewed and the Response Pattern distribution was uniform, to .79 (Case 5), when *quality* was uniform and Response Patterns were Predominantly Pliant. Case 5 reflects distributions that would be advantageous to obtain in order to reveal causal relations between therapy processes and outcomes.

In the simulations described thus far, perfect measurement validity was assumed. The correlations from these simulations are represented in the first column of numbers in Table I. The second column of numbers contains the estimates for each of these correlations under the assumption that the validity coefficients for both the independent variable (*quality*) and the dependent variable (*improvement*) are .80. We provide these adjusted correlations as a reminder that, in addition to the problems we have already addressed, the reliability and validity of the measures can place further constraints on the magnitude of the correlations one can obtain in empirical studies of these phenomena. A validity coefficient of .80 for *improvement* would seem to be achievable, but our guess is that .80 is higher than the validity of even the best psychotherapy process measures, if for no other reason than that the validity coefficient is limited by the reliability of the measure. The resulting correlations (aside from the idealized case) range from .12 to .51. These coefficients, then, represent what are likely to be the upper bounds on findings that relate processes to outcomes. Insofar as a process measure does not capture all of the elements of the therapy process that contribute to change, the expected correlations would be even lower.

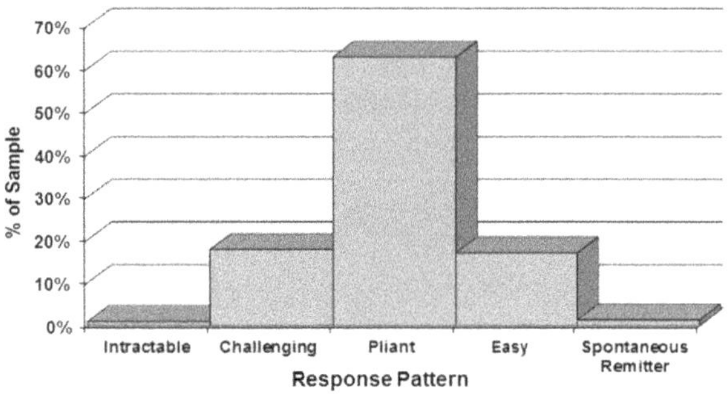

Figure 4. A distribution of Response Patterns that will enhance the likelihood of identifying therapy quality factors that maximize improvement (predominantly Pliant).

The models we tested do not take into account the effects of factors or events that are outside the therapist's control and not related to Response Patterns, such as an unexpected illness in the family, or a contact initiated by a long-lost friend. Lambert (1992) includes these events in his term "extratherapeutic change," to which he attributes 40% of outcome variance. Although these uncontrollable factors may not be as influential, on average, as the 40% figure would suggest, their effects on *improvement* cannot be assumed to be negligible. To the extent that these events do affect *improvement*, each of the correlations in Table I is an overestimate of the relationship that would be obtained between *quality* and *improvement*.

Implications and Considerations for Future Investigations

In the preceding we showed how, in a process-outcome study, the finding of a relation between a causal process and change can depend as much upon the distribution of *quality* and on the make-up of a patient sample as it does on the capacity of the process to promote change. Findings regarding individual therapeutic factors will be similarly affected. For example, if in one study therapists vary considerably in their ability to establish a good therapeutic relationship, a large and significant effect might be obtained between the measure of the relationship and outcome. If, in a replication, all therapists establish good to excellent relationships with their patients, an association between relationship and outcome would likely not be observed. Investigations that aim to characterize the relative importance of two therapy processes, such as therapist adherence to treatment and the therapeutic relationship, can be subject to similar confounds. Even if two processes could be considered equally important in some contexts, a given study in which they are compared could yield results that seem to show that one of them is far more important than the other. For example, the relationship factor might appear to have a stronger association with outcome, relative to the adherence-outcome association, if the therapists vary substantially in their ability to foster a positive relationship but are all similar to each other in their adherence to the treatment.

Attending to the Nature of the Therapist Sample

We have shown that in therapy process studies the strength of process-outcome associations will be constrained insofar as the range of therapy quality is restricted. One implication of this is that information available about the therapist sample should be considered when evaluating the usefulness of the study in assessing process-outcome associations. Another implication is that investigators should consider these features of the sample of therapists and patients who participate in their studies. To the extent it is feasible and ethical, samples of therapists could be identified that represent a broad range on the therapy variables of interest.

Alternatively, process variables can be manipulated experimentally, such as in training studies, in which therapists are assigned randomly to participate, or not participate, in training that emphasizes a potentially important therapy process (Crits-Christoph et al., 2006; Wiles et al., 2013). In an ideal study comparing two processes, therapists would be randomly assigned to a condition without training, a condition with training emphasizing one of the two processes, a condition involving training emphasizing the other process, and a fourth condition in which the two processes are equally emphasized.

Attending to the Nature of the Patient Sample

A finding that a therapeutic process accounts for change is, as we have shown, partially dependent on the nature of the patient sample. Insofar as a sample is composed of patients whose Response Patterns diverge from Pliant, relationships between a process and *improvement* will be obscured. This same principle holds for treatment comparisons. Consider a study with two active treatments and a control condition, where one of the treatments (the "strong" treatment) is able to address the problems presented by more difficult cases, as well as less difficult ones. The "weak" treatment is as effective with less difficult cases, but not as effective with difficult ones. The weak treatment would correspond in our system to a Good *quality* level, whereas the strong treatment would correspond to an Excellent or Highest level of *quality*. Consulting the relationship between *quality* and *improvement* for the Easy patients represented in Figure 2 is illustrative. In a sample composed entirely of Easy patients, the Good treatment will result in 100% *improvement*, and it will lead to much greater *improvement* than will a wait-list control condition (where *quality* is Absent or Modest). An Excellent/Highest *quality* treatment will fare no better than a Good treatment in this sample of patients. This pattern of findings would support the inference that neither treatment is more effective than the other, and that both treatments outperform a control condition. If the study were conducted instead with a sample of Challenging patients, a very different pattern of findings would be obtained. The Excellent/Highest quality treatment would prove superior to the Good treatment, and the Good treatment would not outperform the control condition.

A recent meta-analysis provides an example of how a treatment can be shown to be superior, or not superior, to a control condition, depending on the nature of the sample. The beneficial effects of psychotherapy, relative to placebo, were evident in samples of patients with "high" levels of depressive symptoms, but not in samples of patients with "low" levels of severity (Driessen, Cuijpers, Hollon, & Dekker, 2010). Although the categories "low severity" and "Easy" are not the same, it seems likely that individuals with milder depressions may benefit from a less potent intervention and will not benefit substantially more from a more potent one, which is how we have represented the "Easy" patient.

"The Golden Zone"

The implications are that the nature of the patient sample should be considered when interpreting research or when designing studies. Whereas therapist behaviors can be measured and, to some degree, experimentally manipulated, Response Patterns cannot be measured directly, nor can they be manipulated. This makes it difficult to control the distribution of Response Patterns represented in a sample of patients. Our intuitions tell us that patients vary considerably in the extent to which they require —as well as in how much they would benefit from— high-quality psychotherapy. Attempting to make these judgments after therapy has concluded would confound outcome with predictors of outcome. Although it seems unlikely that a researcher could ever identify with great precision Response Patterns a priori, some patient characteristics indicate a high likelihood that a patient's symptoms will remit spontaneously or that they will not respond to therapy. Characteristics of likely spontaneous remitters include: (a) being in a first episode of depression; (b) a brief episode duration; and (c) mild to moderate symptom levels. Characteristics at the other extreme on some of these same dimensions (i.e., chronic course, severe symptoms, and "treatment resistant") likely indicate patients who will be *intractable* or *challenging*. Excluding patients who appear to be at the extremes in regard to Response Patterns would result in a sample that is similar to the one we modeled as Predominantly Pliant, and therefore would include a relatively low percentage of patients for whom important therapy processes have little to do with their degree of improvement during therapy.

The pharmaceutical industry has taken this approach in the design of placebo-controlled trials. Patients who are expected to be placebo responders are excluded, as are those whose symptoms are so severe that they are not expected to exhibit a good response to active medication. The range in between these two groups, which is the focus of pharmaceutical trials, has been termed the "golden zone" (Thase, 1999; see also Fournier et al., 2010). In our scheme, an analogous effort would result in a focus, to the extent possible and ethical, on the Pliant, and to a lesser extent, the Easy and Challenging patients, to the exclusion of Spontaneous Remitters and Intractable patients. As discussed earlier, there are indications in the outcome literature on psychotherapy for depression that severity might also serve well as a patient-classifying variable in efforts to distinguish active from control psychotherapies (Driessen et al., 2010), suggesting that severity should be considered as a dimension on which to select patients for process-outcome studies.

Using Meaningful Units in Process and Outcome Measures

As we have shown, both the means and the variabilities of the process measures in a study sample need to be accounted for when drawing inferences from their observed associations with outcome. Likewise, comparisons of findings between investigations should take into account any differences in the relevant distributions. The approach we have presented would work best to the extent that measures of *quality* components and *improvement* could be scaled with meaningful units. Arguably, there are outcome measures currently employed for which this is true. For example, the Beck Depression Inventory (BDI-II; Beck, Steer, & Brown, 1996) and the Hamilton Rating Scale for Depression (Hamilton, 1960) are measures for which raw scores are interpretable, with meaningful 0-scores, cutoff scores for mild, moderate, and severe symptom levels, and consensus on the interval that defines a "clinically meaningful" change. We employed percent improvement as our outcome metric in this paper, but the ideas we presented could be adapted to other change metrics, such as a raw change score.

Measures of psychotherapeutic processes tend not to have meaningful units, but rather conform to the idea that "more is better." We recommend that attempts be made to define meaningful intervals, or anchor points, for measures of therapeutic processes. We also recommend measuring multiple process variables with commonly used measures in any given process-outcome study. This would allow for comparisons across studies of the distributions of these measures, and it would provide the opportunity for estimates to be made of the inter-correlations of the components.

Accounting for and Avoiding Confounds in Process-Outcome Investigations

We have shown that typical studies of psychotherapy can be expected to yield process-outcome correlations that are below .30, even if a powerful process has been identified and measured. In this context, with meta-analytic estimates of the alliance-outcome correlation falling in the range of .20 to .30 (Horvath, Del Re, Flückiger, & Symonds, 2011), one might be tempted to conclude that the alliance drives outcome, at least in the short term. However, few of the alliance studies have employed designs that can disentangle cause from consequence (Barber, Khalsa, & Sharpless, 2010; DeRubeis, Brotman, & Gibbons, 2005). We are aware of eight published studies, including four from our lab, in which the investigators controlled for the critical temporal confound. When we combined the results from these studies, and weighted them by study sample size, the resulting estimate of the correlation was .11 (DeRubeis, 2012, October). This suggests that the higher estimates, such as those reported in the Horvath et al. meta-analysis, may have been obtained at least in part because better outcomes lead to better alliances.

Process-outcome designs often contain other confounds that can produce spurious findings. One example occurs when the therapists in the study are represented in multiple dyads, yet these dyads are treated as independent observations. Appropriate analyses of these kinds of data would take into account the non-independence of dyads that share the same therapist. Failing to do so ignores the fact that patients' characteristics or behaviors can influence therapist behaviors, and it may be these same patient factors that promote positive therapeutic change. Estimates of alliance-outcome (Horvath et al., 2011) and adherence-outcome (e.g., DeRubeis & Feeley, 1990; Feeley, DeRubeis, & Gelfand, 1999) relationships may be inflated, therefore, due to the fact that most studies of these processes have not attended to this potential confound (but see Del Re, Flückiger, Horvath, Symonds, & Wampold, 2012, for an exception). For a more extensive discussion of these and other common confounds in process-outcome research, see Crits-Christoph, Connolly Gibbons, and Mukherjee (2013).

Focusing Investigations on Key Moments

We have focused thus far on research methods that could reveal important processes that tend to recur across a course of psychotherapy. However, effective therapy might best be understood as comprising relatively few key moments, or critical sessions, that largely account for change in psychotherapy. This possibility was delineated by Rice and Greenberg (1984), who recommended selecting as study points those moments within a session in which a notable change is observed in one or more key dimensions of the patient's psychological functioning (see also Aspland, Llewelyn, Hardy, Barkham, & Stiles, 2008; Greenberg, 2007; Pascual-Leone, Greenberg, & Pascual-Leone, 2009). Tang and DeRubeis's (1999) "sudden gains" methodology, in which correlates of sizeable single session symptom reductions are examined, is another promising example of this type of approach (see also Tang, DeRubeis, Beberman, & Pham, 2005; Tang, DeRubeis, Hollon, Amsterdam, & Shelton, 2007).

In conclusion, we have presented a framework that, unlike the "variance accounted for" approach, takes into account the potential effects of variation in patient Response Patterns and therapy *quality*. Findings from process-outcome and comparative outcome investigations will be misinterpreted insofar as these effects are not considered. Moreover, studies designed to accommodate these effects explicitly could reveal a more nuanced understanding of the importance of psychotherapeutic processes in the facilitation of positive patient outcomes.

Acknowledgments

We wish to thank Lorenzo Lorenzo-Luaces and Kim de Jong for their helpful comments on an earlier draft of this manuscript.

Notes

1. Skew = −.45; where negative values indicate left-skewed distributions and positive values indicate right-skewed distributions. A value of zero indicates a symmetric distribution.
2. Kurtosis = 1.7 (heavy tailed), where a normal distribution has a kurtosis of 0. Positive values indicate heavy-tailed distributions and negative values indicate light-tailed distributions.

References

Asay, T. P., & Lambert, M. J. (1999). The empirical case for the common factors in therapy: Quantitative findings. In M. A. Hubble, B. L. Duncan, & S. D. Miller (Eds.), *The heart and soul of change: What works in therapy* (1st ed., pp. 23–55). Washington DC: American Psychological Association.

Aspland, H., Llewelyn, S., Hardy, G. E., Barkham, M., & Stiles, W. (2008). Alliance ruptures and rupture resolution in cognitive–behavior therapy: A preliminary task analysis. *Psychotherapy Research, 18*, 699–710. doi:10.1080/10503300802291463

Beck, A. T., Steer, R. A., & Brown, G. K. (1996). *Manual for the Beck Depression Inventory* (2nd ed.). San Antonio, TX: The Psychological Corporation.

Barber, J. P., Khalsa, S., & Sharpless, B. A. (2010). The validity of the alliance as a predictor of psychotherapy outcome. In J. P. Barber, S. R. Khalsa, & B. A. Sharpless (Eds.), *The therapeutic alliance: An evidence-based guide to practice* (pp. 29–43). New York: Guilford Press.

Crits-Christoph, P., Connolly Gibbons, M. B., Crits-Christoph, K., Narducci, J., Schamberger, M., & Gallop, R. (2006). Can therapists be trained to improve their alliances? A preliminary study of alliance-fostering psychotherapy. *Psychotherapy Research, 16*, 268–281. doi:10.1080/10503300500268557

Crits-Christoph, P., Connolly Gibbons, M. B., & Mukherjee, D. (2013). Psychotherapy process-outcome research. In M. J. Lambert (Ed.), *Bergin and Garfield's handbook of psychotherapy and behavior change* (6th ed., pp. 298–340). Oxford: John Wiley & Sons.

Del Re, A. C., Flückiger, C., Horvath, A. O., Symonds, D., & Wampold, B. E. (2012). Therapist effects in the therapeutic alliance-outcome relationship: A restricted-maximum likelihood meta-analysis. *Clinical Psychology Review, 32*, 642–649. doi:10.1016/j.cpr.2012.07.002

DeRubeis, R. J. (2012, October). Mechanism of change in the treatment of depression. In Incorporating Use-Inspired Basic Research into Research on Intervention Efficacy. Symposium conducted at a meeting sponsored by the National Institutes of Health (NIH) Common Fund program on the Science of Behavior Change (SOBC): *Revisiting Pasteur's Quadrant: Use-Inspired Basic Research*, Washington DC.

DeRubeis, R. J., Brotman, M. A., & Gibbons, C. J. (2005). A conceptual and methodological analysis of the nonspecifics argument. *Clinical Psychology: Science and Practice, 12*, 174–183. doi:10.1093/clipsy.bpi022

DeRubeis, R. J., & Feeley, M. (1990). Determinants of change in cognitive therapy for depression. *Cognitive Therapy and Research, 14*, 469–482. doi:10.1007/BF01172968

Driessen, E., Cuijpers, P., Hollon, S. D., & Dekker, J. J. (2010). Does pretreatment severity moderate the efficacy of psychological treatment of adult outpatient depression? A meta-analysis. *Journal of Consulting and Clinical Psychology, 78*, 668–680. doi:10.1037/a0020570

Feeley, M., DeRubeis, R. J., & Gelfand, L. A. (1999). The temporal relation of adherence and alliance to symptom change in cognitive therapy for depression. *Journal of Consulting and Clinical Psychology, 67*, 578–582. doi:10.1037/0022-006X.67.4.578

Fournier, J. C., DeRubeis, R. J., Hollon, S. D., Dimidjian, S., Amsterdam, J. D., Shelton, R. C., & Fawcett, J. (2010). Antidepressant drug effects and depression severity: a patient-level meta-analysis. *The Journal of the American Medical Association, 303*, 47–53. doi:10.1001/jama.2009.1943

Greenberg, L. S. (2007). A guide to conducting a task analysis of psychotherapeutic change. *Psychotherapy Research, 17*, 15–30. doi:10.1080/10503300600720390

Hamilton, M. (1960). A rating scale for depression. *Journal of Neurology, Neurosurgery and Psychiatry, 23*, 56–62. doi:10.1136/jnnp.23.1.56

Horvath, A. O., Del Re, A. C., Flückiger, C., & Symonds, D. (2011). Alliance in individual psychotherapy. *Psychotherapy, 48*, 9–16. doi:10.1037/a0022186

Lambert, M. J. (1992). Psychotherapy outcome research: Implications for integrative and eclectic therapists. In J. C. Norcross & M. R. Goldfried (Eds.), *Handbook of psychotherapy integration* (pp. 94–129). New York: Basic Books.

Lambert, M. J. (2013). The efficacy and effectiveness of psychotherapy. In M. J. Lambert (Ed.), *Bergin and Garfield's handbook of psychotherapy and behavior change* (6th ed., pp. 169–218). Oxford: John Wiley & Sons.

Lambert, M. J., & Barley, D. E. (2001). Research summary on the therapeutic relationship and psychotherapy outcome. *Psychotherapy, 38*, 357–361. doi:10.1037/0033-3204.38.4.357

Lambert, M. J., & Barley, D. E. (2002). Research summary on the therapeutic relationship and psychotherapy outcome. In J. C. Norcross (Ed.), *Psychotherapy relationships that work* (pp. 17–32). New York: Oxford University Press.

Pascual-Leone, A., Greenberg, L. S., & Pascual-Leone, J. (2009). Developments in task analysis: New methods to study change. *Psychotherapy Research, 19*, 527–542 doi:10.1080/10503300902897797

Rice, L. N., & Greenberg, L. S. (1984). The new research paradigm. In L. N. Rice & L. S. Greenberg (Eds.), *Patterns of change: Intensive analysis of psychotherapy process* (pp. 7–24). New York: Guilford Press.

Tang, T. Z., & DeRubeis, R. J. (1999). Sudden gains and critical sessions in cognitive-behavioral therapy for depression. *Journal of Consulting and Clinical Psychology, 67*, 894–904. doi:10.1037/0022-006X.67.6.894

Tang, T. Z., DeRubeis, R. J., Beberman, R., & Pham, T. (2005). Cognitive changes, critical sessions, and sudden gains in cognitive-behavioral therapy for depression. *Journal of Consulting and Clinical Psychology, 73*, 168–172. doi:10.1037/0022-006X.73.1.168

Tang, T. Z., DeRubeis, R. J., Hollon, S. D., Amsterdam, J. A., & Shelton, R. C. (2007). Sudden gains in cognitive therapy of depression and depression relapse/recurrence. *Journal of Consulting and Clinical Psychology, 75*, 404–408. doi:10.1037/0022-006X.75.3.404

Thase, M. E. (1999). How should efficacy be evaluated in randomized clinical trials of treatments for depression? *The Journal of Clinical Psychiatry, 60*, 23–31.

Wiles, N., Thomas, L., Anbel, A., Ridgway, N., Turner, N., Campbell, J., … Lewis, G. (2013). Cognitive behavioural therapy as an adjunct to pharmacotherapy for primary care based patients with treatment resistant depression: results of the CoBalt randomized controlled trial. *The Lancet, 381*, 375–384. doi:10.1016/S0140-6736(12)61552-9

The associations among improvement and alliance expectations, alliance during treatment, and treatment outcome for major depressive disorder

JACQUES P. BARBER[1], SIGAL ZILCHA-MANO[1], ROBERT GALLOP[2], MARNA BARRETT[3], KEVIN S. McCARTHY[4], & ULRIKE DINGER[1,5]

[1]*Derner Institute, Adelphi University, Garden City, NY, USA;* [2]*Statistics, West Chester University, West Chester, PA, USA;* [3]*Psychiatry, University of Pennsylvania, Philadelphia, PA, USA;* [4]*Department of Psychology, Chestnut Hill College, Philadelphia, PA, USA &* [5]*Clinic for General Internal Medicine and Psychosomatics, University of Heidelberg, Germany*

Abstract

Objective: To examine the associations between treatment/outcome expectations, alliance before and during treatment, and the impact of alliance on symptomatic improvement. **Methods:** One hundred and fifty-three depressed patients randomized to dynamic supportive-expressive psychotherapy (SET), antidepressant medication (ADM) or placebo (PBO) + clinical management completed ratings of treatment expectations, therapeutic alliance (CALPAS, WAI-S), and depressive symptoms (HAM-D). **Results:** Pretreatment expectations of the therapeutic alliance were significantly related to alliance later in therapy but did not differ across treatments and did not predict outcome. Alliance development over time differed between treatments; it increased more in SET than in PBO. After controlling for prior symptom improvement, early alliance predicted subsequent depression change. **Conclusions:** Expectations of alliance and of treatment outcome/improvement, measured prior to treatment onset, predicted subsequent alliance.

The therapeutic alliance is one of the most extensively studied concepts in psychotherapy research for three main reasons. First, clinical scholars from different theoretical approaches have noted that a positive treatment relationship is important, and perhaps necessary for the conduct of an effective psychotherapy (Beck, Rush, Shaw, & Emery, 1979; Greenberg, Rice, & Elliott, 1993; Greenson, 1965; Luborsky, 1995; Raue & Goldfried, 1994). Second, early alliance ratings have been repeatedly shown to have a small, but seemingly robust association with therapeutic outcome (Horvath, Del Re, Flückiger, & Symonds, 2011). Third, clinicians and researchers have often suggested that the therapeutic relationship is, in itself, curative (e.g., Lambert & Barley, 2001). For instance, several studies have argued that the universal effect of therapeutic alliance on outcome is likely to account for the equivalency of outcome found in comparative trials of psychotherapy (e.g., Barber, 2009). In this paper we address several unanswered questions regarding the alliance. First, we examine the idea that the therapeutic alliance develops very early in the relationship, possibly even prior to meeting with the therapist, as well as showing changes over time. Second, we examine patients' expectations about treatment as potential influences on early treatment alliance.

Development of Alliance Over Time

When is the therapeutic alliance created? Some studies suggest that alliance is formed early in treatment and remains stable across sessions, as indicated by moderate to strong correlations between alliance ratings early and later in treatment (e.g., Paivio & Bahr, 1998). Even alliance ratings from early assessment sessions before the start of therapy were strong predictors of alliance scores later on (Hilsenroth, Peters, & Ackerman, 2004). Consistent with this notion is the idea that most of the variance in alliance takes place in the first treatment session (Sexton, Hembre, & Kvarme, 1996; Sexton, Littauer, Sexton, & Tømmerås, 2005). In fact, one might argue that at least a portion of the alliance develops very early or even before treatment begins and does not necessarily require much if any therapist-patient interaction. If this is the case, the "starting point" for the development of the therapeutic alliance may depend on general relationship expectations and dispositional tendencies that are independent of and precede patient-therapist encounters. However, few studies have examined this possibility.

In contrast to studies suggesting the stability of alliance, other studies have shown that alliance tends to strengthen throughout treatment, although there are significant differences between patient-therapist dyads (Dinger, Strack, Sachsse, & Schauenburg, 2009). Indeed, several distinct patterns of alliance development have been described in the literature. For example, Kramer, deRoten, Beretta, Michel, and Despland (2008) differentiated three distinct patterns of alliance formation: A group in which alliance increased across sessions, a group in which alliance remained stable throughout treatment, and a group in which the alliance worsened over time. Stiles and colleagues (2004) described four distinct patterns in which alliance was steadily increasing, stable, or steadily decreasing. In addition, a fourth group showed a more rapid early increase with stable alliance scores in the second half of treatment. For very brief treatments of four sessions, U-shaped patterns of alliance development were found with initially high ratings of alliance that decreased during the middle of treatment and then rose again in the last session (Kivlighan & Shaughnessy, 2000). These patterns of alliance development suggest the importance of measuring alliance throughout therapy. However, the majority of researchers have relied on assessments of alliance only during the early phase of therapy (often between session 2 and 5).

Correlation Versus Steps Towards Mapping Causal Relations in Alliance-Outcome Research

Decades of research on alliance in psychotherapy have consistently linked the strength of the therapeutic alliance with therapy outcomes. The most recent meta-analysis combined over 14,000 psychotherapy cases and reported a correlation of .285, with better alliances associated with greater symptomatic improvement (Horvath et al., 2011). Despite such a consistent correlation, the magnitude of the alliance-outcome correlation differs between studies, possibly due to the methodological research strategy employed. For example, if alliance was assessed at only one early session (e.g., session 3), the reported association with overall treatment outcome tended to be lower than when alliance scores were aggregated over several early sessions (Crits-Christoph, Gibbons, Hamilton, Ring-Kurtz, & Gallop, 2011). Although aggregating alliance measures over time is likely to create a more robust and reliable assessment of the alliance, it has the disadvantage of making it hard for researchers to test whether change in symptoms before the measurement of the alliance causes subsequent change in symptoms or whether the change in alliance occurring between the aggregated assessments causes symptom change (Barber, 2009; Crits-Christoph, Connolly Gibbons, & Mukherjee, 2013). In addition, research designs that account for early symptom change (i.e., from intake to early alliance assessment) generally find lower or negligible alliance-outcome correlations than do those not considering early change (Crits-Christoph et al., 2013). Similarly, sudden gains in depressive symptom improvement are at times followed by improvements in the alliance rather than being preceded by alliance improvements (Tang & DeRubeis, 1999). These findings bring into question the causal role of alliance in subsequent symptom change (DeRubeis, Brotman, & Gibbons, 2005). Other studies, however, show that early alliance ratings predict subsequent therapy outcome over and above the effect of previous symptom improvement (Barber, Connolly, Crits-Christoph, Gladis, & Siqueland, 2000; Klein et al., 2003; Zilcha-Mano, Dinger, McCarthy, & Barber, in press). Such divergence among studies calls for more research on the impact of early alliance on outcome while controlling for prior symptomatic improvement (Barber, 2009). Accounting for the correct temporal sequence and for competing influential predictors is the nearest approximation towards establishing a causal relationship that observational studies allow.

Alliance in Different Forms of Treatment

A separate issue regarding the alliance-outcome association is related to treatment modality. Alliance effects have been reported for a broad range of psychotherapies, among them cognitive-behavioral, psychodynamic, interpersonal, and emotion-focused psychotherapy (e.g., Constantino, Arnow, Blasey, & Agras, 2005; Flückiger, Regli, & Grawe, 2005;

Greenberg & Malcolm, 2002; Reis & Grenyer, 2004; Watson, McMullen, Prosser, & Bedard, 2011). Despite some studies reporting lower alliance-outcome correlations for cognitive therapy (CT) and questioning a causal role for alliance in outcome in CT (e.g., Feeley, DeRubeis, & Gelfand, 1999; Strunk, Brotmann, & DeRubeis, 2010; Strunk, Cooper, Ryan, DeRubeis, & Hollon, 2012), a recent meta-analysis found that the alliance-outcome correlation was similar in cognitive behavior therapies (CBT) and other forms of psychotherapies (Flückiger, Del Re, Wampold, Symonds, & Horvath, 2012). However, studies were included in which the alliance assessment preceded the measurement of outcome as well as studies in which the alliance ratings followed outcome assessments.

It is also unclear whether the effect of alliance on outcome is specific to psychotherapy or if it can be found in other forms of mental health treatment. Data from the Treatment of Depression Collaborative Research Study (TDCRP) indicate that alliance correlates with outcome not only in psychotherapy, but also in clinical management of pharmacotherapy and placebo (Krupnick et al., 1994, 1996). However, Strunk, Stewart, et al. (2010) reported that observer-rated early alliance in clinical management of anti-depressant medication use or placebo was not significantly related to subsequent change in depression, although greater clinician support in early sessions predicted a lower rate of improvement with placebo. Thus, studies analyzing patient-rated alliance and controlling for prior symptom improvement are needed in pharmacotherapy and placebo treatments as well as psychotherapy if we are to better understand the role of alliance in treatment outcome.

Alliance and Pretreatment Expectations About Treatment Outcome

Alliance measured early in treatment has been shown to be influenced by patient and therapist characteristics. In addition to attachment patterns and interpersonal style (Diener & Monroe, 2011; Dinger, Strack, Leichsenring, & Schauenburg, 2007), research has found an association between patients' pretreatment expectations and alliance quality. Treatment expectations encompass both expectations about the process of therapy (such as the alliance) as well as expectations about therapy outcome (i.e., symptom change or improvement) (Constantino, Glass, Arnkoff, Ametrano, & Smith, 2011). A recent meta-analysis of 78 studies found a very small, but significant effect (r = .12) of expectations of treatment improvement on subsequent symptom improvement across a variety of psychological disorders and therapeutic approaches (Constantino, Arnkoff, Glass, Ametrano, & Smith, 2011). However, the effect sizes for these comparisons were heterogeneous across studies and the failsafe N indicated that 10 unpublished, non-significant studies would have been necessary to challenge the meaningful association. In addition to the association with outcome, higher expectations for improvement have also shown an association with better alliances, especially if alliance is assessed early in treatment (Connolly Gibbons et al., 2003; Constantino et al., 2005). With several studies showing a meaningful effect of expectations for improvement on symptom improvement, it could be that alliance mediates the effect, at least partially (Constantino et al., 2005; Johansson, Høglend, & Hersoug, 2011; Joyce, Ogrodniczuk, Piper, & McCallum, 2003; Meyer et al., 2002). Accordingly, high expectations for improvement would lead to more favorable alliances, which would then facilitate psychotherapeutic change.

Research Questions

The present study investigated the relation between therapeutic alliance and pre-treatment expectations of improvement in a study of treatments for depression. The data originate from a randomized clinical trial comparing supportive-expressive dynamic psychotherapy (SET), antidepressant medication (MED) plus clinical management, and placebo (PBO) plus clinical management for the treatment of Major Depressive Disorder (MDD; Barber, Barrett, Gallop, Rynn, & Rickels, 2012). All three groups improved throughout the course of treatment, with no significant differences emerging between groups. Such equivalence in outcome encourages examination of whether the underlying mechanisms of change are comparable. The present study examined the following five research questions:

1. How are pretreatment expectations about alliance and improvement related to alliance during the course of treatment?
2. Does the alliance differ between the three treatment groups (supportive-expressive therapy, medication and placebo) over time?
3. Do better alliances predict greater improvement in depression? Does the type of treatment (SET, MED, PBO) moderate the alliance-outcome association?
4. Are pretreatment expectations for improvement a predictor of symptomatic improvement? Is treatment group a moderator for the expectation-outcome association?

5. Is the expectation-outcome association mediated by the therapeutic alliance?

Methods

Participants

Of the original 156 patients with Major Depressive Disorder randomized in the original study, 153 could be included for the present analyses. From the original sample, 149 patients completed at least one alliance questionnaire and 150 rated their outcome expectations. The present sample included 92 (60.1%) females, the mean age was 37.8 (SD 12.11), and about half were ethnic minorities (43.8% African Americans, 2% Asians, 49.0% Caucasians, 5.2% Latinos,). Eighty-five percent of patients had at least one comorbid disorder, including anxiety disorders (45.0%) and current substance abuse or past dependence disorder (35%). In addition, 46.3% had a comorbid axis-2 personality disorder. Diagnoses were obtained through structured clinical interviews conducted by doctoral and Master-level diagnosticians (First, Spitzer, Gibbon, & Williams, 1995). Diagnosticians were blind to treatment conditions.

Treatments

All treatments were provided for 16 weeks. Manualized dynamic SET for depression combines supportive techniques fostering a positive therapeutic relationship with a focus on understanding the patient's problematic relationship patterns. The goal is to help the patient work through his/her core relational difficulties within the context of a positive relationship (Luborsky, 1984, 1995). Patients in this study received 20 sessions of individual psychotherapy, with a frequency of twice weekly for the first 4 weeks and weekly for weeks 5–16. Psychotherapists delivering SET were four experienced clinicians with at least 15 years of clinical experience. Patients and therapists in SET could not be blind to treatment conditions.

The MED and PBO conditions were managed by 10 experienced psychopharmacologists who delivered clinical management (CM) as manualized by Fawcett, Epstein, Fiester, Elkin, and Autry (1987). Patients were seen weekly for the first 6 weeks, after which the psychopharmacologist was permitted to extend the time between visits to 2 weeks. The CM manual prohibited formal psychotherapeutic techniques, but supportive interventions (such as acknowledging gains, reinforcing accomplishments, or offering empathy and warmth) were allowed. Patients in the medication condition were treated with either with sertraline (MED) or placebo (PBO) and psychopharmacologists, patients, and evaluators were blind to the MED or PBO assignment (triple blind). At week 8, patients non-responsive to sertraline were switched to venlafaxine. Patients non-responsive to placebo were switched to a second placebo. Patients responding to treatment maintained the same condition (MED or PBO). Blinding was broken at week 16, and PBO patients were offered 16 weeks of open-label medication.

Measures

Alliance. Quality of the therapeutic alliance was assessed with two questionnaires based on different definitions of the therapeutic alliance.

Patients completed the 12-item Working Alliance Inventory-Short Form (WAI-S; Horvath & Greenberg, 1989; Tracey & Kokotovic, 1989). The WAI-S closely follows the theoretical model proposed by Bordin (1979). Four items assess the agreement between patients and therapists on the goals of treatment, another four assess the agreement on the tasks or interventions of treatment, and four measure the affective bond between the patient and therapist. In this study, the total WAI-S score was used. Items are rated on a 7-point Likert-scale from 1 = "*Never*" to 7 = "*Always*". Internal consistency for the total scale in this study ranged from .92 to .95 at the different time points for assessment.

The California Psychotherapy Alliance Scale (CALPAS; Gaston & Marmar, 1994) is a 24-item questionnaire which is designed to "address the separate contributions of the client and therapist to the alliance and the extent of mutual agreement on the working strategies and goals of therapy" (Hatcher & Barends, 1996, p. 1327). This definition is broader than Bordin's (1979) definition of the alliance. Each item is rated on a 7-point Likert scale, ranging from 1 = "*Not at all*" to 7 = "*Very much so*". The items are grouped into four scales: Patient Working Capacity, Patient Commitment, Therapist Understanding and Involvement, and Working Strategy Consensus. Because these four scales were found to be highly intercorrelated (e.g., Barber et al., 1999), the total CALPAS score was used for analysis. The internal consistency scores of the CALPAS total ranged from .75 to .90 at the different assessment points in the current study.

Expectation of the alliance. Patient expectations for alliance were assessed by the CALPAS and WAI-S, which were obtained prior to meeting with the therapist. The following sentence was added to the instructions for both questionnaires: *"Because you have not yet experienced treatment through this* *study, answer the following questions, thinking about how you expect treatment to be."*

Expectations for improvement. Patient expectations for treatment improvement were assessed at intake, prior to randomization. Patients responded to the question "Overall, how much improvement do you expect to experience as a result of treatment?" on a 7-point scale ranging from 1 = not at all to 7 = great amount. This 1-item measure was taken from the Patient Attitudes and Expectations questionnaire adapted from the Patient Attitudes and Expectations form used in the NIMH Treatment of Depression Collaborative Research Program (Elkin, Parloff, Hadley, & Autry, 1985).

Outcome. Depressive symptoms were assessed with the 17-item version of the Hamilton Rating Scale for Depression ($HRSD_{17}$; Hamilton, 1960; Williams, 1988). The $HRSD_{17}$ is a clinician-administered measure of depression severity. It consists of 17 items with total possible scores ranging from 0 to 52. Higher scores indicate greater severity in depression. Inter-judge reliability for the current study as assessed by intraclass correlation (ICC [2,1]; Shrout & Fleiss, 1979) was .92.

Procedure

Depressive symptoms were assessed at intake and eight times during therapy (weeks 2, 4, 6, 7, 8, 12, 15, and 16). Outcome expectation was measured during the intake assessment. Alliance was assessed at intake before patients met with their therapist for the first time (alliance expectation) as well as during weeks 2, 4, 8, and 16. Due to missing data and patient drop-out, sample size varies at the different time points, and not all patients received and returned questionnaires on the scheduled dates. Including intake alliance, the mean number of usable alliance questionnaires was on average 3.5 alliance questionnaires per patient (SD = 1.45) out of a maximum of five questionnaires. The completion rates of alliance questionnaires varied at the four major time points (intake alliance N = 139, early alliance weeks 2–4 N = 124, mid-treatment alliance weeks 5–11 N = 100, end of treatment alliance weeks 12–16 N = 74).

Statistical Analyses

Correlations among expectations of alliance (assessed at intake), outcome and alliance ratings later in treatment were assessed using Pearson correlations. Analyses of alliance development and symptom change over time were carried out with multilevel models (Raudenbush & Bryk, 2002). All multilevel models were two-level with multiple measurements (level 1) nested within patients (level 2). Time was the only explanatory variable entered as level-1 predictor. Additional predictors were entered on level 2 according to the research question (e.g., alliance, expectation or treatment condition). Treatment condition was entered as categorical variable (MED, SET, PBO); the PBO groups served as reference category. Level-2 predictors were entered as predictors of time slope and therefore are considered two-way interactions of time by predictor. All analyses were carried out with IBM SPSS, version 19.

Results

How are Pretreatment Alliance and Outcome Expectations Related to Alliance Throughout Treatment? How are early and later alliances during treatment related?

At intake, CALPAS and WAI-S alliance expectations were positively correlated (r = .77). In addition, both correlated significantly with the outcome expectation (r_{CALPAS} = .42; r_{WAI} = .43, both p < .001). The correlations between expectation of the alliance at intake and alliance scores later in treatment were significant; the moderate coefficients around r = .50 indicate that about 25% of the variance of alliance levels during treatment is explained by alliance expectations (Table I). The correlations between outcome expectations and alliance were also significant and ranged between low and moderate. Correlations between alliance scores at different time points in therapy were large (ranging from r = .7 to r = .8), showing that more than 50% of the variance of treatment alliances later in treatment was determined by early alliances.

Does Alliance Differ between the three Treatment groups over Time?

All analyses were carried out separately for the CALPAS and the WAI-S alliance measures. Differences failed to be found between the three groups regarding expectations of the alliance at intake, CALPAS: $F(2;130)$ =.57, ns; WAI-S: $F(2;126)$ = .19, ns. Using multilevel modeling, we compared alliance slopes over time for the treatment groups. Multiple measurements were nested within patients. Due to a nonlinear change of individual patient alliance scores over time, a logarithmic transformation of time (weeks) was deemed most appropriate to quantify change in alliance scores (Diggle, Liang, & Zeger, 1994). There was no significant overall effect of time on CALPAS scores. However, the week by

Table I. Correlation of alliance and outcome expectations at intake with alliance scores during treatment

		1.	2.	3.	4.	5.	6.	7.	8.	9.
CALPAS	1. Expectation (N = 133)	1.0								
	2. Early treatment (N = 121)	.59	1.0							
	3. Mid-treatment (N = 99)	.53	.73	1.0						
	4. Termination (N = 60)	.57	.79	.82	1.0					
WAI-S	5. Expectation (N = 129)	.77	.59	.50	.47	1.0				
	6. Early treatment (N = 120)	.43	.88	.64	.69	.55	1.0			
	7. Mid-treatment (N = 99)	.42	.65	.78	.75	.49	.72	1.0		
	8. Termination (N = 58)	.54	.79	.74	.88	.50	.78	.81	1.0	
	9. Outcome expectation	.42	.39	.40	.46	.43	.32	.42	.49	1.0

Note. All depicted correlations significant, with $p < .001$.

treatment interaction ($F(2;127.4) = 5.57$, $p < .005$) indicated that CALPAS slopes differed significantly over the course of time between the groups (Figure 1). For PBO, CALPAS slope estimate decreased over time (–.10, $SE = .044$ per log week, $t(129.4) = -2.35$, $p < .02$). The estimated slope of the alliance in SET increased significantly by .10 CALPAS units ($SE = .045$) per log week ($t(130.8) = 2.20$, $p < .03$). The alliance slope for SET was significantly different from the PBO slope ($t(130.1) = 3.21$, $p < .002$). While the estimated MED slope also differed significantly from PBO ($t(125.7) = 2.38$, $p < .019$), its increase over time was not significant.

The average WAI-S slope increased significantly over time ($F(1;130.6) = 19.12$, $p < .001$) (Figure 2). Although the week by treatment interaction did not reach significance for the WAI-S ($F(2;130.5) = 2.06$, $p < .13$), exploratory post hoc analyses indicated that the increase in alliance was significantly steeper for SET compared to PBO ($t(127.6) = 1.99$, $p < .049$). A significant increase over time was observed for the SET group (slope estimate 2.64 per log week, SE .71, $t(136.6) = 3.72$, $p < .001$) and the MED group (slope estimate 1.96 per log week, SE .69, $t(123.4) = 2.84$, $p < .005$), but not for the PBO group. There were no significant differences in change in alliance between MED and SET on either alliance scales.

Do Better Alliances Predict Greater Change in Depression?

We examined this question in three sets of analyses. The first focused on the expectation of alliance before the patient met the therapist/psychiatrist (alliance expectation at intake), the second focused on the alliance during early phases of treatment (weeks 2–4), and the third looked at early changes in the alliance (from intake through week 4). The multilevel model on change in depression was similar to the main outcome multilevel analysis (Barber et al., 2012), using time as logarithmic transformation of weeks but included alliance as a predictor of the slope (rate of change). In addition, we controlled for depression severity at intake. For all analyses we included the treatment condition as a potential moderator of alliance effects on outcome.

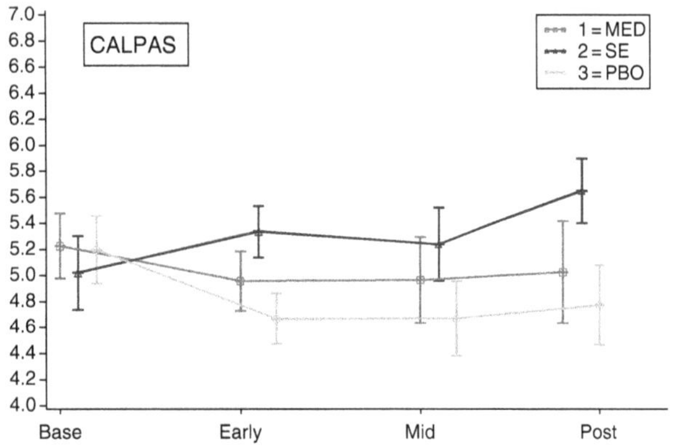

Figure 1. Change in observed CALPAS alliance scores as a function of time and treatment group. The multilevel model assessing group comparison in rate of change per unit of time (time as logarithm of week) showed a significant treatment × time interaction ($F(2;127.4) = 5.57$, $p = .005$).

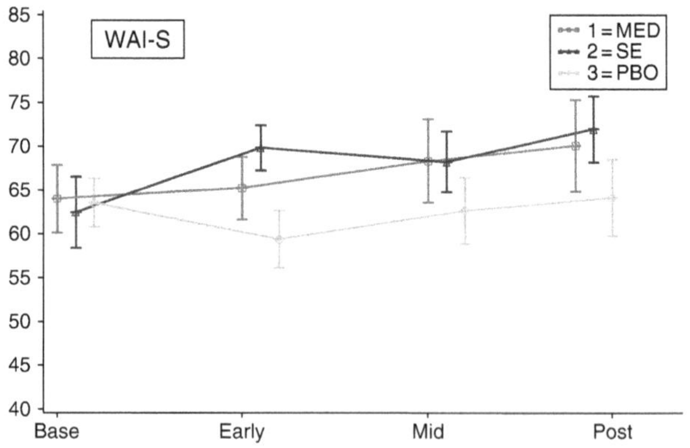

Figure 2. Change in observed WAI-S alliance scores as a function of treatment group. The multilevel model assessing group comparison in rate of change per unit of time (time as logarithm of week) showed a significant average increase over time ($F(1;130.6) = 19.12$, $p < .001$), but no difference in slopes between treatment groups.

Expectation of Alliance

Predicting outcome from the expectation of alliance with the CALPAS showed no significant time by alliance expectation interaction and no significant three-way interaction for time by alliance expectation by treatment group. Together these results indicate that intake CALPAS expectation was not associated with outcome and that the impact of the CALPAS expectation on outcome did not differ per treatment group. In contrast to the CALPAS, the expectation of the alliance measured by the WAI-S was significantly related to symptomatic improvement over the course of therapy (time by alliance expectation: $F(1,108.1) = 6.49$, $p < .012$) but did not differ as a function of treatment. To interpret the impact of the WAI-S alliance expectation, we estimated the change in depression severity for patients with average alliance score, as well as for those who scored one standard deviation above and below the mean (Cohen, Cohen, West, & Aiken, 2003). Table II shows that an individual with an alliance expectation score one standard deviation above the mean changes more in depression severity (1/2 HRSD point per each time period) than patients with an average alliance score.

Predicting Outcome from Alliance During Treatment

We examined the impact of early alliance (weeks 2–4) on subsequent changes in symptoms. The multilevel model on symptom change is restrained to assessments of depressive symptoms after week 4 and controls for initial depression severity. In order to disentangle early alliance from early symptom improvement, we examined the predictive value of alliance both with and without accounting for early change in depressive symptoms. Early symptom improvement was quantified as the subject-specific depression change from intake to the early assessment of the alliance (weeks 2–4, respectively). Early CALPAS alliance was marginally related to subsequent improvement in depression when prior symptom change was not controlled (time by early CALPAS interaction, $F(1,102.9) = 3.61$, $p < .06$) and vanished when early symptom change was controlled ($p = .19$). For both models, there were no significant three-way interactions for time by early alliance by treatment group, indicating that the impact of early CALPAS alliance did not differ between the treatment groups.

A different pattern of results emerged for the WAI-S. Without accounting for prior symptom change, the time by early WAI-S interaction was significant ($F(1,102.5) = 4.94$; $p < .028$). Patients reporting better alliances improved more rapidly during subsequent weeks of treatment. This effect was still significant when controlling for prior symptom improvement ($F(1,95.3) = 4.11$, $p < .045$). There were no significant three-way interactions for time by early WAI-S alliance by treatment group, indicating that the influence of early WAI-S alliance did not depend on the treatment group.

Table II. Estimates of the change in depression as a function of WAI-S at intake (expectation of the alliance)

Label	Estimate	Standard error	*df*	*t*	*p*
Average change	−2.388	.2448	87.7	−9.76	<.001
Average change for +1 SD WAI-S	−2.962	.3299	105.4	−8.98	<.001
Average change for −1 SD WAI-S	−1.816	.3350	106.9	−5.42	<.001

Predicting Outcome from Early Change in Alliance

In the next set of analyses, we focused on the change in alliance from intake through week 4 as a predictor for subsequent improvement in depression. The multilevel model on changes in symptoms is again restrained to assessments of depressive symptoms after week 4. Early change in alliance was quantified as the subject-specific alliance slope from intake to week 4. Initial depression severity was included as a covariate. In addition, the impact of early alliance change was compared for models with and without early improvement in depression (subject-specific depression slope from intake to week 4). Because the pattern of results regarding alliance was similar whether or not early symptomatic improvement was included, only findings for the models including early change in depression are reported. As indicated by the non-significant time by early CALPAS change interaction, change in CALPAS scores from intake to week 4 was not related to later symptom change ($F(1,75.8) = .79$; $p <= .38$). In addition, there was no significant three-way interaction of time by alliance change by treatment group ($F(2,76.9) = .03$; $p <= .98$). Findings looked different for the WAI-S. While there was no direct effect of early WAI-S change on the symptom improvement slope, the three-way interaction of time by alliance change by treatment group interaction was significant ($F(2,89.2) = 4.89$, $p = .01$). To understand the effect, we quantified change in depression as a function of treatment condition at the mean slope estimate in early alliance change, as well as for one

Table III. Slope estimates and within group effect of early change in WAI-S alliance on subsequent change in depressive symptoms

Label	Estimate	Standard error	*df*	*t*	*p*
SET - Average change for mean early WAI-S change	−2.868	.902	96.1	−3.18	.002
SET - Avg change for +1 SD early WAI-S change	−1.701	.979	118.5	−1.74	.085
SET - Avg change for −1 SD early WAI-S change	−4.035	1.123	147.3	−3.59	<.001
Effect in SET	1.167	.544	96.5	2.15	.034
MED - Average change for mean early WAI-S change	−2.505	.896	93.7	−2.80	.006
MED - Avg change for +1 SD early WAI-S change	−3.301	1.014	120.4	−3.26	.001
MED - Avg change for −1 SD early WAI-S change	−1.709	1.701	133.7	−1.59	.113
Effect in MED	−.796	.535	82.1	−1.49	.141
PBO - Average change for mean early WAI-S change	−2.911	.909	98.5	3.20	.002
PBO - Avg change for +1 SD early WAI-S change	−3.480	1.105	141.1	−3.15	.002
PBO - Avg change for −1 SD early WAI-S change	−2.342	.980	119.9	−2.39	.018
Effect in PBO	−.569	.514	86.6	−1.106	.272

standard deviation above and below the mean (Table III). In addition, we estimated the effect of early WAI-S alliance change on subsequent changes in depression within each treatment condition. The slope estimates show a significant effect of early WAI-S change only for SET, indicating that, contrary to expectations, a decrease in early alliance ratings predicted further improvement in depressive symptoms. Although not significant, the effect for the other two conditions MED and PBO is reversed compared to SET, pointing in the expected direction where an increase in alliance is associated with further symptom improvement.

Are Pretreatment Outcome Expectations a Predictor of Symptomatic Improvement?

Next, we examined whether the expectation of treatment improvement/outcome was related to change in depressive symptoms. Similar to the multilevel models with alliance as predictor of outcome, time was modeled as logarithmic transformation of weeks and initial symptom severity was included as a covariate. The time by expectation interaction failed to reach significance ($F(1,108.9) = 2.84$, $p = .095$). The three-way interaction of time by outcome expectation by treatment group was not significant, indicating that the effect of outcome expectations did not differ between the treatment groups.

Is the Improvement Expectation-Outcome Association Mediated by the Therapeutic Alliance?

The last research questions asked whether or not the potential association between expectation for improvement and actual outcome was mediated through the therapeutic alliance. However, as the association between expectations and outcome was not significant, step one of the Baron and Kenny (1986) procedure for mediation analysis was not fulfilled. However, the association between expectations and outcome was not significant. Without a significant and meaningful effect to explain, we decided against a further mediation analysis

Discussion

Using data from an RCT comparing supportive-expressive dynamic psychotherapy with antidepressant medication and placebo (Barber et al., 2012), we investigated the role of expectations for alliance and outcome on the development of the alliance and outcome across these three treatment groups using two different but widely used measures of the therapeutic alliance. Interestingly, our results differed depending on which measure of the alliance was used in the analyses.

In this paper we utilized a measure of what we call alliance expectation, that is, patients were asked to fill out a slightly modified alliance questionnaire before the patient actually met the therapist. A relatively high association was found between alliance expectations and early treatment alliance, suggesting that roughly a quarter of the variance in alliance depends on those pretreatment expectations of the alliance. However, the development of alliance over the course of treatment also impacted subsequent levels of alliance as all correlations among alliance scores over time were highly significant and moderate in magnitude. This finding is consistent with that of earlier studies (e.g., Hilsenroth et al., 2004; Paivio & Bahr, 1998) in which pretreatment alliance expectations as well the ongoing experience of the actual patient-therapist encounter influence the overall alliance.

Patient expectations of good outcome significantly influenced the alliance (see also Connolly Gibbons et al., 2003). This is important as expectations are one of the few patient variables that can potentially be improved by specifically addressing them at the beginning or prior to treatment (Constantino, Ametrano, & Greenberg, 2012). For example, McKee and colleagues (2007) showed that motivation enhancement resulted in higher outcome expectations for cocaine users receiving CBT compared to those individuals who did not receive motivational enhancement.

The next research question concerned potential differences between the process of the three treatments, keeping in mind that outcome failed to differ between the groups. We found that SET patients reported a strengthening of the alliance as measured by the CALPAS over time consistent with findings reported by Dinger et al. (2009). However, the strength of the alliance decreased over time in the PBO condition, suggesting that treatment processes likely differed among the treatments. For example, the more intense and frequent contacts in SET may have accounted for the strengthening of the alliance whereas less intense and frequent contact in the PBO condition may have weakened the alliance. However, the fact that alliance decreased in PBO but remained unchanged in the MED condition is more difficult to explain as both groups received the same intensity of intervention and the same "treatment" as far as the patients were aware. Despite the worsening of the alliance as measured by the CALPAS in PBO, depressive symptoms in PBO patients improved equally well. It is noteworthy that with the WAI-S, all groups showed significant increases over time. Together these findings reflect the fact that the conceptualization of alliance reflected in the CALPAS is broader than that used in the working alliance (WAI-S).

As there are many ways to test the association between alliance and outcome, we focused on three different sets of analyses. The first set examined alliance expectations at intake as potential predictors of outcome. While alliance expectations as measured with the CALPAS were not related to change in depressive symptoms, WAI expectations turned out to be a significant predictor of symptomatic improvement over the course of therapy. Because most of the existing studies on expectations have focused on outcome expectations (often called role expectations), we do not know of any previous studies on alliance expectations predicting treatment outcome. Based on the diverging findings with the two alliance measurements, our data suggest that expectations of the therapeutic alliance following Bordin's (1979) conceptualization of the alliance may be influential in both psychotherapy and clinical management of depression.

The second set of alliance-outcome analyses examined the impact of early treatment alliance on subsequent change in symptoms. Adding to the discussion of whether or not the alliance-outcome correlation is merely an epiphenomenon of prior symptom change, we examined the predictive value of early alliance scores controlling or not controlling for prior symptom change. While early CALPAS scores were not significantly related to outcome (p = .06), early WAI-S scores significantly predicted subsequent symptom change. This association remained true when controlling for prior symptom change, suggesting that alliance is predictive of outcome over and beyond early symptom change. Due to the inclusions of two clinical management conditions, this study is not directly comparable with many of the studies only examining psychotherapy. However, the lack of significant treatment differences in the alliance-outcome relation replicates findings from the NIMH TDCRP using a different alliance rating (Krupnick et al., 1996). Together, those findings provide evidence that the association between alliance and outcome in clinical management might be comparable to the alliance-outcome association found in psychotherapy.

The third set of analyses on the alliance-outcome relation concerned the early slope of the alliance from intake through week 4. The question was whether an initial decline in the therapeutic alliance (as indicated by a negative slope) or an early positive relationship experience (increase in alliance ratings) related to subsequent outcome differences. Similar to the previous analyses, CALPAS was not related to outcome, but WAI-S was related. The significant three-way interaction with treatment type indicated that the impact of early WAI-S slope on alliance was different in SET compared to the two CM conditions. In SET, an initial decrease in alliance was related to subsequent symptomatic improvement. It is important to keep in mind that this finding is about the shape of the alliance curve, not about the alliance-outcome correlation in general. Previous scholars have suggested that moderately U-shaped alliances that start out high, decrease somewhat towards the middle of therapy, and increase again towards the end of therapy might be found in successful psychotherapies (Gelso & Carter, 1994). This relation might be different for CM, where the therapeutic relationship is not an explicit focus of treatment and patients and therapists do not work through interpersonal difficulties together. It is also possible that predicting outcome from alliance measured so late in treatment may be misleading as much of the change had already occurred.

One recurrent finding in our study is that for all analyses between alliance and outcome, the results differed depending on the alliance questionnaire. This was true despite the high intercorrelation at each time point. The findings point to the likelihood that different alliance questionnaires measure different aspects of the broader concept of therapeutic alliance. On the one hand, the WAI-S closely follows Bordin's (1979) model of a working alliance; on the other hand, the CALPAS integrates additional aspects of the relationship such as the patient's and therapist's unique contribution (patient commitment, therapist understanding) and patient working capacity (Gaston & Marmar, 1994). The CALPAS assesses aspects of patient participation in the therapeutic relationship (e.g., idealized relationship and negative aspects of the patient participation) that are not captured by the WAI-S or other measures of alliance (see Hatcher & Barends, 1996). The CALPAS can therefore be viewed as a more comprehensive measure of alliance than the WAI-S and perhaps encompasses a concept broader than the therapeutic alliance. In any case, at least in our sample, its comprehensiveness seems to weaken its ability to predict outcome, perhaps because the additional elements included in the CALPAS are not associated with improved outcome. Moreover, measurement of a broader concept of alliance may result in somewhat lower reliability. In our study, the observed CALPAS reliability scores were somewhat lower than the WAI scores, which may have further contributed to a lower correlation with outcome. In contrast to the CALPAS, the WAI assesses agreement on tasks/goals with eight out of 12 items, thereby emphasizing the agreement aspect more so than the bond component. In line with the findings by Webb et al., (2011), it could also be that the alliance-outcome correlation in general is due more to the agreement on tasks and goals than the bond of the therapeutic relationship. We conclude that the two alliance measures capture unique variance of the therapeutic relationships and are not readily interchangeable (see Tichenor & Hill, 1989; but also see Hatcher & Barends, 1996). A potential consequence is that it may be at times inappropriate to generalize from findings that come from different measures of the alliance.

The most recent meta-analysis of the relation between expectation and outcome (Constantino, Arnkoff, et al., 2011) revealed a very small, but significant effect ($r = .12$). In our fairly large sample of patients, however, we did not find a significant association between outcome expectations and symptomatic improvement. In addition, the association between outcome expectations and change in depression was similar across treatments. Thus, we ruled out the possibility that our PBO group may have had higher expectations, which could have helped explained the lack of significant outcome differences between the groups.

Several limitations have to be considered. Outcome expectation was measured with only one item. Perhaps if we had used more recent, multi-item measures of outcome expectations our results would have been different (Constantino, Glass, et al., 2011) Another limitation regarding generalizability of our results is the fact that patients in our study, like in any RCT, have the bias on being willing to be randomized and were depressed. Furthemore, while recruitment was successful at recruiting an ethnically and socioeconomically diverse sample, the generalizabilty of the findings to non-research settings and non-depressed patients is still limited. Strengths of the current study are the use of multilevel models that can account for missing data as well as frequent measurements of symptoms and alliance throughout therapy.

Acknowledgments

The original study was funded by a NIMH grant R01 MH 061410 to Jacques P. Barber. The sertraline and placebo pills were provided by a grant from Pfizer Corp. Neither sponsor had any role in the study besides funding the study (NIMH) or supplying the sertraline and placebo pills (Pfizer).

References

Barber, J. P. (2009). Towards a working through of some core conflicts in psychotherapy research. *Psychotherapy Research, 19*, 1–12. doi:10.1080/10503300802609680.

Barber, J. P., Barrett, M. S., Gallop, R., Rynn, M. A., & Rickels, K. (2012). Short-term dynamic psychotherapy versus pharmacotherapy for major depressive disorder: a randomized, placebo-controlled trial. *Journal of Clinical Psychiatry, 73*, 66–73. doi:10.4088/JCP.11m06831.

Barber, J. P., Connolly, M. B., Crits-Christoph, P., Gladis, L., & Siqueland, L. (2000). Alliance predicts patients' outcome beyond in-treatment change in symptoms. *Journal of Consulting and Clinical Psychology, 68*, 1027–1032. doi:10.1037/0022-006x.68.6.1027.

Barber, J. P., Luborsky, L., Crits-Christoph, P., Thase, M. E., Weiss, R., Frank, A., ... Gallop, R. (1999). Therapeutic alliance as a predictor of outcome in treatment of cocaine dependence. *Psychotherapy Research, 9*, 54–73. doi:10.1093/ptr/9.1.54.

Baron, R. M., & Kenny, D. A. (1986). The moderator-mediator variable distinction in social-psychological research: Conceptual, strategic and statistical considerations. *Jounral of Personality and Social Psychology, 51*, 1173–1182.

Beck, A. T., Rush, J. J., Shaw, B. F., & Emery, G. (1979). *Cognitive therapy of depression.* New York: Guilford Press.

Bordin, E. S. (1979). The generalizability of the psychoanalytic concept of the working alliance. *Psychotherapy: Theory, Research & Practice, 16*, 252–260. doi:10.1037/h0085885.

Cohen, J., Cohen, P., West, S. G., & Aiken, L. S. (2003). *Applied multiple regression/correlation analysis for the behavioral sciences* (3rd ed.). Mahwah, NJ: Lawrence Erlbaum.

Connolly Gibbons, M. B., Crits-Christoph, P., de la Cruz, C., Barber, J. P., Siqueland, L., & Gladis, M. (2003). Pretreatment expectations, interpersonal functioning, and symptoms in the prediction of the therapeutic alliance across supportive-expressive psychotherapy and cognitive therapy. *Psychotherapy Research, 13*, 59–76. doi:10.1093/ptr/kpg007.

Constantino, M. J., Ametrano, R. M., & Greenberg, R. P. (2012). Clinician interventions and participant characteristics that foster adaptive patient expectations for psychotherapy and psychotherapeutic change. *Psychotherapy, 49*, 557–569. doi:10.1037/a0029440.

Constantino, M. J., Arnkoff, D. B., Glass, C. R., Ametrano, R. M., & Smith, J. Z. (2011). Expectations. *Journal of Clinical Psychology, 67*, 184–192. doi:10.1002/jclp.20754.

Constantino, M. J., Arnow, B. A., Blasey, C., & Agras, W. S. (2005). The association between patient characteristics and the therapeutic alliance in cognitive-behavioral and interpersonal therapy for bulimia nervosa. *Journal of Consulting and Clinical Psychology, 73*, 203–211. doi:10.1037/0022-006x.73.2.203.

Constantino, M. J., Glass, C. R., Arnkoff, D. B., Ametrano, R. M., & Smith, J. Z. (2011). Expectations. In J. C. Norcross (Ed.), *Psychotherapy relationships that work: Evidence-based responsiveness* (2nd ed., pp. 354–376). New York: Oxford University Press.

Crits-Christoph, P., Connolly Gibbons, M. B., & Mukherjee, D. (2013). Psychotherapy process-outcome research. In M. J. Lambert (Ed.), *Bergin and Garfield's handbook of psychotherapy and behavior change* (6th ed.). New York: Wiley.

Crits-Christoph, P., Gibbons, M. B. C., Hamilton, J., Ring-Kurtz, S., & Gallop, R. (2011). The dependability of alliance assessments: The alliance–outcome correlation is larger than you might think. *Journal of Consulting and Clinical Psychology, 79*, 267–278. doi:10.1037/a0023668.

DeRubeis, R. J., Brotman, M. A., & Gibbons, C. J. (2005). A conceptual and methodological analysis of the nonspecifics argument. *Clinical Psychology: Science and Practice, 12*, 174–183. doi:10.1093/clipsy/bpi022.

Diener, M. J., & Monroe, J. M. (2011). The relationship between adult attachment style and therapeutic alliance in individual psychotherapy: A meta-analytic review. *Psychotherapy, 48*, 237–248. doi:10.1037/a0022425.

Diggle, P., Liang, K.-Y., & Zeger, S. L. (1994). *Analysis of longitudinal data.* Oxford: Oxford University Press.

Dinger, U., Strack, M., Leichsenring, F., & Schauenburg, H. (2007). Influences of patients' and therapists' interpersonal problems and therapeutic alliance on outcome in psychotherapy. *Psychotherapy Research, 17*, 148–159. doi:10.1080/10503300600865393.

Dinger, U., Strack, M., Sachsse, T., & Schauenburg, H. (2009). Therapists' attachment, patients' interpersonal problems and alliance development over time in inpatient psychotherapy. *Psychotherapy: Theory, Research, Practice, Training, 46*, 277–290. doi:10.1037/a0016913.

Elkin, I., Parloff, M. B., Hadley, S. W., & Autry, J. H. (1985). NIMH treatment of depression collaborative research program. Background and research plan. *Archives of General Psychiatry, 42*, 305–316.

Fawcett, J., Epstein, P., Fiester, S. J., Elkin, I., & Autry, J. H. (1987). Clinical management – imipramine/placebo administration manual. NIMH Treatment of Depression Collaborative Research Program. *Psychopharmacology Bulletin, 23*, 309–324.

Feeley, M., DeRubeis, R. J., & Gelfand, L. A. (1999). The temporal relation of adherence and alliance to symptom change in cognitive therapy for depression. *Journal of Consulting and Clinical Psychology, 67*, 578–582. doi:10.1037/0022-006x.67.4.578.

First, M. B., Spitzer, R. L., Gibbon, M., & Williams, J. B. W. (1995). The Structured Clinical Interview for DSM-III-R personality disorders (SCID-II): I. Description. *Journal of Personality Disorders, 9*, 83–91. 10.1521/pedi.1995.9.2.83

Flückiger, C., Del Re, A. C., Wampold, B. E., Symonds, D., & Horvath, A. O. (2012). How central is the alliance in psychotherapy? A multilevel longitudinal meta-analysis. *Journal of Counseling Psychology, 59*, 10–17. doi:10.1037/a0025749.

Flückiger, C., Regli, D., & Grawe, K. (2005). Allgemeine Psychotherapie im Gruppensetting: Das Zusammenspiel von gruppen- und interventionsspezifischen Wirkfaktoren [General psychotherapy in the group setting: Interaction between group- and intervention-specific factors]. *Gruppenpsychotherapie & Gruppendynamik, 41*, 306–322.

Gaston, L., & Marmar, C. R. (1994). The California Psychotherapy Alliance Scales. In A. O. Horvath & L. S. Greenberg (Eds.), *The working alliance: Theory, research, and practice* (pp. 85–108). Oxford, England: John Wiley & Sons.

Gelso, C. J., & Carter, J. A. (1994). Components of the psychotherapy relationship: Their interaction and unfolding during treatment. *Journal of Counseling Psychology, 41*, 296–306. doi:10.1037/0022-0167.41.3.296.

Greenberg, L. S., & Malcolm, W. (2002). Resolving unfinished business: Relating process to outcome. *Journal of Consulting and Clinical Psychology, 70*, 406–416. doi:10.1037/0022-006x.70.2.406.

Greenberg, L. S., Rice, L. N., & Elliott, R. (1993). *Facilitating emotional change: The moment by moment process.* New York: Guilford Press.

Greenson, R. R. (1965). The working alliance and the transference neurosis. In R. R. Greenson (Ed.), *Explorations in psychoanalysis* (pp. 199–224). New York: International Universities Press.

Hamilton, M. (1960). A rating scale for depression. *Journal of Neurology, Neurosurgery & Psychiatry, 23*, 56–61. doi:10.1136/jnnp.23.1.56.

Hatcher, R. L., & Barends, A. W. (1996). Patient's view of the alliance of psychotherapy: Exploratory factor analysis of three alliance measures. *Journal of Consulting and Clinical Psychology, 64*, 1326–1336.

Hilsenroth, M. J., Peters, E. J., & Ackerman, S. J. (2004). The development of therapeutic alliance during psychological assessment: patient and therapist perspectives across treatment. *Journal Of Personality Assessment, 83*, 332–344. 10.1207/s15327752jpa8303_14

Horvath, A. O., Del Re, A. C., Flückiger, C., & Symonds, D. (2011). Alliance in individual psychotherapy. *Psychotherapy, 48*, 9–16. doi:10.1037/a0022186.

Horvath, A. O., & Greenberg, L. S. (1989). Development and validation of the Working Alliance Inventory. *Journal of Counseling Psychology, 36*, 223–233. doi:10.1037/0022-0167.36.2.223.

Johansson, P., Høglend, P., & Hersoug, A. G. (2011). Therapeutic alliance mediates the effect of patient expectancy in dynamic psychotherapy. *British Journal of Clinical Psychology, 50*, 283–297.

Joyce, A. S., Ogrodniczuk, J. S., Piper, W. E., & McCallum, M. (2003). The alliance as mediator of expectancy effects in short-term individual therapy. *Journal of Consulting and Clinical Psychology, 71*, 672–679. doi:10.1037/0022-006x.71.4.672.

Kivlighan, D. M., & Shaughnessy, P. (2000). Patterns of working alliance development: A typology of client's working alliance ratings. *Journal of Counseling Psychology, 47*, 362–371. doi:10.1037/0022-0167.47.3.362.

Klein, D. N., Schwartz, J. E., Santiago, N. J., Vivian, D., Vocisano, C., Castonguay, L. G., ... Keller, M. B. (2003). Therapeutic alliance in depression treatment: Controlling for prior change and patient characteristics. *Journal of Consulting and Clinical Psychology, 71*, 997–1006. doi:10.1037/0022-006x.71.6.997.

Kramer, U.,de Roten, Y., Beretta, V., Michel, L., & Despland, J.-N. (2008). Patients' and therapists' views of early alliance building in dynamic psychotherapy: Patterns and relation to outcome. *Journal of Counseling Psychology, 55*, 89–95. doi:10.1037/0022-0167.55.1.89.

Krupnick, J. L., Elkin, I., Collins, J., Simmens, S., Sotsky, S. M., Pilkonis, P. A., & Watkins, J. T. (1994). Therapeutic alliance and clinical outcome in the NIMH Treatment of Depression Collaborative Research Program: Preliminary findings. *Psychotherapy: Theory, Research, Practice, Training, 31*, 28–35. doi:10.1037/0033-3204.31.1.28.

Krupnick, J. L., Sotsky, S. M., Simmens, S., Moyer, J., Elkin, I., Watkins, J., & Pilkonis, P. A. (1996). The role of the therapeutic alliance in psychotherapy and pharmacotherapy outcome: Findings in the National Institute of Mental Health Treatment of Depression Collaborative Research Program. *Journal of Consulting and Clinical Psychology, 64*, 532–539. doi:10.1037/0022-006x.64.3.532.

Lambert, M. J., & Barley, D. E. (2001). Research summary on the therapeutic relationship and psychotherapy outcome. *Psychotherapy: Theory, Research, Practice, Training, 38*, 357–361. 10.1037/0033-3204.38.4.357

Luborsky, L. (1984). *The principles of psychoanalytic psychotherapy.* New York: Basic Books.

Luborsky, L. (1995). Supportive-expressive dynamic psychotherapy of depression: A time-limited version. In J. P. Barber & P. Crits-Christoph (Eds.), *Dynamic therapies for psychiatric disorders* (pp. 41–83). New York: Basic Books.

McKee, S. A., Carroll, K. M., Sinha, R., Robinson, J. E., Nich, C., Cavallo, D., & O'Malley, S. (2007). Enhancing brief cognitive-behavioral therapy with motivational enhancement techniques in cocaine users. *Drug and Alcohol Dependence, 91*(1), 97–101.

Meyer, B., Pilkonis, P. A., Krupnick, J. L., Egan, M. K., Simmens, S. J., & Sotsky, S. M. (2002). Treatment expectancies, patient alliance and outcome: Further analyses from the National Institute of Mental Health Treatment of Depression Collaborative Research Program. *Journal of Consulting and Clinical Psychology, 70*, 1051–1055. doi:10.1037/0022-006x.70.4.1051.

Paivio, S. C., & Bahr, L. M. (1998). Interpersonal problems, working alliance, and outcome in short-term experiential therapy. *Psychotherapy Research, 8*, 392–407. doi:10.1093/ptr/8.4.392.

Raudenbush, S. W., & Bryk, A. S. (2002). *Hierarchical linear modeling* (2nd ed.). Thousand Oaks, CA: Sage.

Raue, P. J., & Goldfried, M. R. (1994). The therapeutic alliance in cognitive-behavior therapy. In A. Horvath & L. S. Greenberg (Eds.), *The working alliance: Theory, research, practice* (pp. 131–152). New York: Wiley.

Reis, S., & Grenyer, B. F. S. (2004). Fearful attachment, working alliance and treatment response for individuals with major depression. *Clinical Psychology & Psychotherapy, 11*, 414–424. doi:10.1002/cpp.428.

Sexton, H. C., Hembre, K., & Kvarme, G. (1996). The interaction of the alliance and therapy microprocess: A sequential analysis. *Journal of Consulting and Clinical Psychology, 64*, 471–480. doi:10.1037/0022-006x.64.3.471.

Sexton, H. C., Littauer, H., Sexton, A., & Tømmerås, E. (2005). Building an alliance: Early therapy process and the client–therapist connection. *Psychotherapy Research, 15*, 103–116. doi:10.1080/10503300512331327083.

Shrout, J., & Fleiss, J. L. (1979). Intraclass correlations: Uses in assessing rater reliability. *Psychological Bulletin, 86*, 420–428.

Stiles, W. B., Glick, M. J., Osatuke, K., Hardy, G. E., Shapiro, D. A., Agnew-Davies, R., ... Barkham, M. (2004). Patterns of alliance development and the rupture-repair hypothesis: Are productive relationships U-shaped or V-shaped? *Journal of Counseling Psychology, 51*, 81–92. doi:10.1037/0022-0167.51.1.81.

Strunk, D. R., Brotmann, M. A., & DeRubeis, R. J. (2010). The process of change in Cognitive Therapy for Depression: Predictors of early inter-session symptom gains. *Behaviour Research and Therapy, 48*, 599–606. 10.1016/j.brat.2010.03.011

Strunk, D. R., Cooper, A. A., Ryan, E. T., DeRubeis, R. J., & Hollon, S. D. (2012). The process of change in cognitive therapy for depression when combined with antidepressant medication: Predictors of early intersession symptom gains. *Journal of Consulting and Clinical Psychology, 80*, 730–738. doi:10.1037/a0029281.

Strunk, D. R., Stewart, M. O., Hollon, S. D., DeRubeis, R. J., Fawcett, J., Amsterdam, J. D., & Shelton, R. C. (2010). Can pharmacotherapists be too supportive? A process study of active medication and placebo in the treatment of depression. *Psychological Medicine, 40*, 1379–1387. doi:10.1017/s0033291709991553.

Tang, T. Z., & DeRubeis, R. J. (1999). Sudden gains and critical sessions in cognitive-behavioral therapy for depression. *Journal of Consulting and Clinical Psychology, 67*, 894–904. doi:10.1037/0022-006x.67.6.894.

Tichenor, V., & Hill, C. E. (1989). A comparison of six measures of working alliance. *Psychotherapy, 26*, 195–199.

Tracey, T. J., & Kokotovic, A. M. (1989). Factor structure of the Working Alliance Inventory. *Psychological Assessment: A Journal of Consulting and Clinical Psychology, 1*, 207–210. doi:10.1037/1040-3590.1.3.207.

Watson, J. C., McMullen, E. J., Prosser, M. C., & Bedard, D. L. (2011). An examination of the relationships among clients' affect regulation, in-session emotional processing, the working alliance, and outcome. *Psychotherapy Research, 21*, 86–96. doi:10.1080/10503307.2010.518637.

Webb, C. A., DeRubeis, R. J., Amsterdam, J. D., Shelton, R. C., Hollon, S. D., & Dimidjian, S. (2011). Two aspects of the therapeutic alliance: Differential relations with depressive symptom change. *Journal of Consulting and Clinical Psychology, 79*, 279–283. doi:10.1037/a0023252.

Williams, J. B. (1988). A structured interview guide for the Hamilton Depression Rating Scale. *Archives of General Psychiatry, 45*, 742–747. doi:10.1001/archpsyc.1988.01800320058007.

Zilcha-Mano, S., Dinger, U., McCarthy, K. S., & Barber, J. P. (in press). Does alliance predict symptomatic change, or is it the other way around? *Journal of Counseling and Clinical Psychology.*

How does the therapeutic alliance develop throughout cognitive behavioral therapy for panic disorder? Sawtooth patterns, sudden gains, and stabilization

MICHAL WEISS*, YOGEV KIVITY*, & JONATHAN D. HUPPERT

Psychology, The Hebrew University of Jerusalem, Jerusalem, Israel

Abstract

Objective: There has been little research on the development of the therapeutic alliance in cognitive behavioral therapy (CBT). This study aims to examine the development of therapeutic alliance in CBT for panic disorder. **Method:** Nineteen patients were treated with CBT for panic disorder. Pre- and post-session data of the therapeutic alliance and panic symptoms and cognitions were collected. **Results:** Several patterns were observed, including a sawtooth pattern (within-session improvements followed by decline between sessions; 63% of the patients), sudden gains in the alliance (58%), and late stabilization (89%). The sawtooth pattern was related to less symptom reduction between sessions (explained variance = 20–48%). Though not statistically significant, there were moderate effect sizes for the relationships between outcomes and early alliance and sudden gains (explained variance = 13–17%). **Conclusions:** Overall, results suggest that intensive data collection is likely to yield understanding of the relationship between therapy processes and outcomes.

Research on the importance of the therapeutic alliance in psychotherapy outcome has established a relationship between alliance and outcome, regardless of disorder (Flückiger, Del Re, Wampold, Symonds, & Hovarth, 2012; Horvath, Del Re, Flückiger, & Symonds, 2011; Martin, Garske, & Davis, 2000; Muran & Barber, 2010). Most of the research on the therapeutic alliance has been conducted with therapies that emphasize the relationship as an essential mechanism of change (e.g., psychodynamic or humanistic orientations), but results appear to be similar for treatments that do not emphasize the relationship as the main mechanism of change (e.g., CBT: Castonguay, Constantino, McAleavey, & Goldfried, 2010). Given its importance, there is a need to better understand in depth the development of the therapeutic alliance, as well as the influence of such developmental patterns on proximal (session) and distal (posttreatment) outcomes.

Examining session-by-session changes, and the way such changes relate to outcome, is one method of deepening our understanding of the mechanisms and development of the therapeutic alliance. Most studies to date have investigated the outcome-alliance correlation by examining whether high levels of alliance at a given time point predict treatment outcome, rather than examining whether *change* in alliance predicts treatment outcome (Barber et al., 2001; Crits-Christoph et al., 2006; Flückiger et al., 2012). By examining a single-point level rather than a session-by-session change in alliance, one cannot infer the contribution of the temporal dynamics of the alliance that occur during therapy to outcome (Kazdin, 2007). While a number of studies have examined alliance and symptoms at multiple time points (e.g., Crits-Christoph, Gibbons, Hamilton, Ring-Kurtz, & Gallop, 2011; Kivlighan & Shaughnessy, 1995; Klein et al., 2003), we are aware of

*The first and second authors contributed equally to this manuscript.

only one study that examined session-by-session change in symptoms and alliance throughout treatment (Marker, Comer, Abramova, & Kendall, 2013). Using latent growth modeling, Marker and colleagues found a reciprocal relationship of change in alliance and change in symptoms in CBT for child anxiety. The current study attempts to add to this literature by examining pre- and post-session changes in symptoms and alliance in CBT for panic disorder in adults.

In addition to examining the alliance-outcome relationship per se, it is also important to examine the development of the alliance during therapy, in order to better understand how it is established, what can prevent it from progressing, and how different patterns in its development are related to treatment outcome (Stiles & Goldsmith, 2010). In their review of studies that have examined the development of alliance over time, Stiles and Goldsmith (2010) report that many studies examine either a linear, curvilinear, or U-shaped development of the alliance, with mixed results regarding the presence of each of these patterns, and some studies suggesting stable alliances from early on in treatment. There are some preliminary findings about the emergence of V- or U-shaped patterns signifying "rupture and repair" in the alliance in CBT, and the importance of the repair in order to resume a proper therapeutic alliance (e.g., Castonguay et al., 2004; Constantino et al., 2008). Some studies examined the relationship of the U-pattern to treatment outcomes, with mixed results (Westra, Constantino, & Aviram, 2011). However, there is little research examining alliance development and its relationship to treatment course in CBT and we are not aware of studies that looked at patterns of development of the alliance and their relationship to outcome of CBT for anxiety disorders.

Given previous findings in a large study of CBT for panic disorder that alliance was related to outcome (Huppert et al., 2014), we decided to examine the development of alliance patterns in that treatment. In an unpublished case study that was carried out in our lab, a patient was treated with CBT for panic disorder, and therapeutic alliance and panic symptoms were collected before and after each session, in order to try and examine patterns of alliance development and symptom improvement at a high resolution. The development of this patient's alliance during therapy is shown in Figure 1. As the figure shows, some interesting patterns of the alliance development over time were observed. The first was the sawtooth pattern, in which alliance improved during a session, and then deteriorated to some degree by the beginning of the next session. It appeared that there was an overall increase in the alliance during treatment, though not purely linear

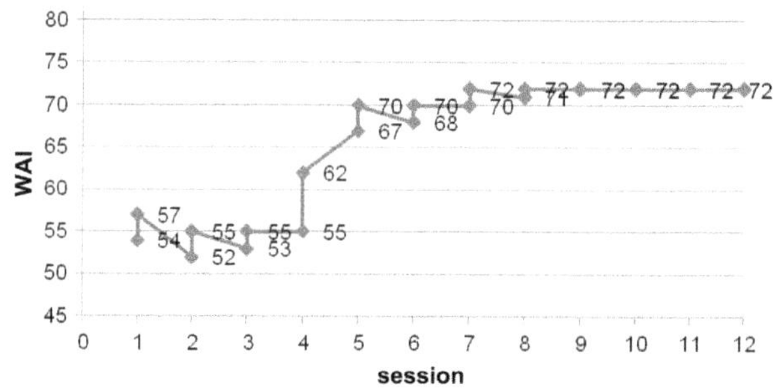

Figure 1. Development of the Working Alliance Inventory (WAI) in a single case of cognitive behavioral therapy for panic disorder. Vertical lines indicate changes within session, and diagonal/horizontal lines, between sessions. A sawtoothed pattern is evident in sessions 1, 2, 3, 5, 6, 7, and 8. A sudden gain is evident in session 4. Stabilization is evident by sessions 8–12. More details are described in the text.

or curvilinear. We also noticed a significant elevation in alliance within session that occurred in the middle of treatment. This phenomenon is reminiscent of Tang & DeRubeis's (1999) concept of "sudden gains," described as a large between-session improvement in depressive symptoms. We therefore adopted Tang and DeRubeis's definition of sudden gains, with some adaptations.[1] In addition, we observed a stabilization of the alliance in the later sessions of treatment, so that the alliance had reached a high level and tended to stay on the same level until treatment termination.

Given that the patterns of development of the therapeutic alliance and their relationship to treatment outcome have not been studied before in CBT for panic disorder to our knowledge, our observations of this patient's alliance were the motivation for the current study. We examined data collected in the context of intensive case studies (cf., Fishman, 2000). As recommended by many researchers (e.g., Barlow, Bullis, Comer, & Ametaj, 2013; Hayes, Laurenceau, Feldman, Strauss, & Cardaciotto, 2007; Kazdin, 2007), we integrated single-case and group-level analyses in our dataset by intensively collecting data on the alliance on the individual level (pre and post every session). This study is innovative in its use of intensive data collection that enables more fine-grained resolution than typically used in research on the alliance, as measures of the therapeutic alliance and panic-related cognitions were obtained before and after each session. The advantage of this method is that it allows us to examine the relationship of the changes that occur in alliance and symptoms both within and between sessions.

Our hypotheses were based on the individual case study described above. While there are drawbacks in using case studies to derive hypotheses, it is necessary in a clinical study that lacks theoretical background (Barlow et al., 2013; Borckardt et al., 2008;

Stiles & Goldsmith, 2010), which was the case in the current research because of the novel data collection method used.

Based on our case study, we hypothesized that the sawtooth pattern, sudden gains, stabilization towards the end of treatment, and rapid elevation in the beginning of treatment will be evident in the therapeutic alliance for most patients (more than 50%) in CBT for panic. We expected to find a pattern of rapid elevation (i.e., a large improvement in alliance occurring from the beginning of the first session until the beginning of the second session), even though it was not evident in our case study, because studies have reported finding it in the past (Stiles et al., 2004). We expected the presence of sawtooth patterns and sudden gains to be predictive of greater symptom reduction during therapy. We further hypothesized that sudden gains in alliance will be associated with greater symptom reduction in the session in which they occurred, compared to the sessions before and after the sudden gain, and compared to the rest of the sessions (cf., Tang & DeRubeis, 1999), and that it would be related to better outcomes.

We also tested the alliance-outcome association at a higher resolution than typically reported in literature (Flückiger et al., 2012; Horvath et al., 2011; Martin et al., 2000; Muran & Barber, 2010). As a first step, we replicated traditional analyses in which we hypothesized that a high level of alliance early in treatment (i.e., average scores in the first four sessions) will predict treatment outcome. In addition, our intensive data collection allowed us to examine change in the working alliance as a predictor of change in symptoms in therapy. We hypothesized that change in alliance, both within and between sessions, will predict change in symptoms both within and between sessions. However, given that evidence regarding the causal direction of alliance-outcome correlation is lacking (Barber, 2009), we also examined the opposite direction (symptoms predicting alliance). To better assess causality, we controlled for temporal order by conducting lagged analyses in which change in alliance predicted change in symptom in the next session, and vice versa.

Finally, there are few studies examining the relationship between pre-treatment symptoms and therapeutic alliance with mixed results (e.g., Connolly Gibbons et al., 2003; Eaton, Abeles, & Gutfreund, 1998; Gaston, Marmar, Thompson, & Gallagher, 1988; Hersoug, Monsen, Havik, & Høglend, 2002; Klein et al., 2003). However, none of these studies have looked at the relationship between pretreatment symptoms and the possible patterns of sawtooth or sudden gains in alliance. In this study, we examined the possible correlation of these patterns with pre-treatment panic symptoms in an exploratory manner.

Method

Participants

Twenty-two patients who responded to advertisements (via flyers and the internet) to receive free treatment for panic disorder in the context of a research study were recruited. Inclusion criteria were a DSM-IV diagnosis of panic disorder as the primary disorder, over 18 years old, not in concurrent therapy, and no history of a full course of CBT for panic disorder, and a PDSS-IE rating of 10 or above at intake. Exclusion criteria included history of psychosis, mania, recent history of substance abuse or dependence, and current suicidal ideation or history of suicide attempts. Data regarding respondents to advertisements who were not appropriate for this study were not saved, as the study was not designed as a randomized controlled trial, but rather as a naturalistic study. They all signed informed consent to participate in the study that was approved by the University's Ethics Board. Patients were diagnosed using the Mini International Neuropsychiatric Interview 4.5 (MINI-4.5; Sheehan et al., 1998), a structured interview of axis-I disorders of the DSM-IV-TR, and the Panic Disorder Severity Scale – Independent Evaluator Version (PDSS-IE; Shear et al., 1997, 2001), a valid and reliable measure for assessing the severity of the panic disorder. These were administered to them by their future therapist and the therapist's supervisor. The presence of these two interviewers in each interview was important in order to strengthen the reliability of diagnoses made during the interview. All participants were informed that the goal of the study was to understand the process of treatment and that they would be asked to complete a number of forms online before and after each session as part of the study. Data were collected between the years 2008 and 2012. In the first year of the study, three patients were included who were diagnosed as having secondary panic disorder and either primary personality disorders ($n = 2$) or social anxiety disorder ($n = 1$), based on the clinical judgment of the supervisor on the basis of the patient's behavior and reports of emotion regulation difficulties in terms of anger and their interpersonal difficulties in many areas of life. These patients were removed from data analyses, as panic was not their primary disorder. Thus, all analyses were conducted on a final sample of 19 patients (11 females, 57.9%) with primary diagnosis of panic disorder, aged 22 to 63 ($M = 31$, $SD = 11.32$). Comorbid disorders in this final sample were evident in 13 patients (68.4%), and included other anxiety disorder (N = 8, 42.1%), depressive disorders (N = 4, 21.0%), and ADHD (N = 1, 5.3%). The prototypic case study that initiated this study is one of the 19 patients we refer to here.

Therapists

Data were collected in the context of a research seminar on psychotherapy process and outcome for students studying for their Masters in clinical psychology, in which they conducted CBT for panic disorder. The data accrued over the years in the context of the seminar were intended to serve as a database for examining processes of CBT in panic disorder. This is the first published analysis of this dataset. Therapists were 19 first-year clinical psychology students (eight females), who were already treating other patients in their practicum sites. All therapists were in their late 20s or early 30s. Each therapist treated only one patient as part of the study. They were trained and received supervision from a clinical psychologist with extensive experience in the treatment of panic disorder (JDH). All in-office treatment sessions were videotaped in order to supervise the therapists and monitor protocol adherence, and the supervisor provided group supervision after viewing part or all of the sessions (formal assessments of therapists' adherence and competence were not carried out).

Treatment

Treatment was based on Barlow and Craske's (2007) protocol for treating panic disorder with additions (Huppert & Baker-Morisette, 2003). It included 12 sessions. The first sessions (sessions 1 to 3 approximately) were dedicated to psychoeducation and cognitive restructuring, the next sessions (3–5 approximately) were focused on interoceptive exposures (formal exercises which elicit various bodily sensations similar to panic sensations), and the later sessions were dedicated to in-vivo exposures (some combined with interoceptive exposures), and consolidation of gains and relapse prevention. Patients were asked to indicate lessons learned at the end of each session. They also received homework after each session (e.g., repeat the interoceptive exposure exercises at home, conducting an in-vivo exposure on their own such as drinking coffee and running and then driving alone in the car).

Measures

All measures were translated into Hebrew from English and then back-translated to ensure proper translation of the measures.

Panic Disorder Severity Scale – Self-Report Version (PDSS-SR). The PDSS-SR is a self-report version of the respective independent evaluator measure, which has been shown to have good psychometrics and sensitivity to change (Houck, Spiegel, Shear, & Rucci, 2002). Cronbach's α coefficients in the present study showed good internal consistency (α = .76–.96 over the various time points).

Anxiety Sensitivity Index-3 (ASI-3). The ASI-3 is an 18-item self-report scale used to evaluate anxiety focused on panic-related bodily sensations. Each item is rated on a 0 (very little) to 4 (very much) scale. It has been used extensively in research on panic disorder, and has been found to have strong psychometrics (Taylor et al., 2007). Cronbach's α coefficients in the present study showed very good internal consistency (α = .82–.97 over the various time points).

Working Alliance Inventory – Short Form (WAI-SF). The WAI-SF (Tracey & Kokotovic, 1989) is a 12-item self-report scale used to assess the therapeutic relationship between therapist and client. In the present study, we used the client version of the scale (WAI-C). Each item is rated on a 1 (never) to 7 (always) scale. Given our small sample size and given the high inter-correlations between subscales (all r values > .68 in the measurement after the first session), we only analyzed total scores in order to minimize the number of analyses. The psychometrics of the WAI-C have been found to be very strong (Tracey & Kokotovic, 1989). Cronbach's α coefficients in the present study showed excellent internal consistency (α = .92–.99 over the various time points).

Procedure

Patients who responded to the advertisements were first screened by a clinical psychology student on the telephone. Those who were found suitable were invited to come for the full clinical interview, which included the MINI 4.5 (Sheehan et al., 1998) and the PDSS-IE. Patients who met inclusion and exclusion criteria and agreed to treatment began therapy after a staggered baseline period (ranging from 1 to 6 weeks). During therapy, patients completed questionnaires before and after each session (ASI, WAI-C; the PDSS was only administered at the beginning of each session, as it refers to panic severity in the last week). Therapy typically lasted up to 12 sessions with one session per week. Supervision was conducted on a weekly basis.

Data Analytic Approach

Data were analyzed using linear multi-level models in SPSS Version 17.0. Analyses were adjusted for repeated measures with random intercepts and slopes at the patient level with the full maximum likelihood estimation method. Intra-Class Correlation (ICC) estimates showed that 59% of the variance in PDSS scores, 59% in ASI scores, and 39% in WAI scores were attributed to the patient level, thus justifying the use of a multi-level modeling approach. Fitting of level one (time level) growth curves and the choice of covariance structure were performed using deviance tests performed on model fit estimates (−2 log likelihood). Using this approach, a linear growth curve was chosen for all analyses, with a first-order autoregressive covariance structure.

Quantifying treatment outcome and change in alliance scores during treatment. In all analyses, we used the ASI and not the PDSS as the sole symptom measure, as it was obtained before and after each session and thus enabled us to examine within- and between-session changes separately. We nevertheless report change in PDSS during treatment, to allow for comparability to other studies in the field.

Treatment outcome was quantified as the average change during each week of therapy in the PDSS and ASI scores measured before each session. In addition, because the ASI was also measured after each session, we were also able to break the weekly change into within- and between-session changes (cf., Foa & Kozak, 1986) using piecewise modeling (Raudenbush & Bryk, 2002). We also looked at change in WAI scores in a similar way. We did not control for baseline symptom levels because, in contrast to other studies (e.g., Huppert et al., 2014), in our sample these were not predictive of outcome.

Examining the outcome-alliance correlation. To examine whether the working alliance predicts treatment outcome, we first tested whether early alliance scores predict change in ASI scores (ASI scores pre and post each session were averaged in this analysis). For each patient, early alliance was calculated as the average of all WAI measurements between the first session and the fourth session (excluding the WAI measurement immediately before the first session) centered on the sample mean. This analysis closely resembles the way studies have approached this issue in the past (Barber et al., 2001; Huppert et al., 2014), and thus enables us to directly compare our results to those of past studies while taking into account recent suggestions for increasing the reliability of alliance measurement (Crits-Christoph et al., 2011). As a next step, to better control for time precedence, we added early change in ASI as a predictor to the model. Early change in ASI was calculated as the slope of change in ASI in sessions one to four.

We were also interested in session by session changes in the WAI. Therefore, using a similar approach to the one used by Baldwin, Wampold, and Imel (2007),[2] we partitioned between variance within and between patients in the WAI and the way these variances predict changes in ASI. To model within-patient variance in the WAI, we calculated two WAI change scores for each patient and for each session: Change in the WAI within and between sessions. These scores where then patient-centered and entered as time-level predictors. To model between-patient variance in the WAI we separately averaged within- and between-session changes in the WAI scores of each patient and centered these scores on the sample mean. This procedure resulted in two scores for each patient: Mean change in WAI within sessions (i.e., WAI within-session changes averaged across all of the patient's sessions) and mean change in WAI between sessions (i.e., WAI between-session changes averaged across all of the patient's sessions). These two scores were then entered as predictors at the patient level. Note that in these analyses we were mainly interested in the interaction between WAI scores (at the time level and at the patient level) and the two ASI slopes (within- and between-session change).

In addition, to better assess causality, we controlled for temporal order by conducting lagged analyses in which WAI scores at a given session were used to predict ASI scores in the following session. In these analyses, we did not enter WAI scores at the patient level, as these are averaged across therapy and are identical to the scores used in the simultaneous prediction.

Finally, to test a complementary explanation according to which outcome predicts alliance (in addition to or instead of alliance predicting outcome), we used the same approach just described to test whether ASI scores predict changes in WAI scores.

Exploring patterns of development in the WAI and their relation to treatment outcome. The frequency of patterns of alliance development (sawtooth, sudden gains, rapid elevation, and stabilization) was determined using a priori definitions described below. Patterns that showed enough variability in our sample (i.e., existed in more than half and less than two-thirds of the patients) were used to predict outcome by entering them as patient-level predictors of within- and between-session changes in ASI scores.

Effect sizes. Effect Sizes (ES) for multi-level analyses were calculated from likelihood ratio statistics (Lipsitz, Leong, Ibrahim, & Lipshultz, 2001) and are reported in a percent reduction in variance (R^2) metric.[3]

Results

Was the Treatment Effective?

The mean PDSS score at the beginning of therapy was M = 11.95, SD = 4.71 (above the clinical cut score for panic disorder; Shear et al., 2001) with a significant decrease of .64 points in each week during therapy ($p < .001$), resulting in a mean post-treatment PDSS score of M = 6.21, SD = 5.56. The mean ASI score at the beginning of therapy was M = 57.53, SD = 10.22 (higher than the clinical population mean of 32.6 reported in Taylor et al., 2007) with a significant decrease of 1.94 points each week ($p < .001$), resulting in a mean post-treatment ASI score of M = 38.05, SD = 13.81. Using a piecewise model, the weekly ASI decrease was broken into a significant decrease of 1.33 points in ASI within each session ($p < .001$) and a non-significant decrease of .61 points between sessions ($p = .07$), suggesting that most of the symptom change occurred during sessions.[4]

The treatment had a large effect size both on PDSS scores (ES = 36.73%) and on ASI scores (ES = 66.34%). In addition, we determined the number of patients achieving reliable change and end-state functioning (Jacobson & Truax, 1991). We determined cut scores using data from published norms for the PDSS-SR (Monkul et al., 2004) and ASI (Taylor et al., 2007) and used test-retest reliability data from Houck et al. (2002) to determine reliable change for the PDSS-SR. Whereas there are no published test-retest reliability data for the ASI-3, the internal consistency coefficient data from the current sample were used to calculate reliable change. To be considered "recovered" a patient's post-treatment score had to be lower than 6 for the PDSS-SR and lower than 34 for the ASI-3. To be considered "improved," a patient's score had to decrease from pre- to post-treatment by at least 2.9 points for the PDSS-SR and at least 5.7 points for the ASI-3. Using these criteria for the PDSS-SR, 11 patients (58%) were classified as "recovered," two patients (10.5%) were classified as "improved but not recovered," and six patients (31.5%) were classified as "unchanged." According to the ASI, seven patients (37%) were classified as "recovered," six patients (31.5%) were classified as "improved but not recovered" and six patients (31.5%) were classified as "unchanged."

In sum, the results show that the treatment was effective in reducing both panic severity and panic cognitions, with large effect sizes.

Did Alliance Scores Change During Treatment?

At the beginning of therapy the mean WAI score was 59.82, with a significant increase of 1.82 points each week ($p < .001$). Change in alliance scores during therapy accounted for a large portion of the total variability in alliance scores (ES = 54.14%). Using a piecewise model, we broke the weekly WAI increase into a significant increase of 3.86 points in WAI within each session ($p < .001$) and a significant *decrease* of 2.11 points between sessions ($p < .001$).[5]

Put together, the results show that alliance scores generally increased during therapy, but this increase was not purely linear: Scores increased within sessions and, to a lesser extent, decreased between sessions.

Do Early Alliance Scores Predict Outcome of Therapy?

Using multi-level modeling, we found that average early alliance scores did not predict the mean weekly decrease in ASI scores ($b = -.05$, $p = .10$, ES = 13.54%). However, the effect size was indeed within the range expected by meta-analyses (Flückiger et al., 2012; Horvath et al., 2011; Martin et al., 2000) and consistent with Huppert et al. (2014), with higher early alliance scores predicting greater decreases in ASI scores during treatment (for each point above the mean WAI score, the mean weekly ASI decrease was larger by .05 points).

Including early change in ASI as a predictor in the model did not change the effect size of early alliance ($b = -.05$, $p = .09$, ES = 13.99%), even though early changes in ASI were predictive of overall change in ASI in treatment ($b = .37$, $p = .05$, ES = 18.56%).

In sum, in contrast to our hypothesis, early alliance did not significantly predict change in panic cognitions during therapy, although the effect size was moderate even after controlling for change in cognitions prior to the last measurement of the alliance.

Does Within- and Between-Patient Variability in Alliance Predict Within- and Between-Session Changes in Panic Cognitions?

Our analyses showed that within-patient variability in the WAI did not predict within-session changes in the ASI (b = −.07, p = .43, ES = .01%), nor did it predict between-session changes in the ASI (b = .07, p = .42, ES = .14%). At the patient level (between-patient variability), within- or between-session changes in the WAI did not predict within (b = (−.07)–(−.57), p > .15, ES = .02–2.10%) or between (b = .26–.42, p > .29, ES = 10.47–11.99%) session changes in the ASI.

One-session time-lagged analyses yielded similar results. Within-patient variability in the WAI did not predict within-session changes in the ASI in the following session (b = .02, p = .80, ES = .47%) or between-session changes in the ASI in the following session (b = −.03, p = .71, ES = .04%).

In sum, in contradiction to what we hypothesized, variability in alliance did not predict within- or between-session changes in panic cognitions, either simultaneously or in a one-session time-lag.

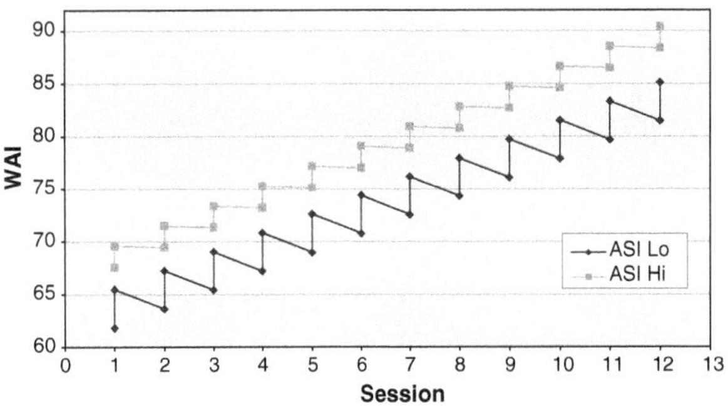

Figure 2. An illustration of the significant relationship between the development of alliance during therapy and the mean reduction in panic cognitions between sessions. The figure shows the estimated development of the Working Alliance Inventory (WAI) among patients exhibiting either large between-session decreases (2 points reduction) in Anxiety Sensitivity Index (ASI) scores ("ASI Hi" group), or no change in ASI between sessions ("ASI Lo" group). Vertical lines indicate changes in WAI within session; diagonal lines indicate change in WAI between sessions.

Does Within- and Between-Patient Variability in Panic Cognitions Predict Within- and Between-Session Changes in Alliance?

Within-patient variability in ASI scores did not predict within-session changes in the WAI (b = −.07, p = .58, ES = .47%), nor did it predict between-session changes in the WAI (b = .06, p = .65, ES = .07%).

At the patient level (between-patient variability), within-session changes in ASI did not predict within (b = −.22, p = .56, ES = .35%) or between (b = .34, p = .34, ES = 4.55%) session changes in the WAI. However, between-session changes in the ASI predicted within (b = .79, p = .01, ES = 47.70%) and between (b = −.84, p < .01, ES = 20.32%) session changes in the WAI. Patients who showed greater average decrease in ASI between sessions tended to show less increase in WAI within sessions, but also less decrease between sessions. This finding is illustrated in Figure 2 by plotting estimated within- and between-session changes in the WAI among patients who did not show any decreases in ASI between sessions on average (ASI between = 0) and among patients who showed an average decrease of 2 points in ASI between sessions (ASI between = −2). As this illustration shows, although both groups showed similar increases in WAI overall in therapy, the group that showed greater average decrease in ASI between sessions had a more stable development of the WAI, with smaller increases within sessions and smaller decreases between sessions. Note that the main effect of group is insignificant.

One-session time-lagged analyses yielded similar results. Within-patient variability in ASI scores did not predict within-session changes in the WAI in the following session (b = .02, p = .86, ES = .10%) or between-session changes in the WAI in the following session (b = −.12, p = .31, ES = .30%).

Summarizing the findings in this sub-section, in support of our hypothesis, average reductions in panic cognitions between sessions predicted a more stable development of alliance. However, in contrast to our hypothesis, other sources of variability in cognitions did not predict changes in alliance (simultaneously or in a one-session time-lag).

Which Patterns of WAI Development Were Observed in Our Sample and Were They Predictive of Treatment Outcome?

Sawtooth. A priori criteria for identifying sawtooth pattern included an elevation in WAI score within a session of at least 3 points, followed by a decrease between that session and the session that followed by at least 1 point. This pattern had to exist in at least two sessions in a row, and the overall trend of the WAI throughout therapy was of elevation.

An overall sawtooth pattern was observed when averaging WAI scores of all patients in each time point. As reported before, we found a significant increase in WAI within each session and a significant *decrease* between sessions, and an overall increase in WAI during treatment. Mean WAI scores of all patients in each time point are shown in Figure 3. Using our proposed criteria, we found that the sawtooth pattern was observed in 12 patients (63%). The sawtooth pattern appeared on average in 3.13 consecutive sessions (with a range of 2–6 consecutive sessions), and in different time points throughout treatment across different patients. Three patients showed the pattern twice during the course of their treatment.

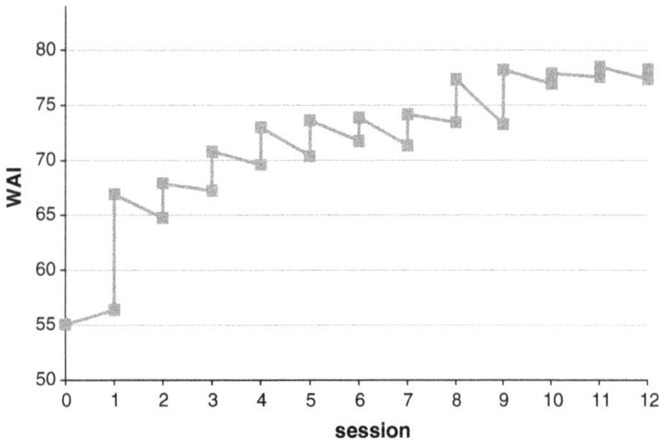

Figure 3. Mean Working Alliance Inventory (WAI) across all 19 patients during cognitive behavioral therapy for panic disorder. Vertical lines reflect in-session change while diagonal lines reflect between-session change.

As for treatment outcome, patients who exhibited the pattern had significantly lower pre-treatment ASI scores ($b = -12.32$, $p = .01$, ES = 28.54%; signifying a difference of 12 points between groups). The existence of the sawtooth pattern was not predictive of within-session changes in ASI ($b = -.63$, $p = .27$, ES = .07%) and between-session changes in ASI ($b = 1.26$, $p = .06$, ES = 17.32%). However, as we have reported earlier, greater average decreases in ASI between sessions were predictive of a more stable pattern of WAI development (lower increases in WAI within sessions, and lower decreases in WAI between sessions) or, in other words, less sawtooth pattern. This may suggest that the current analysis was underpowered by treating the sawtooth pattern as a dichotomous phenomenon rather than a sequential one. Indeed the effect size in this analysis is in the medium-large range, though insignificant.

Put together, in partial support of our hypotheses, the sawtooth patterns was observed for most of the patients and it was predictive of lower pretreatment panic cognitions, but not of change in cognitions (even though the effect size for between-session change in cognitions was medium to large).

Sudden gains. A priori criteria of sudden gains were based on the original criteria of Tang and DeRubeis (1999). First, the gain had to be of at least 6 points in the WAI scale. Second, there could not be a drop in WAI of more than 3 points in the session that followed. Lastly, there had to be a significant difference in the mean WAI score of three sessions before the sudden gain compared with that of three sessions that follow it. A rapid elevation in WAI at the beginning of treatment was not considered as sudden gain, and it is a common pattern in many treatments (see Stiles & Goldsmith, 2010), and is the phase when patient and therapist are first gaining trust and stabilize their relationship.

Sudden gains in the alliance were observed in 11 patients (58%). Examining whether sudden gains are related to high impact sessions, we found that within-session changes in the ASI were not significantly different between session of sudden gains, sessions before the sudden gain, sessions after the sudden gain, and the rest of the sessions ($F(3,115) = .38$, $p = .77$, partial $\eta^2 = .01$). Sudden gains were not predictive of pre-treatment ASI scores ($b = -4.24$, $p = .39$, ES = 5.41%), within-session changes in ASI ($b = .28$, $p = 0.49$, ES = .59%) and between-session changes in ASI ($b = -1.14$, $p = .07$, ES = 16.39%).

Collectively, in partial support of our hypotheses, the sudden gains were observed for most of the patients but they were not related to pretreatment panic cognitions, change in cognitions, or high impact sessions.

Other patterns. Rapid elevation criteria were an increase of at least 8 points on the WAI scale by the beginning of the second session. Rapid elevation was observed in 14 patients (74%). Criteria for alliance stabilization were high scores on WAI (minimum of 72) at the last three sessions of therapy, with little or no fluctuations in this score (no more than 2 points in each direction). Stabilization of alliance was observed in 17 out of 19 patients (89%). The two patients who did not show the pattern were occupied with their adherence to treatment (one dropped out). Given the small number of patients who did not exhibit these patterns, we did not examine outcome with them.

On the whole, in support of our hypotheses, rapid elevations and late stabilizations were observed for most of the patients, but we could not examine whether they predict outcome and pretreatment cognitions because there was not enough variability in them.

Discussion

We conducted an in-depth analysis of the development of the alliance in CBT for panic disorder and its relation to treatment outcome. Alliance and cognitions were measured before and after each session, enabling us to disentangle within- and between-session changes. Our results indicated that the treatment had large effect sizes on panic severity and cognitions, and that most of the change in cognitions occurred within and not between sessions. We observed an increase in alliance within sessions with a smaller decrease between sessions, resulting in an overall increase during therapy.

As we hypothesized, we found a number of patterns of alliance development which have not been described before in the psychotherapy research literature (sudden gains and a sawtooth pattern) in addition to some other patterns that have been described in the literature (rapid elevation, a flattening/stabilization late in treatment, and an overall either linear or curvilinear improvement in alliance over time; cf., Stiles & Goldmith, 2010). Contrary to our expectations, we did not find that early alliance (with and without controlling for early change in cognitions), changes in alliance (simultaneously or in one-session time-lag), or patterns of alliance were significant predictors of outcome in our small sample. However, the effect sizes for early alliance and between-patient variability in the alliance were of a reasonable magnitude, suggesting that with a larger sample size and more statistical power, these variables may significantly predict treatment outcome. This would support previous findings about the alliance-outcome relationship (Barber, Connolly, Crits-Christoph, Gladis, & Siqueland, 2000; Emmerling & Whelton, 2009; Klein et al., 2003), and broaden the accumulated knowledge by shifting the focus to the role of the development and process of alliance on outcome, rather than its mere level at a single time point. These issues should be researched further with larger sample sizes.

Consistent with our hypotheses, a sawtooth pattern was observed on average across all patients over the full course of treatment (when averaging WAI scores of all patients in each time point) and, when examined separately for each single case, most patients met the criteria. As far as we know, this finding is the first of its kind. Apparently, individuals develop a positive view of the therapist/alliance during the session, but this view is not completely stable. Instead, as the course of the week goes by, there is degradation in their view of the alliance, though not a complete deterioration. More research is needed to determine whether this is a unique characteristic of the treatment (i.e., CBT), the patient population (i.e., panic), or the therapist population (i.e., novice therapists).

Orlinsky and Geller (1993) suggested that during therapy sessions, patient–therapist interactions may challenge their cognitive-emotional schemas and cause a change in the patients' symptoms. Based on these in-session experiences, the patients gradually internalize the therapists' representation and the schema's modification becomes more and more present outside the clinic. A possible explanation of the sawtooth pattern phenomena is that during the session, patients often feel well understood and therefore close to the therapist, leading to alliance increases. However, between early and middle sessions, their internalizations of the therapeutic principles (such as thought-challenging, probability-cost matrices, and not avoiding fearful situations) and of the therapist are not yet stable and this leads to a decrease in the alliance as they have trouble regulating their anxiety when not in the presence of the therapist. As treatment progresses, the principles of CBT become internalized, resulting in a more stable alliance, as can be seen toward the late stage of treatment. This possible explanation should be further studied by assessing the internalization directly or by using the components of the alliance (i.e., task, goal and bond; Webb et al., 2011) as indicators for internalizing the treatment principles (task and goal) and internalizing the therapist (bond).

In this context, it is important to distinguish the sawtooth pattern from the rupture repair (or U-shaped pattern) already known in literature: The sawtooth pattern is identifiable in a single session period, where an elevation in therapeutic alliance occurs during this session, followed by a decrease between that session and the one that follows, and so forth. The U-shaped pattern refers to alliance at the macro-level of treatment, and is characterized by a strong alliance in early stages of treatment, a decrease in alliance during the middle phase, and an elevation towards the end of the treatment (Stiles & Goldsmith, 2010). More work will need to be done to examine the relationship between saw-toothed development of the relationship (which occurs at an intermediate level between micro and macro) and rupture-repair findings (which can be defined variably at the micro or macro level, but most often are used on a micro-level within sessions; Safran, Muran, & Eubanks-Carter, 2011). However, it seems that many rupture-repair episodes should occur even within a single session, making it necessary to examine the dynamics within a session more than between sessions.

The fact that the sawtooth pattern is a common experience suggests that therapists should be aware of the vicissitudes of the alliance as it develops, even between and within sessions. The sawtooth pattern suggests that there are processes taking place both during a session and between sessions. This finding may help therapists improve their outcomes by understanding the way the alliance develops. For example, therapists may consider communicating with patients between sessions to facilitate internalizations of the principles of CBT and minimize decreases in alliance.

We found that patients who had less severe pre-treatment panic cognitions tended to exhibit more of a sawtooth pattern in their therapeutic alliance. This finding may indicate that the more severe the panic cognitions are before treatment, the more stable the alliance development is. It could be that patients with fewer pre-treatment panic cognitions feel less need for treatment, which then leads them to be more skeptical about whether the treatment will meet their needs during the initial phase of therapy, resulting in unstable alliance scores.

It was also found that the more that panic cognitions reduce between sessions, the less the alliance increased within session and the less it decreased between sessions. In other words, the more the cognitions reduced between sessions, the less a saw-tooth pattern was evident. It is possible that patients who better internalize and generalize the principles of CBT outside the session are better able to further build between sessions on the cognitive change that occurred within session, and therefore are able to form a more stable alliance. This conclusion extends Hartmann, Orlinsky, and Zeeck's (2011) finding of patients with more positive intersession experiences forming a better therapeutic alliance.

Consistent with our hypotheses, sudden gains in alliance within session were evident in our sample. Sudden gains were not related to treatment outcome; however, the effect size for prediction of between-session decrease in ASI was considerable (16.4%), suggesting that more research in this area is worthwhile. At the same time, change in cognition during the session of the sudden gain was not different from change in cognitions in other sessions. Therefore, it is not clear what drives sudden gains of alliance and whether they are related to symptom change in any way (cf., Lutz et al., 2013; Tang & DeRubeis, 1999).

Overall, our findings partially support our hypothesis of a positive relationship between alliance and symptom improvement. The effects sizes for prediction of treatment outcome using early alliance scores and using between-patient variability in the alliance were in the expected range. However, within-patient variability in the alliance did not predict outcome, either simultaneously or at a one-session time-lag. Thus, although obtaining alliance measures before and after each session is a step forward in establishing the alliance as a candidate mediator of change in therapy (Kazdin, 2007), we were not able to show that session-by-session changes in alliance preceded changes in symptoms. Therefore, it is still unclear whether change in symptoms leads to high levels of alliance or vice versa (cf., Klein et al., 2003; Marker et al., 2013). We believe that this preliminary study provides a better methodological framework than those used in previous studies in order to test this question. The innovation in our study lies in examining the change in alliance in a session-by-session context, both before and after each session, and with time-lagged analyses. While causality cannot be determined on the basis of such relationships, stronger evidence of temporality can be established, which is a necessary criterion for inferring potential causal mechanisms of change related to outcome.

An important concern arises from our results: Although we found a reasonable effect size for early alliance prediction of panic symptoms during treatment (though not significant), there was no evidence whatsoever for a time-lag prediction. If alliance and outcome are correlated, but there is no way of determining which predicts which in a time-lagged analysis, it may raise the question of whether alliance and outcome are inextricably confounded. This suspicion must be verified in future studies, in order to better understand the nature of the relationship between alliance and outcome.

Some limitations of the study should be considered. Our findings rely on a small sample size of patients who had panic disorder as their primary diagnosis. Therapists were all first-year graduate students conducting their first CBT case and still at the beginning of their training, all under the supervision of the same person. We cannot know if these patterns were unique to this context of the patient-therapist dyads or generalize to more experienced therapists, different treatment orientations, and/or CBT for different patient populations. In addition, the study included one treatment group only, without a control group. Therefore, the changes that occurred with time in the therapeutic alliance and in panic cognitions cannot be definitively attributed to the CBT intervention. Nevertheless, the demonstrated efficacy of CBT for panic disorder (Mitte, 2005) strengthens the possibility that the changes are due to the treatment and not merely due to the passage of time. Further studies examining these hypotheses a priori in larger samples and using fine-grained analyses will be needed to fully understand the different patterns of alliance development and their relation to treatment. Another interesting avenue for future studies is using hierarchical cluster analysis to examine which of the above-mentioned patterns tend to cluster together and how these clusters relate to outcome. As such, the current study mainly emphasizes the importance of integrating single-case and group-level analyses, using intensive data collection methods (i.e., pre and post each session), and conducting longitudinal analyses examining the relationship of the alliance and outcomes (ideally cross-lagged in both directions). This approach seems to hold a great promise for psychotherapy process research.

Acknowledgment

The authors would like to thank Robert Gallop for his invaluable assistance with statistical advice for this manuscript

Notes

[1] We considered the gains that occurred within session, since we had measured alliance both before and after each session, and theoretically it makes sense that alliance changes would occur mostly within session. We also modified the criteria suggested by Tang and DeRubeis (1999) in order to fit the alliance scale. These modifications are reported in the method section.

[2] However, our approach is different from that of Baldwin et al. (2007) in that Baldwin et al.'s dataset included therapist and patient levels. Therefore, they calculated therapist-level WAI scores by averaging patient-level WAI scores for each therapist separately. Our dataset, on the other hand, includes patient and time levels. Therefore, we calculated patient-level WAI scores by averaging time-level WAI scores for each patient separately.

[3] Note that although the effect sizes are reported as percentages they do not represent the percentage of patients responding to the therapy but rather the percent of variance explained by a given predictor.

[4] To assess the degree of mutli-collinearity between the two slopes, we fit multilevel models predicting change in ASI/WAI between sessions from the respective change in the session that preceded it. The results showed that change within a given session explained only a small proportion of the variance in change between sessions (8.77% for WAI; 6.45% for ASI), corresponding to a modest correlation only (−.30; −.25).

[5] Note that due to some missing post-session data, the sum of the within- and between-session changes (1.75) resembles but is not entirely equal to the weekly changes in WAI (1.82).

References

Baldwin, S. A., Wampold, B. E., & Imel, Z. E. (2007). Untangling the alliance-outcome correlation: Exploring the relative importance of therapist and patient variability in the alliance. *Journal of Consulting and Clinical Psychology, 75*, 842–852. doi:10.1037/0022-006X.75.6.842

Barber, J. P. (2009). Toward a working through of some core conflicts in psychotherapy research. *Psychotherapy Research, 19*, 1–12. doi:10.1080/10503300802609680

Barber, J. P., Connolly, M. B., Crits-Christoph, P., Gladis, M., & Siqueland, L. (2000). Alliance predicts patients' outcome beyond in-treatment change in symptoms. *Journal of Consulting and Clinical Psychology, 68*, 1027–1032. doi:10.1037/0022-006X.68.6.1027

Barber, J. P., Luborsky, L., Gallop, R., Crits-Christoph, P., Frank, A., Weiss, R. D., ... Siqueland, L. (2001). Therapeutic alliance as a predictor of outcome and retention in the National Institute on Drug Abuse Collaborative Cocaine Treatment Study. *Journal of Consulting and Clinical Psychology, 69*, 119–124. doi:10.1037/0022-006X.69.1.119

Barlow, D. H., Bullis, J. R., Comer, J. S., & Ametaj, A. A. (2013). Evidence-based psychological treatments: An update and the way forward. *Annual Review of Clinical Psychology, 9*(1), 1–27 doi:10.1146/annurev-clinpsy-050212-185629

Barlow, D. H., & Craske, M. G. (2007). *Mastery of your anxiety and panic* (4th ed.). New York: Oxford University Press.

Borckardt, J. J., Nash, M. R., Murphy, M. D., Moore, M., Shaw, D., & O'Neil, P. (2008). Clinical practice as natural laboratory for psychotherapy research: A guide to case-based time-series analysis. *American Psychologist, 63*, 77–95.

Castonguay, L. G., Constantino, M. J., McAleavey, A. A., & Goldfried, M. R. (2010). The alliance in cognitive-behavioral therapy. In J. C. Muran & J. P. Barber (Eds.), *The therapeutic alliance: An evidence-based approach to practice and training*. New York: Guilford Press.

Castonguay, L. G., Schut, A. J., Aikins, D. E., Constantino, M. J., Laurenceau, J. P., Bologh, L., & Burns, D. D. (2004). Integrative cognitive therapy for depression: A preliminary investigation. *Journal of Psychotherapy Integration, 14*, 4–20. doi:10.1037/1053-0479.14.1.4

Connolly Gibbons, M. B., Crits-Christoph, P., de la Cruz, C., Barber, J. P., Siqueland, L., & Gladis, M. (2003). Pretreatment expectations, interpersonal functioning, and symptoms in the prediction of the therapeutic alliance across supportive–expressive psychotherapy and cognitive therapy. *Psychotherapy Research, 13*, 59–76. doi:10.1093/ptr/kpg007

Constantino, M. J., Marnell, M. E., Haile, A. J., Kanther-Sista, S. N., Wolman, K., Zappert, L., & Arnow, B. A. (2008). Integrative cognitive therapy for depression: A randomized pilot comparison. *Psychotherapy Theory, Research, Practice, Trining, 45*, 122–134. doi:10.1037/0033-3204.45.2.122

Crits-Christoph, P., Gibbons, M. B. C., Crits-Christoph, K., Narducci, J., Schamberger, M., & Gallop, R. (2006). Can therapists be trained to improve their alliances? A preliminary study of alliance-fostering psychotherapy. *Psychotherapy Research, 16*, 268–281. doi:10.1080/10503300500268557

Crits-Christoph, P., Gibbons, M. B. C., Hamilton, J., Ring-Kurtz, S., & Gallop, R. (2011). The dependability of alliance assessments: The alliance–outcome correlation is larger than you might think. *Journal of Consulting and Clinical Psychology, 79*, 267. doi:10.1037/a0023668

Eaton, T. T., Abeles, N., & Gutfreund, M. J. (1988). Therapeutic alliance and outcome: Impact of treatment length and pretreatment symptomatology. *Psychotherapy, 25*, 536–542. doi:10.1037/h0085379

Emmerling, M. E., & Whelton, W. J. (2009). Stages of change and the working alliance in psychotherapy. *Psychotherapy Research, 19*, 687–698. doi:10.1080/10503300902933170

Fishman, D. B. (2000). Transcending the efficacy versus effectiveness research debate: Proposal for a new, electronic "Journal of Pragmatic Case Studies." *Prevention & Treatment, 3*, Article 8. Posted May 3, 2000. http://journals.apa.org/prevention/.

Flückiger, C., Del Re, A. C., Wampold, B. E., Symonds, D., & Hovarth, A. O. (2012). How central is alliance in psychotherapy? A multilevel longitudinal meta-analysis. *Journal of Counseling Psychology, 59*, 10–17. doi:10.1037/a0025749

Foa, E. B., & Kozak, M. J. (1986). Emotional processing of fear: Exposure to corrective information. *Psychological Bulletin, 99*, 20–35. doi:10.1037/0033-2909.99.1.20

Gaston, L., Marmar, C. R., Thompson L. W., & Gallagher, D. (1988). Relation of patient pretreatment characteristics to therapeutic alliance in divers psychotherapies. *Journal of Consulting and Clinical Psychology, 56*, 483–489. doi:10.1037/0022-006X.56.4.483

Hartmann, A., Orlinsky, D., & Zeeck, A. (2011). The structure of intersession experience in psychotherapy and its relation to the therapeutic alliance. *Journal of Clinical Psychology, 67*, 1044–1063. doi:10.1002/jclp.20826

Hayes, A. M., Laurenceau, J.-P., Feldman, G. C., Strauss, J. L., & Cardaciotto, L. (2007). The shape of change: Discontinuous and nonlinear patterns of change in psychotherapy. *Clinical Psychology Review, 27*, 715–723. doi:10.1016/j.cpr.2007.01.008

Hersoug, A. G., Monsen, J. T., Havik, O. E., & Høglend, P. (2002). Quality of early working alliance in psychotherapy: Diagnoses, relationship and intrapsychic variables as predictors. *Psychotherapy and Psychosomatics, 71*, 18–27. doi:10.1159/000049340

Horvath, A. O., Del Re, A., Flückiger, C., & Symonds, D. (2011). Alliance in individual psychotherapy. *Psychotherapy, 48*, 9–16. doi:10.1037/a0022186

Houck, P. R., Spiegel, D. A., Shear, M. K., & Rucci, P. (2002). Reliability of the self-report version of the panic disorder severity scale. *Depression and Anxiety, 15*, 183–185. doi:10.1002/da.10049

Huppert, J. D., & Baker-Morrisette, S. L. (2003). Going beyond the manual: An insiders guide to Panic Control Treatment. *Cognitive and Behavioral Practice, 10*, 2–12. doi:10.1016/S1077-7229(03)80003-2

Huppert, J. D., Kivity, Y., Barlow, D. H., Shear, M. K., Gorman, J. M., & Woods, S. W. (2014). Therapist effects and the outcome-alliance correlation in cognitive behavioral therapy for panic disorder and agoraphobia. *Behaviour Research and Therapy, 52*(1), 26–34.

Jacobson, N. S., & Truax, P. (1991). Clinical significance: A statistical approach to defining meaningful change in psychotherapy research. *Journal of Consulting and Clinical Psychology, 59*, 12–19. doi:10.1037/0022-006X.59.1.12

Kazdin, A. E. (2007). Mediators and mechanisms of change in psychotherapy research. *Annual Review of Clinical Psychology, 3*, 1–27. doi:10.1146/annurev.clinpsy.3.022806.091432

Kivlighan, D. M., & Shaughnessy, P. (1995). Analysis of the development of the working alliance using hierarchical linear modeling. *Journal of Counseling Psychology, 42*, 338–349. doi:10.1037/0022-0167.42.3.338

Klein, D. N., Schwartz, J. E., Santiago, N. J., Vivian, D., Vocisano, C., Castonguay, L. G., ... Keller, M. B. (2003). Therapeutic alliance in depression treatment: Controlling for prior change and patient characteristics. *Journal of Consulting and Clinical Psychology, 71*, 997–1006. doi:10.1037/0022-006X.71.6.997

Lipsitz, S. R., Leong, T., Ibrahim, J., & Lipshultz, S. (2001). A partial correlation coefficient and coefficient of determination for multivariate normal repeated measures data. *Journal of the Royal Statistical Society: Series D (The Statistician), 50*, 87–95. doi:10.1111/1467-9884.00263

Lutz, W., Ehrlich, T., Rubel, J., Hallwachs, N., Röttger, M., Jorasz, C., ... Tschitsaz-Stucki, D. (2013). The ups and downs of psychotherapy: Sudden gains and sudden losses identified with session reports. *Psychotherapy Research, 23*, 14–24. doi:10.1080/10503307.2012.693837

Marker, C. D., Comer, J. S., Abramova, V., & Kendall, P. C. (2013). The reciprocal relationship between alliance and symptom improvement across the treatment of childhood anxiety. *Journal of Clinical Child and Adolescent Psychology, 42*, 22–33. doi:10.1080/15374416.2012.723261

Martin, D. J., Garske, J. P., & Davis, M. K. (2000). Relation of the therapeutic alliance with outcome and other variables: A meta-analytic review. *Journal of Consulting and Clinical Psychology, 68*, 438–450. doi:10.1037/0022-006X.68.3.438

Mitte, K. (2005). A meta-analysis of the efficacy of psycho- and pharmacotherapy in panic disorder with and without agoraphobia. *Journal of Affective Disorders, 88*(1), 27–45. doi:10.1016/j.jad.2005.05.003

Monkul, E. S., Tural, Ü., Onur, E., Fidaner, H., Alkın, T., & Shear, M. K. (2004). Panic Disorder Severity Scale: reliability and validity of the Turkish version. *Depression and Anxiety, 20*(1), 8–16. doi:10.1002/da.20011

Muran, J. C., & Barber, J. P. (Eds.). (2010). *The therapeutic alliance: An evidence-based approach to practice and training.* New York: Guilford Press.

Orlinsky, D. E., & Geller, J. (1993). Patients' representations of their therapists and therapy: New measures. In *Psychodynamic treatment research: A handbook for clinical practice* (pp. 423–466). New York: Basic Books.

Raudenbush, S. W., & Bryk, A. S. (2002). *Hierarchical linear models: Applications and data analysis methods* (2nd ed.). Thousand Oaks, CA: Sage.

Safran, J. D., Muran, J. C., & Eubanks-Carter, C. (2011). Repairing alliance ruptures. *Psychotherapy, 48*, 80–87. doi:10.1037/a0022140

Shear, M. K., Brown, T. A., Barlow, D. H., Money, R., Sholomskas, D. E., Woods, S. W., ... Papp, L. A. (1997). Multicenter collaborative panic disorder severity scale. *American Journal of Psychiatry, 154*, 1571–1575.

Shear, M. K., Rucci, P., Williams, J., Frank, E., Grochocinski, V., Vander Bilt, J., Houck, P., & Wang, T. (2001). Reliability and validity of the Panic Disorder Severity Scale: Replication and extension. *Journal of Psychiatric Research, 35*, 293–296. doi:10.1016/S0022-3956(01)00028-0

Sheehan, D. V., Lecrubier, Y., Sheehan K. H., Amorim, P., Janavs, J., Weiller, E., ... Dunbar, G. C. (1998). The Mini-International Neuropsychiatric Interview (M.I.N.I.): The development and validation of a structured diagnostic psychiatric interview for DSM-IV and ICD-10. *Journal of Clinical Psychiatry, 59*, 22–33.

Stiles, W. B., Glick, M. J., Osatuke, K., Hardy, G. E., Shapiro, D. A., Agnew-Davies, R., Rees, A., & Barkham, M. (2004). Patterns of alliance development and the rupture-repair hypothesis: Are productive relationships U-shaped or V-shaped? *Journal of Counseling Psychology, 1*, 81–92. doi:10.1037/0022-0167.51.1.81

Stiles, W. B., & Goldsmith, J. Z. (2010). The alliance over time. In J. C. Muran & J. P. Barber (Eds.), *The therapeutic alliance: An evidence-based approach to practice and training* (pp. 44–62). New York: Guilford Press.

Tang, T. Z., & DeRubeis, R. J. (1999). Sudden gains and critical sessions in cognitive- behavioral therapy for depression. *Journal of Consulting and Clinical Psychology, 67*, 894–904. doi:10.1037/0022-006X.67.6.894

Taylor, S., Zvolensky, M. J., Cox, B. J., Deacon, B., Heimberg, R. G., Ledley, D. R., ... Cardenas, S. J. (2007). Robust dimensions of anxiety sensitivity: Development and initial validation of the Anxiety Sensitivity Index-3. *Psychological Assessment, 19*, 176–188. doi:10.1037/1040-3590.19.2.176

Tracey, T. J., & Kokotovic, A. M. (1989). Factor structure of the Working Alliance Inventory. *Psychological Assessment: A Journal of Consulting and Clinical Psychology, 1*, 207–210. doi:10.1037/1040-3590.1.3.207

Webb, C. A., Derubeis, R. J., Amsterdam, J. D., Shelton, R. C., Hollon, S. D., & Dimidjian, S. (2011). Two aspects of the therapeutic alliance: Differential relations with depressive symptom change. *Journal of Consulting and Clinical Psychology, 79*(3), 279–283.

Westra, H. A., Constantino, M. J., & Aviram, A. (2011). The impact of alliance ruptures on client outcome expectations in cognitive behavioral therapy. *Psychotherapy Research, 21*, 472–481. doi:10.1080/10503307.2011.581708

The therapeutic relationship in action: How therapists and clients co-manage relational disaffiliation

PETER MUNTIGL[1,2] & ADAM O. HORVATH[2]

[1]*Linguistics Department, Ghent University, Ghent, Belgium & [2]Faculty of Education, Simon Fraser University, Burnaby, British Columbia, Canada*

Abstract
Over the past three decades a great deal of energy has been invested in examining the consequences of relational stresses and their repair. Less work has been done to examine how therapists and clients actually achieve re-affiliation through verbal and non-verbal resources, how such affiliation becomes vulnerable and at risk, and how therapists attempt to re-establish affiliative ties with the client—or fail to do so. We utilize the method of Conversation Analysis (CA) to examine clinical cases that involve extended episodes of disaffiliation. Clients with different styles of disaffiliation—confrontation and withdrawal—are compared. We show how disaffiliation is interactionally realized in different ways and how this is followed by more or less successful attempts at repair.

Interest in the dynamics of the relationship between therapist and client has been central from the earliest days of psychotherapy (Freud, 1994) and continues to occupy center stage in more recent conceptualizations of psychological treatments (e.g., Bohart, Elliott, Greenberg, Watson, & Norcross, 2002; Rogers, Gendlin, Kiesler, & Truax, 1967). Over the last three decades empirical research has provided robust support for the general claim that the quality of the therapeutic relationship bears a ubiquitous and significant relation to treatment outcome across the breadth of client problems and variety of treatment approaches (Norcross, 2002, 2011). While the value of the relationship in therapy has been clearly documented, the existence of this positive link between elements of the therapy relationship and outcome, in and of itself, provides only one part of the information we need to improve our services. In addition to appreciating the value of a solid alignment with their clients, psychotherapists also need to better understand how various aspects of the relationship are realized in clinical practice, such as what makes these elements therapeutic and how they can be improved (Ribeiro et al., 2014). The next generation of research needs to move toward the closer exploration of the relational processes from the clinician's perspective (Bordin, 1994). For instance, the robust linkage between the quality of the alliance and outcome is only the starting point in the quest to better understand how therapists can use their understanding of the importance of the alliance to provide more effective treatments. The clinically crucial follow-up questions include: How do therapists gain clients' enthusiastic participation in the tasks of treatment? What are some of the signs as treatment unfolds that clients use to communicate anxiety, reluctance, or resistance to the direction the therapist is taking? How does the actual deterioration or breakdown (rupture) of the close alignment between therapist and client dynamically unfold in the session? How do therapists interact with their clients to effectively re-negotiate their affiliation and re-align themselves with the client, re-build a sense of joint purpose and resume productive work? How do therapists adjust their stance and re-position themselves to overcome the rift between themselves and the client?

These "next generation of questions" we proposed in the preceding paragraphs all pertain to *how* these relational processes are realized in the dialogical interactive context of therapy. As far back as 1994, Bordin suggested that the management of relational stresses constitutes a core therapeutic opportunity because it has the potential of providing the client with transformative experiences: "the collaborative process represents an arena in which the patient once more encounters his self defeating propensities.... In therapy the patient struggles with these problems with the therapist" (p. 18). He further proposed that understanding the *hows* of relational stresses in therapy, which he called "the basic science" of psychotherapy, is the next important challenge for psychotherapy researchers (Bordin, 1994). In a similar vein, Safran and Muran (2006) argue that relational enactments between therapist and client are at the core of the healing experience for clients and the better understanding of how these events are negotiated is of prime interest.

Most of the research on the therapy relationship to date has used quantitative methods drawn from clients, therapists or observers' appraisal. A great majority of the data researchers have examined are based on questionnaires or checklist-type measures. These sources and methods tend to yield assessments indexing the quality, quantity, presence or absence of relational elements summed up over one or more sessions. (Elvins & Green, 2008; Norcross, 2002, 2011). Much less energy has been committed to the detailed examination of the specifics of in-therapy events that aggregate over time to produce effective therapy experiences, whether they are assessed from the perspective of empathy, alliance or positive regard. There are, however, efforts to fill this gap in our qualitative understanding of how the therapy relationship works to facilitate change. Safran and colleagues (Safran & Muran, 1996, 2000; Safran, Muran, & Samstag, 1994; Safran, Muran, Samstag, & Stevens, 2001) have examined episodes of relational stresses between therapist and client and have developed a taxonomy of client responses to relational misalignments classified as confrontational or withdrawal ruptures.[1] Lepper and Mergenthaler (2007) researched patterns of lexical coherence and its relation to the therapeutic bond, while Sutherland and Strong (2011) have investigated discursive practices of a master therapist to better understand how therapists invite collaboration from clients in couples therapy.

While each of these (and other) investigators explored how relational stresses are managed and function in treatment, the focus has been on over-session or longer-term relational stress. Much less work has been done on examining how therapists and clients jointly work locally, turn-by-turn, to (1) find ways to accommodate the inevitable differences in expectations of what needs to be achieved, (2) find consensus on what kinds of things they could do together to foster change, and (3) achieve a therapeutic bond (Orlinsky, 2010). The goal of the project we report on is to make an inroad in providing better descriptions of the way this kind of work is dialectically realized, and also to explore, in the near term and in dynamic detail, *how* the therapy relationship becomes strained, the dynamic unfolding of repair work, and the way clients' styles of disaffiliation color the way these interactions unfold.

In order to shed more light on how relational stresses are realized at the level of therapist-client interaction, we use the methods of Conversation Analysis (CA) (Sacks, 1992; Schegloff, 2007). CA is a qualitative approach to studying naturally occurring talk in both everyday and institutionalized contexts. A general aim in CA research is to explore the orderly methods or practices through which speakers produce social interaction. According to this view, talk is an ongoing accomplishment that is predicated on speakers' abilities to (1) co-ordinate their turns at speaking (Sacks, Schelgoff, & Jefferson, 1974); (2) organize their actions in patterned sequences, as for example answers following questions, acceptance following invitations and agreement following assessments (Atkinson & Heritage, 1984; Sacks, 1992; Schegloff & Sacks, 1973); and (3) use organized methods for solving problems in understanding in order to get the conversation back on track (Schegloff, Jefferson, & Sacks, 1977). This cooperative management of turns and actions allows speakers to stay intersubjectively aligned throughout a conversation (Heritage, 1984), but also helps them to get various interactional agendas or projects under way (Schegloff, 2007, p. 244). Turns and actions, thus, form the building blocks for achieving mutual understanding, for getting things done and for forming social relations. As Schegloff (2006, p.70) has put it, interaction is "the primordial site of sociality."

The organization of talk, in general, is argued to be biased so as to promote social solidarity and avoid conflict (Brown & Levinson 1987; Enfield, 2006; Goffman 1967; Heritage 1984; Levinson 1983). This bias is realized not only in the overwhelming tendency for speakers to produce pro-social actions (e.g., agreement, compliance), but also in specific kinds of linguistic and interactional practices used to mitigate potential threats to the self-other relationship: For example, disagreements and refusals tend to be softened through various linguistic markers and delay tactics (Atkinson & Drew, 1979; Heritage, 1984; Pomerantz, 1984). Even in contexts in which social cohesion may be placed at risk, such as in everyday conflict episodes, speakers tend to maintain social bonds by formulating their disagreements in increasingly less aggravating ways (Muntigl & Turnbull, 1998). Degrees of cooperativeness and mutual levels of affect between speakers have been conceptualized within CA using the following terms:

Affiliation and *alignment* (Stivers, 2008; Stivers, Mondada, & Steensig, 2011). The term affiliation refers, in general, to the affective level of interaction in which speakers work together in harmony by producing pro-social actions. Affiliative actions generally convey "agreement" with the prior speaker, but may also be explicitly empathic and thus display a keen understanding of what the speaker had said. Alignment, on the other hand, refers to cooperative interaction in which the relevant tasks or activities at hand are successfully accomplished. Aligning responses display a willingness to co-participate in a given activity. Moreover, alignment does not necessarily imply *agreement*; that is, one can disagree but still cooperate with the general aims of the interaction. *Dis*affiliation and *dis*alignment, by contrast, are distinguished by interactions in which social harmony, empathy and cooperation are placed at risk.

For this paper, we examine two cases of extended disaffiliation and disalignment between two different therapists and clients. Our research questions are as follows:

- How are disaffiliations and disalignments between clients and therapists interactively realized at the discursive level in therapy conversations?
- What kinds of interactional resources and conversational moves do clients use to indicate disaffiliation or disalignment?
- What kind of conversational work done by therapists leads to successful re-affiliation and also how does unsuccessful repair work unfold?
- Can we identify sequential patterns that lead to successful re-affiliation and re-alignment as opposed to those that do not?

Rather than attempt to make generalizations across cases or therapies, our aim is to show how an important therapeutic process is managed at the "ground level," through the specific interactional practices of the client and therapist. Thus, our main contribution is to provide an interactional perspective on what is loosely conceptualized in the psychotherapy literature as relationship stresses. Through the lens of CA we are able to track the turn-by-turn interactive development in which disaffiliation between therapist and client occurs and, subsequently, is or is not repaired. By adopting the methods of CA, we are able to study what clients and therapists actually do within the institutionalized framework of therapy, while operating within a certain therapeutic mode of practice. These practices include not only speakers' verbal utterances, but also non-verbal actions including gesture, gaze and body movements. Therefore, the study of interactional practices that constitute the "management of affiliation" between therapist and client is of interest to therapists and complements our knowledge of the therapy process.

Participants and Case Selection

Our sample draws from the York I Depression Study (Greenberg & Watson, 1998) and consists of videotaped treatments of severely depressed clients who underwent Emotion-focused Process Experiential Therapy (PET/ EFT; Greenberg 2002; Greenberg, Rice, & Elliot, 1993). Three sessions each from two different cases (total = six sessions) in which the clients completed the required 20 sessions of therapy were examined. The sessions were selected from the beginning, middle and late stages of therapy. Outcome was derived from the following measures: BDI (Beck Depression Inventory), IIP (Inventory of Interpersonal Problems), GSI (Global Severity Index) and RSE (Rosenberg Self-Esteem Scale). We rank ordered the cases in terms of outcome using the sum of each of the outcome measures (standardized) and chose cases from the bottom (poorer) quartile. We chose these relatively less successful cases because it was hypothesized that these therapies would provide us with a rich variety of episodes in which disalignment and repair work were evident. The two therapists and clients (the pseudonyms used were Kristina and Sophia) in our sample were female. The clients were suffering from depression and the therapists were experienced, trained and supervised in the use of Emotion-focused Process Experiential Therapy.[2]

This material has offered several advantages for our inquiry: The treatment prioritized the management of the therapist-client relation, the clients had similar concerns, the therapists were well trained, the techniques at the therapist's disposal were known to us (we knew the techniques they were trying to implement) and treatment fidelity was supervised. The segments we chose for analysis were not selected randomly but with a view to exploring events that provided good examples of the interactive processes we were interested in examining. Both cases we use as illustrations provided us with clear instances of stress and repair sequences; one case (Sophia) was selected as an exemplar of a client with a confrontational disaffiliative style. The other client (Kristina) was a good exemplar of the person whose style in situations of relational stress was more passive.

Analytic Procedure

Transcription. A prerequisite for conversation analysis is to work at obtaining a detailed transcript

Extract 1:

014.13

	Kris:	I- I don't have the strength really to uh- to uh: leave the marriage.
		I was thinking about it, why is it- why it didn't come to
		(1.1)
	Kris:	a conclusion.
		(3.5)
F→	Ther:	.hhh >so you don't have the < strength to leave- to break out.
	Kris:	mm [hm.]
	Ther:	[yeah.] mm hm,
		(6.7)
	Kris:	hm.
		(0.4)
F→	Ther:	.hhh break out've the prison. mm(h)heh

that illustrates not only *what* speakers are saying, but also *how* they are saying it. For this reason, prosodic features such as emphasis, intonation, syllable lengthening, quiet speech, and so on are included in transcriptions. Moreover, other potentially important information such as silences and non-verbal displays (e.g., gaze, gestures, nodding) are also included. The transcribing conventions used in this paper are illustrated in the Appendix (a complete list of CA transcription conventions is outlined in Jefferson, 2004). In order to make the examples in this paper easier to read and comprehend, we provide an abridged and simplified version of the original transcribed material.

Focus. For our next step, we followed the common analytic practice in CA of identifying action sequences and exploring the cohesive relations between action pairs such as question-answer, assessment-agreement, request-compliance, and so on (Schegloff, 2007). Sequence analysis is optimally suited for examining naturally occurring social interaction (see also Peräkylä, 2004) and has been shown to shed light on many interesting features of psychotherapy interactions (see Peräkylä, Antaki, Vehviläinen, & Leudar, 2008; Voutilainen, Peräkylä, & Ruusuvuori, 2011): First, sequence analysis places the focus on client-therapist interaction and how each of the speakers responds to and shapes what the other will say (Heritage, 1984), rather than on single decontextualized expressions or utterances. Thus, for clients and therapists, sequences are resources for action and inference-making, intention attribution and coming to mutual understandings (Enfield, 2006). Second, a sequence represents a specific interactional context that facilitates a comparison between different instances. Third, once a corpus of sequence types has been obtained, further analysis can target whether differences in action types may be noted or if the same action is observed, but expressed in different ways.

From our initial overview of the session transcriptions, we decided to focus our investigation on *formulation* sequences, the main reason being that a number of client disaffiliations were found in this specific sequential context. Formulations are generally characterized as actions that reflect back what someone has said. They can merely provide the gist of prior talk (i.e., summarizing) or they may do slightly more by stating an implication of that talk (Antaki, 2008; Heritage & Watson, 1979). A formulation bears similarity to what Stiles (1992) has termed *reflection*; that is, a therapist's formulation adopts the client's frame of reference and, consequently, maintains the client's ownership of experience. However, while in Stiles's sense formulations are reflective, we understand them to be also transformative and often move talk in a more therapeutically relevant direction. Consider extract (1), involving the client Kristina (F = Formulation).

In this example, Kristina talks about her lack of strength to leave the marriage. The therapist first summarizes or reflects back what Kristina had said ("so you don't have the strength to leave"), but then elaborates on her turn by transforming the meaning "to leave" to the potentially more therapeutically relevant meaning "to break out" and, later in line 12, to "break out've the prison." The therapist's *re*formulation of Kristina's talk is interesting because it adds another layer of meaning to what Kristina had said: *Breaking out* implies a greater exertion of force than does Kristina's prior expression of *leaving.*

Formulations, as they are being described here, are empathic because they (1) maintain a close semantic (and often a grammatical) tie with the client's prior utterance and, in doing so, (2) imply a client's rather than a therapist's perspective. In the example above, the therapist's formulation begins by closely matching the original wording of the client's utterance and then, at the end, offers a slight, but relevant, modification in meaning to the term "to leave." Although not all formulations have this tight grammatical matching,

Extract 2:

304.07

	Sofia:	before the nervous breakdown. (0.4) I could feel (0.3) sad.
		but never sad (0.3) to the point, of wanting to ɲcry!
F→	Ther:	mm hm. [so this is more recent.]
	Sofia:	[never that sad.]
I→	Ther:	.hhh >and I imagine it has something to do with < not feeling
		connected.

there does exist a degree of linguistic cohesion between client's and therapist's utterances.

By attempting to uphold the client's perspective of the personal event under discussion, formulations make no allusions to the *therapist's* point of view and thus are not considered *interpretations* (cf., Stiles, 1992). We can differentiate between these two practices: Work in CA has shown that interpretations are designed much differently than formulations (Bercelli, Rossano, & Viaro, 2008; Peräkylä, 2005). Consider extract 2, involving a different client, Sofia (I = Interpretation).

Sofia recounts a recent change in her behavior in which emotional experiencing of sadness has now become intensified, "to the point, of wanting to ɲcry!" As a response, the therapist begins with a formulation by reflecting back the temporal relevance of Sofia's disclosure ("so this is more recent"). However, the therapist continues her turn by emphasizing her own perspective ("I imagine") and, subsequently, by providing an explanation for why she now feels this way. In this example, the grammatical expression "I imagine" flags the therapist's subjective view; that is, what is about to be said is derived from the therapist, it is a subjective inferential leap, and not necessarily bound to what they client may have specifically said, or meant to say.

Disaffiliation and disalignment following formulation. We have argued that from a therapeutic standpoint, formulations constitute a therapeutically important form of empathic reflection. Although formulations tend to be followed by agreement (Antaki, 2008; Heritage & Watson, 1979; Muntigl, 2004), they are sometimes responded to with disaffiliative actions such as disagreement or with disaligning actions, such as when clients simply ignore the therapist and continue to pursue their agenda. We draw attention to two general discursive features of formulations that help to explain this. First, although formulations are closely connected to clients' talk, they still transform this talk. Thus, clients may feel that their version of experience has been altered to the point that they may no longer endorse it or even that they have begun to lose ownership of this experience. Second, formulations may function to move talk in a specific therapeutically relevant direction. Clients, however, may choose to disalign with the therapist's agenda and, also, may prefer to continue with their own agenda instead. It should also be noted that disaffiliation, as expressed through some form of disagreement, tends to implicate a disalignment; that is, when clients disagree with the therapist's formulation of their talk, this will often imply that the client is not endorsing the therapeutic trajectory that has been initiated by the therapist.

It is important to emphasize that disaffiliation and disalignment *are not* being used as normative or value-laden terms here; that is, they are not considered as "bad" practices and are not to be equated with resistance or non-compliance. Client disagreement, for example, may signal the client's hesitation to engage in therapeutic work, but it could also imply that if the therapist provided more empathy, the client may be prepared to re-join the process. Irrespective of whether client disagreement is indexing resistance, hesitation or a lack of therapist empathy, what we aim to highlight is the social interactional relevance of disaffiliating and disaligning and how these actions create a momentary relational strain between the therapist and client. Further, the therapist has the next turn at talk and, thus, it becomes incumbent on the therapist to address this strain. We will show that the therapist orients to two related interpersonal tasks when responding. The first is to work at achieving re-affiliation between herself and the client and the second is to display empathy by attempting to understand the client's divergent position. For the remainder of this paper, we explore the interactional practices that two therapists have used to repair disaffiliation, how some practices were less successful than others and how extended disaffiliation occurs within the context of two different styles of client disaffiliation (confrontation and withdrawal).

Results

Disaffiliation

We found that client disaffiliation can strain the therapist-client relationship in three important ways:

Extract 3a:

014.04(2b)

	01	Kris:	((lip smack)) well (0.8) we- we have common debts, hhh.hhh definitely
	02		the practical (0.9) parts, are here as well,
	03		(5.6)
	04	Kris:	(an then) we have a chi:ld,
	05		(4.0)
	06	Kris:	an she really (.) loves her father,
	07		(12.8)
	08	Kris:	.hhh an there's not everything that I mind about him there are some
	09		(0.6) positive charact(h)er(h)ist(h)ics he has as well,
	10		(9.2)
F→	11	Ther:	((lip smack)) so somehow thes:e.hh these things seem.hh worth
F→	12		(2.3) sacrificing your happiness for?
	13		(1.5)
F→	14	Ther:	or worth the pain?
D→	15	Kris:	.hhh well th- th- my question is I don't know what's on the other side.
D→	16		would I- would I be any happier?
	17		(1.6)
D→	18	Kris:	I don't know.

First, the client's response does not endorse the therapist's version of the client's situation, thus placing the affective relation between them at risk. Second, disaffiliation often has the consequence of hindering or resisting the therapist's agenda—and, by implication, of potentially promoting the client's usual (pathogenic) way of conceptualizing or dealing with the situation—thus causing a disalignment with respect to the direction in which therapeutic work should be taking. Third, disaffiliation may imply that the therapist has not provided or communicated empathy with the client's prior talk.

Client disaffiliation is shown in extract 3a. Prior to this sequence of talk, the client Kristina had reported her unhappiness in her marriage to the therapist. She then proceeds to list a number of reasons why she and her husband should be together: They have common debts, they have a child who loves the father and—said in an ironic, joking manner—the husband does have some redeeming qualities (D = Disaffiliation).

When formulating, the therapist draws an implication from Kristina's prior talk: By weighing up being unhappy and being "in pain" against her reasons for staying in the relationship, it is inferable that Kristina is ultimately sacrificing her happiness and inflicting punishment on herself. Thus, the formulation attempts to shift the focus of talk from Kristina's rationalization for staying in the relationship to the negative emotional consequences that this line of action might have (e.g., unhappiness, pain). The therapist, thus, offers an alternative perspective through which Kristina may view her situation. The therapist does not, however, position herself as an expert when doing so: She uses epistemic downgraders such as "somehow" and rising intonation to seek confirmation from the client rather than assert own view. Thus, the formulation is clearly designed in terms of what Labov and Fanshel (1977) call a *B-event*, in which epistemic primacy, or knowledge of personal experience, lies within the client's domain.

The therapist's formulation also places a number of constraints on Kristina's response. Thus, Kristina has the option not only of confirming or disconfirming the formulation, but also of accepting or denying the assumption that she will be happier and in less pain if she leaves her husband. Kristina then responds by producing what Stivers and Hayashi (2010) have termed an *agenda transforming answer*; that is, she does not produce a "yes" or "no" but instead denies the assumption and counters the therapist's shift of perspective (i.e., from the husband's tolerable features to the clients self-defeating schema) by highlighting the uncertainty involved in taking such a course of action ("would I be any happier?"). Through this disagreement, the client asserts greater rights in defining what the most relevant aspects are for her, if she were to disband the relationship. The disagreement thus creates a momentary epistemic impasse; that is, divergent views have been laid on the table and this lack of consensus somehow needs to be resolved. Kristina's response of disagreement also disaligns with the therapist's attempt at getting her to explore the emotional repercussions of her behavior. Kristina's action is disaligning because it blocks the exploration of the client's experiential state and instead projects the conversation along more rhetorical lines in which the pros and cons of leaving the relationship (or staying in the relationship) may be debated. The issue of whether alignment occurs or not is

Extract 3b:

014.04(2b)

	15	Kris:	.hhh well th- th- my question is I don't know what's on the other side.
	16		would I- would I be any happier?
	17		(1.6)
	18	Kris:	I don't know.
	19		(2.0)
R→	20	Ther:	mm ∩hm! ∩yeah! so that's a big unknown.
	21		(0.7)
R→	22	Ther:	maybe (2.4) maybe ye just- would just be the same.
	23		(2.1)
R→	24	Ther:	an then =
R→	25	Kris:	=or- or y'know or maybe end product would be the same. the
	26		circumstances would be different?
	27		(3.8)
R→	28	Ther:	the end product meaning you'd still be [unhap]py.
	29		[my::]
R→	30	Kris:	.hhh m- yes. hhh
	31	Ther:	uh huh,

important, because if the client disaligns, the therapist's local goal of focusing on the client's self-defeating pattern may be delayed or even hindered.

These local impasses in the conversation involving affiliation and alignment, brought about by the client's disaffiliation, are very relevant social interactional matters that require attention from both participants, but especially the therapist. Successful repair of this interactional tension/disruption depends a great deal on what happens subsequently. In these situations, therapists are called upon to use interactional resources to gain re-affiliation and mutual understanding with the client. We examine specific contexts in which disaffiliation is managed by clients and therapists. We begin by showing how disaffiliation is immediately resolved. Next, we turn our attention to situations where disaffiliation is extended, by comparing an example of a client who persistently confronts the therapist with an example of a client who persistently withdraws.

Resolving the Disaffiliation in immediately Subsequent Turns

Disaffiliation creates a number of interactional challenges for the therapist. First, disagreements may place stress on the therapist-client relationship; second, if not successfully resolved, they may hinder important therapeutic work; third, they provide an opportunity for therapists to better understand and display empathy with the client's experience. Thus, disaffiliation need not be obstructive to therapeutic work, but instead may be a chance or resource for achieving effective therapeutic exploration of the client's problem (cf., Safran et al., 2001; Stiles et al., 2004).

From our corpus, we found a frequent pattern in which re-affiliation was successfully accomplished immediately subsequent to client disaffiliation. The general pattern was as follows: Therapists would endorse the client's contrasting position, which would lead to client agreement and thus to mutual affiliation and alignment. Endorsement from the therapist was realized through discursive markers of agreement or consensus (e.g., "yeah," "mm hm," "right") or through actions that worked with the client's position such as formulations. To illustrate how re-affiliation is achieved in this manner, consider extract 3b, which is a continuation of extract 3a (R = Reaffiliation).

Following Kristina's disaffiliation, the therapist delays her response for two seconds. This form of delay was consistently observed in these environments, helping therapists to retreat from their own position and to make room for clients to assert and develop their own position instead (Muntigl, Knight, & Watkins, 2012). Following the silence, the therapist first expresses strong agreement—as realized through sharp, emphatically voiced rising-falling intonation ("mm ∩hm!," "∩yeah!"). Next, the therapist utters a formulation that voices an upshot to Kristina's prior disagreement; that is, not knowing "what's on the other side" or if she would "be any happier?" implies "a big unknown" on Kristina's part. The formulation, however, does not procure immediate agreement from Kristina—note the 0.7 ensuing pause in line 21—which then leads the therapist to continue by softening ("maybe") and elaborating upon her formulation ("would just be the same."). In doing so, the therapist is able to align herself more closely with Kristina's initially expressed doubt that changing her life situation will make a difference. Following this, the speakers gradually move towards re-affiliation through a process of mutually elaborating each other's turns. Kristina begins by adding more specificity to what would remain the same (i.e., the end product) and what would not (i.e., the circumstances) in that hypothetical situation. The therapist, in turn, continues in this vein by specifying the end product ("you'd still be unhappy"). This is then followed by successive expressions of agreement from both parties ("yes," "uh huh"). Thus, through interactional practices of softening, recycling each other's words ("maybe," "same," "end product") in a mutually collaborative manner and explicitly endorsing the client's position, the therapist was able to initiate a resolution to the relational stress by actively re-affiliating with the client.

This extract has shown how, following client disaffiliation, the therapist and client work at securing a context of re-affiliation. This was primarily achieved through discursive practices such as agreement, formulation and elaboration, in which the therapist and client would endorse and work with each other's viewpoint. The therapist's responses were also explicit in displaying understanding of the client's diverging position. This was important not only for expressing empathy, but also for helping to develop the client's experiential state and, thus, for moving therapeutic work forwards.

Challenges in Resolving Dissafiliation

Therapists were not always successful in immediately securing re-affiliation with clients. In these contexts of extended disaffiliation, clients and therapists were found to constantly move in and out of affiliation over time. Our interest, therefore, is in mapping these shifts and in examining the type of eventual outcome this sort of negotiation might have for the participants of therapy.

We were able to identify distinctive kinds of interactional patterns that tended to maintain rather than repair the disaffiliation. These patterns resulted from the collaborative production of both therapists and clients. It was clients, however, who first drew attention to the relational strain by disaffiliating with the therapist's formulation. What we observed was that the client's *manner* of disaffiliating tended to recur throughout the extended disaffiliation sequence. Furthermore, this manner of disaffiliating was found to roughly correspond to Safran and Muran's (1996) description of client *confrontation* vs. *withdrawal*. In our data, client confrontation was generally realized through oppositional practices such as explicit disagreement or interruption, but withdrawal was marked by frequent delays or silences, downgraded disagreement or evasive answers. The confrontational client would make her disagreement of the therapist's view explicit and would articulate a clear contrasting view. The withdrawing client, on the other hand, would express opposition more weakly or tentatively and, when therapists responded by pursuing affiliation from them, the client would subtly resist these attempts by delaying affiliation through expressions of weak agreement; that is, the withdrawing client would continue to weaken her opposition but, at the same time, would refrain from fully engaging with the therapist. Therapists' responses to disaffiliation were found to lie on a continuum in which, at the one end, they displayed a high degree of empathy and, at the other end, they contrasted with or in some way opposed the client's prior disaffiliative action. Further, whereas the empathic responses tended to facilitate re-affiliation and further therapeutic exploration, the non-empathic acts often maintained a context of opposition and, as a result, clients tended to respond in kind by continuing to disaffiliate.

In order to identify and provide a map of the moment-by-moment shifts in affiliation, we examine two extended sequences of talk that span over several minutes and that involve recurring episodes of disaffiliation; one from a client whose disaffiliative style is confrontational and one from a client who tends to withdraw. Furthermore, for the former we show how the therapist is unsuccessful at regaining re-affiliation and, for the latter, how successful re-affiliation is achieved. Both sessions were taken from the middle range of the overall therapy.

Client Practices of Confrontation

In the following extracts, we show how disaffiliation is built up around a conflict of views between the therapist and client. At the core of these interactions is a *disalignment*—in which therapist and client are pursuing different agendas—that becomes realized in opposing action plans, with the therapist attempting to explore the client's needs and the client repeatedly resisting that trajectory by claiming not to have needs (i.e., she is independent and tough). Whereas the client Sofia is particularly assertive in blocking the therapist's pursuit of her agenda through explicit disagreements, elaborated arguments for her own position and interruptions, the therapist seems unable to make cogent empathic displays. Thus, these extended disaffiliation sequences were, in part, spurred on by a battle over who has primary rights in reflecting on the reasons or motives governing the client's actions.

Introducing the topic of Sofia's needs: Conflicting agendas. Prior to extract 4a, Sofia and the therapist had been discussing Sofia's past affair with another man and that Sofia had "found a bunch of other things in this other relationship" that were very positive. The therapist then shifts the topic

Extract 4a:[3]

304.07(5)

	01	Ther:	and d'you remembe:r like as a kid?
	02		(0.7)
	03	Ther:	ha- like
	04	Sofia:	w-when I [when I:?]
	05	Ther:	[d'ya] >I mean d'you think < this goes back to when you were a
	06		child? th-it sort've (0.5).hhh r-it I mean is that s- s-[is this] always been true
	07	Sofia:	[m-]
	08	Ther:	of you? kinda needing a lot of.hhh (0.50) lo:ve, an: (0.5) suppo:rt?
	09		(2.3)
D→	10	Sofia:	<if I always needed a lot of love [and support? >]
	11	Ther:	[mm hm,] mm hm.
	12		(1.9)
D→	13	Sofia:	uh::, (2.1) no I don't remember myself as being,
D→	14		(0.7) uh: I remember myself (1.1) when I was a little (0.3) girl?
	15	Ther:	[mm hm,]
D→	16	Sofia:	[between] ages five? (0.6) an thirteen?
			S: looks at T
	17		[(0.4)]
			[*T: double nod*]
D→	18	Sofia:	being very independent.
	19	Ther:	mm hm.
			T: double nod
D→	20	Sofia:	an being (0.7) uh:: wild.
	21		(0.3)
			T: smiles
D→	22	Sofia:	an being outside outdoor all the time,.hhh a:nd uh: I neve:r
			T: slow multiple nods
	23		(0.7)
D→	24	Sofia:	I wasn't a per- eh- a child that needed a lot of attention?
	25		(0.3)
D→	26	Sofia:	[no.]
			S: shakes head
F→	27	Ther:	[yeah.] (0.6) no. (0.3) you [were] just really wild
	28	Sofia:	[no.]
F→	29	Ther:	and happy.
	30		(1.1)
	31	Sofia:	m'yeah.
			S: multiple nods
	32		[(0.3)]
			[*T: shallow multiple nods*]
	33	Sofia:	mm hm, no I'm not- never. never that type (0.2) of- of- of person
	34		that is very sensitive or.hhh

by drawing a connection between Sofia's childhood and her strong need of love and support during that time. Sofia, however, assertively resists that interpretation and the therapist then works quickly to affiliate with Sofia's contrasting viewpoint.

This extract begins with the therapist asking a question that seeks confirmation as to whether Sofia needed a lot of love and support as a child. Initial disaffiliation from the client begins in line 10 with a *disagreement implicative other-initiated repair* (Schegloff, 2007); that is, Sofia's question as to whether she "always needed a lot of love and support?" is not, in the first instance, a request for clarification, but an action that presages disagreement. Sofia's actual disagreement then becomes heralded in through various discursive features such as prefatory silences, hesitations ("uh::") and the negation marker "no." She then continues on with a lengthy account of why the therapist is mistaken by claiming not to remember anything of the sort that the therapist is suggesting and, instead, by remembering a set of contrasting attributes that forcefully speak against having needs: *Being very independent, wild, not needing a lot of attention.*

Thus, the therapist's view is that the client is not having her needs of having love and support met and that (1) this may have a history that extends back into her childhood; and (2) it may explain why she sought this out in another man. The client resists this view and instead presents herself as not having needs, as being independent and wild. At this point in the interaction, the speakers are disaffiliated; that is, Sofia

Extract 4b:

	75	Sofia:	she:::, (0.7) I remember her. (0.3) from the (.) time that I was
	76		little (0.3) I was three years old?
	77		(0.5)
	78	Ther:	mm hm.
	79	Sofia:	that's as far as I can remember from my granma..hhh an she always
	80		(0.4)
	81	Sofia:	I always remember her teaching me to be tough.
	82		(0.2)
F→	83	Ther:	mm:. so (.) you [show people that] you (.) [can handle it] or you
	84	Sofia:	[she never grew] [she:::]
	85		(0.3)
	86	Sofia:	she did? (1.0) gave me a lot of uh sensitivity (0.4) °s:ensitivity°
	87		in many ways.
	88		[(0.9)] [T: shallow nod]
			. . .
D→	104	Ther:	but it was also like the message was be tough on the outside right?
	105	Sofia:	uh:m.
	106		(0.2)
D→	107	Ther:	and [I'd imagine don't] show your feelings on the [in]
D→	108	Sofia:	[be- be tough.] [not-] not only not show
D→	109		your feelings.
	110	Ther:	yeah.
D→	111	Sofia:	more than that is: not don't have them.
	112	Ther:	[°uh huh,°]
D→	113	Sofia:	[des come on.] get up an (.) an do your
D→	114		[y- do you] keep going on life an (0.5) don't cry.
	115	Ther:	[uh huh.] *T: multiple nods* ——————————>
	116		[(0.2)] [——————————>] [*S: raises eyebrows, smiles at T*]
	117	Ther:	ye:s. right. right. = *T: multiple nods, smiles*
	118	Sofia:	= that was the message [my granmother,]

has actively rejected the therapist's suggestion through a range of oppositional practices. The therapist then responds with affiliation in line 27 by displaying agreement ("yeah") and by producing a summary formulation of Sofia's talk ("you were just really wild and happy"). Further, minimal displays of mutual affiliation occur at the end of the extract, as seen by Sofia's return agreement and their mutual displays of nodding (Muntigl, Knight, & Watkins, 2012). In the last couple of lines, however, Sofia returns to her previous claim of not having needs by stating that she is not "very sensitive." Her use of the present tense also seems to bring the topic of needs to her present-day situation and away from her childhood. Thus, by expanding on her prior disaffiliative position of not having needs, Sofia moves back into an oppositional frame, thereby calling on more affiliative work from the therapist. Thus, the therapist's attempt to help Sofia gain access to the ways that she needs love, support and attention are not met with success.

Extended disaffiliation and disalignment

The client's continued opposition to the therapist's attempt at pursuing the topic of Sofia's needs is shown in extract 4b. Sofia, however, now shifts the focus of her argumentation on her grandmother, claiming that it was the grandmother that socialized her into being tough and, by implication, not having emotional needs.

At the beginning of this extract, Sofia mentions the grandmother's important role in teaching Sofia to be tough. The therapist then immediately seeks affiliation with that position through an upshot formulation (line 83). Sofia, however, ignores the formulation as expressed through her overlapping speech and continues to develop her account of the grandmother's role by stating that she also provided Sofia with "sensitivity." It should be noted that this meaning of "sensitivity" differs from the original usage back in extract 4a. There, "sensitivity" was associated with "having needs," whereas here it refers to "artistic expression" such as being able to appreciate music and dancing (not shown here in transcript). The therapist displays affiliation with Sofia's position by nodding (line 88) and then, some lines later, she tries to re-introduce the topic of "needs." The therapist's contrastive "but" at the beginning of her turn is disaffiliative, implying that there is an additional meaning or interpretation to the grandmother's message to Sofia. That an interpretive action is going on is further strengthened by the therapist's use of "I'd imagine" in line 107, which clearly expresses that this is *her* view and not the client's. The therapist's turn also includes talk that is designed to repair relational stress brought on by disaffiliation: She tries to accommodate Sofia's view with her own. She does this by juxtapositioning "being tough on the outside" (Sofia's position) with "don't show your feelings on the inside" (the therapist's position); further, there is an implication that if Sofia does not show her feelings, certain needs may not be met, such as Sofia may not get the love and support that she requires.

Sofia, again, responds in a confrontational manner. Opposition is realized in a number of ways: First, she cuts the therapist off through overlapping speech (line 108). Next, she resists the implication that she needs to express feelings by upgrading "don't' show your feelings" to "don't have them"; that is, if you somehow block out your feelings, you will not need love and support from others. This contrasting claim is then further strengthened when she claims the grandmother's voice as her own and animates this voice by articulating a series of commands directed at Sofia: "come on. get up an (.) an do your... don't cry." At the end of this extract, Sofia also explicitly counters the therapist's attempt at defining the grandmother's message; that is, by ending her turn with "that was the message m-granmother" Sofia is able to appropriate the therapist's initial use of the term, by stating what the grandmother's message *really* was.

Faced with the client's disaffiliation and repeated opposition to her attempt to re-introduce the topic of her needs, the therapist again retreats from this practice and works instead to minimally endorse the client through nodding, smiling and expressions of agreement (line 117). These interactions demonstrate that the pursuit of a certain agenda can have mixed results when (1) a client tends to respond with confrontation, rather than positively engaging with the therapist's interventions, and (2) the therapist is unable to sufficiently empathize with the client's talk. It may be that different kinds of interactional strategies could have helped, rather than hindered, the therapist's continued pursuit of her own agenda and could have resulted in further exploration of the client's experience or deepened emotional reflection. Safran and Muran (1996) have suggested that, in situations of client resistance, therapists may opt to bring the conversation towards a meta-discursive level, by topicalizing the client's resistance in the here and now of therapy and by emphasizing the therapist's own responsibility for the impasse; as for example, an utterance such as "you (Sofia) seem to have a very clear idea of the kind of person you are, and I seem to be having difficulty in tuning in with you. We don't yet share the same vision..." would have done. Or, the therapist could have worked much harder to endorse and validate the client's claim that she is independent and tough as in "so your grandmother taught you not to have feelings, and that's been important to you ever since." This could have led the therapist to gain increased knowledge of the client's thoughts, feelings and motives, but it might also have led to more cooperation from the client in terms of Sofia considering, if only briefly, how the therapist's perspective may have some relevance for her. As our examination of the interactions between Sofia and the therapist has shown, pursuing her agenda in this way provoked further confrontation from the client and thus worked to deepen disaffiliation, making it increasingly difficult for them to achieve common ground and a closer social relationship.

Client Practices of Withdrawal

Disaffiliation may also occur, not because the client is actively confrontational, but instead withdraws from engaging with the therapist's formulations. In these contexts, clients withhold their ratification of what the therapist has proposed through a range of evasion practices. In this section, we show how client withdrawal works to disaffiliate with a therapist and display uncertainty or reluctance with her line of therapeutic inquiry. We also show how this reluctance can be overcome through therapist practices that work to convey understanding of the client's perspective. We will show how these practices lead to the client's willingness to talk about an important personal matter and to heightened mutual affiliation between the speakers.

Client withdrawal as disaffiliating with the therapist's mode of inquiry. An example illustrating client disaffiliation and withdrawal is shown in extract 5a. The client is Kristina and, as in the previous extract with this client, the topic involves her relationship with her husband and the advantages or disadvantages of becoming divorced.

Kristina begins this extract by problematizing the interpersonal relation between her and her husband; that is, the husband may behave in whatever manner he wishes towards Kristina (by implication, even if the husband's acts are cruel), but

Extract 5a:

014.13(6)

	01	Kris:	so I think no matter- ((stops speaking to wipe nose)) ((sniffs))
	02		who my husband is o:r how he behaves, or whatever I should be able to: (0.4)
	03	Ther:	((nods))
	04	Kris:	u:h (0.6) lĭberate <myself. >
			((several lines omitted))
F→	08	Ther:	.hhh so you should be able to overcome
	09		(2.4)
F→	10	Ther:	whatever obstacles. (1.3) he places in your path. >no matter what he's like. <
F→	11		you should be able to
D→	12	Kris:	m-↑yeah!s. don't you think so?
	13		(0.8)
D→	14	Kris:	hhheh (0.6) heh hehheh.hhh ((sniffs))
	15		(1.6)
	16	Kris:	.hhh uh:m.
	17		(2.4)
	18	Kris:	[why]
F/I→	19	Ther:	[so] sounds like you're angry at yourself, that you can't ↑do this.
	20		(10.7)
D→	21	Kris:	n'I'm st- hhh hehheh.hhh (0.4) still reluctant..hhh ↓uh;
	22		(1.0)
D→	23	Kris:	an to admit that I would be angry with myself,
	24		(0.9)
	25	Ther:	wha maybe you're not I mean I'm just it's just an observation.
	26	Kris:	.hhh yeah uh y-y:
			K: nods, throws palm out then pulses hand and nods at T.
	27		(5.4)
	28	Ther:	((lip smack)) maybe it's not anger maybe its just determination you know
	29		or I will (1.6) overcome this at some point or. I dunno.
	30		(13.1)
D→	31	Kris:	((lip smack)) yeah. I- I <haven't decided. >

Kristina should in some way rise above these acts ("lĭberate <myself. >"). The therapist responds by summarizing and slightly elaborating Kristina's talk. Thus "liberating" is transformed into the upgraded version of "overcoming obstacles" unconditionally ("no matter what he's like").

Although Kristina's response is disaffiliative (line 12), the manner of her response differs strikingly from Sofia's. Kristina's response—and her subsequent responses—not only expresses covert or mitigated disagreement, it also displays a reluctance to engage with the therapist's proposition. The initial part of her turn expresses ostensible agreement ("↑yeah!s"), but the rest of her utterance clearly disaffiliates with the therapist. Her ironic "don't you think so?" followed by ensuing laughter is expressed in a mocking tone. In a way, Kristina ridicules not only her own stance towards her husband's behavior, but also the therapist's attempt at merely reflecting back Kristina' portrayal of the relationship dynamic. Thus, rather than engage with the therapist's formulation, it is treated as "non serious." In this way, Kristina withdraws from having to work with the therapist's prior talk. The ironic manner in which Kristina responds, however, does offer the therapist "access" to how she may be emotionally experiencing everyday situations with her husband. Thus, the utterance "don't you think so" and the ensuing laughter may be disclosing and recreating her sense of frustration at always having to endure unacceptable behaviors.

The therapist then reacts by drawing attention to the affective component of what Kristina had said; that is, she is angry with herself at always tolerating the husband's actions, rather than acting differently, perhaps more confrontationally ("that you can't ↑do this"). The therapist's reaction marks a substantial inferential leap from Kristina's original utterance and, thus, is no longer reflecting back Kristina's own words, but extrapolates to her present (as opposed to hypothetical future) emotional state. The therapist's utterance, therefore, borders on interpretation and thus may be considered as more a reflection of the therapist's than the client's perspective. That the therapist has perhaps taken her interpretation of the client's state too far may be indicated by Kristina's response. Her disagreement that she is angry with herself is inexplicit and couched within a mitigating expression that she may be "reluctant to admit" what the therapist proposed, thus indicating that this may still be open to negotiation. Here, Kristina is being evasive in her manner of disagreeing.

Extract 5b:

	32		(20.5)
	33	Kris:	well with this haze hhh (h)in my head I'm ch(h)heh definitely.hhh more in
	34		touch with my emotions than u-uhm, (1.3) without it,
	35	Ther:	mm hm?
	36		(12.5)
	37	Ther:	well? they have something to say,
	38		(1.6)
	39	Kris:	mm [hm.]
	40	Ther:	[your] emotions, ((nods))
	41		(45.4)
	42	Kris:	.hhhh I think the- n the the nee:d to see my situation from distance. (4.2)
	43		i is that I would see ↑away (1.0) which I don't see because I'm so clo:se.
			((several lines omitted))
	53	Kris:	.hh I probably am am not uh (6.7) even allowing u:h (1.6) mys:- even- not even
	54		in in theory h(hh)eh.hh e allowing myself the the happiness. y'know? an uh
	55		(0.8) the joy of life. =
	56	Ther:	=mm hm.
	57		(1.2)
	58	Ther:	mm hm.
	59	Kris:	u:hm.
	60	Ther:	mm hm
	61		(7.3)
	62	Ther:	yeah that sounds very important. (2.5) to look at. how::.hh how you
	63		stop yourself (1.3) how you disallow yourself
	64	Kris:	mm hm.
	65	Ther:	sounds really important.
	66		(2.1)
	67	Kris:	.hh I think its probably (3.3) because I'm protecting myself from a
	68		disappointment (1.8) uh so (9.2) so in a way its (1.5) I think I
	69		(1.9) ah hold myself [ba:ck.
	70	Ther:	[mm:::.
	71		(1.0)
	72	Kris:	so that a:h (0.4) um I don't get hurt.
	73	Ther:	mm hm. mm hm.
			((lines omitted))
F→	78	Ther:	.hhh so it's like how do you oppress yourself.
	79		(0.6)
	80	Kris:	((lip smack)) yes: hhh hehheh.hhh sounds like a title of a(h) [heh novel heh]
			K: smiles. T: nods. K: laughing. K: faces T, laughing
	81	Ther:	[mm h:m.]
			T: smiles at K
	82	Ther:	mm ↑hm!
			T: smiling
	83	Kris:	.hhh (0.3) u[h]
	84	Ther:	[.hhh] see wu- this is ↑wonderful because there's a lot of
	85		↑hope in that. >because if it< is in fact something that you do to yourself
	86		then it is something that you can.hh come to understand, and have some more
	87		(0.8)
	88	Kris:	°°uh huh,°° yes: =
	89	Ther:	=once you understand it better an then (0.6) be aware of what you're doing
	90		when you're doing it, and (0.3) potentially make some choices and stop doing
	91		it.
	92		(2.4)
	93	Kris:	sounds very n[ice hhheh hehheh].hhh ((sniffs))
	94	Ther:	[mm ↑hm! mm hm.]

The therapist then opts to retreat from her standpoint that the client is angry with herself ("wha maybe you're not"). Various mitigation strategies are also employed by the therapist such as modality ("maybe") and repair in which she frames her turn as stemming from her own personal perspective ("I mean I'm just it's just an observation"). Sofia, however, responds with ambivalence: She does not ratify the therapist's assertion, as evidenced by the disagreement markers (Pomerantz, 1984), such as the inbreath and the aborted attempt at producing more talk, surrounding her minimal agreement. But, her use of non-verbal resources such as nodding and placing her palm outwards towards the therapist implies a minimal endorsement of the therapist's utterance. The therapist then proceeds to further retreat from her claim that the client experiences anger and instead suggests that "determination" may explain her behavior. With this move, the therapist backs away from a potentially conflictual theme and attempts to secure affiliation around a different theme, one that positions the client as an *agent* who resolutely tries to overcome difficulties rather than a passive participant who feels anger due to her lack of agency.

However, the therapist's attempt at securing affiliation is, at best, only partially successful. The wording of the client's utterance is relevant here because, on the one hand, the client asserts primary rights to interpret her own experience, and, on the other hand, she remains non-committal. By emphasizing "I" in "*I- I* <haven't decided. >," Kristina asserts that any interpretations regarding her personal experience (e.g., what emotions are at play, whether she is an agent of certain events) clearly rest with her and not the therapist. But, because she refuses to decide on this issue, she blocks any further progress to explore her anger or determination. By not committing herself, Kristina withdraws from cooperatively negotiating the reasons behind her inability to confront the husband. On a more productive note, however, the client's disagreement is very weak (line 31) and may be signaling that the prior negotiation over her emotional state has garnered some acceptance from the client and that if the therapist is able to gain and display further understanding of the client's experience, then more exploration and therapeutic work may be accomplished.

Stepwise transition to re-affiliation. In extract 5b, we show how the therapist and client gradually move towards increased forms of mutual affiliation. We also illustrate how this re-affiliation is a joint effort. On the one hand, the client works to engage more with her personal issue and, on the other hand, the therapist continues to draw from a range of interactional resources to affiliate with the client and prompt her to continue speaking.

Brief affiliation is achieved at the beginning of this extract. Following a lengthy silence (line 32), Kristina then takes up a slightly new topical thread by claiming that she has lately been more "in touch with her emotions." Given that the therapist had previously been trying to secure Kristina's affiliation around "her anger," this may be seen as a concession from Kristina, in which she now introduces a topic that both may affiliate with. The therapist first responds with a *continuer* "mm hm?" (Schegloff, 1982) that attempts to get Kristina to expand on her talk about her emotions. However, after no further talk from Kristina is forthcoming, the therapist then affiliates with Kristina by stressing an emotion's relevance ("they have something to say"), which encourages Kristina to say more about her emotions. Later on, mutual affiliation is displayed at a surface level, through which Kristina produces an agreement token ("mm hm."), followed by the therapist's ratifying nod.

It is at this point that the interaction progressively moves towards greater mutual affiliation and exploration of the topic that was initially introduced back in extract 5a: *Why Kristina sacrifices her happiness*. This shift is prefaced by a very long silence that lasts 45 s, in which Kristina presumably takes time to reflect on her prior interaction with the therapist. Kristina then begins by accounting for why it is so difficult for her to understand her situation; that is, she does not possess the necessary objective distance ("because I'm so clo:se") to gain this understanding. Shortly thereafter, however, she makes the suggestion that she holds herself back from experiencing happiness ("I probably am am not uh (6.7) even allowing u:h (1.6) mys..."). The therapist's responses play a key role not only in explicitly endorsing Kristina's suggestion, but also in signaling to her that what she said is relevant and needs to be expanded. For example, the therapist produces a number of continuers (lines 56, 58, 60) that prompt her to say more about how she does not allow herself happiness. Endorsement is further upgraded through the specific positive appraisal "sounds very important." Kristina then continues to develop her line of reasoning, which suggests that the therapist's practices had been effective. Thus, motives are provided such as "she is protecting herself from disappointment and hurt" and the therapist, in turn, displays positive appreciation (lines 70, 73) of how Kristina is developing her understanding of her own situation.

The last part of this extract shows how Kristina and the therapist work at strongly affiliating with each other. To begin, the therapist provides a summary formulation of the client's prior talk ("so it's like how do you oppress yourself"), which slightly upgrades Kristina's original wording of "not allowing" to "oppress." Kristina affiliates with the formulation through agreement and laughter. The non-verbal interaction seems especially important here: Kristina smiles and laughs as she produces her turn and this is met with the therapist's upgraded confirmations and return smiles. The speakers' coordinated production of these verbal and non-verbal actions shows mutual affiliation and a progressive strengthening of their affective bonds (Bänninger-Huber, 1992). The remainder of this segment of conversation shows how the therapist and client work at maintaining this intensified degree of affiliation between them. The therapist, for instance, produces positive appraisals ("this is ↑wonderful"), upgraded confirmation (line 94) and provides Kristina with a perspective of hope and a solid direction through which she will be able to work out her personal issues. Kristina, in turn, affiliates with the therapist through agreement (line 88), laughter and positive appraisal ("sounds very nice").

Discussion

Therapeutic conversation unfolds in an institutionally constrained social context in which therapists make use of a specialized set of interactional practices (Peräkylä et al., 2008; Viklund, Holmqvist & Nelson, 2012). In this way, effective therapists manage to closely affiliate and collaborate with their clients to engage in conversations that extend the client's horizons, create new more viable ways to view themselves and engage with the world (Horvath, 2007; Ribeiro et al., 2014; Ribeiro, Gonçalves, & Horvath, 2009; Stiles, 2011). In this research we systematically explored how therapists and clients struggle to develop, maintain, and repair a close collaborative relationship at the level of the actual practices that constitute "therapy talk." The negotiation of interpersonal distance / alignment was examined as an interactional achievement that can be observed by the various ways in which clients and therapists use language and non-verbal resources. We argue that the insights that emerge from looking closely at the social interactional level of therapy are an important complement to more meta-level psychotherapy process inquiries.

Our research also illustrates how different research perspectives can be used to provide complementary and additive insights. Over the years, there have been a number of intensive analyses of York I study data that have yielded many insights into narrative change processes in clients suffering from major depression (for examples of more recent studies see Angus, 2012; Boritz, Angus, Monette, Hollis-Walker, & Warwar, 2011; Mendes et al., 2011). Our research provides a unique perspective on this process: Disaffiliation or contexts in which the client does not endorse the therapist's line of action or perspective. We felt this area of investigation was important because disaffiliation indexes a potential interactional roadblock and, if not resolved, may have undesirable effects leading to more "distance" between client and therapist or even episodes of conflict, likely implicating a breach in the alliance. Thus, disaffiliation offers a relevant context to explore the therapeutic relationship.

Our analysis throws some light on how disaffiliation is managed in the subsequent actions between therapist and client, by focusing on a specific sequential context (formulation sequences). We observed two distinct ways formulation sequences leading to disaffiliation can unfold: First, disaffiliation may be repaired quickly when therapists achieve successful re-affiliation in the next or a following turn. We have shown how this may be realized in practice, when therapists respond with conciliatory moves such as agreement or other actions that endorse and work with the client's divergent position. An important consequence of this kind of repair work is that the therapist's attempt at moving the client's talk in a certain direction becomes aborted. Thus affiliation is repaired, but at the "cost" of the therapist's having to abandon what may have been a therapeutically profitable line of discourse in which mutual elaboration and development of a certain issue or a new innovative perspective could have been achieved (Gonçalves & Ribeiro, 2012).

Second, disaffiliation may be extended, occurring over a series of turns and sometimes even continuing for over several minutes (e.g., Sofia). It was observed that—in a manner consistent with Safran and Muran's classification (1996)—clients can disaffiliate or resist in two stylistically distinct ways: Confrontation and withdrawal. Extended transcripts from sessions of two clients were examined to illustrate these practices of protracted disaffiliation and to explore how therapists are able to manage these two distinct disaffiliating styles. Sofia was shown to repeatedly disaffiliate through confrontational moves such as disagreement or interruption. Further, the therapist also seemed to contribute to the disaffiliation by responding with oppositional moves involving disagreement and by not effectively engaging with and displaying understanding of the client's perspective. Thus, a recursive cycle of disaffiliation was created in which client disaffiliation was followed by therapist disaffiliation, which was again followed by client disaffiliation. In our transcripts the therapist would, however, occasionally suspend the cycle by affiliating with the client, but the cycle would again begin anew when the therapist used the same moves to try to re-introduce her agenda. The interactions between the therapist and client also indexed a battle between divergent goals to pursue in the interaction and thus were constitutive of a disalignment (the therapist's agenda of exploring Sofia's needs vs. Sofia's resistance to exploring her needs within the conceptual frame introduced by the therapist) and, at a deeper level, a conflict involving epistemic rights: Sofia would actively block the therapist's attempt at elaborating on—or, Sofia may well view this as redefining—and "re-storying" Sofia's self-narrative (Angus, Lewin, Bouffard, & Rotondi-Trevisan, 2004). Through her direct forms of opposition, Sofia was able to maintain exclusive epistemic primacy over her domain of experience. The cost of the ensuing relational strain was the exclusion of the therapist from making any substantive contributions to the dialogue. In fact, as the disaffiliation escalated, the client "invited" a powerful ally—the grandmother—who acted as a witness to support her position against the therapist. As the therapist does not have access to this witness of Sofia's past, she becomes excluded from the dialogue.

The client Kristina, by contrast, was shown to resist in a less confrontational, more passive manner. Her responses tended to be evasive and her disagreements were mitigated. Kristina's responses, however, did provide the therapist with some room to engage with her; Kristina's reluctance to engage with the therapist's formulation did not completely prevent the therapist from elaborating on her talk about her relationship, her emotions and the reasons for her not wanting change. Once the therapist explicitly engaged with the client's disaffiliative move, there was a gradual transition to more reflection on Kristina's part and to more mutual affiliation between her and the therapist. Towards the end, Kristina began to discuss the possible motives behind her not wanting to leave her husband. These interactions were also marked by strong mutual affiliative displays that were expressed through agreements and non-verbal actions such as nodding, laughter and smiling. Thus, in comparison to the Sofia case, it appears that this therapist was able to develop stronger empathic ties with the client. By carefully designing her formulation to empathically connect with Kristina's disaffiliation and by strategically withholding from speaking, thus allowing Kristina many opportunities to consider and comment on the therapist's talk, client and therapist were able to come out of this interaction with a developed sense of why Kristina is "sacrificing her happiness" and with stronger affectual bonds.

Limits and Future Directions

The research we present is exploratory in nature. Our illustrations of how client disaffiliation unfolds in the dialogical context of psychotherapy, and how this is managed in subsequent talk, were limited to the detailed analysis of two clients with different styles of responding to the therapist's formulations. While these two styles closely resemble the bivariate classification developed by Safran and colleagues (Safran & Muran, 1996) we have no grounds to claim that there may be no other important client response variables or, more likely, that there are no further important subclasses within these categories, each, perhaps, with unique clinically relevant features. Moreover, by narrowly concentrating on how these processes dialogically unfold in selected specific instances, we did not tackle the question of how these successful or unsuccessful negotiations of affiliation aggregate to effect outcome in the longer term. Are therapists who experience difficulties with one client likely to have similar struggles with other patients? Our project is but a first step in addressing these issues. More generally, the type of conversation analysis we brought to bear on our research questions depends on intensive analysis of exemplars purposely selected to exemplify certain practices of interest. Thus we cannot extrapolate these findings to the "universe of possible forms of client therapist disaffiliation." Indeed this was not our goal.

In order to gain more insight into the full range of practices used to manage extended disaffiliation and gain re-affiliation, more data will need to be collected. For instance, we looked for, but were unable to locate, instances where the therapist made meta-discursive moves to topicalize the client's resistance and shift the accountability on the therapist to resolve relational stress—an important strategy recommended by Safran and colleagues (2001). Finally, disaffiliation management has not yet been considered with respect to specific therapeutic modes of practice. We hope that future research, based on diverse types of therapies and different kinds of client issues, will be implemented to further clarify the effective modes of minimizing and resolving these immediate relational disturbances.

Clinical Implications

The fine-grained examination of how stresses or ruptures in the therapist-client relationship are realized and how the process of repair works in the dialogical flow of therapeutic conversation points to some tentative clinical implications: First, it seems that, depending on the client's style, the indications of disaffiliation can be quite subtle and muted, including small delays in speech, prosodic signals and mitigated expressions. Second, an immediate response to signs of disaffiliation by withdrawing from a prior formulation can be effective. There has been some recent research on the importance of balancing support with exploration of new and innovative conceptualizations (Ribeiro et al., 2009). Our findings are consistent with these notions; it seems strategically better to wait until the affiliation is fully repaired before pushing ahead and introducing material that may challenge the client's current perspectives, risking further problems in affiliation (Muntigl, Knight, Watkins, Horvath, & Angus, 2013). Third, the analysis highlights the importance of being highly sensitive to a client's epistemic rights. An opportunity to comment on or negotiate the client's experience from a novel perspective requires willingness on the client's part. The interactions with Sophia were good illustrations of this: If the client directly opposes (i.e., disagrees or ignores) and refuses to invite therapist reflections of their own talk, any further attempts by the therapist to continue pursuing the opposed agenda may be ineffectual *at that time* and may significantly damage the therapy relationship. Last, it is our hope that our research would provide therapists with a useful additional perspective to reflect on their work: A chance to view the relational ebb and flow in terms of the dynamic unfolding of mutual influences at the verbal, prosodic and nonverbal levels.

Acknowledgements

This research is supported by a standard research grant from the Social Sciences and Humanities Research Council of Canada (410-2009-0549). We also wish to thank Les Greenberg and Lynne Angus for having provided important feedback on a previous version of this paper

Notes

[1] In much of the literature, particularly in relation to the concept of alliance, the term "rupture" is used to identify disturbances in the relationship. We, along with Bordin (1989, 1994) and Safran (2012), find the terminology potentially misleading, as the events in question range in severity from minor disruptions to actual severance of the relation; thus our preferred term in this context is "stress." However, in this research we examine disturbances in many aspects of the therapy relationship, not only in alliance. Thus we will use the broader concepts of (dis)alignment and (dis)affiliation, as will be defined later.

[2] For more detailed information on the client and therapist demographics see Greenberg, L.S., & Watson, J. (1998).

[3] In this example and the ones to follow, non-verbal information such as "nod," "smile," etc. is added within the lines of the transcript in italics below the concurrent verbal text (for more information on how non-verbal information is presented in transcripts, see Muntigl, Knight, & Watkins, 2012, and Muntigl, Knight, Horvath, & Watkins, 2012). We mainly included non-verbal resources that played a role in displaying affiliation.

References

Angus, L. (2012). Toward an integrative understanding of narrative and emotion processes in Emotion-focused therapy of depression: Implications for theory, research and practice. *Psychotherapy Research, 22*, 367–380. doi:10.1080/10503307.2012.683988

Angus, L., Lewin, J., Bouffard, B., & Rotondi-Trevisan, D. (2004). "What's the story?" Working with narrative in experiential psychotherapy. In L. Angus & J. McLeod (Eds.), *The handbook of narrative psychotherapy: Practice, theory, and research* (pp. 87–102). London: Sage.

Antaki, C. (2008). Formulations in psychotherapy. In A. Peräkylä, C. Antaki, S. Vehviläinen & I. Leudar (Eds.), *Conversation analysis and psychotherapy* (pp. 26–42). Cambridge: Cambridge University Press.

Atkinson, J. M., & Drew, P. (1979). *Order in court.* Atlantic Highlands, NJ: Humanities.

Atkinson, J. M., & Heritage, J. (Eds.) (1984). *Structures of social action: Studies in conversation analysis.* Cambridge: Cambridge University Press.

Bänninger-Huber, E. (1992). Prototypical affective microsequences in psychotherapeutic interactions. *Psychotherapy Research, 2*(4), 291–306. doi:10.1080/10503309212331333044

Bercelli, F., Rossano, F., & Viaro, M. (2008). Clients' responses to therapists' reinterpretations. In A. Peräkylä, C. Antaki, S. Vehviläinen & I. Leudar (Eds.), *Conversation analysis and psychotherapy* (pp. 43–61). Cambridge: Cambridge University Press.

Bohart, A. C., Elliott, R., Greenberg, L. S., Watson, J. C., & Norcross, J. C. (2002). Empathy. In J. Norcross (Ed.), *Psychotherapy relationships that work* (pp. 89–108). New York, NY: Oxford University Press.

Bordin, E. S. (1989, June). Building therapeutic alliances: The base for integration. Paper presented at the Society for Psychotherapy Research Conference. Berkley, CA.

Bordin, E. S. (1994). Theory and research on the therapeutic working alliance: New directions. In A. O. Horvath & L. S. Greenberg (Eds.), *The working alliance: Theory, research, and practice.* New York, NY: Wiley.

Boritz, T., Angus, L., Monette, G., Hollis-Walker, L., & Warwar, S. (2011). Narrative and emotion integration in psychotherapy: Investigating the relationship between autobiographical memory specificity and expressed emotional arousal in brief emotion-focused and client-centred treatments of depression. *Psychotherapy Research, 21*, 16–26. doi:10.1080/10503307.2010.504240

Brown, P., & Levinson, S. C. (1987). *Politeness: Some universals in language usage.* Cambridge: Cambridge University Press.

Enfield, N. J. (2006). Social consequences of common ground. In N. J. Enfield & S. C. Levinson (Eds.), *Roots of human sociality: Culture, cognition and interaction* (pp. 399–430). Oxford: Berg.

Elvins, R., & Green, J. (2008). The conceptualization and measurement of therapeutic alliance: An empirical review. *Clinical Psychology Review, 28*(7), 1167–1187. doi:10.1016/j.cpr.2008.04.002

Freud, S. (1994). The dynamics of transference Essential papers on transference analysis (pp. 5–17). Lanham, MD: Jason Aronson.

Goffman, E. (1967). *Interaction ritual: Essays on face-to-face behavior.* Garden City: Doubleday.

Gonçalves, M. M., & Ribeiro, A. P. (2012). Narrative processes of innovation and stability within the dialogical self. In H. J. M.

Hermans, & T. Gieser (Eds.), *Handbook of dialogical self* (pp. 301–318). Cambridge: Cambridge University Press.
Greenberg, L. (2002). *Emotion-focused therapy: Coaching clients to work through feelings*. Washington, DC: American Psychological Association Press.
Greenberg, L. S., Rice, L. N., & Elliot, R. (1993). *Facilitating emotional change: The moment-by-moment process*. New York, NY: Guildford Press.
Greenberg, L. S., & Watson, J. (1998). Experiential therapy of depression: differential effects of client-centered relationship conditions and process-experiential interventions. *Psychotherapy Research, 8*, 210–224.
Heritage, J. (1984). *Garfinkel and ethnomethodology*. Cambridge: Polity Press.
Heritage, J., & Watson, D. (1979). Formulations as conversational objects. In G. Psathas (Ed.), *Everyday language: Studies in ethnomethodology* (pp. 123–163). New York, NY: Irvington.
Horvath, A. O. (2007). The alliance in context: Accomplishments, challenges, and future directions. *Psychotherapy: Theory, Research, Practice, Training, 43*(3), 258–263.
Jefferson, G. (2004). Glossary of transcript symbols with an introduction. In G. Lerner (Ed.), *Conversation analysis: Studies from the first generation* (pp. 13–31). Amsterdam: John Benjamins.
Labov, W., & Fanshel, D. (1977). *Therapeutic discourse: Psychotherapy as conversation*. New York, NY: Academic Press.
Lepper, G., & Mergenthaler, E. (2007). Therapeutic collaboration: How does it work? *Psychotherapy Research, 15*, 433–444. doi:10.1080/10503300500091587
Levinson, S. (1983). *Pragmatics*. Cambridge: Cambridge University Press.
Mendes, I., Ribeiro, A., Angus, L., Greenberg, L., Sousa, I., & Goncalves, M. (2011). Narrative change in emotion-focused psychotherapy: A study on the evolution of reflection and protest innovative moments. *Psychotherapy Research, 21*, 304–315. doi:10.1080/10503307.2011.565489
Muntigl, P. (2004). *Narrative counselling: Social and linguistic processes of change*. Amsterdam: John Benjamins.
Muntigl, P., & Turnbull, W. (1998). Conversational structure and facework in arguing. *Journal of Pragmatics, 29*(3), 225–256. doi:10.1016/S0378-2166(97)00048-9
Muntigl, P., Knight, N., Horvath, A. O., & Watkins, A. (2012). Client affectual stance and therapist-client affiliation: A view from grammar and social interaction. *Research in Psychotherapy: Psychopathology, Process and Outcome, 15*(2), 117–130
Muntigl, P., Knight, N., & Watkins, A. (2012). Working to keep aligned in psychotherapy: using nods as a dialogic resource to display affiliation. *Language and Dialogue, 2*(1), 9–27. doi:10.1075/ld.2.1.01mun
Muntigl, P., Knight, N., Watkins, A., Horvath, A. O., & Angus, L. (2013). Active retreating: Person-centered practices to repair disaffiliation in therapy. *Journal of Pragmatics, 53*, 1–20. doi:10.1016/j.pragma.2013.03.019
Norcross, J. C. (Ed.) (2002). *Psychotherapy relationships that work: Therapist contributions and responsiveness to patients*. New York, NY: Oxford University Press.
Norcross, J. C. (Ed.) (2011). *Psychotherapy relationships that work: Evidence-based responsiveness* (2nd ed.). New York, NY: Oxford University Press.
Orlinsky, D. E. (2010). The "Generic Model of Psychotherapy" after 25 years: Evolution of a research-based metatheory. *Journal of Psychotherapy Integration, 19*, 1–23.
Peräkylä, A. (2004). Reliability and validity in research based on naturally occurring social interaction. In D. Silverman (Ed.), *Qualitative research: Theory, method and practice* (pp. 283–304). Amsterdam: John Benjamins.
Peräkylä, A. (2005). Patients' responses to interpretations: A dialogue between conversation analysis and psychoanalytic theory. *Communication & Medicine, 2*, 164–176.
Peräkylä, A., Antaki, C., Vehviläinen, S., & Leudar, I. (2008). *Conversation analysis and psychotherapy*. Cambridge: Cambridge University Press.
Pomerantz, A. (1984). Agreeing and disagreeing with assessment: Some features of preferred/dispreferred turn shapes. In J. M. Atkinson & J. Heritage (Eds.), *Structure of social action: Studies in conversation analysis* (pp. 79–112). Cambridge: Cambridge University Press.
Ribeiro, E., Gonçalves, M., & Horvath, A. O. (2009, Oct.). Therapeutic alliance as a balance of therapist and client's complementary actions. Paper presented at the European Society for Psychotherapy Research Conference. Bolzano, Italy.
Ribeiro, A. P., Ribeiro, E., Loura, J., Gonçalves, M. M., Stiles, W. B., Horvath, A. O., & Sousa, I. (2014). Therapeutic collaboration and Resistance: Describing the nature and quality of the therapeutic relationship within ambivalence events using the Therapeutic Collaboration Coding System. *Psychotherapy Research, 24*, 346–359. doi:10.1080/10503307.2013.856042
Rogers, C. R., Gendlin, G. T., Kiesler, D. V., & Truax, L. B. (1967). *The therapeutic relationship and its impact: A study of psychotherapy with schizophrenics*. Madison: University of Wisconson Press.
Sacks, H. (1992). *Lectures on conversation, Volumes 1 & 2*. Oxford: Basil Blackwell.
Sacks, H., Schegloff, E., & Jefferson, G. (1974). A simplest systematics for the organization of turn-taking for conversation. *Language, 50*, 696–735. doi:10.2307/412243
Safran, J. D., (June, 2012) Personal communication.
Safran, J. D., & Muran, J. C. (1996). The resolution of ruptures in the therapeutic alliance. *Journal of Consulting and Clinical Psychology, 64*, 447–458. doi:10.1037/0022-006X.64.3.447
Safran, J. D., & Muran, J. C. (2006). Has the concept of the therapeutic alliance outlived its usefulness? *Psychotherapy: Theory, Research, Practice, Training, 43*(3), 286–291. doi:10.1037/0033-3204.43.3.286
Safran, J. D., Muran, J. C., & Samstag, W. L. (1994). Resolving therapeutic ruptures: A task analytic investigation. In A. O. Horvath & L. S. Greenberg (Eds.), *The working alliance: Theory, research, and practice* (pp. 225–255). New York, NY: Wiley.
Safran, J. D., Muran, J. C., Samstag, L. W., & Stevens, C. (2001). Repairing alliance ruptures. *Psychotherapy: Theory, Research, Practice, Training, 38*(4), 406–412. doi:10.1037/0033-3204.38.4.406
Schegloff, E. A. (1982). Discourse as an interactional achievement: Some uses of 'uh huh' and other things that come between sentences. In D. Tannen (Ed.), *Analyzing discourse: Text and talk. Georgetown University Roundtable on Languages and Linguistics* (pp. 71–93). Washington, DC: Georgetown University Press.
Schegloff, E. A. (2006). Interaction: The infrastructure for social institutions, the natural ecological niche for language, and the arena in which culture is enacted. In N. J. Enfield & S. C. Levinson (Eds.), *Roots of human sociality: Culture, cognition and interaction* (pp. 70–96). Oxford: Berg.
Schegloff, E. A. (2007). *Sequence organization in interaction*. Cambridge: Cambridge University Press.
Schegloff, E. A., Jefferson, G., & Sacks, H. (1977). The preference for self-correction in the organization of repair in conversation. *Language, 53*, 361–382.
Schegloff, E. A., & Sacks, H. (1973). Opening up closings. *Semiotica, 8*, 289–327. doi:10.1515/semi.1973.8.4.289
Stiles, W. B. (1992). *Describing talk. A taxonomy of verbal response modes*. London: Sage.

Stiles, W. B. (2011). Coming to terms. *Psychotherapy Research*, *21*, 367–384. doi:10.1080/10503307.2011.582186

Stiles, W., Glick, M., Osatuke, K., Hardy, G., Shapiro, D., Agnew-Davies, R., Rees, A. & Barkham, M. (2004). Patterns of alliance development and the rupture-repair hypothesis: Are productive relationships U-shaped or V-shaped? *Journal of Counseling Psychology*, *51*, 81–92. doi:10.1037/0022-0167.51.1.81

Stivers, T. (2008). Stance, alignment and affiliation during storytelling: When nodding is a token of affiliation. *Research on Language and Social Interaction*, *41*(1), 31–57. doi:10.1080/08351810701691123

Stivers, T., & Hayashi, M. (2010). Transformative answers: One way to resist a question's constraints. *Language in Society*, *39*, 1–25. doi:10.1017/S0047404509990637

Stivers, T., Mondada, L., & Steensig, J. (2011). Knowledge, morality and affiliation in social interaction. In T. Stivers, L. Mondada, & J. Steensig (Eds.), *The morality of knowledge in conversation* (pp. 3–24). Cambridge: Cambridge University Press.

Sutherland, O., & Strong, T. (2011). Therapeutic collaboration: a conversation analysis of constructionist therapy. *Journal of Family Therapy*, *33*, 256–278. doi:10.1111/j.1467-6427.2010.00500.x

Voutilainen, L., Peräkylä, A., & Ruusuvuori, J. (2011). Therapeutic change in interaction: Conversation analysis of a transforming sequence. *Psychotherapy Research*, *21*(3), 348–365. doi:10.1080/10503307.2011.573509

Viklund, E., Holmqvist, R., & Nelson, K. Z. (June, 2012). Two ways of analyzing clients' accounts of important events in therapy. Paper presented at the Society for Psychotherapy Research Conference. Virginia Beach, VA.

Appendix: Transcription Symbols

Symbol	Meaning
[	Starting point of overlapping speech
]	Endpoint of overlapping speech
(1.5)	Silence measured in seconds
(.)	Silences less than 0.2 s
wo:rd	Prolongation of sound
(word)	Transcriber's guess
wo-	Speech cut off in the middle of the word
word =	Latching (no audible break between words).
word	Spoken slowly
<word >	Spoken slowly
>word <	Spoken quickly
°word°	Spoken quietly
Word	Emphasis
.hhh	Audible inhalation
Hhh	Audible exhalation
wo(h)rd	Laugh particle (or outbreath) inserted within a word
Heh	Laugh particle
↓word	Marked falling intonation (not phrase final)
↑word	Marked rising intonation (not phrase final)
.	Falling intonation at end of utterance
?	Rising intonation at end of utterance
,	Continuing intonation at end of utterance
∪word	Fall-rising intonation
∩word	Rise-falling intonation
((sniffs))	Audible non-speech sounds
Italics	Non-verbal behavior (actor indicated by initial)

Simplified from Jefferson (2004).

Therapeutic collaboration and resistance: Describing the nature and quality of the therapeutic relationship within ambivalence events using the Therapeutic Collaboration Coding System

ANTÓNIO P. RIBEIRO[1], EUGENIA RIBEIRO[1], JOANA LOURA[1], MIGUEL M. GONÇALVES[1], WILLIAM B. STILES[2], ADAM O. HORVATH[3], & INÊS SOUSA[4]

[1]*School of Psychology, University of Minho, Braga, Portugal;* [2]*Psychology, Miami University, Oxford, OH, USA;* [3]*Faculty of Education, Simon Fraser University, Burnaby, BC, Canada &* [4]*Mathematics and Applications, University of Minho, Guimaraes, Portugal*

Abstract

Objectives: We understand ambivalence as a cyclical movement between two opposing parts of the self. The emergence of a novel part produces an innovative moment, challenging the current maladaptive self-narrative. However, the novel part is subsequently attenuated by a return to the maladaptive self-narrative. This study focused on the analysis of the therapeutic collaboration in episodes in which a relatively poor-outcome client in narrative therapy expressed ambivalence. **Method:** For our analysis we used the Therapeutic Collaboration Coding System, developed to assess whether and how the therapeutic dyad is working within the therapeutic zone of proximal development (TZPD). **Results:** Results showed that when the therapist challenged the client after the emergence of ambivalence, the client tended to invalidate (reject or ignore) the therapist's intervention. **Conclusions:** This suggests that in such ambivalence episodes the therapist did not match the client's developmental level, and by working outside the TZPD unintentionally contributed to the maintaining the client's ambivalence.

Therapists of all orientations report phenomena that can be understood as resistance (Wachtel, 1982, 1999). We conceptualize resistance as an interpersonal phenomenon that reflects both the client's ambivalence, or degree of internal conflict regarding change, and the way the therapist responds to this ambivalence (Moyers & Rollnick, 2002). The therapist's response to the client's expressions of ambivalence is critical because robust empirical evidence indicates that higher levels of resistance are consistently associated with poor therapy outcomes, as well as premature termination of treatment (for a review, see Beutler, Rocco, Moleiro, & Talebi, 2001).

Wachtel (1999) claimed that the quality of the therapeutic relationship plays a central role in determining the level of resistance. Increased resistance can be a sign that the patient feels unsafe, which can reflect the therapist relating to the client in a way he or she experiences as threatening (Wachtel, 1993). Attention to the therapeutic relationship is thus a crucial factor in reducing resistance (Wachtel, 1999).

We used a moment-to-moment analysis of therapeutic collaboration of a case of a relatively poor-outcome client in narrative therapy to study ambivalence and resistance with the *Therapeutic Collaboration Coding System* (TCCS; Ribeiro, Ribeiro, Gonçalves, Horvath, & Stiles, 2013). The TCCS was developed to assess whether and how the therapeutic dyad is working within the *therapeutic zone of proximal development* (TZPD). TZPD is the interval between the client's actual developmental level and the potential developmental level that can be achieved in collaboration with the therapist. We shall elaborate this concept in a later section.

Our Theoretical Framework of the Self and Concept of Change

We construe narratives as tools individuals use to join together life events into coherent units (Dimaggio et al., 2003). Human beings are able to reconstruct their experiences in the form of narratives and then use them as schemata to make sense of the continuous flow of events.

These narratives are the result of the continuous dialogue between multiple parts of the self, which we describe as internal *voices*. Theoretically, voices are constructed from the traces of the person's experiences, including experiences passed to them though other people by signs and stories (Stiles, 2011). Each voice is agentic and possesses its own characteristics and ways of being in the world (Hermans, 1996, 2001a, 2001b; Hermans & Dimaggio, 2007; Hermans & Kempen, 1993; Leiman, 1997, 2002; Osatuke et al., 2004). Insofar as the self is composed of voices, each utterance or action by a person is the action of some internal voice or the coordinated action of several voices.

In line with the assimilation model (Stiles, 2002, 2011), we consider that constellations of similar or related internal voices become linked or *assimilated* and constitute a *community of voices*. This community is experienced by the person as their usual sense of self, personality, or center of experience. Theoretically, psychological distress is a product of the disconnection or exclusion of certain voices from community. The self-narrative is the *meaning bridge* among members of the community of voices. A meaning bridge is a semiotic framework—a system of words and other signs that can represent, link, and encompass the previously separated voices, binding the experiences/voices together, thus allowing smooth mutual access to experiential resources, and enabling joint action (Stiles, 2011). An experience/voice may be disconnected from the community, and thus problematic, if the self-narrative is too rigid and excludes it (Ribeiro, Bento, Salgado, Stiles, & Gonçalves, 2011). For example, if a self-narrative has no place for active self-promotion, then experiences of ambition may be unrecognized, distorted, or distressing. Viewed from this theoretical perspective, a client's initial (presenting) dominant self-narrative may be maladaptive because it fails to acknowledge important parts of the client's life experience.

In line with Gonçalves and co-workers' narrative perspective, instances in which unassimilated voices express themselves constitute exceptions to the maladaptive self-narrative and are identified as *innovative moments* (IMs) (Gonçalves, Matos, & Santos, 2009; see also Gonçalves, Ribeiro, Mendes, Matos, & Santos, 2011). The accumulation and elaboration of IMs facilitate the development of an alternative self-narrative; when unassimilated voices express themselves, the dominance of the current community of voices is disrupted, at least temporarily, opening an opportunity for *meaning bridges* to develop.

In sum, we construe change in psychotherapy as a developmental process in which clients move from a maladaptive self-narrative—ways of understanding and experiencing that are dysfunctional since they exclude important internal voices—to a more functional self-narrative, one that integrates the previously excluded problematic voice. Such narratives are co-constructed through psychotherapeutic dialogue by building meaning bridges.

Ambivalence as a Reaction to IMs

We have proposed that the emergence and elaboration of IMs in therapy challenge and destabilize the maladaptive self-narrative, threatening the client's sense of self-stability. This threat often generates an increased level of anxiety which in turn evokes a self-protective response in which the client returns to the maladaptive self-narrative, suppressing the innovative way of feeling, thinking. In such cases we may observe that the client minimizes, depreciates, or trivializes the IM's meaning or significance. Such actions work to reinstate the maladaptive self-narrative, promoting stability at the cost of change, and eventually lead to therapeutic failure (Gonçalves, Ribeiro Stiles, et al., 2011; Gonçalves & Ribeiro, 2012; Ribeiro, Cruz, Mendes, Stiles, & Gonçalves, 2012).

We conceptualize this cyclical movement between opposing parts of the self—the client's currently dominant but maladaptive self-narrative and IMs—as ambivalence. This cyclical movement interferes with the development of an inclusive and coherent system of meanings in therapy in which these internal voices respectfully listen to each other and engage in joint action (cf., Brinegar, Salvi, Stiles, & Greenberg, 2006).

We have developed a measure of therapeutic ambivalence that grew from our observations of therapy passages in which an IM was immediately followed by a return to the maladaptive self-narrative. We label these events a *return-to-the-problem's marker* (RPM; Gonçalves, Ribeiro, Stiles, et al., 2011). The following is an example of such event:

> Client: I've been facing my issues, bringing them into the open ... and that is fine (IM), but then I feel that going beyond that point, confronting people is dangerous ... dangerous in terms of losing God knows what (RPM).

Research on cases of Emotion-Focused Therapy, Client-Centered Therapy, and Narrative Therapy showed that the incidence of IM-RPM sequences decreased across therapy in good-outcome cases, whereas it remained unchanged and consistently high in poor-outcome cases (Ribeiro, 2012). This suggests that ambivalence between the maladaptive self-narrative and the alternative perspective may interfere with therapeutic progress or at least that it is associated with therapeutic stagnation.

The TCCS and the Therapeutic Zone of Proximal Development

The TCCS (Ribeiro et al., 2013) was designed to micro-analyze the TCCS which emerges from a negotiation and meshing of therapists' and clients' contributions to the alliance (Hatcher, 1999; Safran & Muran, 2000, 2006). It offers a way to assess how ambivalence is addressed and dealt with within the therapeutic relationship. The TCCS is conceptually based on our integration of the assimilation model (Stiles, 2001, 2011) and the IMs model (Gonçalves et al., 2009). A central theoretical concept in the construction and application of the TCCS was the notion of the *therapeutic zone of proximal development* (TZPD; see Leiman & Stiles, 2001).

The TZPD is an extension of Vygotsky's (1978) concept of the *zone of proximal development* (ZPD). The TZPD assumes that progress in therapy proceeds along a developmental sequence such as that described by the assimilation model (Stiles, 2002, 2011). According to the assimilation model, problematic voices pass through some part of a sequence of stages that ranges from completely disconnected and alienated from the self to completely integrated and part of the self as they are assimilated in successful psychotherapy: Warded off/dissociated, unwanted thoughts/active avoidance, vague awareness/emergence, problem statement/clarification, understanding/insight, application/working through, resourcefulness/problem solution, and integration/mastery. The TZPD is the segment of this therapeutic developmental continuum that extends from the client's current or *actual* developmental level to the *potential* developmental level that can be achieved in collaboration with the therapist at a particular moment in therapy. Theoretically, then, productive therapeutic work takes place within the client's TZPD. The TZPD itself continues to shift to higher levels in the therapeutic developmental sequence as progress is made. Therapeutic interventions within the TZPD are likely to succeed, whereas interventions outside it are likely to fail.

Therapeutic Interventions and the TZPD

In line with our conceptualization of the TCCS (Ribeiro et al., 2013), clients usually enter therapy with a limited capacity for experiencing the world in alternative ways. As a consequence, the intrusion of new or unassimilated voices, that is, IMs, is most often painful or threatening. Therapists need to develop a climate in which new experiences can be better tolerated, considered, and integrated. Thus therapists must balance the activities of *supporting* and *challenging* (see Table II). In our model supporting consists of working closer to the client's actual level within the TZPD; confirming and elaborating upon the client's perspective of his or her experiences. If the client feels that the therapist validates his or her experience, he or she will likely experience a sense of *safety*. Supporting can be focused on the current (maladaptive) self-narrative that brought the client to therapy, as when the therapist tries to understand the role the problem plays in the client's life from the client's perspective. Alternatively, therapists may focus on emerging novelties in supportive ways, as when the therapist tries to understand how IMs emerged. Support focused on the current self-narrative, however, is more likely to generate safety than is support focused on IMs, whereas focusing on IMs is likely to be experienced as *risky*.

Challenging is conceptualized as working closer to the TZPD potential level within the TZPD, i.e., moving beyond the client's maladaptive narrative. However, focusing on the new or unassimilated voices (IMs) may amplify the contrast with the current framework, triggering a felt sense of contradiction or self-discrepancy, challenging the old framework and creating dysphoric feelings of unpredictability and uncontrollability (Arkovitz & Engle, 2007).

The success of supportive or challenging interventions depends on the therapist's ability to correctly assess the client's tolerance for risk, that is, the limits of the client's TZPD. The client's response to the therapeutic intervention may indicate whether the therapist worked within, outside, or at the limit of the TZPD. In the following examples we explore these interactional possibilities. We theorize that these components of collaboration must remain in balance. The therapist must keep working within a zone in which the client feels safe but is also able to explore the emerging different perspectives. Too much support risks maintaining the client's maladaptive narrative, precluding change; too much challenge risks creating excessive anxiety, fostering resistance.

The point of balance between support and challenge evolves as therapy progresses along a developmental continuum. As the client's self-narrative gains flexibility in accommodating the client's emerging experiences, the TZPD moves, turning what was formerly a potential level into an actual one and extending the client's potential level towards greater ability to accommodate the challenging novelties.

Clients' Responses as Indicators of the TZPD

Scoring categories for the TCCS, along with the rationale for each category, have been presented elsewhere (Ribeiro et al., 2013). In this section we provide a summary of the salient features of the instrument.

Working Within the TZPD

When the therapy discourse is within TZPD, clients feel either *safe* or at *tolerable risk* following supporting or challenging interventions. In either case, clients tend to validate the therapist's intervention. *Validation* refers to the client explicitly or implicitly accepting the therapist's support or invitation to look at his or her experience from the proposed (new) perspective (see Table III).

The client may validate the therapist's intervention implicitly by responding within the TZPD near the developmental level proposed by the therapist (see Figure 1):

(1) The client may respond at the same developmental level as the therapist. For example, if both therapist and client are closer to the *actual developmental level*, a sequence might be as follows: The client elaborates the currently maladaptive self-narrative; the therapist supports it; and the client keeps elaborating that framework. If therapist and client are closer to the *potential developmental level*, the sequence might be as this: The client elaborates upon the maladaptive self-narrative; the therapist challenges; the client accepts the therapist's intervention, elaborating an IM and extending it.

(2) The client may provide a response that lags behind the level of the therapist's intervention. For example, if the therapist is closer to the *potential developmental level*, whereas the client is closer to the *actual developmental level*, a sequence might be as follows: The

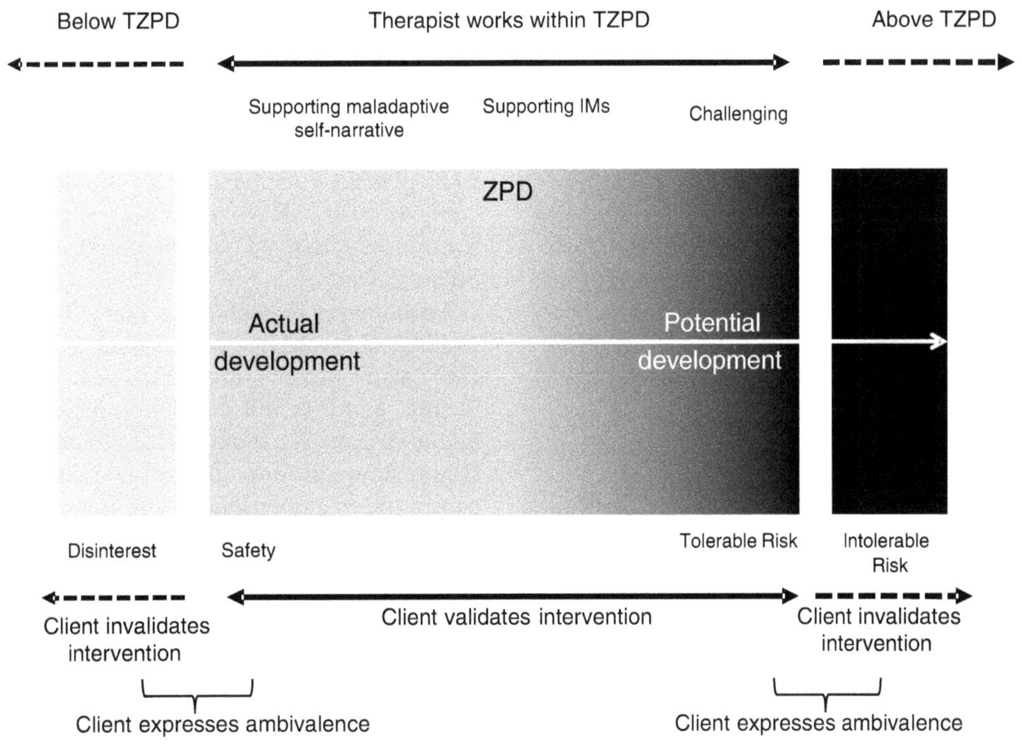

Figure 1. Segment of the therapeutic developmental continuum showing the therapeutic zone of proximal development (TZPD).
Note. From: *How collaboration in therapy becomes therapeutic: The therapeutic collaboration coding system*, by E. Ribeiro et al. (2013). Adapted with permission.

client elaborates upon the maladaptive self-narrative; the therapist challenges it; the client accepts the therapist's intervention, elaborating an IM, but does not extend it.

(3) Finally, the client may provide a response that moves beyond the level the therapist proposes. For example, if the therapist is closer to the *actual developmental level* whereas the client is closer to the *potential developmental level*, then a sequence might be as this: The client elaborates upon the maladaptive self-narrative; the therapist supports it; the client accepts the therapist's intervention but follows up by raising an IM.

Working Outside the TZPD

We theorize that when the therapist works outside the TZPD, the client will probably invalidate the intervention. *Invalidation* refers to declining an invitation to look at his or her experience from the perspective offered by the therapist (see Table III).

When the therapist pushes the client above the upper limit of the TZPD, the client is likely to experience *intolerable risk* and, thus, will invalidate therapist's intervention, for example by changing the subject, misunderstanding, or becoming defensive as a self-protective mechanism. Invalidation may also occur when the therapist works below the lower limit of the TZPD, since the client may feel that the therapist is being redundant (not getting anywhere) and may become bored and disengaged.

The TZPD constantly evolves throughout the therapy; its limits are redefined moment by moment. What was risky (closer to the potential level) for the client early in therapy may later become safe (closer to actual level). On the other hand, as setbacks inevitably occur (Caro-Gabalda & Stiles, 2009, 2013), what seemed safe at one moment may become risky in the next. New perspectives co-constructed in psychotherapy are fragile, and the safety experienced by the client is usually temporary or provisional.

Working at the Upper or Lower Limit of the TZPD

We argue that when the therapist works at the limit of the TZPD, the client is more likely to exhibit ambivalence than invalidation—to begin to accept the perspective proposed by the therapist but then take an opposite perspective. This can happen whether the therapist is working at the upper limit or at the lower limit of the TZPD.

If the therapist works closer to the upper limit of the TZPD, by challenging the client or supporting IMs, the client's ambivalence response may indicate he or she lags behind the proposed level, *moving towards safety*. Such behaviors are akin to what we described above as an RPM (Gonçalves & Ribeiro, 2012; Gonçalves, Ribeiro, Stiles, et al., 2011). IMs and TCCS markers of ambivalence are equivalent, although the IMs formulation is intrapersonal, whereas the TCCS one is interpersonal.

In contrast, if the therapist works closer to the lower limit of the TZPD, by supporting the maladaptive self-narrative, the client's ambivalence response may indicate he or she extends beyond the level proposed by the therapist, *moving towards risk*.

Study Goals and Questions

Our purpose in this study was to assess and improve our theoretical understanding of the impact of the therapist's responses in situations where clients present evidence of ambivalence (RPMs). We were particularly interested in exploring the impact of these interventions on the collaboration between client and therapist in these situations.

This was a theory-building case study (Stiles, 2009). The theory we are building is our account of how self-narratives change in psychotherapy. It is based on our integration of the IMs model and the assimilation model. This model was also used to construct the TCCS (described above and in Ribeiro et al., 2013). Theory-building case studies can make use of rich clinical material to assess and improve theories. Whereas statistical hypothesis-testing compares observations on many cases with one theoretically derived statement, theory-building case studies compare many observations on one case with many theoretically derived statements (Campbell, 1979; Stiles, 2009).

To obtain a rich cross section of events demonstrating ambivalence, we selected a case with relatively poor outcome, one which presented the lowest incidence of IMs and the highest incidence of RPMs in our sample. We thought that a poor-outcome case might show us how therapists may inadvertently contribute to ambivalence by responding at inappropriate TZPD levels.

We focused on three questions:

(1) Which types of therapeutic intervention precede the emergence of RPMs (understood as empirical markers of ambivalence)?
(2) How did the therapist respond to the client's RPMs? In other words, how did the therapist try to restore collaboration or keep the dyad within the TZPD?

(3) How did the client react to the therapist's response to RPMs? To put in another way, was the therapist's intervention successful in restoring collaboration or placing the dyad within the TZPD?

Method

Data for the current study were drawn from the Matos, Santos, Gonçalves, and Martins (2009) sample of IMs in narrative therapy. This relatively poor-outcome case of narrative therapy had been previously coded for RPMs by Gonçalves, Ribeiro, Stiles, et al. (2011). Relevant parts of these studies' method are summarized here; please see Gonçalves et al. (2011) for further details.

Client

Maria was a 47-year-old retired industrial worker, married for 20 years. Maria's treatment outcome was relatively poor, as compared to the rest of a sample of women who were victims of intimate violence (Matos et al., 2009). Maria was recommended for therapy by an institution for crime victims. She presented severe symptoms of depression (e.g., sadness, hopelessness, social withdrawal, isolation). She also had relational problems with her oldest son, and she blamed herself for not being a good mother. Her intent was to leave home with her youngest child and move to a temporary crime victims' shelter. Her main obstacles were lack of financial independence and the impossibility of taking her oldest son with her.

Therapy and Therapist

Maria attended psychotherapy in a Portuguese university clinic, where she received individual narrative therapy (White & Epston, 1990). This case involved 15 sessions, initially four weekly sessions and then twice a month, plus one follow-up (after 6 months). She was treated by a female therapist who had a master's degree in Psychology and 5 years of experience in psychotherapy with battered women. The therapist was supervised to ensure adherence to the narrative model.

Planned therapy interventions included (i) externalization of problems, (ii) identification of the cultural and social assumptions that support women's abuse, (iii) identification of unique outcomes (the narrative therapy term for IMs), (iv) therapeutic questioning around these unique outcomes, trying to create a new alternative to the narrative that was externalized, and (v) consolidation of the changes through social validation, trying to make more visible the way change happened (see Matos et al., 2009, for a detailed description of the narrative therapy guidelines).

Researchers

The TCCS analysis was conducted by the first author, co-author of TCCS, and the third author, a master's student in clinical psychology. The fourth author served as auditor of the TCCS coding, reviewing and checking the judgments made by the judges.

Measures

Brief Symptom Inventory (BSI). The BSI (Derogatis & Melisaratos, 1983) is a 53-item self-report rating scale of distress, using a 5-point Likert scale. We used the Portuguese adaptation by Canavarro (2007), which has good psychometric characteristics (Cronbach's alpha for the nine symptom subscales ranges from .62 to .80).

Severity of Victimization Rating Scale (SVRS). The SVRS (Matos, 2006) assesses abusive actions received (physical, psychological, and/or sexual), their frequency, and their severity on a 3-point scale (low, medium, high); it is completed by the therapist based on the client's report.

Working Alliance Inventory (WAI). The WAI (Horvath, 1982) is a 36-item questionnaire, which uses a 7-point Likert scale to assess therapeutic alliance quality. The Portuguese version (Machado & Horvath, 1999) has good internal consistency (Cronbach's alpha .95).

Return-to-the-Problem Coding System (RPCS). The RPCS (Gonçalves, Ribeiro, Santos, Gonçalves, & Conde, 2010) is a qualitative system that assesses the re-emergence of the maladaptive self-narrative immediately after the emergence of an IM. Previous studies using the RPCS (e.g., Gonçalves, Ribeiro, Stiles, et al., 2011; Ribeiro et al., 2011, 2012) reported a reliable agreement between judges on RPM coding, with a Cohen's kappa between .85 and .93.

Therapeutic Collaboration Coding System (TCCS). The TCCS is a transcript-based coding system designed to analyze therapeutic collaboration on a moment-to-moment basis. An initial study (Ribeiro et al., 2013) showed good reliability, with mean Cohen's kappa values of .92 for therapist interventions and .93 for client responses. Sequences of therapist's intervention and client's response categories are interpreted as reflecting the position of the exchange relative to the TZPD.

Procedure

Analytical strategy. Our research strategy involved the analysis of therapeutic exchanges immediately before and after RPMs using the TCCS. This comprised three tasks: (i) categorization of the therapist's intervention that occurred immediately before the client's RPMs; (ii) categorization of therapist's intervention that occurred immediately after the client's RPMs; and (iii) categorization of the client's reaction to it (interpreted as its impact on therapeutic collaboration).

Outcome and alliance measures administration. The BSI was administered in sessions 1, 4, 8, 12, and 16 and at 6-month follow-up. This study used the Global Severity Index (GSI) of the BSI, which considers responses to all items; this index is considered to be the best single predictor of level of distress (Derogatis, 1993). Like the BSI, the SVRS was recorded every fourth session, starting with the first. The WAI was administered in sessions 4, 8, 12, and 14 and at 6-month follow-up. Versions for client (WAIc) and observers (WAIo) (two independent observers, who were psychotherapists with 2 years of clinical experience, coded recordings of sessions) were applied (see Table I).

Criteria for case categorization and selection. Maria was considered a relatively poor-outcome case because: (i) although her symptom intensity declined from her initial to post-therapy assessments, it had returned to clinical levels at follow-up (initial GSI 2.66; final GSI = .62; follow-up GSI =1.64; GSI cut-off score of ≤ 1.32; Matos, 2006); and (ii) there was no change in the level of intimate violence measure (SVRS) from the beginning to the end of therapy. In comparison to the rest of the sample, Maria showed the highest value on the GSI at the follow-up session (Matos et al., 2009). The quality of alliance assessed by both the self-report and observer version of the WAI was high and stable across therapy (see Table I).

Table I. Outcome and alliance measures

	BSI(GSI)	WAI Observer A	WAI Observer B	WAI Client
Session 1	2.66			
Session 4	1.35	5.4	5.3	5.71
Session 8	1.2	5.5	6	6.41
Session 12	1.41	5.7	5.9	6.11
Session 15	0.62	6.2	5.5	6.55
Follow-up	1.64	6.5	5.9	6.63

Note: BSI: Brief Symptom Inventory; GSI: General Severity Index; WAI: Working Alliance Inventory.

RPMs coding and reliability. Two trained judges independently coded session video recording, analyzing IMs for the presence of RPMs, following the RPCS manual. The reliability of identifying RPMs, assessed by Cohen's k, was .90 (Gonçalves, Ribeiro, Stiles, et al., 2011).

TCCS coding and reliability. Two trained judges (the first and third authors) watched the video recordings of each session in their entirety and read the transcripts. The judges then independently listed the client's problems (themes from the maladaptive self-narrative that brought the client to therapy) and met to discuss their assessment of the client's maladaptive self-narrative. Following this, the client's maladaptive self-narrative was consensually characterized in a way that remained faithful to the client's words. Next, the judges independently classified each therapist's speaking turn before and after each episode in which there was an IM followed by an RPM, into a Supporting subcategory or a Challenging subcategory (see Table II). For Supporting subcategories, they further decided whether it focused on the maladaptive self-narrative or focused on the IM.

Finally, the judges independently classified the client's speaking turn after each therapist response to an RPM, into a Validation/Invalidation subcategory (see Table III). In coding a Validation category, judges further assessed whether clients *lagged behind* the intervention on the therapeutic developmental continuum, responded *at the same level* as the intervention, or extended *beyond the level* of the intervention, using the specific subcategories of client response shown in Table III. In coding an Invalidation category, judges assessed whether the therapist worked below the lower limit or above the upper limit of the TZPD (the distinctive feature of exchanges below the TZPD is the presence of markers that indicated that the client experienced the therapist as being redundant).

Sessions 8 and 9 were not coded due to technical problems with the video. The follow-up session was not analyzed, since its nature, goals and structure were very different from the regular sessions. The last session was not coded for therapist's interventions and client's responses because it did not include any RPMs. The pair of judges met after coding each session to assess their rating's reliability (using Cohen's kappa) and to note any differences in their perspectives on their coding. When differences were

Table II. Therapist intervention coding subcategories

Supporting subcategories	Definitions
Reflecting	The therapist reflects the content; meaning or feeling present in the client's words. He or she uses his/her or the client's words but doesn't add any new content in the reflection, asking for an implicit or explicit feedback.
Confirming	The therapist makes sure he/she understood the content of the client's speech, asking the client in an explicit and direct mode.
Summarizing	The therapist synthesizes the client's discourse, using his/her own and the client's words, asking for feedback (implicit or explicit)
Demonstrating interest/ attention	The therapist shows/ affirms interest on client's discourse.
Open questioning	The therapist explores the client's experience using open questioning. The question opens to a variety of answers, not anticipated and/or linked to contents that the client hasn't reported or only reported briefly. This includes the therapist asking for feedback on the session or on the therapeutic task.
Minimal encouragement	The therapist makes minimal encouragement of the client's speech, repeating the client's words, in an affirmative or interrogative mode (ambiguous expressions with different possible meanings aren't codified, like a simple "Hum ... hum" or "ok").
Specifying information	The therapist asks for concretization or clarification of the (imprecise) information given by the client, using closed questions, specific focused questions, asking for examples.
Challenging subcategories	**Definitions**
Interpreting	The therapist proposes to the client a new perspective over his or her perspective, by using his or her own words (instead of the client's words). There is, although, a sense of continuity in relation to the client's previous speaking turn.
Confronting	The therapist proposes to the client a new perspective over his or her perspective or questions the client about a new perspective over his or her perspective. There is a clear discontinuity (i.e., opposition) in relation to the client's speaking turn.
Inviting to adopt a new perspective	The therapist invites (implicitly or explicitly) the client to understand a given experience in an alternative way.
Inviting to put into practice a new action	The therapist invites the client to act in a different way, in the session or out of the session.
Inviting to explore hypothetical scenarios	The therapist invites the client to imagine hypothetical scenarios, i.e., cognitive, emotional and/or behavioral possibilities that are different from the client's usual way of understanding and experiencing.
Changing level of analysis	The therapist changes the level of the analysis of the client's experience from the descriptive and concrete level to a more abstract one or vice versa.
Emphasizing novelty	The therapist invites the client to elaborate upon the emergence of novelty.
Debating client's beliefs	The therapist debates the evidence or logic of the client's believes and thoughts.
Tracking change evidence	The therapist searches for markers of change, and tries to highlight them.

Note: From: *How collaboration in therapy becomes therapeutic: The therapeutic collaboration coding system*, by E. Ribeiro et al. (2013). Adapted with permission.

detected, they were resolved through consensual discussion. Reliability of identifying therapist's intervention, assessed by Cohen's k, was .95. Reliability of identifying client's response, assessed by Cohen's k, was .95. The consensus version of the TCCS coding was audited by an external auditor (the fourth author) who then met with the pair of judges to discuss his feedback. His role was one of "questioning and critiquing" (Hill et al., 2005, p. 201).

RPMs' Evolution Across Therapy

In the previous study involving this case, 114 RPMs were identified (Gonçalves, Ribeiro, Stiles, et al., 2011). The frequency of RPMs showed an increasing trend, as shown in Figure 2, except that the last session did not include any RPMs. The authors interpreted this pattern as suggesting that ambivalence was not resolved in this case. The absence of RPMs in the final session appeared not to reflect ambivalence resolution but instead to reflect the nature of the last session: The dyad reviewed the client's change process and did not engage in specific therapeutic work (Gonçalves, Ribeiro, Stiles, et al., 2011).

Results

Which Type of Therapeutic Intervention Precedes the Emergence of RPMS?

The results are presented in Figure 3, in which the y axis represents the proportion of therapeutic interventions and the x axis therapy sessions over time. Results indicated that challenging was the most common type of therapeutic intervention preceding

Table III. Client response coding subcategories

Validation subcategories	Definitions
Confirming	The client agrees with the therapist's intervention, but does not extend it.
Extending	The client not only agrees with the therapist's intervention, but expands it (i.e., going further).
Giving information	The client provides information according to the therapist's specific request.
Reformulating one's own perspective	The client answers the therapist's question or reflects upon the therapist's prior affirmation and, in doing so, reformulates his or her perspective over the experience being explored.
Clarifying	The client attempts to clarify the sense of his or her response to the therapist's prior intervention or clarify the sense of the therapist's intervention itself.
Invalidation subcategories	**Definition**
Expressing confusion	Client feels confused and/or states his or her inability to answer the therapist's question.
Focusing/persisting on the maladaptive self-narrative	Client persists on looking at a specific experience or topic from his or her standpoint.
Defending one's own perspective and/or disagreeing with the therapist's intervention	Client defends his/her thoughts, feelings, or behavior by using self-enhancing strategies or self-justifying statements.
Denying progress	Client states the absence of change (novelty) or progress.
Self-criticism and/or hopelessness	Client is self-critical or self-blaming and becomes absorbed in a process of hopelessness (e.g., client doubts about the progress that can be made).
Lack of involvement in response	Client gives minimal responses to therapist's efforts to explore and understand client's experience.
Shifting topic	Client changes topic or tangentially answers the therapist
Topic/focus disconnection	The client persists in elaborating upon a given topic despite the therapist's efforts to engage in the discussion of a new one.
Non-meaningful storytelling and/or focusing on others' reactions	Client talks in a wordy manner or overly elaborates non-significant stories to explain an experience and/or spends an inordinate amount of time talking about other people.
Sarcastic answer	The client questions the therapist's intervention or is ironic towards the therapist's intervention.

Note: From: *How collaboration in therapy becomes therapeutic: The therapeutic collaboration coding system*, by E. Ribeiro et al. (2013). Adapted with permission.

the emergence of an RPM (mean = 92.6%). Supporting IMs preceded only 7.4% of the RPMs. There were no occurrences of RPM following an intervention coded as supporting the current (maladaptive) self-narrative. The following example illustrates the most frequent type of therapeutic exchange preceding RPMs. This and the examples in the next two sections are successive excerpts from the same interaction in session 1 (translated from Portuguese by the first author), selected to illustrate our main results compactly and coherently.

T: *You said that 'partly' there's a voice that says there's no use making any effort because you will never get anywhere* [The therapist refers to the dominant community of voices]. *But is there another voice* [The therapist challenges the client by searching for alternative voices—emphasizing novelty subcategory]?

C: *Yes, there's another part that seems [to say] that I can [do] everything!* [The client elaborates an IM, by acknowledging the existence of an alternative voice] ***But suddenly, it falls down! Like a castle of cards that we build and then suddenly falls apart!*** [The client elaborates an RPM by emphasizing the alternative voice's lack of power].

How does the Therapist Respond to the Client's RPMs?

As shown in Figure 4, results indicated that the therapist more often responded to RPM using a challenging intervention (mean = 75.0%) than using a supporting maladaptive self-narrative (mean = 11.2%) or a supporting IMs intervention (mean = 9.1%).

The following excerpt illustrates the most common type of therapist intervention following RPMs:

C: *I would be less impaired if this voice's strength were 5 and the other 5 too (...)* [The client elaborates an IM, by reflecting upon the importance of both the dominant community of voices and the unassimilated voice expressing themselves and guiding her action] ***But the other voice is so weak, so weak ... my husband has destroyed me! And If I leave him, he will try to convince everybody that it was my fault!*** [The client elaborates an RPM, by expressing hopelessness and emphasizing the negative consequences of leaving the abusive relationship].

T: *I understand this is important to you, but look ... if you are prepared to fight him, even if he does that he will*

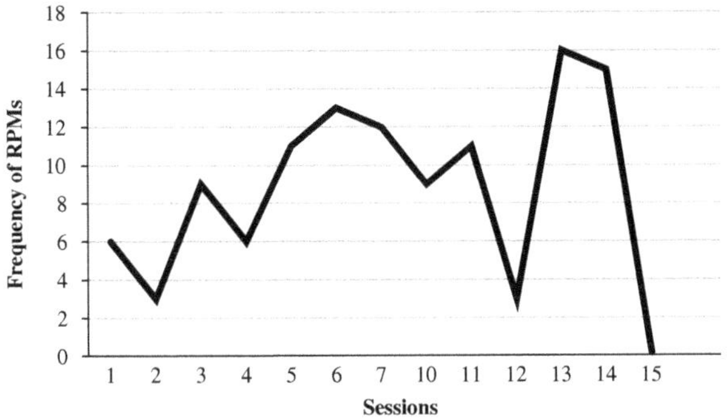

Figure 2. Emergence of return-to-the-problem markers (RPMs) across therapy.

not be able to destroy you. You have to create some defenses, some barriers [The therapist challenges the client—*confronting* subcategory; she proposes to the client a new perspective and there is a clear discontinuity (i.e., opposition) in relation to the client's prior speaking turn].

How Does the Client Respond to the Therapist's Intervention Following RPMs?

When the therapist responded to RPMs by challenging the client, as in the previous excerpt, the client tended to invalidate the therapist's intervention (mean = 61.8%), which may indicate she experienced intolerable risk. The following client response, which occurred immediately after the therapist intervention above, illustrates this pattern:

C: *I just can't, he has a lot of power … I can't leave him; it is not worth it … I just can't!* [The client invalidates therapist intervention—*expressing hopelessness* sub category; she doubts about the progress that can be made].

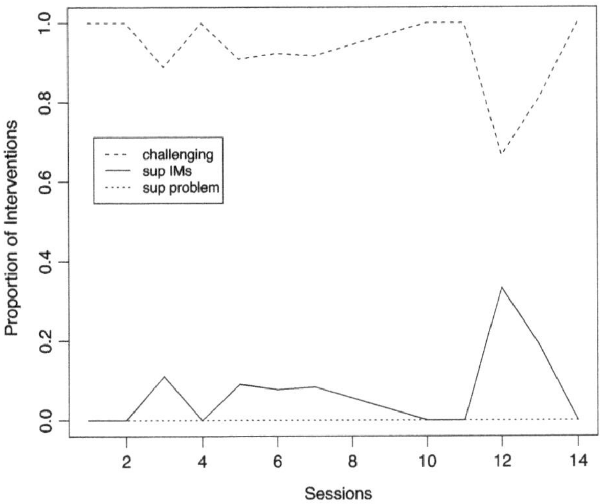

Figure 3. Therapeutic intervention before return to the problem markers (sup = supporting; IMs = innovative moments).

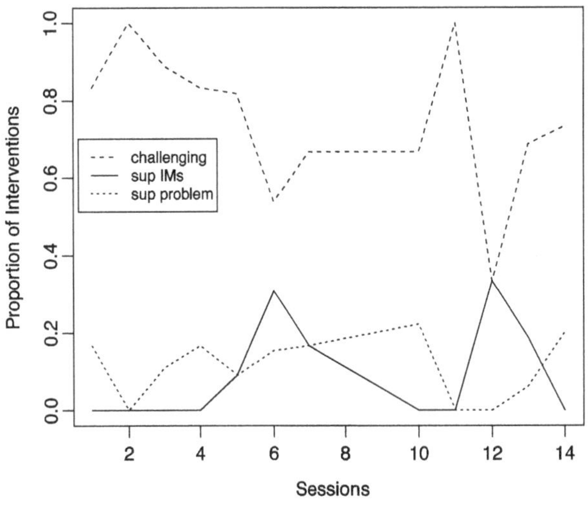

Figure 4. Therapeutic intervention after return to the problem markers (sup = supporting; IMs = innovative moments).

Alternatively, the client minimally validated therapist intervention (mean = 33.1%), lagging behind the level proposed by the therapist, as in the example below. Only, 3.9% of the times did the client respond at the level proposed by the therapist, by elaborating an IM.

T: Let's explore the voice whose strength is 10. Let's try to reduce its strength because it makes you suffer [The therapist challenges the client by emphasizing the need to reduce the constraining power of the dominant community of voices so that the unassimilated voices can emerge and express themselves—*Inviting to put into practice a new action* subcategory].

C: Yes [The client agrees with the therapist's intervention, but does not extend it—confirming subcategory].

As shown in Table IV, results indicated that when the therapist responded to RPMs by supporting the current (maladaptive) self-narrative, the client invariably validated the therapist's intervention (100%), which likely indicates that she experienced safety, working at the level proposed by the therapist.

When the therapist responded to RPMs by supporting IMs, Maria tended to validate the therapist's intervention (mean = 61.7%), which may indicate she experienced safety, working at the level proposed by the therapist. Alternatively, Maria expressed ambivalence, by elaborating a new RPM (mean = 21.7%), lagging behind the level proposed by the therapist and moving towards safety.

Discussion

Maria's ambivalence responses (RPMs) tended to emerge after challenging interventions, that is, when the therapist worked close to her potential

Table IV. Therapist intervention and subsequent client response

		Supporting maladaptive self-narrative Mean	Supporting IMs Mean	Challenging Mean
Client's response	Safety	100%	61.67%	33.14%
	Tolerable risk		6.67%	3.90%
	RPM		21.67%	1.19%
	Intolerable risk		10.00%	61.77%

Note: IMs: innovative moments; RPMs: return-to-the-problem markers.

developmental level (upper limit of the TZPD). This pattern is consistent with our hypothesis that RPMs act as a self-protective mechanism to manage the felt risk of contradicting the maladaptive self-narrative. These observations add confidence to our theoretical model of therapeutic collaboration.

Most often, the therapist responded to Maria's RPMs with further challenging. Interestingly, after instances in which the therapist responded to an RPM with a challenging intervention, the therapeutic dialogue tended to move out of the TZPD, producing an escalation of the clients' felt level of risk. That is, not only did the therapist fail to restore collaboration, but she also seemingly contributed to a (momentary) deterioration in the quality of the therapeutic collaboration. There were also instances in which the client only minimally validated the therapist's intervention, lagging behind the level proposed by the therapist within the TZPD. In both of these types of therapeutic exchange, the therapist worked beyond the client's level. These alternatives elaborate the theoretical suggestion that therapy is most likely to be effective within the TZPD.

Our observations converge with previous work in suggesting that when therapists challenge their clients, trying to stimulate or amplify IMs in ways that do not match the clients' developmental level, they may unintentionally contribute to ambivalence; to the oscillatory cycle between the IMs and the maladaptive self-narrative (Santos, Gonçalves, & Matos, 2010). Also they may unintentionally reinforce the dominance of the maladaptive self-narrative. If therapists respond to a clients' RPMs by insisting that they revise their maladaptive self-narrative or by trying to convince them that they are changing, the clients may feel misunderstood, invoking a "strong reactance on the part of the client, often hardening the client's stuck position" (Engle & Arkovitz, 2008, p. 390). This is consistent with research suggesting that higher levels of therapist demand or directiveness toward change are associated with higher levels of client resistance, whereas more supportive approaches diminish resistance (Miller, Benefield, & Tonigan, 1993; Patterson & Forgatch, 1985; see also Beutler, Harwood, Michelson, Xiaoxia, & Holman, 2011, for a meta-analysis of the interaction between client reactance and therapist directiveness).

Maria's invalidation responses could be interpreted as a marker of needing more support before being able to accept challenges. Supportive responses were relatively successful. Both supporting interventions that focused on the maladaptive self-narrative and supporting interventions that focused on the IMs were followed by responses on the level proposed by the therapist. That is, when the therapist supported Maria's IMs she seemed able to keep working within the TZPD, validating the therapeutic intervention and even extending it, responding with tolerable risk.

It is important to note that Maria evaluated the therapy as being helpful and did not prematurely terminate the process. Perhaps Maria needed more time to change. As suggested by developmental models of change (Prochaska & DiClemente, 1982; Stiles et al., 1990), our results illustrate how a poor-outcome case began with lower readiness for change and might have benefited from a greater amount of therapeutic work.

Maria's positive informal evaluation of her therapy and her consistently high ratings on the WAI contrast with her relative failure to maintain gains on the GSI at follow-up and the continuing problems indicated on the SVRS. Our findings were consistent with the latter; she exhibited high levels of IM-RPM sequences throughout therapy, and there were many events in which Maria showed the signs of not being able to cope with the levels of risk generated by her therapist's interventions. How do we reconcile this relatively negative TCCS description of the process with Maria's positive reports of her experience of therapy and the alliance? One possibility is that this was simply a discrepancy between external and internal perspectives—behavioral resistance to therapeutic progress even though the alliance was strong. Some studies on alliance ruptures have found similar discrepancies between observer systems and client self-report perspectives on quality of alliance (Eubanks-Carter, Gorman, & Muran, 2012; Safran, Muran, & Eubanks-Carter, 2011; see also Coutinho, Ribeiro, Sousa, & Safran, 2013). Perhaps Maria's deference or compliance toward the therapist protected her view of the therapeutic relationship, yielding strong alliance ratings in spite of the resistance to change and transient breakdowns in the collaboration. Most of the time the dyad worked within the TZPD, and perhaps Maria's global perception of alliance was based on her spending most of the time in the collaborative zone of the TZPD. If so, her global perception was confirmed by the observers, who also gave high WAI ratings (see Table I). That said, the discrepancy remains a conundrum that deserves further empirical and theoretical attention.

Implications, Limitations and Future Directions

Client resistance in the ongoing therapy process on a moment-to-moment basis is a consistently potent predictor of treatment outcomes (Aviram, Westra, & Kertes, 2010). Thus, building a better understanding of the process of maintaining resistance, as we have attempted in this study, is an important research priority. Insofar as theory-building case studies do not assess isolated hypotheses, all generalization is through the theory (Stiles, 2009). The present study supports aspects of our theory and, through the theory, allows us to draw some implications for training and practice.

Maria's therapist offered more empathy to Maria's alternative perspective or unassimilated voice than to her maladaptive self-narrative or dominant community of voices. Stiles and Glick (2002) suggested that therapists should adopt an attitude toward client's multiple internal voices similar to multilateral partiality in family therapy (Boszormenyi-Nagy & Spark, 1973), in order that conflicting internal voices can be heard and come to respect each other, a central step on the way to developing internal meaning bridges. To do so, with Engle and Arkovitz (2008), we might suggest "therapists need to monitor their frustration" and "resist the temptation to 'help' the client by pushing for change" (p. 391).

In particular, a therapist may "direct his or her efforts toward an understanding of what it is in the client's experience that prevents easy change" (Engle & Arkovitz, 2008, p. 391; Ahmed, Westra, & Constantino, 2010; Binder & Strupp, 1997; Miller & Rollnick, 2002). Put differently, therapists whose clients show resistance by continually returning to the perspective of a maladaptive self-narrative may need to decrease the level of risk experienced by the client by reducing the degree of challenging, and increasing the degree of supporting.

Of course, we cannot be confident that if Maria's therapist had responded to her RPMs by supporting her perspective instead of challenging it that this would lead to a positive outcome. Further research is needed. Intensive analysis of how therapists responded to RPMs in cases in which RPMs decreased across treatment might support our suggestion. It would aid such research if alliance and outcome measures were administered at every session.

Although the TCCS was developed as a research tool, we think that it might also be useful for training. It could be used to help sensitize trainees to the dyad's position in relation to the TZPD, allowing them to intervene accordingly. Likewise it might, with further validation and development, serve as a diagnostic tool to identify challenges that are mis-timed or too threatening for clients, or, conversely, situations where there are opportunities for more challenging exploration.

Funding

This article was supported by the Portuguese Foundation for Science and Technology (FCT) by the grant [PTDC/ PSI-PCL/121525/2010] (Ambivalence and unsuccessful psychotherapy, 2011–2014) and by the Postdoctoral research grant [SFRH/BPD/ 84157/2012].

References

Ahmed, M., Westra, H. A., & Constantino, M. J. (2010). *Interpersonal process during resistance in CBT associated with high vs low client outcome expectations: A micro-process analysis*. Paper presented at the annual meeting of the Society for Psychotherapy Research, Asilomar.

Arkovitz, H., & Engle, D. (2007). Understanding and working with resistant ambivalence in psychotherapy. In S. G. Hofmann & J. Weinberg (Eds.), *The art and science of psychotherapy* (pp. 171–190). New York: Routledge.

Aviram, A., Westra, H. A., & Kertes, A. (2010). *The impact of motivational interviewing on resistance in CBT for GAD: A process analysis*. Paper presented at the annual meeting of the Society for Psychotherapy Research, Asilomar.

Beutler, L. E., Harwood, T. M., Michelson, A., Xiaoxia, S., & Holman, J. (2011). Reactance/resistance level. In J.C. Norcross (Ed.), *Psychotherapy relationships that work: Evidence-based responsiveness* (2nd ed., pp. 261–278). New York: Oxford University Press.

Beutler, L. E., Rocco, F., Moleiro, C. M., & Talebi, H. (2001). Resistance. *Psychotherapy: Theory, Research, Practice, Training, 38*, 431–436. doi:10.1037/0033-3204.38.4.431

Binder, J. L., & Strupp, H. H. (1997). "Negative process": A recurrently discovered and underestimated facet of therapeutic process and outcome in the individual psychotherapy of adults. *Clinical Psychology: Science and Practice, 4*, 121–139. doi:10.1111/j.1468-2850.1997.tb00105.x

Boszormenyi-Nagy, I., & Spark, G. M. (1973). *Invisible loyalties: Reciprocity in intergenerational family therapy*. Hagerstown, MD: Harper & Row.

Brinegar, M. G., Salvi, L. M., Stiles, W. B., & Greenberg, L. S. (2006). Building a meaning bridge: Therapeutic progress from problem formulation to understanding. *Journal of Counseling Psychology, 53*, 165–180. doi:10.1037/0022-0167.53.2.165

Campbell, D. T. (1979). "Degrees of freedom" and the case study. In T. D. Cook & C. S. Reichardt (Eds.), *Qualitative and quantitative methods in evaluation research* (pp. 49–67). Beverley Hills, CA: Sage.

Canavarro, M. C. (2007). Inventário de Sintomas Psicopatológicos (BSI): Uma revisão crítica dos estudos realizados em Portugal. In M. R. Simões, C. Machado, M. M. Gonçalves, & L. S. Almeida (Eds.), *Avaliação Psicológica: Instrumentos validados para a população portuguesa* – Vol. III (pp. 305–331). [Psychological assessment: Validated instruments for the Portuguese population – Vol. III]. Coimbra: Quarteto.

Caro-Gabalda, I., & Stiles, W. B. (2009). Retrocessos no contexto de terapia linguística de avaliação [Setbacks in the context of linguistic therapy of evaluation]. *Análise Psicológica, 27,* 199–212.

Caro-Gabalda, I., & Stiles, W. B. (2013). Irregular assimilation progress: Setbacks in the context of Linguistic Therapy of Evaluation. *Psychotherapy Research, 23,* 35–53.

Coutinho, J., Ribeiro, E., Sousa, I., & Safran, J. D. (2013). Comparing two methods of identifying alliance rupture events: The Working Alliance Inventory versus the Rupture Resolution Rating System. *Psychotherapy.* doi:10.1037/a0032171.

Derogatis, L. R. (1993). *BSI – Brief Symptom Inventory. Administration, scoring, and procedures manual* (4th Ed.). Minneapolis, MN: National Computer Systems.

Derogatis, L. R., & Melisaratos, N. (1983). The Brief Symptom Inventory: An introductory report. *Psychological Medicine, 13,* 595–605. doi:10.1017/S0033291700048017

Dimaggio, G., Salvatore, G., Azzara, C., Catania, D., Semerari, A., & Hermans, H. J. M. (2003). Dialogical relationships in impoverished narratives: From theory to clinical practice. *Psychology and Psychotherapy: Theory, Research and Practice, 76,* 385–409. doi:10.1348/147608303770584746

Engle, D., & Arkowitz, H. (2008). Viewing resistance as ambivalence: Integrative strategies for working with ambivalence. *Journal of Humanistic Psychology, 48,* 389–412. doi:10.1177/0022167807310917

Eubanks-Carter, C., Gorman, B. S., & Muran, J. C. (2012). Quantitative naturalistic methods for detecting change points in psychotherapy research: An illustration with alliance ruptures. *Psychotherapy Research, 22,* 621–637. doi:10.1080/10503307.2012.893772.

Gonçalves, M. M., Matos, M., & Santos, A. (2009). Narrative therapy and the nature of "innovative moments" in the construction of change. *Journal of Constructivist Psychology, 22,* 1–23. doi:10.1080/10720530802500748

Gonçalves, M. M., & Ribeiro, A. P. (2012). Narrative processes of innovation and stability within the dialogical self. In H. J. M. Hermans & T. Gieser (Eds.), *Handbook of dialogical self* (pp. 301–318). Cambridge: Cambridge University Press.

Gonçalves, M. M., Ribeiro, A. P., Mendes, I., Matos, M., & Santos, A. (2011). Tracking novelties in psychotherapy process research: The innovative moments coding system. *Psychotherapy Research, 21,* 497–509. doi:10.1080/10503307.2011.560207

Gonçalves, M. M., Ribeiro, A. P., Santos, A., Gonçalves, J., & Conde, T. (2010). *Manual for the Return to the Problem Coding System – version 2.* Unpublished manuscript, University of Minho, Braga, Portugal.

Gonçalves, M. M., Ribeiro, A. P., Stiles, W. B., Conde, T., Santos, A., Matos, M., & Martins, C. (2011). The role of mutual in-feeding in maintaining problematic self-narratives: Exploring one path to therapeutic failure. *Psychotherapy Research, 21,* 27–40. doi:10.1080/10503307.2010.507789

Hatcher, R. (1999). Therapists' views of treatment alliance and collaboration in therapy. *Psychotherapy Research, 9,* 405–423.

Hermans, H. J. (1996). Opposites in a dialogical self: Constructs as characters. *Journal of Constructivist Psychology, 9,* 1–26. doi:10.1080/10720539608404649

Hermans, H. J. M. (2001a). The construction of a personal position repertoire: Method and practice. *Culture & Psychology, 7,* 324–366.

Hermans, H. J. M. (2001b). The dialogical self: Toward a theory of personal and cultural positioning. *Culture & Psychology, 7,* 243–281. doi:10.1177/1354067X0173001

Hermans, H. J. M., & Dimaggio, G. (2007). Self, identity, and globalization in times of uncertainty: A dialogical analysis. *Review of General Psychology, 11,* 31–61. doi:10.1037/1089-2680.11.1.31

Hermans, H. J. M., & Kempen, H. J. G. (1993). *The dialogical self: Meaning as movement.* San Diego, CA: Academic Press.

Hill, C. A., Knox, S., Thompson, B. J., Nutt Williams, E., Hess, S. A., & Ladany, N. (2005). Consensual qualitative research: An update. *Journal of Counseling Psychology, 52,* 196–205. doi:10.1037/0022-0167.52.2.196

Horvath, A. O. (1982). *Users' manual of the working alliance inventory.* Unpublished manuscript, Simon Fraser University, Burnaby, Canada.

Leiman, M. (1997). Procedures as dialogical sequences: A revised version of the fundamental concept in cognitive analytic therapy. *British Journal of Medical Psychology, 70,* 193–207. doi:10.1111/j.2044-8341.1997.tb01899.x

Leiman, M. (2002). Toward semiotic dialogism. *Theory and Psychology, 12,* 221–235. doi:10.1177/0959354302012002631

Leiman, M., & Stiles, W. B. (2001). Dialogical sequence analysis and the zone of proximal development as conceptual enhancements to the assimilation model: The case of Jan revisited. *Psychotherapy Research, 11,* 311–330. doi:10.1080/713663986

Machado, P. P., & Horvath, A. O. (1999). Inventário da aliança terapêutica WAI. In M. R. Simões, M. M. Gonçalves, & L. S. Almeida (Eds.), *Testes e provas psicológicas em Portugal* – Vol. II (pp. 87–94). [Tests and psychological instruments in Portugal – Vol. II]. Braga: APPORT.

Matos, M. (2006). Violência nas relações de intimidade. Estudo sobre a mudança psicoterapêutica da mulher [Violence in intimate relationships: A research about the psychotherapeutic change in women]. Unpublished doctoral dissertation, University of Minho, Braga.

Matos, M., Santos, A., Gonçalves, M. M., & Martins, C. (2009). Innovative moments and change in narrative therapy. *Psychotherapy Research, 19,* 68–80. doi:10.1080/10503300802430657

Miller, W. R., Benefield, R. G., & Tonigan, J. S. (1993). Enhancing motivation for change in problem drinking: a controlled comparison of two therapist styles. *Journal of Consulting and Clinical Psychology, 61,* 455–461. doi:10.1037/0022-006X.61.3.455

Miller, W. R., & Rollnick, S. (2002). *Motivational interviewing: Preparing people for change.* New York: Guilford Press.

Moyers, T. B., & Rollnick, S. (2002). A motivational interviewing perspective on resistance in psychotherapy. *Journal of Clinical Psychology,* 58, 185–193. doi:10.1002/jclp.1142

Osatuke, K., Glick, M. J., Gray, M. A., Reynolds, D. J., Humphreys, C. L., Salvi, L. M., & Stiles, W. B. (2004). Assimilation and narrative: Stories as meaning bridges. In L. E. Angus & J. Mcleod (Eds.), *The handbook of narrative psychotherapy: Practice, theory and research* (pp. 87–102). London: Sage.

Patterson, G. R., & Forgatch, M. S. (1985). Therapist behavior as a determinant for client noncompliance: A paradox for the behavior modifier. *Journal of Consulting and Clinical Psychology, 53,* 846–851. doi:10.1037/0022-006X.53.6.846

Prochaska, J. O., & DiClemente, C. (1982). Transtheoretical therapy: Toward a more integrative model of change. *Psychotherapy: Theory, Research and Practice, 19,* 276–288. doi:10.1037/h0088437

Ribeiro, A. P. (2012). *Maintenance and transformation of self-narratives in brief psychotherapy: Theoretical and empirical advances* (Unpublished doctoral thesis). University of Minho, Braga, Portugal.

Ribeiro, A. P., Bento, T., Salgado, J., Stiles, W. B., & Gonçalves, M. M. (2011). A dynamic look at narrative change in psychotherapy: A case-study tracking innovative moments and protonarratives using state-space grids. *Psychotherapy Research*, *21*, 34–69. doi:10.1080/10503307.2010.504241

Ribeiro, A. P., Cruz, G., Mendes, I., Stiles, W. B., & Gonçalves, M. M. (2012). Ambivalence in client-centered therapy. Manuscript in preparation

Ribeiro, E., Ribeiro, A. P., Gonçalves, M. M., Horvath, A. O., & Stiles, W. B. (2013). How collaboration in therapy becomes therapeutic: The therapeutic collaboration coding system. *Psychology and Psychotherapy: Theory, Research and Practice*, *86*, 294–314. doi:10.1111/j.2044-8341.2012.02066.x.

Safran, J. D., & Muran, J. C. (2000). *Negotiating the therapeutic alliance, a relational treatment guide*. New York: Guilford Press.

Safran, J. D., & Muran, J. C. (2006). Has the concept of the therapeutic alliance outlived its usefulness? *Psychotherapy: Theory, Research, Practice, Training*, *43*, 286–291. doi:10.1037/0033- 3204.43.3.286.

Safran, J. D., Muran, J. C., & Eubanks-Carter, C. (2011). Repairing alliance ruptures. *Psychotherapy*, *48*, 80–87. doi: 10.1037/a0022140.

Santos, A., Gonçalves, M. M., & Matos, M. (2010). Innovative moments and poor-outcome in narrative therapy. *Counselling and Psychotherapy Research*, *11*, 129–139. doi:10.1080/14733140903398153

Stiles, W. B. (2001). Assimilation of problematic experiences. *Psychotherapy*, *38*, 462–465.

Stiles, W. B. (2002). Assimilation of problematic experiences. In J. C. Norcross (Ed.), *Psychotherapy relationships that work: Therapist contributions and responsiveness to patients* (pp. 357–365). New York: Oxford University Press.

Stiles, W. B. (2009). Logical operations in theory-building case studies. *Pragmatic Case Studies in Psychotherapy*, *5*, 9–22.

Stiles, W. B. (2011). Coming to terms. *Psychotherapy Research*, *21*, 367–384. doi:10.1080/10503307.2011.582186

Stiles, W. B., & Glick, M. J. (2002). Client-centered therapy with multivoiced clients: Empathy with whom? In J. C. Watson, R. Goldman, & M. S. Warner (Eds.), *Client-centered and experiential therapy in the 21st century: Advances in theory, research, and practice* (pp. 406–414). London: PCCS Books.

Stiles, W. B., Elliott, R., Llewelyn, S. P., Firth-Cozens, J. A., Margison, F. R., Shapiro, D. A., & Hardy, G. (1990). Assimilation of problematic experiences by clients in psychotherapy. *Psychotherapy*, *27*, 411–420. doi:10.1037/0033-3204.27.3.411

Vygotsky, L. (1978). *Mind in Society: the development of higher psychological processes*. Cambridge, MA: Harvard University Press.

Wachtel, P. L. (Ed.). (1982). *Resistance: Psychodynamic and behavioral approaches*. New York: Plenum.

Wachtel, P. L. (1993). *Therapeutic communication: Knowing what to say when*. New York: Guilford Press.

Wachtel, P. L. (1999). Resistance as a problem for practice and theory. *Journal of Psychotherapy Integration*, *9*, 103–118. doi:10.1023/A:1023262928748

White, M., & Epston, D. (1990). *Narrative means to therapeutic ends*. New York: Norton.

Investigating the impact of alliance-focused training on interpersonal process and therapists' capacity for experiential reflection

JEREMY SAFRAN[1], J. CHRISTOPHER MURAN[2], ANTHONY DEMARIA[1], CATHERINE BOUTWELL[1], CATHERINE EUBANKS-CARTER[3], & ARNOLD WINSTON[4]

[1]*Clinical Psychology Program, New School for Social Research, New York, NY, USA;* [2]*Derner Institute for Adv Psy Studies, Adelphi University, Garden City, NY, USA;* [3]*Ferkauf Graduate School of Psychology, Yeshiva University, Bronx, NY, USA &* [4]*Department of Psychiatry, Beth Israel Medical Center, New York, NY, USA*

Abstract

Objective: In this article we present preliminary findings from a research program designed to investigate the value of *alliance-focused training* (AFT), a supervision approach designed to enhance therapists' ability to work constructively with negative therapeutic process. **Method:** In the context of a multiple baseline design, all therapists began treating their patients using *cognitive therapy* and then joined AFT supervision groups at either session 8 or 16 of a 30 session protocol. Study I investigated the impact of AFT on patient and therapist interpersonal process as assessed through the Structural Analysis of Social Behavior (SASB). Study 2 investigated the impact of AFT on therapists' tendency to reflect on their relationships with their patients in an experientially grounded fashion, as assessed via the Experiencing Scale (EXP). Since one of the goals of AFT is to train therapists to use their own emerging feelings as important clues regarding what may be taking place in the therapeutic relationship, we hypothesized that they would show increased levels of EXP after undergoing AFT. **Results and Conclusion:** The results of both studies 1 and 2 were for the most part consistent with hypotheses. Implications and future research directions are discussed.

One of the most consistent findings emerging from psychotherapy research is that the quality of the therapeutic alliance is a robust predictor of outcome across a range of different treatments and that, conversely, weakened alliances are correlated with unilateral termination by the patient (e.g., Horvath, Del Re, Flückiger, & Symonds, 2011). In addition, there is now evidence that some therapists consistently have better alliances, along with better outcomes (see Baldwin, Wampold, & Imel, 2007; Wampold, 2001). There is also a growing body of evidence suggesting that therapists often respond to patient hostility with counter-hostility, and that this type of "negative process" is associated with poor outcome (Anderson, Knobloch-Fedders, Stiles, Ordonez, & Heckman, 2012; Binder & Strupp, 1997; Safran, Muran, Samstag, & Stevens, 2001).

The empirical focus on negative process emerged in tandem with the growing empirical interest in the therapeutic alliance. A key impetus was Hans Strupp's efforts to make sense of the Vanderbilt I study's finding that seasoned professional therapists were no more helpful to patients than a group of college professors who had received no clinical training (Strupp & Hadley, 1979). Strupp's subsequent use of a series of research-informed case studies comparing good and bad outcome cases from the Vanderbilt I study led him to what was to become the central theme of his research career: the attempt to grapple with the problem of training therapists to work constructively with negative therapeutic process. As he said at the time, "In our study, we failed to encounter a single instance in which a difficult patient's hostility and negativism were successfully confronted or resolved … therapists' negative responses to difficult patients are far more common and far more intractable than has been generally recognized" (Strupp, 1980, p. 954).

In the last two decades, there has emerged a "second generation" of alliance research that integrates work on the alliance with attention to negative process by focusing on improving therapists' abilities to repair ruptures in the alliance when they occur (see Eubanks-Carter, Muran, & Safran, 2010; Safran et al., 2001; Safran, Muran, & Eubanks-Carter, 2011, for reviews). A number of studies have evaluated the effectiveness of treatment interventions and training procedures designed specifically to improve therapists' abilities to work constructively with weakened alliances and negative therapeutic process. In a recent meta-analysis, Safran et al. (2011) found a moderate and significant effect size for studies of this type when examining pre-post effect sizes. However, the average between-group effect size, though still significant, was relatively modest.

The lack of large differences between treatments targeting problems in the alliance should come as no surprise. One of the most common findings in psychotherapy research is the "therapeutic equivalence effect," i.e., the failure to find that one form of treatment is consistently more effective than others (Luborsky et al., 2002; Wampold et al., 1997). Various hypotheses have been advanced to account for this effect. One is that group averages in randomized clinical trial studies can mask the fact that not all patients in a given treatment condition show equal benefit and that not all therapists are equally effective. The situation is further complicated by the fact that even if we were able to control for both patient and therapist variables, we would also need to take into account the patient-therapist interaction variable (i.e., factors unique to the specific therapeutic dyad). Another way of framing this issue is in terms of Stiles' notion of therapeutic responsiveness (Stiles, Honos-Webb, & Surko, 1998): Therapists and patients are always influencing and responding to one another on an ongoing basis. Thus, every therapeutic dyad is unique, and their style of mutual responsiveness will vary at different points in time.

Although it is impossible to control for all of these variables at the same time, there are ways of controlling for more of them than we normally do. For example, both Strupp and colleagues (Bein et al., 2000; Henry, Strupp, Butler, Schacht, & Binder,1993; Strupp, 1993) in the Vanderbilt II study and Crits-Christoph et al. (2006) evaluated the effectiveness of training programs designed specifically to improve therapists' abilities to enhance the alliance and work constructively with negative therapeutic process. Both studies evaluated the therapeutic outcomes obtained by the same therapists with different cohorts of patients pre- and post-training. In this way, they were able to reduce the degree of variance attributable to individual therapists by holding the therapist variable constant. Although the results of Crits-Christoph et al.'s study were more promising than Strupp et al.'s, they were still somewhat equivocal. Moreover, it is important to bear in mind that both studies attempted to control for the therapist variable while failing to control for the patient variable. Thus one cannot, for example, rule out the possibility that the patients treated after training were in some ways more difficult to work with than the patients treated before training.

In a pilot study designed to test the effectiveness of an alliance-focused intervention with patients who were potential treatment failures, Safran, Muran, Samstag, and Winston (2005) attempted to reduce the degree of patient variance by including only patients with whom therapists had difficulty establishing a good therapeutic alliance in the first phase of the study. These challenging patients were reassigned to a different set of therapists working in either an alliance-focused modality or a control condition in the second phase of the study. Although the results of this study provided promising support for the alliance-focused treatment, the sample was too small to draw any definitive conclusions. Moreover, in contrast to the Vanderbilt II and Crits-Christoph et al. (2006) studies, Safran et al. (2005) focused on reducing patient variance, while neglecting to control for the therapist variable.

In this article, we present preliminary findings emerging from an ongoing research project currently under way at the Beth Israel Psychotherapy Research Program (see Muran, 2002, for background) designed to investigate the effectiveness of a training protocol to enhance therapists' abilities to detect and work constructively with alliance ruptures and negative therapeutic process. The training protocol, which we will refer to as alliance-focused training (AFT), is based upon the principles of the alliance-focused treatment we have described elsewhere (e.g., Muran, Safran & Eubanks-Carter, 2010; Muran, Safran, Samstag, & Winston, 2005; Safran & Muran, 2000; Safran et al., 2005) and will discuss briefly below. This project was designed to control for variance attributable to patient, therapist, and patient-therapist interactional sources. In order to evaluate whether changes taking place after the implementation of AFT were attributable to AFT or to other factors (e.g., an improvement in therapist skill due to increased experience or greater familiarity with a specific patient), we employed a multiple baseline design. In this design, all therapists began treating a case with CBT while receiving CBT supervision, and then at predetermined points (at session 8 or at session 16) switched from CBT supervision to AFT. By introducing AFT at different time intervals, we were able to control for time or maturation effects. We were then able to evaluate whether theoretically predictable changes on a variety of dimensions occurred after the implementation of AFT. By testing for differences within, rather than between patient-therapist dyads, we were able to control for patient and therapist individual differences as well as differences specific to each dyad.

This project consisted of two phases. In the first phase therapists (who were primarily graduate students in clinical psychology) received 1 year of training in CBT and completed one 30-session CBT case while attending weekly CBT supervision sessions. Therapists were required to demonstrate adherence to the CBT protocol in order to enter the second phase of the study. In this phase, therapists began treating a second case with CBT, while continuing to attend CBT supervision. After either eight or 16 sessions of CBT (the timing was determined by random assignment), therapists were transferred from the CBT supervision group to an AFT supervision group, where they learned how to augment CBT with AFT principles while continuing to work with the same patient. Because all therapists in the second phase began AFT at some point (albeit at different time intervals), we did not necessarily expect to find differences in ultimate outcome between therapeutic dyads who switched to AFT at session 8 versus session 16. Our focus was thus on proximal outcome (including changes in theoretically relevant processes) rather than ultimate outcome. It may ultimately be the case that dyad-specific differences in proximal outcome prove to be predictive of ultimate outcome, but this question was not examined in the studies that follow. All data collected in the two studies described below came from an ongoing investigation designed to examine the impact of augmenting CBT with AFT training. Because of missing data the cases analyzed in the two studies were only partially overlapping.

Training Conditions

Cognitive-Behavioral Therapy (CBT: Turner & Muran, 1992; Turner, Muran, & Ochoa, 2004). The cognitive-behavioral therapy condition is designed to treat patients presenting with anxious, fearful, and avoidant Cluster C personality disorders and with personality disorders "not otherwise specified" according to DSM-IV in a 30-session, one 45-minute session/week protocol. It is largely based on Beck, Freeman, and associates' (1990) adaptation of cognitive therapy to the treatment of personality disorders, and incorporates Persons and Silberschatz's (1988) case formulation approach. According to this treatment model, personality and behavior are understood as organized by underlying belief systems or schemas. The treatment process involves the application of various cognitive and behavioral strategies to reduce symptoms and change schemas, including in-session tasks (e.g., breathing retraining, applied relaxation, role-playing, exposure exercises, eliciting and testing automatic thoughts, cognitive restructuring, and rehearsal) and extra-session tasks in the form of homework assignments (e.g., self-monitoring with thought records, scheduling activities, in vivo exposure exercises, and behavioral experiments).

Training consisted of a weekly 90-minute group supervision format. It entailed teaching a cognitive-behavioral conceptualization of anxiety, depression, and personality, how to establish a case formulation and identify core schemas, and how to implement the two intervention phases: (1) symptom reduction and (2) schema change. Training also involved a didactic component, observation of videotapes of skilled cognitive therapists, feedback on videotapes of trainees' therapy cases, and role-playing exercises. These role-playing exercises were used to help therapists develop basic skills such as agenda setting, eliciting automatic thoughts and abstracting underlying schemas, and the use of various cognitive and behavioral strategies for challenging cognitive distortions and dysfunctional attitudes.

CBT training began with a 4-month-long didactic seminar on CBT taught by a psychologist who has an extensive background as a CBT therapist, including a 1-year postdoctoral fellowship at the Beck Institute, and 15 years of clinical experience. She is a fellow of the Academy of Cognitive Therapy. Following the seminar, trainees were assigned to supervision groups ranging in size from six to eight participants. The majority of trainees participated in groups led by the same psychologist who had led the didactic seminar. Approximately 20% of trainees participated in group supervision led by a second psychologist, trained as a cognitive therapist, with 20 years of clinical experience.

Alliance-focused training (AFT: Muran et al., 2010; Safran & Muran, 2000; Safran, Muran, Stevens, & Rothman, 2008). The principles of AFT derive from our ongoing research program on resolving therapeutic alliance ruptures (see Safran et al., 2001, 2011 for reviews) as well as contemporary developments in relational psychoanalysis (e.g.,

Aron, 1996; Benjamin, 1990; Bromberg, 1998; Goldfried, 1994; Harris, 2011; Mitchell, 1988; Pizer, 1998; Safran 2002, 2012; Safran & Muran, 2006a Stern, 1998). Safran and Muran's (2000) *Negotiating the therapeutic alliance: A relational treatment guide* was used as a training manual. This was supplemented with the training DVD *Resolving therapeutic impasses* (Safran & Muran, 2006b). The training included introducing an array of strategies to resolve alliance ruptures from explaining the rationale of the treatment, clarifying misunderstandings, and changing a task or goal, to exploring core relational themes.

Some of the key features of AFT are as follows: (a) it assumes that alliance ruptures result from patients and therapists becoming unwittingly embedded in negative interpersonal cycles with one another (e.g., hostility and counter-hostility), (b) therapists are taught to recognize that all interventions are relational acts, (c) therapists are trained to monitor what is taking place in the therapeutic relationship on an ongoing basis, (d) therapists are taught to take responsibility for their own contributions to what is taking place in the therapeutic relationship and to recognize that they are often contributing in ways that they do not fully recognize, (e) therapists are taught to use their own emerging feelings as important clues regarding what may be taking place in the therapeutic relationship, and (f) an important emphasis is placed on training therapists to explore their own emerging experience in a non-defensive fashion. As indicated above, this type of self-exploration is considered crucial since therapists' feelings are viewed as a potentially valuable source of information about what may be taking place in the therapeutic relationship. Moreover, to the extent that therapists have difficulty fully acknowledging their own experience, their actions will be motivated by dissociated feelings and they are more likely to remain embedded or locked into pernicious transference-countertransference enactments (Safran & Muran, 2000).

Training was conducted in a weekly 90-minute group supervision format, consisting of a didactic component, videotaped demonstrations, and experiential exercises. The didactic component involved readings and lectures provided by supervisors regarding the definition and identification of ruptures and various rupture resolution strategies, with particular emphasis on the principles of therapeutic metacommunication. Metacommunication (i.e., communicating about implicit relational communications) is a commonly used intervention (Kiesler, 1996; Safran & Muran, 2000). Therapists are trained to invite patients to collaborate with them in the process of exploring how both partners in the therapeutic relationship are contributing to recurring patterns that are playing out. Metacommunication may involve exploring links between what is taking place in the therapeutic relationship and other patterns in the patient's life, but therapists are trained to bear in mind that interventions of this type (traditionally referred to as transference interpretations) are relational acts as well. Depending on what the patient feels this act means, and what motivates the therapist's intervention, patients may or may not find a particular metacommunication helpful

Alliance-focused training emphasizes experiential learning and self-exploration. Therapists were trained to attend to and explore their own feelings as important sources of information about what is going on in the therapeutic relationship. Role-playing exercises are used in AFT in order to bring to life interactions moments in treatment trainees have described to the group or illustrated through video-recordings. The objective of the role-plays is not only to experiment with intervening in different ways, but also to provide trainees with the opportunity to explore their own feelings and internal conflicts as they emerge in the moment. These exercises are referred to as "awareness-oriented role-plays" (Muran et al., 2010; Safran & Muran, 2000; Safran et al., 2008). Supervisors monitor the role-plays carefully and intervene at critical moments to direct therapists' attention to their inner experience, and to encourage them to put unarticulated feelings and intuitions into words. In some cases, this process deepens into an exploration of internal conflicts that play a role in the therapist's contribution to the rupture. In other cases, the supervisor helps the trainee explore feelings emerging in the context of a role-play and then encourages him or her to verbalize these feeling in the role-play as part of a metacommunication process.

Supervision sessions also employed mindfulness training for the purpose of helping therapists refine their capacity to observe their own inner experience as well as the nature of their own contributions to interaction. All supervision sessions devoted some time to mindfulness training, and therapists were encouraged to develop an ongoing mindfulness practice on their own between training sessions. Metacommunication is conceptualized as a type of "mindfulness in action" (Safran & Muran, 2000). In other words, therapists are taught to view metacommunication as an extension of mindfulness practice in which the goal is to attend to what is happening in the here-and-now, both in the therapeutic relationship and in their own emerging internal experience, with an attitude of curiosity and nonjudgmental acceptance.

Unlike the CBT supervision condition, AFT supervision did not begin with a didactic course in AFT. Instead trainees were reassigned from their ongoing CBT supervision to an AFT training group when the design dictated that it was time for them to begin augmenting CBT with AFT training. AFT supervision groups ranged in size from four to eight participants. Each group was led by one of the two main developers of the AFT approach, with support in some of the groups from a more junior PhD psychologist, who had received 2 years of AFT training and supervision while on predoctoral internship and postdoctoral fellowship.

Augmenting CBT with AFT

Once therapists transitioned from CBT supervision into alliance-focused training, they were instructed to begin incorporating principles of AFT into their work with their patients in a fashion that felt appropriate for their particular case. The precise pace and extent to which they used specific AFT interventions (e.g., metacommunication, therapists' exploration of their own contributions to enactments, in-depth exploration of patients' emerging feelings in context of the therapeutic relationship) were worked out collaboratively with their supervisors. In some cases, where it became apparent that there were well-defined ruptures in the alliance, therapists were encouraged to begin collaboratively exploring these ruptures with their patients soon after transitioning to AFT. In other cases, where ruptures were more subtle or it was not clear that ruptures of any type were taking place, therapists were encouraged simply to begin the process of paying closer attention to their own feelings while interacting with their patients, and to reflect internally and during supervision on subtle patterns that may have been playing out in the therapeutic relationship.

In cases where patients appeared to be benefiting from the use of cognitive-behavioral interventions, therapists were encouraged to continue using these interventions, while at the same time becoming more mindful of distinctive relational patterns or subtle enactments that might be playing out between them and their patients in sessions. In other cases, where the use of CBT interventions appeared to be problematic, therapists were encouraged to modify their approach more dramatically—in some cases actually abandoning the use of cognitive-behavioral interventions in order to focus more intensively on the use of relational interventions.

Given the individually tailored nature of the shift to AFT and the fact that this transition was often gradual and more subtle in nature, therapists were not instructed to tell their patients that they were beginning a new form of treatment. They were, however, instructed to provide their patients with rationales for employing interventions they had not used up until that point (e.g., explicitly exploring what is going on in the here and now of the therapeutic relationship). This process of providing rationales when relevant was considered to be important for purposes of maintaining a therapeutic alliance.

Study 1

The aim of Study 1 was to evaluate whether the introduction of AFT would result in changes in patient and therapist interpersonal process that are predictable on theoretical grounds, and that have been established as predictive of ultimate outcome. To assess for differences between the CBT and AFT conditions in therapist and patient interpersonal process, we employed a simplified version of the Structural Analysis of Social Behavior (SASB; Benjamin, 1974) coding system (described below). The SASB is a circumplex model that allows interpersonal behaviors to be coded along three dimensions: Interpersonal focus (focus on other, focus on self in relation to the other, or focus on self in relationship to the self), affiliation (friendliness vs. hostility), and interdependence (differentiation vs. enmeshment). The SASB model allows predictions to be made about complementary behaviors that are likely to emerge in an interpersonal interaction (Benjamin, 1974, 1994). The simplified version of the SASB we employed enabled us to code videotapes of sessions as a whole, in terms of the octant versions of Surface 1 (Focus on Self in Relation to the Other) and Surface 2 (Focus on Other) of the SASB. Below we describe the differences in interpersonal process that we hypothesized would emerge between the CBT and AFT phases.

Hypotheses

1. Given the more directive nature of CBT relative to AFT, we hypothesized that therapists in AFT would display less evidence of friendly, controlling interpersonal processes (AFT therapists < *Watching & Controlling* and *Nurturing & Protecting*) than they did in CBT training. We also anticipated a complementary pattern of patients displaying less evidence of friendly, submissive interpersonal process (patients < *Deferring & Submitting* and < *Trusting & Relying*) in AFT than in CBT.
2. Because AFT tends to be more exploratory and process-oriented in nature than CBT, and because AFT places an emphasis on encouraging patients to explore any concerns

they have about the therapy or therapeutic relationship and to express wishes or needs that they feel are not being met by the therapist, we hypothesized that therapists in AFT would be more empathic and understanding and more encouraging of patient autonomy than they were during CBT training. We hypothesized that this would be reflected in an increase in therapist empathic understanding in AFT (therapists > *Affirming & Understanding*). For patients, we hypothesized a corresponding shift in AFT toward a greater degree of patient self-exploration (AFT patients > *Disclosing & Expressing)*, and more self-assertion in the context of the therapeutic relationship (AFT patients > *Asserting & Separating)* than in CBT training.

3. Because therapeutic metacommunication (which involves therapist self-disclosure) plays an important role in AFT, we predicted more evidence of therapist self-disclosure (therapists > *Disclosing & Expressing*) in AFT than in the CBT phase of training. Based on our prior work on rupture resolution (see Safran & Muran, 2000), we predicted that greater therapist self-disclosure would also contribute to the increase in patient self-disclosure (patients > *Disclosing & Expressing*) noted above.
4. Finally, since AFT emphasizes the importance of therapists reflecting on and making constructive use of their own countertransference rather than expressing it unconsciously through their actions, we hypothesized that they would display less hostile interpersonal process (therapists < *Belittling & Blaming* and < *Ignoring & Neglecting*) in AFT than in CBT. We also hypothesized that patients would show a complementary decrease in hostile interpersonal process (patients < *Sulking & Scurrying* and < *Walling-off & Distancing*) during AFT.

For purposes of clarity we have stated our hypotheses as a series of specific shifts in therapist interpersonal stance, each followed by a specific shift in patient interpersonal stance. It is important to bear in mind, however, that in reality we anticipated that any links between shifts in therapist and patient interpersonal stance would operate in a more holistic fashion. For example, we anticipated that patients in AFT would show increased levels of self-disclosure as a function of a number of shifts in therapist process, including decreased controlling process, increases in friendly autonomy-granting process, and increased levels of therapist self-disclosure.

Method

Therapy cases used in the present study were selected from the ongoing research project described above. All patients entered into the project study met criteria for an Axis II diagnosis of either Cluster C or PD-NOS. Consistent with the multiple baseline design described earlier, therapists began weekly AFT supervision at either session 8 or session 16 to control for a time effect (e.g., change resulting from therapists becoming more experienced, or developing more experience with the particular patient in the study, or changes which might be attributable to the stage of the treatment).

To analyze the study data and make use of the multiple baseline design, six sessions were coded for each dyad. Two sessions were selected from each of the following phases of treatment: the early phase (defined as sessions 6–8), mid-phase (defined as sessions 14–16), and late phase (defined as sessions 22–24) to allow for an analysis of both within-group differences (i.e., changes attributable to training modality), and between-group differences (i.e., change attributable to the time factor) The two sessions for each phase were selected within a range of three sessions to accommodate missing data (see Figure 1). In cases where three sessions were available, two were randomly selected.

Sample. Twenty-two patients were selected for the study based on availability of video data. Of these patients, 12 were male and 10 female with a mean age of 45.13 (*SD* = 10.23). Seventeen patients included in the present study were White (77.3%), two African-American (9.1%), and three of Asian-Pacific Island descent (13.6%). Regarding primary Axis I diagnoses, 10 patients had a diagnosis of Major Depressive Disorder (45.5%), three met criteria for Dysthymia (13.6%), three met for Generalized Anxiety Disorder (13.6%), one Panic Disorder with Agoraphobia (4.5%), one Panic Disorder without Agoraphobia (4.5%), one Social Phobia (4.5%), and three had no Axis I diagnosis (13.6%). All patients in

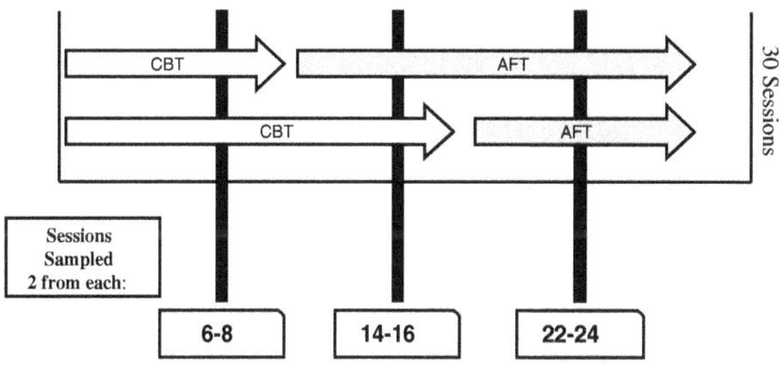

Figure 1. Study design, showing CBT and AFT (alliance-focused training) phases for the group that switched at session 8 (top row of arrows) and the group that switched at session 16 (bottom row of arrows).

the study had a Cluster C or a PD-NOS diagnosis on Axis II. Nine patients (40.9%) met criteria for PD-NOS (two with Negativistic PD, one with Depressive PD), seven for Avoidant PD (31.8%), and six for Obsessive-Compulsive PD (27.2%).

Therapists were 22 externs, who were doctoral candidates in clinical psychology. These therapists received 20 weeks of CBT didactic training before completing a 30-session CBT therapy case to assess treatment modality competency and adherence. Therapists received weekly CBT group supervision throughout treatment. Upon case completion, they were assigned a second case beginning in CBT, and switching to AFT at either session 8 or session 16 (11 in each condition). Eighteen of the therapists were female (82%) and four were male (18%), with a mean age of 29.55 (SD = 3.42). Eighteen of the therapists were White (82%), two Hispanic (9%), and two of Asian-Pacific Island descent (9%).

Measures. The SASB is typically used to code process at the level of thought units (i.e., portions of speech corresponding to one complete thought). An important advantage of this procedure is that it allows for a fine-grained analysis of turn-by-turn shifts in interpersonal process. This coding process is, however, relatively labor intensive and, consequently, researchers often restrict themselves to coding samples of process presumed to be representative (e.g., 15–30 minutes of the third session [Henry, Schacht, & Strupp, 1986]). For the present study, we reasoned that global ratings of entire sessions would be a meaningful and adequate unit of analysis. This rendered SASB coding less labor intensive, thus allowing us to code more sessions of potential interest, including multiple sessions per dyad, and to code entire sessions rather than samples of sessions. We thus traded off the potential value of a more fine-grained analysis for the gain of being able to increase the degree of representativeness of the material coded.

Using a working group of 10 graduate student coders, a number of videotapes of psychotherapy sessions were viewed, and the team gradually refined its sense of how best to code these videotapes at a global level. Ultimately the decision was made to code using the octant level of the SASB for both Surface 1 (Focus on Self) and Surface 2 (Focus on Other).

This resulted in 16 possible codes or dimensions that coders were instructed to rate on a 5-point scale borrowed from Baranackie and Crits-Christoph's (1992) QUAINT methodology, with 1 meaning not present and 5 meaning very present. Both patients and therapists were rated on each of these 16 dimensions, thus resulting in a total of 32 codes (16 for patients and 16 for therapists). Therapy sessions were broken into 5-minute intervals which served as the units of coding. Ratings for each of the 5-minute intervals were then averaged to provide a total of 32 SASB dimension ratings for each session coded. Reliability was calculated at the session level. Approximately 15 weeks of coding training were required to attain inter-rater reliability.

Data analysis. After the 15-week training period, inter-rater reliability on therapy sessions that were not included in this study was assessed using intraclass correlation coefficients (ICCs; two-way random effects model with absolute agreement on single measures). Groups were judged to be reliable after attaining ICC scores above .70 for each SASB item for five consecutive codings. Following this, pairs of raters independently coded the sessions included in this study. Mean scores of pairs were retained if the two raters were reliable with each other (ICC > .70). One session in the present study's data set received an ICC below .70 (.67). This session was coded by a third coder, and the two most reliable scores were retained for the session's composite SASB scores. The present study's average ICC score for all sessions included was .78.

We hypothesized that any differences between CBT and AFT in interpersonal process would be evident regardless of whether AFT was implemented at session 8 or 16. In other words, we hypothesized that any differences in interpersonal process would be attributable specifically to training modality rather than the number of sessions that had taken place in the treatment. Moreover, we did not anticipate any training modality × time interval (8 or 16) interaction. In other words, we did not anticipate that shifts in interpersonal process would be moderated by time interval. To control for non-independence of observations, a Generalized Estimating Equations (GEE) analysis and repeated measures design was utilized for each item of the SASB.

Because of the large number of SASB items and the associated concerns about incurring Type I error, 17 items with minimal variance were not included in the analysis. These items largely corresponded to "Focus on Self" items for therapists, and "Focus on Other" items for patients. This is not surprising—due to the nature of the therapeutic relationship, the "Focus on Self" surface is rarely coded for therapist, and the "Focus on Other" surface is rarely coded for patients (Henry et al., 1986, 1993). In addition there were a few codes that were rarely used because of their extreme degree of intensity with respect to the affiliation dimension (e.g., therapist codes of *attacking & rejecting* or *ignoring & neglecting*). This left a total of 15 items for analysis (see Table I for descriptive data).

Table I. Patient and therapist mean SASB scores across the entire treatment.

SASB item	Therapist Mean (*SD*)	Patient Mean (*SD*)
Surface 1: Focus on Other		
Freeing & Forgetting	1.00 (.00) [i]	1.00 (.00) [i]
Affirming & Understanding	2.67 (.77)	1.00 (.00) [i]
Loving & Approaching	1.07 (.13)	1.00 (.00) [i]
Nurturing & Protecting	2.18 (.84)	1.00 (.00) [i]
Watching & Controlling	1.23 (.37)	1.02 (.07)
Belittling & Blaming	1.02 (.06)	1.05 (.18)
Attacking & Rejecting	1.00 (.00) [i]	1.00 (.00) [i]
Ignoring & Neglecting	1.00 (.00) [i]	1.00 (.00) [i]
Surface 2: Focus on Self		
Asserting & Separating	1.02 (.03)	1.28 (.50)
Disclosing & Expressing	1.31 (.38)	2.93 (.80)
Joyfully Connecting	1.00 (.00) [i]	1.20 (.16)
Trusting & Relying	1.00 (.00) [i]	1.65 (.67)
Deferring & Submitting	1.00 (.00) [i]	1.20 (.34)
Sulking & Scurrying	1.00 (.00) [i]	1.12 (.21)
Protesting & Recoiling	1.00 (.00) [i]	1.00 (.00) [i]
Walling off & Distancing	1.00 (.00) [i]	1.20 (.41)

[i] Not included in analyses because of lack of variance.

Results

Several significant shifts in both therapist and patient interpersonal process emerged after CBT was augmented with AFT (see Tables II and III for statistical results). All significant differences in therapist interpersonal process (except for *Disclosing & Expressing*) emerged on the "other" or "transitive" surface of the SASB (Surface 2). All significant differences in patient interpersonal process emerged on the "self-focused" or "intransitive" surface of the SASB (Surface 1).

1. Consistent with hypothesis 1, therapists in AFT showed significantly less evidence of both *Watching & Controlling* (Cluster 5, Surface 2) and *Nurturing & Protecting* (Cluster 4, Surface 2) interpersonal process than they did in CBT training. Complementing this shift in therapist interpersonal process, patients in AFT showed significantly less evidence of *Deferring & Submitting* process (Cluster 5, Surface 1) than they did in CBT. Further, patients in AFT displayed significantly less evidence of *Trusting & Relying* (Cluster 4, Surface 1) process than they did in CBT.
2. Consistent with hypothesis 2, therapists in AFT showed more evidence of *Affirming & Understanding* (Cluster 2, Surface 2) process than they did in CBT training. Also, consistent with hypothesis 2, patients in AFT showed more evidence of *Disclosing & Expressing* (Cluster 2, Surface 2) process than they did in CBT. In addition, patients in AFT showed more evidence of self-assertion, i.e. *Asserting & Separating* (Cluster 1, Surface 1) than they did in CBT.
3. Consistent with hypothesis 3, therapists in AFT showed more evidence of *Disclosing & Expressing* (Cluster 2, Surface 1) process than they did in CBT training. As noted above, patients in AFT also demonstrated an increase in *Disclosing & Expressing* process.
4. Our findings did not support the first part of hypothesis 4: Therapists in AFT did not show less evidence of the hostile interpersonal processes of *Belittling &Blaming* (Cluster 6, Surface 2) or *Ignoring & Neglecting* (Cluster 8, Surface 2) than they did in CBT training. Consistent with the second part of hypothesis 4, however, patients in AFT did show decreases in hostile interpersonal processes of both *Walling off & Distancing* (Cluster 8, Surface 1) and *Sulking & Scurrying* (Cluster 6, Surface 1).

Consistent with our hypotheses, the majority of significant differences between training modalities in both therapist and patient interpersonal processes emerged regardless of time of implementation of

Table II. Analysis of changes in therapist SASB scores from CBT to AFT phases.

SASB item	Significant model effect	Wald x^2	CBT mean	AFT mean	95% Wald CI (grand mean) Lower	Upper
Affirming & Understanding	Training condition	169.29**	2.12	3.23	2.54	2.81
Nurturing & Protecting	Training condition	106.34**	2.78	1.59	2.04	2.31
Watching & Controlling	Training condition	47.88**	1.48	1.02	1.17	1.32
Disclosing & Expressing	Training condition	39.35**	1.09	1.51	1.24	1.36
Asserting & Separating	N/A	1.10	1.01	1.00	0.09	1.00
Loving & Approaching	N/A	1.97	1.04	1.08	1.03	1.08
Belittling & Blaming	N/A	2.90	1.03	1.00	0.99	1.03

Note. No significant findings had interaction effects. $^*p \leq .05$. $^{**}p \leq .01$.

Table III. Analysis of changes in patient SASB scores from CBT to AFT phases.

SASB item	Significant model effect	Wald x^2	CBT mean	AFT mean	Lower	Upper
Disclosing & Expressing	Training Condition	149.91**	2.27	3.52	2.78	3.01
Trusting & Relying	Training Condition	51.96**	2.07	1.21	1.52	1.76
Deferring & Submitting	Training Condition	33.60**	1.33	1.01	1.11	1.22
Sulking & Scurrying	Training Condition	21.22**	1.20	1.02	1.07	1.15
Walling Off & Distancing	Training Condition	4.16*	1.29	1.04	1.05	1.28
Joyfully Connecting	N/A	0.29	1.07	1.08	1.04	1.10
Belittling & Blaming	N/A	0.53	1.08	1.04	1.01	1.12
Watching & Controlling	N/A	1.96	1.02	1.00	0.99	1.03

SASB Item	Significant Model Effect	Wald x^2	Time of AFT	Modality	Mean	95% Wald CI	
						Lower	Upper
Asserting & Separating	Interaction (Condition × Time of Implementation)	4.46*	8	CBT	1.17	0.99	1.36
				AFT	1.38	1.13	1.63
			16	CBT	1.04	.99	1.09
				AFT	1.63	1.29	1.95

Note. No significant findings but Asserting & Separating had interaction effects. $*p \leq .05$. $**p \leq .01$.

AFT (session 8 or session 16). Moreover, there were for the most part no training modality × time interactions. The one exception was *Asserting & Separating* (Cluster 1, Surface 1). Here we found that patients whose therapists switched to AFT in session 8 displayed significantly more evidence of *Asserting & Separating* process than patients whose therapists switched to AFT in session 16.

Discussion

The majority of the findings were consistent with our hypotheses. Although we have summarized our results sequentially in a fashion that corresponds to our hypotheses, it may be useful at this point to discuss their implications as a whole (see Figures 2 & 3). Therapists in AFT were less likely to display controlling interpersonal process than they were during CBT training. They showed less evidence of both *Watching & Controlling* process (controlling interpersonal process that is neutral with respect to the affiliation dimension) and less evidence of *Nurturing & Protecting* process (controlling process that is friendly in nature). Therapists in the AFT phases were also more *Affirming & Understanding* (a friendly autonomy-granting behavior) than they were in CBT training. Finally, therapists in AFT tended to self-disclose (*Disclosing & Expressing*) more than they did in CBT training.

Patients in the AFT phases tended to display complementary shifts in interpersonal process. First, they displayed less submissive interpersonal process, both (1) less friendly-submissive process (*Trusting & Relying*) and (2) less submissive process that is neutral with respect to affiliation (*Deferring & Submitting*). They also displayed more interpersonal process of a self-disclosing nature. Finally, consistent with therapists' shift towards a less controlling and more autonomy-encouraging stance, patients in AFT displayed an increase in *Asserting & Separating* interpersonal process.

It is worth noting that some previous studies (e.g., Henry et al., 1986; Henry, Schacht, & Strupp, 1990) found that patient interpersonal process that is coded as *Asserting & Separating* on the SASB was associated with poor outcome. In this particular context, however patient movement in the direction of greater self-assertion is consistent with the goals of AFT. There are two reasons for this: First, facilitating patient self-assertion in relationship to the therapist is considered to be an important component of the rupture resolution process (Safran & Muran, 1996, 2000). Especially in the context of alliance ruptures, it is considered important for patients to have the experience of telling their therapists what they want from them and from the treatment, rather than hiding their feelings and concerns for fear of alienating their therapists. Second, it is important to bear in mind that the patients in this study were primarily cluster C patients, who tend to present with problems with excessive compliance, deference, and avoidance. For this particular subgroup of patients, movement in the direction of increased self-assertion is likely to be a desirable outcome of therapy.

The finding that this difference was even more pronounced when AFT commenced at the earlier time interval (session 8), while not anticipated, is also not surprising. It stands to reason that the process of being able to assert oneself in relationship to the

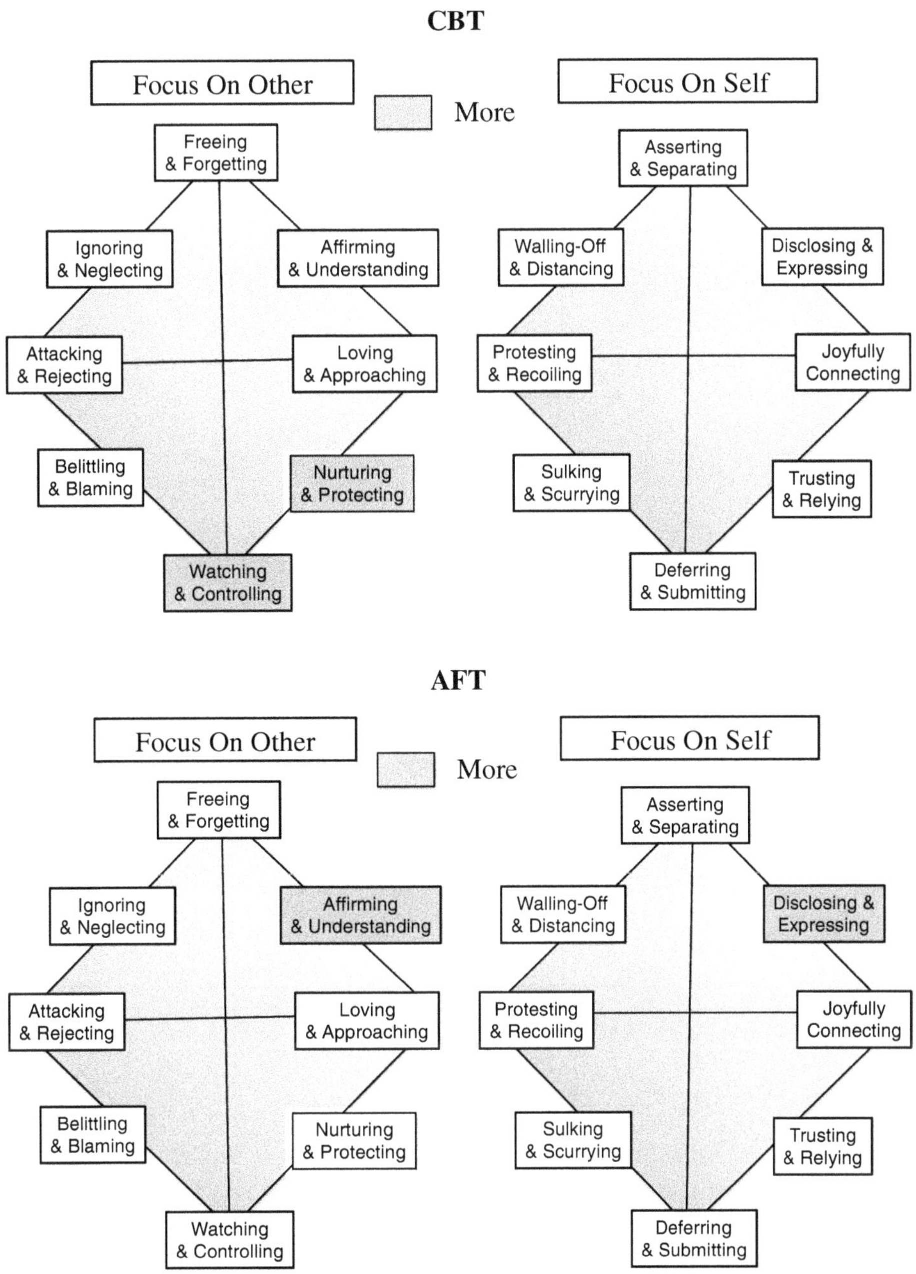

Figure 2. Therapist results on the Focus on Other and Focus on Self surfaces of the SASB. Shaded items in the top two figures were rated significantly higher in the CBT phase relative to the AFT phase of treatment. Shaded items in the bottom two figures were rated significantly higher in AFT than CBT.

therapist may take more time, especially with this population. A possible explanation is that, while therapists may be able to change their interpersonal stance in a direction that encourages greater patient self-assertion after as few as 14 sessions of AFT (i.e., when AFT begins at session 16), and while patients may be able to begin to shift their stances in corresponding fashion, additional time may help to strengthen or facilitate patients' ability to assert themselves.

As previously stated, although these changes have been described separately for simplicity, in actuality they occurred in a more holistic fashion. This type of process can be illustrated with the following clinical example. In one session in the CBT phase, the patient expressed difficulty with the previous session's homework assignment and apprehension about therapy tasks. The therapist adopted a friendly yet dominant stance, and explained the rationale for the homework and therapy tasks, indicating how they would help alleviate the patient's symptoms. The therapist's stance was coded as *Nurturing & Protecting*. The patient, who loudly sighed and expressed both doubts and anxiety with therapy tasks, ultimately complied.

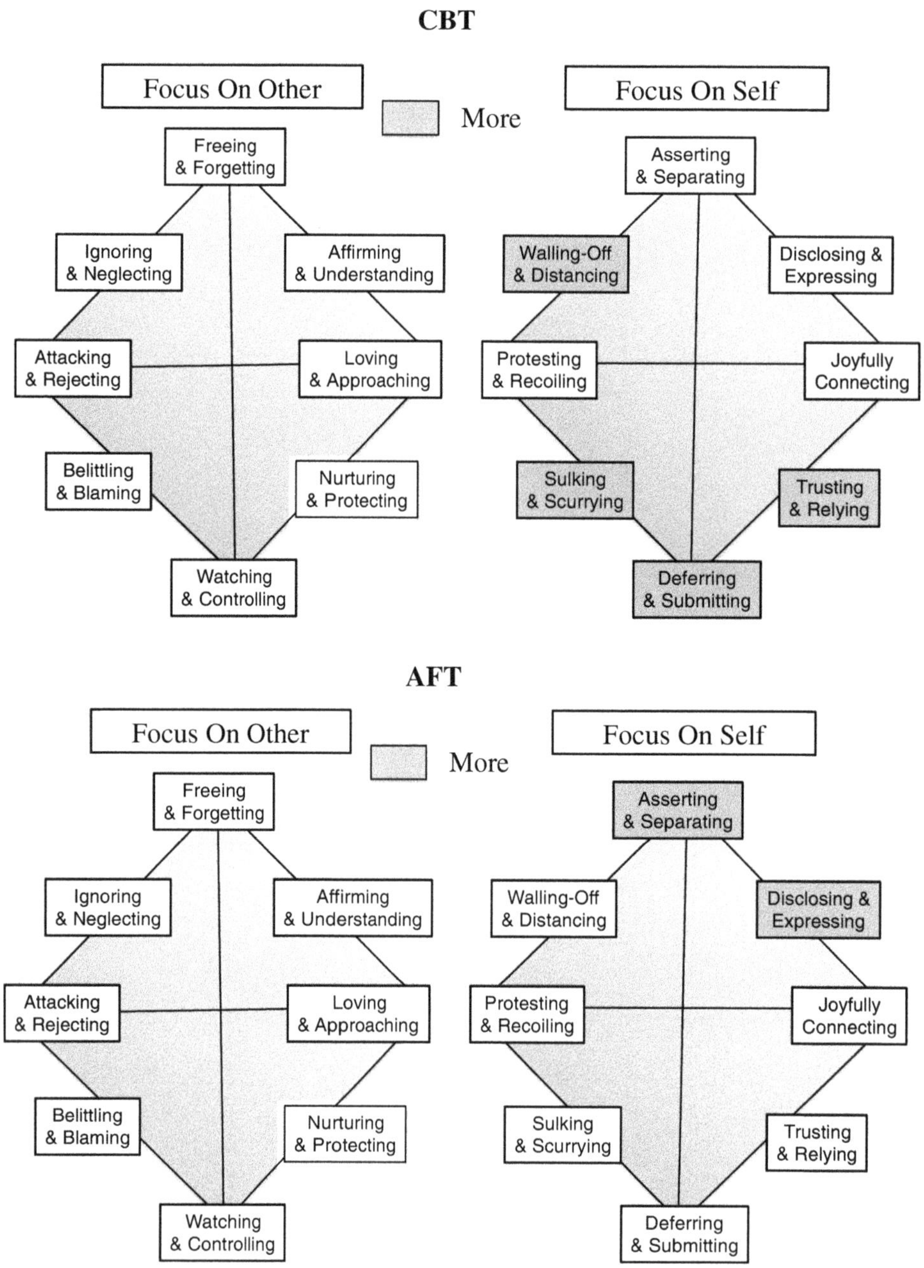

Figure 3. Patient results on the Focus on Other and Focus on Self surfaces of the SASB. Shaded items in the top two figures were rated significantly higher in the CBT phase relative to the AFT phase of treatment. Shaded items in the bottom two figures were rated significantly higher in AFT than CBT.

The patient's reluctant submission was captured through a code of *Sulking & Scurrying*.

In contrast, during the AFT phase, when the patient experienced a similar apprehension about therapy tasks, the therapist metacommunicated the following: "I'm getting the sense that this feels really difficult. Almost like I'm asking you to face what you fear the most." This utterance, coded as therapist *Disclosing & Expressing*, was not dominating of the other as in the previous example. The patient did not submit or display self-focused hostility as in the previous example, but rather disclosed her experience in a friendly and autonomous way, which was coded as *Disclosing & Expressing*: "Yeah… I don't know… it is like, I can hold onto the fact that I know that it'll be helpful, but it really is tough for me."

Finally, while we did not find that therapists in the CBT phases were more likely to display hostile interpersonal process than they did in AFT, we did find more evidence of hostile patient interpersonal process in CBT phases. However, it is possible that the therapist dominance seen in CBT (as in the clinical example above) represents a subtle form of hostility that is difficult to detect using the SASB, which requires that codes be made purely based on observable behavior. It was not uncommon for therapists in the AFT phases to retrospectively report in supervision groups that they had been experiencing subtle feelings of frustration and irritation towards their patients during CBT phases of treatment that they had not discussed extensively with their CBT supervisors. It is possible that such feelings had been leaking out in the form of subtle nonverbal manifestations of hostility which were sensed at some level by their patients, thus contributing to their tendency towards hostility (albeit of a self-focused or intransitive nature).

It is worth noting that these patients did not show the type of other-focused hostility (*Belittling & Blaming, Attacking & Rejecting, Ignoring & Rejecting* that has been found to be associated with poor outcome (e.g., Henry et al., 1986, 1990). However, both *Walling Off & Distancing* and *Sulking & Scurrying* acts are still forms of hostile patient interpersonal process that are associated with poor outcome (Henry et al., 1986, 1990). In this respect, it is important to bear in mind that the distinction between hostility coded on the *self-focused* versus the *other-focused* surfaces of the SASB is not one of intensity, but rather one of directionality. In other words, hostile interpersonal behavior coded on the other-focus surface is directed *at* the therapist, whereas hostility on the self-focused surface of the SASB tends to be less direct (examples will be given in the final discussion). Another way of looking at it is that this self-focused form of hostility is more likely to manifest as what we have termed a withdrawal rupture, in which the patient moves away from the therapist, than a confrontation rupture, in which the patient moves against the therapist. Again, this is not surprising given this particular population of patients.

Study 2

Our aim in study 2 was to explore whether AFT had any impact on therapists' tendency to engage in the type of experientially grounded self-reflection about their relationships with their patients that AFT attempts to promote. It has been theorized that therapists who have difficulty becoming aware of their own negative countertransference feelings may inadvertently engage in hostile or complex communications outside their awareness and, as a consequence, perpetuate a vicious circle of hostility and counterhostility (Safran & Muran, 2000). In addition, a failure to fully attend to one's own countertransference feelings can play an important role in keeping therapists embedded in negative transference/countertransference enactments (Safran & Muran, 2000; Safran & Reading, 2008).

As previously indicated, an important component of AFT involves training therapists to attend to their own internal experience and to accept it in a nonjudgmental fashion. This study examined the impact of AFT on therapists' capacity for experientially grounded reflection and awareness. We hypothesized that AFT would enhance therapists' capacity to explore and make constructive use of their own affectively grounded experience with their patients. Using interview data collected at time intervals that capitalized on the multiple baseline design, we tested the hypothesis that therapists would demonstrate an increase in their tendency to engage in experientially grounded reflection about their relationships with their patients after undergoing AFT, regardless of whether they began the training after session 8 (in which case they received AFT for 22 sessions) or session 16 (in which case they received AFT for 14 sessions).

This dimension of therapists' reflective style was assessed with the use of a semi-structured interview designed to probe for therapists' tendency to reflect on their own internal experience when responding to questions about their relationships with the patients they were treating in the study. This interview, known as the Therapist Relationship Interview (TRI; Safran & Muran, 2007) was then coded with the Experiencing Scale (EXP; Klein, Mathieu, Gendlin, & Kiesler, 1969). Although the EXP Scale is typically used for the purposes of coding patient material in therapy sessions, we reasoned that it could serve as a meaningful measure of the relevant therapist processes in the current context. Furthermore, in a previous study using the same measures, we found that higher levels of therapist EXP on the TRI were associated with an increased proportion of resolved to unresolved alliance ruptures over the course of treatment (Kazariants, 2011).

Method

Therapist Relationship Interviews (TRIs) were conducted with all therapists before the switch from CBT to AFT, and at the end of treatment. Specifically, therapists who switched from CBT to AFT after session 8 were interviewed at session 8, and therapists who switched from CBT to AFT after session 16 were interviewed at session 16. All therapists were also administered the TRI at termination. The aim of this design was to enable us to evaluate whether increases in EXP were attributable specifically to AFT rather than maturation effects. Increases in therapists' capacity for experientially grounded reflection were not expected to be contingent on the amount of time spent in AFT.

Sample. Due to missing TRI data for many of the cases used in Study 1 (at either termination, or at session eight or 16), only 10 of the cases from that study could be included in the present study. These 10 cases were augmented with an additional 13 cases from the larger ongoing study that had complete TRI data. The resulting sample included 13 cases that switched from CBT supervision to AFT at session 8, and 10 cases that switched at session 16. The sample included 11 men and 12 women patients (N = 23) ranging from 23 to 67 years of age (M = 48.35, SD = 13.77). Most patients identified as White (78.3%), and one as African American (4.3%), while others did not specify (17.4%). The majority of the patients met criteria for an Axis I diagnosis (78.3%), with seven meeting for major depression (30%), two for generalized anxiety disorder (8.7%), one for dysthymia (4.3%), one panic disorder with agoraphobia (4.3%), four for past episode of major depression (17%), and one eating disorder in full remission (4.3%). The remaining patients (21.7%) were not given an Axis I diagnosis. All patients in this study had a Cluster C or PD-NOS diagnosis on Axis II. Seven met for Avoidant PD (30%), eight met for Obsessive Compulsive PD (35%), and eight for Personality Disorder not otherwise specified (35%, with one Depressive PD). Therapists were 22 clinical psychology externs and one psychiatry resident. Eight of the therapists were male (34.8%) and 15 female (65.2%), and they ranged in age from 26 to 39 (M = 29.22, SD = 3.37). Most therapists identified as White (87%), two therapists identified as Hispanic/Latino (8.7%), and one as Asian or Pacific Islander (4.3%).

Measures. The *Therapist Relationship Interview* (TRI; Safran & Muran, 2007) is a semi-structured interview designed to probe for therapists' memories, thoughts, and reflections about a specific patient they have been treating. It consists of nine open-ended questions and a number of follow-up questions asking about the therapist's experience of his or her relationship with the patient. Administration time is 45–60 minutes. The objective of the TRI is to elicit a sample of therapists' verbal account of their experiences, which can then be coded for quality and style of reflection. For example, therapists are asked to choose five adjectives that reflect how they feel about the patient and to then elaborate on each adjective. Additional questions ask therapists whether there is anything about this specific patient that they find puzzling. Considerable attention in the TRI is given to moments of tension in the therapeutic relationship, and to negative process. Examples of relevant questions include: "Did you experience any moments of conflict, disagreement, misunderstanding, or tension in your relationship with your patient; or a particular time when you felt rejected, attacked, or criticized by your patient?" "Can you describe a specific time that happened?" "When did this occur? What did you do? How did your patient respond? What was your understanding of the cause? What was your initial feeling or experience of it?" "Have you ever felt your patient would end therapy?" and "Have you ever felt criticized, rejected or attacked by your patient?"

The questions in the TRI are open-ended; they give therapists the freedom to respond in a fashion that is as personal, emotionally distant, or factual as they wish. Each TRI was videotaped and administered by the program's research assistants, who were instructed to closely follow the protocol with minimal use of personal judgment. TRIs were administered by trained interviewers twice: Once at the point of the switch from CBT into AFT (either session 8 or 16), in order to assess the impact of CBT on their tendency to reflect on the work with their patients in an experientially grounded fashion, and a second time at the end of treatment (session 30), to determine whether their tendency to reflect on the therapeutic relationship increased after undergoing AFT.

The Experiencing Scale (EXP; Klein, Mathieu-Coughlan, & Kiesler, 1986) is an observer rated coding system that assesses the extent to which an individual makes sense of events by reflecting on internal experience. EXP measures the level to which one attends to feelings as they emerge and integrates these feelings into a personally involved appraisal of external events. EXP assesses the quality of an individual's verbalizations along a 7-point scale. On the lower end of the scale, the person's narratives focus on the description of other people or events in which they themselves are not personally involved. At the higher end of the EXP scale, the speaker struggles to elaborate on his or her implicit, felt sense of what is going on in a given event. The quality of the narrative is described in a personally involved fashion with attention placed on feelings in order to expand the speaker's understanding of the personal meaning of the event. Coders give an EXP rating for each of the interviewee's speech turns. For this study, the mode and the peak EXP ratings for each interview were entered into the analyses.

The coders consisted of 10 Master's level psychology graduate students who attended weekly didactic trainings over 1 year led by one of the co-authors. Experiencing ratings have been shown to be equivalent whether determined by audio recordings or printed transcriptions (Mathieu-Coughlan & Klein, 1984). Consistent with the guidelines contained in

Klein et al's. (1969) training manual, coders were trained until they reached reliability (ICC > .70) with the gold standard audio recordings across 20 segments. Once reliability was achieved using the gold standard as provided by the manual, coders then rated transcripts of TRIs that were not included in this study until the coders reached an ICC of .70 (two-way random effects model with consistency agreement on average measures) three times in a row. At that point, coders began coding the study data. Five coders independently coded each interview, and their ratings were averaged to form the mode and peak scores for each case.

Results

We used a mixed-design ANOVA in which the within-groups factor represented changes in therapists' EXP levels on the TRI following AFT (regardless of whether they began AFT after sessions 8 or 16), and the between-groups factor represented time interval (i.e., whether AFT began after session 8 or 16). The means and standard deviations are presented in Table IV. Consistent with our hypothesis, we found a significant main effect for training modality on both mode and peak EXP scores. Mode EXP scores were significantly higher for therapists administered TRIs after AFT phases of training than after CBT phases of training, regardless of whether AFT began after session 8 or 16, $F(1,21) = 5.015$, $p = .036$. The same finding emerged for EXP peak scores for TRI interviews after the AFT phase compared to peak EXP scores after the CBT phase, $F(1,21) = 4.613$, $p = .044$. As predicted, there were no significant main effects for time interval on either EXP mode ($F(1,21) = .008$, $p = .93$) or peak ($F(1,21) = 1.832$, $p = .19$), and no training modality by time interval interaction on either EXP mode ($F(1,21) = 1.73$, $p = .203$) or peak ($F(1,21) = .018$, $p = .895$). Results were consistent with the hypothesis that after receiving AFT, therapists would demonstrate a greater tendency during TRI interviews to reflect on their relationships with their patients in a personally involved, experientially grounded fashion than they did after receiving CBT training. The absence of a significant main effect for time interval (session 8 or 16) on EXP mode or peak suggests that therapists' increase in EXP was not likely to be simply a function of (1) receiving more supervision of any type or (2) working with and becoming familiar with a specific patient. The absence of a significant interaction between training modality and time interval for either mode or peak EXP suggests that therapists who switched at session 8 and received 22 sessions of AFT did not have significantly higher mode or peak EXP scores at termination than therapists who switched at session 16 and received only 14 sessions of AFT.

Discussion

This study investigated the impact of alliance-focused training on therapists' tendency to reflect on their relationships with their patients in a personally involved and experientially grounded fashion. We hypothesized that following alliance-focused training, therapists would be more likely to respond to an interview protocol designed to probe for their reflections about their therapeutic relationships with higher levels of EXP than they would following CBT training (and before commencing AFT). Results were consistent with our hypotheses. After receiving AFT therapists were more inclined to explore and share their own personal feelings and reactions to their patients with interviewers than they were following CBT training. In other words, they showed a greater tendency to reflect on their relationships with their patients in a fashion that made reference to their own felt experience in an attempt to make sense of these relationships.

For example, during the Therapist Relationship Interview (TRI) administered at the end of the CBT phase, when one therapist in this sample was asked, "Is there anything that puzzles you or that you find challenging in your work with your patient?" she gave the following response: "... it's been hard to pin down what she [the patient] wants to get out of the entire endeavor. It's clear that she was in a great deal of pain when she came in, and she would like for that pain to be eased, but she has had real difficulty conceptualizing what she wants to be happening."

Table IV. Mean EXP mode and peak scores (standard deviations)

	EXP mode		EXP peak	
Condition	Interview 1 (post CBT)	Interview 2 (post AFT)	Interview 1 (post CBT)	Interview 2 (post AFT)
Switch at 8 (n = 13)	2.18 (.27)	2.50 (.34)	3.30 (.41)	3.53 (.58)
Switch at 16 (n = 10)	2.28 (.35)	2.37 (.44)	3.08 (.40)	3.35 (.38)
Total (N = 23)	2.22 (.31)	2.44 (.39)	3.20 (.41)	3.45 (.50)

The therapist's response was coded as level two on the EXP scale because personal feelings, thoughts and reflections were not referred to directly, but the beginning of a personal perspective on therapeutic events was beginning to emerge.

During the second TRI, which occurred after AFT, the same therapist responded to the question above by explicitly disclosing her own inner thoughts and feelings, "I guess initially I felt that it was hard to create a comfortable place for Susan (a pseudonym for the patient) to share and disclose with me and I guess I felt a little hesitant to force disclosure … I guess I felt like it was hard to be flexible and I felt that Susan needed a lot of flexibility on my part. I also felt like there were times in our work together when I had no idea what was going to happen when Susan came in …." After AFT the therapist's remarks were coded at level four on the EXP scale: The "quality of involvement or 'set' shifts to the speaker's attention to the subjective felt flow of experience as referent, rather than events or abstractions" (Klein et al., 1969, p. 23).

The absence of significant main effects for time interval suggests that our findings are not likely to be solely attributable to maturation effects. The absence of a significant interaction between training modality and time interval suggests that receiving an additional eight sessions of AFT did not have an incremental effect on therapists' tendency towards experientially grounded reflection over and above the first 8 sessions of AFT. Although the interaction between training interval and time interval was not significant, a graphical representation of the interaction does suggest a trend towards higher EXP levels for those therapists who received more alliance-focused training, and it is possible that a larger sample with more statistical power would have yielded a significant interaction. Certain features of the design also precluded our exploration of other types of training modality × time interactions. For example, the absence of a pure CBT training modality with TRI interviews administered at sessions 8, 16 and at termination makes it impossible to examine whether therapist EXP levels on the TRI increase over time as a result of CBT training in and of itself. To summarize, the present study provides preliminary evidence that alliance-focused training has the capacity to enhance a style of therapist reflection hypothesized to be advantageous in the context of therapeutic interactions that are vulnerable to negative therapeutic process or potentially problematic transference-countertransference enactments, and that has been found to be related to the process of alliance rupture resolution (Kazariants, 2011).

General Discussion and Conclusion

Taken together, the findings of studies 1 and 2 provide intriguing preliminary evidence regarding the potential of alliance-focused training to have a positive impact on both in-session interpersonal process, and on therapists' capacity to reflect on the therapeutic relationship in a fashion that incorporates their own felt experience. One possible methodological limitation worth considering is the question of whether SASB and EXP coders were able to distinguish between therapeutic modalities (and the TRIs associated with them) and if so whether this might have biased their coding. While we cannot rule out the possibility that they were able to distinguish between CBT versus AFT material, they were blind to study hypotheses.

A second question concerns the degree of variability in the ways therapists implemented the AFT aspects of treatment. Given the fact that supervisors worked collaboratively with trainees to tailor the timing and degree of implementation of AFT-related interventions, our general sense is that there was considerable variability in this respect. While the finding of modality-specific differences in SASB codes provide us with a global picture of how therapists intervened during AFT phases relative to CBT phases, a more detailed picture of the various ways that therapists blended CBT and AFT interventions will need to be obtained through the examination of treatment adherence ratings that assess the extent to which different therapists incorporated various blends of CBT and AFT interventions into their treatments.

And finally, further research will be essential to evaluate whether differences in SASB and EXP ratings are related to ultimate outcome. As we indicated earlier, since all patients received some combination of CBT and AFT, we did not expect to find between-group differences in treatment outcome. It will, however, be critical to examine whether differences in treatment process are meaningfully related to one another and predictive of treatment outcome. At the present time, we continue to enter more patients and therapists into the larger, ongoing research project, and will be in the position to examine these questions in the future.

Funding

The research was supported by a grant from the National Institute for Mental Health [MH071768] (Principal Investigator: J. Christopher Muran).

References

Anderson, T., Knobloch-Fedders, L. M., Stiles, W. B., Ordonez, T., & Heckman, B. D. (2012). The power of subtle hostility in psychotherapy: A speech acts analysis. *Psychotherapy Research, 22,* 348–362. doi:10.1080/10503307.2012.658097

Aron, L. (1996). *A meeting of minds: Mutuality in psychoanalysis.* Hillsdale, NJ: Analytic Press.

Baldwin, S. A., Wampold, B. E., & Imel, Z. E. (2007). Untangling the alliance-outcome correlation: Exploring the relative importance of therapist and patient variability in the alliance. *Journal of Consulting and Clinical Psychology, 75,* 842–852. doi:10.1037/0022-006X.75.6.842

Baranackie, K., & Crits-Cristoph, P. (1992). *The Quantitative Assessment of Interpersonal Themes (QUAINT) Rater Manual.* Unpublished manuscript.

Beck, A. T., Freeman, A. M., & Associates. (1990). *Cognitive therapy of personality disorders.* New York: Guilford Press.

Bein, E., Anderson, T., Strupp, H., Henry, W. P., Schacht, T. E., Binder, J., & Butler, S. (2000). The effects of training in Time-Limited Dynamic Psychotherapy: Changes in therapeutic outcome. *Psychotherapy Research, 10,* 119–132. doi:10.1080/713663669

Benjamin, J. (1990). An outline of intersubjectivity: The development of recognition. *Psychoanalytic Psychology 7* (Suppl.), 33–46. doi:10.1037/h0085258

Benjamin, L. S. (1974). Structural analysis of social behavior. *Psychological Review, 81,* 392–425. doi:10.1037/h0037024

Benjamin, L. S. (1994). SASB: A bridge between personality theory and clinical psychology. *Psychological Inquiry,* 5, 273–316. doi:10.1207/s15327965pli0504_1

Binder, J. L., & Strupp, H. H. (1997). "Negative process": A recurrently discovered and underestimated facet of therapeutic process and outcome in the individual psychotherapy of adults. *Clinical Psychology: Science and Practice, 4,* 121–139. doi:10.1111/j.1468-2850.1997.tb00105.x

Bromberg, P. (1998). *Standing in the spaces: Essays on clinical process, trauma, and dissociation.* Hillsdale, NJ: Analytic Press.

Crits-Christoph, P.,Gibbons, M. B. C.,Crits-Christoph, K., Narducci, J.,Schamberger, M., &Gallop, R. (2006). Can therapists be trained to improve their alliances? A preliminary study of alliance-fostering psychotherapy. *Psychotherapy Research, 16,* 268–281. doi:10.1080/10503300500268557

Eubanks-Carter, C., Muran, J. C., & Safran, J. D. (2010). Alliance ruptures and resolution. In J. C. Muran & J. P. Barber (Eds.), *The therapeutic alliance: An evidence-based approach to practice and training* (pp. 74–94). New York, NY: Guilford Press.

Goldfried, M. R. (1994). Considerations in developing a core assessment battery. In H. H. Strupp, L. M. Horowitz, & M. J. Lambert (Eds.), *Measuring patient changes* (pp. 99–116). Washington DC: American Psychological Association.

Harris, A. E. (2011). The relational tradition: Landscape and canon. *Journal of the American Psychoanalytic Association, 59,* 701–735. doi:10.1177/0003065111416655

Henry, W. P., Schacht, T. E., & Strupp, H. H. (1986). Structural analysis of social behavior: Application to a study of interpersonal process in differential psychotherapeutic outcome. *Journal of Counseling and Clinical Psychology, 54,* 27–31. doi:10.1037/0022-006X.54.1.27

Henry, W. P., Schacht, T. E., & Strupp, H. H. (1990). Patient and therapist introject, interpersonal process, and differential psychotherapy outcome. *Journal of Consulting and Clinical Psychology, 58,* 768–77. doi:10.1037/0022-006X.58.6.768

Henry, W. P., Strupp, H. H., Butler, S. F., Schacht, T. E., & Binder, J. L. (1993). Effects of training in time-limited dynamic psychotherapy: Changes in therapist behavior. *Journal of Consulting and Clinical Psychology, 61,* 434–440. doi:10.1037/0022-006X.61.3.434

Horvath, A. O., Del Re, A. C., Flückiger, C., & Symonds, D. (2011). Alliance in individual psychotherapy. *Psychotherapy, 48,* 9–16. doi:10.1037/a0022186

Kazariants, G. (2011). *The relationship between therapist capacity for experientially grounded reflection on the therapeutic relationship and alliance rupture resolution.* ProQuest, UMI Dissertation Publishing.

Kiesler, D. J. (1996). *Contemporary interpersonal theory and research: Personality, psychopathology and psychotherapy.* New York: John Wiley & Sons.

Klein, M. H., Mathieu, P. L., Gendlin, E. T., & Kiesler, D. J. (1969). *The experiencing scale: A research and training manual.* Madison: University of Wisconsin Extension Bureau of Audio-visual Instruction.

Klein, M. H., Mathieu-Coughlan, P., & Kiesler, D. J. (1986). The Experiencing Scales. In W. P. Pinsof & L. S. Greenberg (Eds.), *The psychotherapeutic process: A research handbook* (pp. 21–71). New York, NY: Guilford Press.

Luborsky, L., Rosenthal, R., Diguer, L., Andrusyna, T. P., Berman, J. S., Levitt, J. T., Seligman, D. A., & Krause, E. D. (2002). The Dodo bird verdict is alive and well - mostly. *Clinical Psychology: Science and Practice, 9,* 2–12. doi:10.1093/clipsy/9.1.2

Mathieu-Coughlan, P., & Klein, M. H. (1984). Experiential psychotherapy: Key events in client-therapist interaction. In L. N. Rice & L. S. Greenberg, (Eds.), *Patterns of change.* New York: Guilford Press.

Mitchell, S. A. (1988). *Relational concepts in psychoanalysis.* Cambridge, MA: Harvard University Press.

Muran, J. C. (2002). A relational approach to understanding change: Plurality and contextualism in a psychotherapy research program. *Psychotherapy Research, 12,* 113–138.

Muran, J. C., Safran, J. D., & Eubanks-Carter, C. (2010). Developing therapist abilities to negotiate alliance rupture. In J. C. Muran & J. P. Barber (Eds), *The therapeutic alliance: An evidence-based guide to practice* (pp. 320–340). New York: Guilford Press.

Muran, J. C., Safran, J. D., Samstag, L., & Winston, A. (2005). Evaluating an alliance-focused treatment for personality disorders. *Psychotherapy, 42,* 512–531. doi:10.1037/0033-3204.42.4.532

Persons, J. B., & Silberschatz, G. (1998). Are results of randomized controlled trials useful to psychotherapists? *Journal of Consulting and Clinical Psychology, 66,* 126–135. doi:10.1037/0022-006X.66.1.126

Pizer, S. A. (1998). *Building bridges: The negotiation of paradox in psychoanalysis.* Hillsdale, NJ: Analytic Press.

Safran, J. D. (2002). Brief relational psychoanalytic treatment. *Psychoanalytic Dialogues, 12,* 171–195. doi:10.1080/10481881209348661

Safran, J. D. (2012). *Psychoanalysis and psychoanalytic therapies.* Washington DC: American Psychological Association.

Safran, J. D., & Muran, J. C. (1996). The resolution of ruptures in the therapeutic alliance. *Journal of Consulting and Clinical Psychology, 64,* 447–458. doi:10.1037/0022-006X.64.3.447

Safran, J. D., & Muran, J. C. (2000). *Negotiating the therapeutic alliance: A relational treatment guide.* New York: Guilford Press.

Safran, J. D., & Muran, J. C. (2006a). Has the concept of the alliance outlived its usefulness? *Psychotherapy, 43,* 286–291. doi:10.1037/0033-3204.43.3.286

Safran, J. D., & Muran, J. C. (2006b). *Resolving therapeutic impasses.* CustomFlix. http://www.amazon.com.

Safran, J. D., & Muran, J. C. (2007). *Therapist Relational Interview: Administration manual.* Unpublished manuscript.

Safran, J. D., & Reading, R. (2008). Mindfulness, metacommunication and and affect regulation in psychoanalytic treatment. In S. Hick & T. Bien (Eds.), *Mindfulness and the therapeutic relationship* (pp. 112–140). New York, NY: Guilford.

Safran, J. D., Muran, J. C., Samstag, L., & Stevens, C. (2001). Repairing therapeutic alliance ruptures. *Psychotherapy*, *38*, 406–412. doi:10.1037/0033-3204.38.4.406

Safran, J. D., Muran, J. C., Samstag, L. W., & Winston, A. (2005). Evaluating an alliance focused treatment for potential treatment failures. *Psychotherapy*, *42*, 512–531.

Safran, J. D., Muran, J. C., & Eubanks-Carter, C. (2011). Repairing alliance ruptures. *Psychotherapy*, *48*, 80–87. doi:10.1037/a0022140

Safran, J. D., Muran, J. C., Stevens, C., & Rothman, M. (2008). A relational approach to supervision: Addressing ruptures in the alliance. In C. A. Falender & E. P. Shafranske (Eds.), *Casebook for clinical supervision: A competency-based approach* (pp. 137–157). Washington DC: APA Books.

Stern, D. B. (1998). *Unformulated experience: From dissociation to imagination in psychoanalysis*. Hillsdale, NJ: Analytic Press.

Stiles, W. B., Honos-Webb, L., & Surko, M. (1998). Responsiveness in psychotherapy. *Clinical Psychology: Science and Practice*, *5*, 439–458. doi:10.1111/j.1468-2850.1998.tb00166.x

Strupp, H. (1980). Success and failure in time-limited psychotherapy. *Archives of General Psychiatry*, *37*, 947–954. doi:10.1001/archpsyc.1980.01780210105011

Strupp, H. (1993). The Vanderbilt psychotherapy studies: synopsis. *Journal of Consulting and Clinical Psychology*, *61*, 431–433. doi:10.1037/0022-006X.61.3.431

Strupp, H. H., & Hadley, S. W. (1979). Specific vs. nonspecific factors in psychotherapy: Controlled study of outcome. *Archives of General Psychiatry*, *36*, 1125–1136. doi:10.1001/archpsyc.1979.01780100095009

Turner, A. E., & Muran, J. C. (1992). *Cognitive-behavioral therapy for personality disorders: A treatment manual.* San Diego, CA: Social & Behavioral Documents.

Turner, A. E., Muran, J. C., & Ochoa, E. (2004). *Cognitive-behavioral therapy for personality disorders: A treatment manual (Updated Version)*. New York: Beth Israel Medical Center.

Wampold, B. E. (2001). *The great psychotherapy debate: Model, methods, and findings*. Mahwah, NJ: Lawrence Erlbaum.

Wampold, B., Mondin, G. W., Moody, M., Stich, F., Benson, K., & Ahn, H. (1997). *Psychological Bulletin*, *122*, 203–215. doi:10.1037/0033-2909.122.3.203

To be or not to be immediate with clients: The use and perceived effects of immediacy in psychodynamic/interpersonal psychotherapy

CLARA E. HILL[1], CHARLES J. GELSO[1], HAROLD CHUI[1], PATRICIA T. SPANGLER[1], ANN HUMMEL[1], TERESA HUANG[1], JOHN JACKSON[1], RUSSELL A. JONES[2], BEATRIZ PALMA[1], AVANTIKA BHATIA[1], SHUDARSHANA GUPTA[1], STACIE C. AIN[1], BETH KLINGAMAN[2], ROBERT H. LIM[2], JINGQING LIU[1], KAYI HUI[2], MATTHEW M. JEZZI[2], & JOSEPH R. MILES[2]

[1]*Psychology Department, University of Maryland, College Park, MD, USA & [2]College of Education, University of Maryland, College Park, MD, USA*

Abstract

The purpose of this study was to investigate the use and perceived effects of immediacy in 16 cases of open-ended psychodynamic psychotherapy. Of 234 immediacy events, most were initiated by therapists and involved exploration of unexpressed or covert feelings. Immediacy occurred during approximately 5% of time in therapy. Clients indicated in post-therapy interviews that they remembered and profited from immediacy, with the most typical observed consequences being clients expressing feelings about the therapist/therapy and opening up/gaining insight. Amount of immediacy was associated with therapists' but not clients' ratings of session process and outcome. Therapists focused more on feelings and less on ruptures, and initiated immediacy more often with fearfully than with securely attached clients. Implications for practice, training, and research are offered.

Regardless of theoretical orientation, most therapists and researchers agree about the importance of the therapeutic relationship for the process and outcome of psychotherapy (see Gelso & Samstag, 2008; Horvath, Del Re, Fluckiger, & Symonds, 2011; Martin, Garske, & Davis, 2000; Norcross & Wampold, 2011). There is still much to be learned, however, about how the therapeutic relationship unfolds over time, how different events in the relationship contribute to process and outcome, and how client and therapist factors contribute to the therapeutic relationship.

In the present study we focused on the role of immediacy as a way of establishing, maintaining, and repairing the therapeutic relationship. We defined immediacy as a discussion of the therapeutic relationship by both the therapist and client in the here-and-now, involving more than social chitchat (e.g., "It's nice to see you."). Our definition is similar to that for therapeutic immediacy used by Kuutmann and Hilsenroth (2011): "any discussion within the therapy session about the relationship between therapist and patient that occurs in the here-and-now, as well as any processing of what occurs in the here-and-now patient-therapist interaction." Immediacy is also similar to metacommunication (Kiesler, 1988), or disclosing to the client about perceptions of and reactions to client actions. Kiesler distinguished metacommunication from disclosures of historical or factual information because metacommunications relate specifically to the therapist's experience of the client. Kiesler noted that metacommunication is helpful because it is different from the way that others typically respond to the client. Other phrases or descriptions that have been used for immediacy are relational events, processing the therapeutic relationship, discussions about the here-and-now in the here-and-now, disclosures about the therapeutic relationship, self-involving self-disclosures, in vivo work, and present-focused work.

One key relational construct that is at times conflated with immediacy is that of transference interpretation. Although there may be considerable overlap between the two concepts, they can be theoretically differentiated. Transference interpretations are typically used to make a connection between the client's reactions to the therapist and experiences in earlier significant relationships. In this sense, transference may be seen as a carryover or displacement from earlier significant relationships into the present therapeutic relationship (Gelso & Bhatia, 2012). Immediacy, on the other hand, may or may not be transferential, as it may include all here-and-now interactions about the therapeutic relationship, including, for example, interactions pertaining to the working alliance and the real or personal relationship.

Research on the Frequency and Consequences of Immediacy

Research suggests that immediacy varies widely across cases. For example, in a study of eight cases of brief psychotherapy conducted by experienced therapists from across a range of orientations, Hill et al. (1988) found that only 1% of therapist interventions involved "disclosure" (a category that included both disclosure of historical material and immediacy). In contrast, immediacy was used much more frequently in three recent case studies, all conducted by experienced therapists who had strong interpersonal orientations. Kasper, Hill, and Kivlighan (2008) coded 34% of the therapist's and 37% of the client's speaking turns as immediacy in a 12-session case. In Hill et al.'s (2008) 17-session case study, 5% of the client's speech and 12% of the therapist's speech were coded as immediacy. Finally, in an investigation of a 4-year case of psychodynamic psychotherapy (Mayotte-Blum et al., 2012), 25% of all speech was coded as immediacy. Thus, immediacy seems to range from less than 1% to about 35% of time in cases, with more frequent use by interpersonally and psychodynamically oriented therapists.

Perceived consequences of immediacy were studied intensively in the three case studies. In their quantitative and qualitative analyses, Kasper et al. (2008) suggested that the client felt validated and cared for when the therapist expressed positive feelings toward her. Immediacy also seemed to help the therapist and client negotiate the boundaries of their relationship, provide a corrective relational experience for the client, and lower the client's defenses. The client sometimes, however, was confused by the immediacy and felt pressured to respond. In their qualitative analyses of immediacy events with the highest depth ratings, Hill et al. (2008) found that immediacy events seemed to help the therapist and client negotiate their relationship, help the client express immediate feelings to the therapist, and provide the client with corrective relational experiences. Finally, Mayotte-Blum et al. (2012), in their qualitative analysis of the 11 most salient immediacy events in one case, found that immediacy seemed to facilitate the client's ability to experience painful feelings, provide a corrective relational experience for the client, allow the therapist to show care and concern for the client, and allow the client to communicate positive feelings such as gratitude to the therapist. Across the three case studies, then, therapist immediacy consistently was judged as facilitating client emotional awareness or insight, helping to resolve problems as they arose in the therapeutic relationship, facilitating a correlative relational experience, and providing a model for how clients could resolve relationship problems outside therapy. Although there were occasional negative consequences, none were consistent across the three clients.

These three cases provide strong evidence of the potential therapeutic impact of immediacy. Further research is needed, however, given that all three therapists were studied specifically because they were reputed to be master therapists who used immediacy extensively. Perhaps immediacy only has such positive effects if used by master therapists.

Client Variables that Might Influence the Frequency and Consequences of Immediacy

In addition, it appears that immediacy is more frequent and helpful with some clients than others. In Kuutmann and Hilsenroth's (2011) examination of 76 cases of short-term psychodynamic psychotherapy, therapeutic immediacy was used more often with clients who had personality pathology, distressing interpersonal problems, a cold/distant interpersonal style, and low self-esteem.

One client characteristic that has been related to therapy process and outcome and that may be relevant to the use and consequences of immediacy is attachment style (e.g., Levy, Ellison, Scott, & Bernecker, 2011; Mikulincer, Shaver, Cassidy, & Berant, 2009). Specifically, Mallinckrodt (2010) suggested that successful therapists moderate "therapeutic distance" (i.e., "the level of transparency and disclosure in the psychotherapy relationship from both client and therapist, together with the immediacy, intimacy, and emotional intensity of a session," p. 266), depending on clients' attachment styles and timing in therapy. With a client who has an insecure, avoidant attachment style, the therapist might initially gratify the client's need for distance in the relationship, but increasingly use immediacy as the work progresses in order to decrease therapeutic distance. With a client who has an insecure, anxious style, in contrast, the therapist might initially gratify the client's need for closeness, but gradually begin to use immediacy to increase therapeutic distance. Mallinckrodt's theorizing thus suggests that client attachment is an important characteristic to study in relation to therapists' use of immediacy.

Purposes of the Present Study

Our overall purpose was to provide a description of immediacy events so that we can have a better idea of what these events involve in psychodynamic/interpersonal psychotherapy as conducted by advanced doctoral student therapists. More specifically, our first set of objectives involved examining the frequency and duration of immediacy events. We operationalized *amount* as the number of immediacy events as well as the amount of time spent on immediacy. We were also interested in whether the therapist or client typically initiated the immediacy. In addition, we investigated whether there were different types of immediacy as suggested by Kasper et al. (2008) and Hill et al. (2008). We used the four *types* of immediacy identified in the Kasper et al. and Hill et al. case studies: (a) negotiation of the tasks and goals of therapy, (b) exploration of unexpressed feelings or making the covert overt, (c) drawing parallels between other relationships and the therapy relationship, and (d) attempts to repair ruptures by talking about what is going on between the therapist and client. Finally, we also judged *quality* by having trained judges evaluate the appropriateness, timing, and relevance of the immediacy within the context of the case.

Our second set of objectives involved examining the perceived consequences of therapeutic immediacy. To do this, we trained judges to observe consequences evidenced in sessions. In addition, we investigated client descriptions during post-therapy interviews of their experiences of immediacy. Furthermore, although not as clearly linked to consequences of immediacy (other variables could easily have influenced the results), we also examined the association between immediacy and client and therapist evaluations of session process and outcome (i.e., perceptions of session quality, the working alliance, and the real relationship), as well as the association between immediacy and overall treatment outcome in terms of changes in interpersonal functioning.

Our third and final set of objectives in the current study involved examining the use of therapeutic immediacy with different types of clients. Given the importance of attachment in relation to client process and outcome (e.g., Levy, 2011; Mikulincer et al., 2009), and the potential of immediacy as a tool for modulating therapeutic distance (Mallinckrodt, 2010), we were specifically interested in examining whether amount, type, and quality of immediacy differed depending on the client's level of attachment security and the client's attachment to the therapist.

Many people have written about the value of case studies for the exploration of complex phenomena (e.g., Dattilio, Edwards, & Fishman, 2010; Stiles, 2007, 2009). The previously cited studies (Hill et al., 2008; Kasper et al., 2008; Mayotte-Blum et al., 2012) successfully used case studies to investigate immediacy, so this method seemed like a valuable approach to capture the richness of the phenomenon within the context of the entire case. In the present study, however, we wanted to go beyond using single cases so that we could examine consistencies across cases and differences among cases. Furthermore, in the previous studies, researchers specifically selected cases because they were likely to have or did have considerable immediacy. In contrast, in this study, we did not select cases on the basis of proclivity toward using immediacy, although doctoral student therapists received some training in immediacy.

Like the previous studies on immediacy (Hill et al., 2008; Kasper et al., 2008; Mayotte-Blum et al., 2012), we used a mixed quantitative-qualitative method. Because the judgments of immediacy required considerable clinical expertise, we required that all judges were at least advanced doctoral students who had participated in training on immediacy. Rather than requiring judges to code independently into predetermined categories, we relied on the qualitative method of consensus among judges to arrive at all judgments. We wanted judges to use their clinical expertise to arrive at judgments, under the assumption that considerable discussion and exposure to multiple viewpoints result in more trustworthy judgments (see also Hill, 2012).

Method

Data Set

In this study, we analyzed 16 cases conducted within a psychology department clinic that provided low-fee individual open-ended psychotherapy to community clients. Because we wanted to study cases in which clients had an opportunity to develop secure attachments with their therapists, and because previous researchers suggest that clients have had a reasonable opportunity to do so by session 8 (Mallinckrodt, Porter, & Kivlighan, 2005), we included only those cases that had at least eight sessions past intake (some of the cases were planned terminations and some were dropouts, but all had terminated from the psychotherapy). Data were collected over a 3-year period. The 16 cases used for this study represented all of the completed cases that had met for at least eight sessions available in the clinic at the time of the study. Number of sessions per case ranged from 10 to 59 ($M = 24.44$, $SD = 12.57$).

Participants

Clients. Sixteen clients (eight female, eight male; 11 European American, three Hispanic American, one African American, one Asian American), ranging in age from 21 to 60 years ($M = 34.56$, $SD = 12.77$) at intake, participated in the study. Presenting problems (some clients described more than one) described during screening included relationship concerns (11 clients), anxiety or depression (five clients), career concerns (one client), coming out concerns (one client), and immigration issues (one client). No formal diagnoses were determined.

Therapists. The therapists were nine counseling psychology doctoral students (five female, four male; five European Americans, one Asian American, one Asian international, one Chilean international, one African American) ranging in age from 26 to 50 years ($M = 31.78$, $SD = 7.46$). Therapists were in a doctoral program that emphasized learning all the different theoretical orientations and developing their own personal orientation. All therapists had completed at least two practica prior to working in the clinic, and all espoused a psychodynamic/interpersonal orientation at least moderately. Therapists engaged in weekly individual supervision and biweekly group supervision with experienced, psychodynamically oriented supervisors. Therapists worked in the clinic for 1 to 3 years, and each conducted therapy with one to three of the clients in this study.

Judges. Judges were two professors (one female, one male; both European American) and 15 doctoral students (10 female, five male; six European American, five Asian international, two Asian American, one African American, one Chilean international), all of whom had a psychodynamic and interpersonal orientation. All but two judges were also therapists or supervisors in this study. In terms of biases, judges all valued immediacy at least moderately but they ranged considerably in their comfort with using it.

Measures

The **Inventory of Interpersonal Problems–32** (IIP; Barkham, Hardy, & Startup, 1996) is a widely-used 32-item self-report instrument of interpersonal distress (shortened from the original 127-item measure developed by Horowitz, Rosenberg, Baer, Ureno, & Villasenor, 1988). Items are scored on a 5-point Likert scale from 0 (*not at all*) to 4 (*extremely*). We used the total score (the average of all items), where high scores indicate more distressed interpersonal functioning. Adequate validity and reliability have been reported for this widely used measure (Barkham et al., 1996). For the present sample, the internal consistency (alpha) for the IIP completed after session 8 was .93.

The **Experiences in Close Relationships Scale** (ECR; Brennan, Clark, & Shaver, 1998) assesses client attachment prior to the start of treatment. The ECR is a 36-item measure that asks respondents about their relationships in general. It has two subscales: Anxiety and Avoidance, and all items are rated on a 7-point Likert scale from 1 (*disagree strongly*) to 7 (*agree strongly*). The Avoidance subscale of the ECR assesses respondents' discomfort with emotional closeness and interdependence in close relationships (e.g., "I prefer not to show others how I feel deep down."). The Anxiety subscale assesses excessive desire for closeness, and fear of rejection, neglect, or abandonment (e.g., "I often want to merge completely with others, and this sometimes scares them away."). Validity of this measure has been supported in a wide range of studies. In previous studies, internal consistency estimates ranged between .91 and .94 for the Avoidance subscale, and between .90 and .91 for the Anxiety subscale (Brennan et al., 1998; Marmarosh, Gelso, Markin, & Majors, 2009; Mohr, Gelso, & Hill, 2005). For the current study, internal consistency (alpha) was .91 for the Avoidance subscale and .92 for the Anxiety subscale.

The **Working Alliance Inventory-Short Revised** (WAI-SR; Hatcher & Gillaspy, 2006) is a 12-item measure that assesses client perceptions of the working alliance. Items are rated on a 5-point scale from 1 (*seldom*) to 5 (*always*). Hatcher and Gillaspy developed this version through extensive factor analyses and item response theory of the original 36-item WAI (Horvath & Greenberg, 1986); they reported that the three subscales (bond, task, goal) and total scale had adequate internal consistency ($\alpha > .85$) and were related to other alliance measures. A comparable 10-item therapist version developed by Hatcher and Gillaspy was used in this study. Internal consistency alphas were .91 for the client form and .94 for the therapist form in the present study.

The **Session Evaluation Scale** (SES; Hill & Kellems, 2002) assesses client and therapist perceptions of the quality of the session. We used the 5-item version of the SES, as suggested by Lent et al. (2006), who added a fifth item ("Rate the overall effectiveness of the session") to the original four items ("I am glad I attended this session," "I did not feel satisfied with what I got our of this session," "I thought the session was helpful," and I did not think the session was valuable") to increase the variability of scores. The items are rated on 5-point Likert scales from 1 (*strongly disagree*) to 5 (*strongly agree*); the negative items are reverse scored. Validity was demonstrated by correlations with similar measures such as the Session Evaluation Questionnaire (Hill & Kellems, 2002). Internal consistency (alpha) for the present sample was .86 for clients and .91 for therapists.

The **Real Relationship Inventory-Therapist and the Real Relationship Inventory-Client** (RRI-T and RRI-C; Gelso et al., 2005; Kelley, Gelso, Fuertes, Marmarosh, & Lanier, 2010) are 24-item measures, each using a 5-point scale from 1 (*strongly disagree*) to 5 (*strongly agree*), which assess perceptions of the strength of the real relationship in terms of realism and genuineness. The therapist and client forms have been found to relate in theoretically predicted ways to other process variables, as well as to treatment progress and outcome (e.g., Fuertes et al., 2007; Gelso et al., 2012; Lo Coco, Gullo, Prestano, & Gelso, 2011; Marmarosh et al., 2009). Because high internal consistency has been found in previous studies, and because we wanted to reduce the amount of time that it takes to complete the measures after each session, for the current study we chose the 12 items that we believed best represented the theoretical components of the measure. In comparison with another data set of long-term psychotherapy, we found correlations of .91 and .96, respectively between the shortened versus full-length client and therapist forms.

The **Client Attachment to Therapist Scale** (CATS; Mallinckrodt, Gantt, & Coble, 1995) is a 36-item measure of respondents' perceptions of their relationship with their therapist. The CATS items are rated on a 6-point Likert scale from 1 (*strongly agree*) to 6 (*strongly disagree*). The CATS contains three subscales: Secure, Preoccupied-Merger, and Avoidant-Fearful. The Secure subscale assesses the client's perception of the therapist as an emotionally available secure base for exploring difficult material (e.g., "My counselor is sensitive to my needs."). The Preoccupied-Merger subscale assesses the client's preoccupation with the therapist and desire to expand the boundaries of the relationship (e.g., "I wish my counselor could be with me on a daily basis."). The Avoidant-Fearful subscale assesses the client's perception of the therapist as disapproving and the client's reluctance to disclose when speaking to the therapist (e.g., "Talking over my problems with my counselor makes me feel ashamed or foolish."). In previous studies, internal consistency estimates have ranged from .51 to .81 for Secure, .81 to .88 for Preoccupied-Merger, and .63 to .86 for Avoidant-Fearful (Janzen, Fitzpatrick, & Drapeau, 2008; Mallinkrodt et al., 1995; Woodhouse, Schlosser, Crook, Ligiero, & Gelso, 2003). For the current study, internal consistency (alpha) for the CATS subscale scores ranged from .63 to .78 for Secure, .46 to .87 for Preoccupied-Merger, and .65 to .80 for Avoidant-Fearful.

Quality of immediacy was determined by judges based on listening to the immediacy events within the context of the entire case. Judges used 5-point scales, ranging from 1 (*poor*) to 5 (*excellent*), to rate each immediacy event on four dimensions: depth, appropriateness, resolution, and quality. Judges independently rated each event and then discussed their ratings until they reached consensus. Because of high positive intercorrelations (.76 to .92) among all teams on the four items, these items were combined into a construct we called *quality*.

Procedures for Data Collection

Therapist recruitment and training. Therapists were recruited via announcements in the doctoral program housing the clinic. Therapists read about immediacy (Cashdan, 1988; Hill, 2009; Safran & Muran, 2000; Teyber, 2006) and then attended a 4-hour workshop each year devoted to immediacy, with discussions and role plays of the four types of immediacy. In addition, immediacy was a major focus of the weekly individual supervision and bi-weekly group supervision.

Client recruitment, screening, pre-therapy assessment, and intake. Clients were recruited through an internet website, local therapists, physicians, local agencies, newspapers, and word of mouth. When potential clients contacted the clinic, they were screened by phone to determine eligibility. Those who were eligible (i.e., they were over 18, experiencing interpersonal problems, not exhibiting psychotic symptoms, not suicidal, not currently substance abusing or addicted, not currently in other individual psychotherapy, not more appropriate for marital or family therapy, and have been on psychotropic medicine for 2 months if using it) were scheduled for an intake. When they arrived for the intake, clients first signed a consent form, completed the IIP and the ECR (and other measures not included in this study), and met with a therapist for an intake session. During the intake, the therapist asked the client to explore presenting problems and history. The therapist then assessed whether the client was willing to work with him or her, be videotaped, work on relational aspects of her/his problems, and pay a fee of $25 to $50 (there was no charge for the intake). After the intake, the client again completed the IIP. Clients and therapists were assigned code numbers for all data to protect confidentiality. Those people who were not eligible at any step of the process were offered referrals to other providers.

Treatment. Therapy was conducted from a psychodynamic/interpersonal perspective, although departures were made when clinically appropriate. Therapists were encouraged to establish a therapeutic relationship, conceptualize and treat presenting problems according to a psychodynamic/interpersonal framework, and to be aware of when problems arose in the relationship and address these problems using immediacy when appropriate. All 45–60-minute weekly sessions were videotaped. No limit was placed on the number of sessions, although seven cases were terminated when therapists left the clinic for another externship or internship.

Post-session assessment. Following all sessions, clients completed the WAI-SR, RRI-C, and SES in a random order. After the third session, clients completed the CATS. After every eight sessions (e.g., sessions 8, 16, 24 . . .) clients completed the IIP and CATS.

Therapists completed the WAI, RRI-T, and SES after sessions. They also responded "Yes" or "No" to the question: "Did you use immediacy in today's session (i.e., did you disclose about your feelings about the client, yourself in relation to the client, or the relationship)?"

Post-therapy assessment. Approximately 1 week after terminating therapy, clients completed the IIP and were interviewed by a researcher about their experiences. Five of the clients who dropped out of treatment did not respond to repeated contacts and thus did not complete the post-therapy assessment.

Procedures for Data Coding

Coding immediacy. Given the complexity of clinical phenomena and the value of voicing and hearing multiple perspectives, all judgments related to immediacy were made by consensus among judges after (at times considerable) discussion. In this method, which has been referred to consensual qualitative research-cases (CQR-C; Jackson, Chui, & Hill, 2012), consensus among judges is considered more relevant than independent ratings because clinical intuition, reasoning, and thoughtful discussion of many viewpoints are encouraged and hopefully result in more effective judgments and ratings. Considerable attention is given to making sure that each person feels comfortable talking and providing his or her viewpoint, with consensus then being used to construct a final shared viewpoint.

The entire research team met for 3 hours and observed several events to refine the definition of an immediacy event (i.e., it had to be about the therapeutic relationship, both people had to participate in the discussion, had to be more than social chit chat) and to develop criteria for judgments. The distinction between immediacy and social chit-chat was included because in watching the sessions from the Hill et al. (2008) case, it was clear that the therapist and client typically engaged in social chit-chat (e.g., "It's so nice to see you today"), which helped to establish the relationship but had little to do with negotiating the therapeutic relationship.

Three-person teams were then randomly constituted with at least one person on each team who had rated immediacy in a previous study. Therapists were not assigned to their own cases. Each team coded one to four cases over 18 months, with some change in team membership over time to ensure that teams were coding similarly.

Teams first watched the intake session and read the intake notes for the assigned case. Next, they watched the DVD of each session involving immediacy events (as identified at post-session by the therapist). In addition, based on reading the therapist's progress notes for all sessions, teams watched the DVDs of sessions where they suspected that there might have been unreported immediacy events. Because one case had more sessions than others (59 versus 10 to 39), we coded only 35 (first 10, 15–20, 25–30, 35–40, 45–50, and 54–59) sessions of the 59-session case so that a relatively similar numbers of sessions were coded across cases.

As the team watched and listened to the session, they stopped the DVD after each immediacy event. To ensure that they understood the event, they went back and listened to the entire event again and wrote a description of the event. They then calculated the duration of the event and coded whether the therapist or client initiated the event. After considerable discussion, they then coded the type of event (negotiation of the tasks and goals of therapy, exploration of unexpressed feelings or making the covert overt, drawing parallels between other relationships and the therapy relationship, and attempts to repair ruptures by talking about what is going on between the therapist and client). Next, they independently rated the depth, appropriateness, resolution, and quality, using 5-point scales from 1 (*poor*) to 5 (*excellent*), and then discussed their ratings until they reached consensus (these scales were later combined and called *quality* given high positive intercorrelations of .76 to .92). Next, each team consensually wrote a narrative account of the consequences of the immediacy event. At the end of the entire session, teams consensually described the consequences of all the immediacy events within the sessions. Finally, after observing all the immediacy events in the entire case, the team wrote a final summary of the effects of immediacy in the entire case.

To ensure consistency across cases in terms of describing the consequences of immediacy, a new team was then composed of five of the judges who had served on different initial teams. These five judges met and reviewed the narrative accounts of the initial teams and inductively derived 10 categories of consequences (see Table I). Once the categories were stabilized (i.e., no new categories emerged as new narrative accounts were reviewed), three-person teams coded each narrative account into categories of consequences for each event (relying on data from the narratives for the event and session) and for the entire case (relying on data from the narratives for the case). More than one consequence could apply for each event and case.

Results

Description of Immediacy Events (Frequency Duration, Quality, Initiator, and Type)

Analyses revealed a total of 234 immediacy events (ranging from three to 40 events per case). For the descriptive data, we first computed means across sessions for each case and then computed averages across cases (thus controlling for the different number of sessions across cases).

Across the 16 cases, the average number of immediacy events per session was .61 (SD=.31, ranging from .14 to 1.00 per session per case), the average duration of events was 285 seconds (SD = 114 seconds, ranging from 98 seconds to 508 seconds per event), and the average amount of time spent in immediacy was 5% (SD = .04, ranging from .5% to 14% per case) of the entire case. On a 5-point Likert scale ranging from 1 (*poor*) to 5 (*excellent*), the average quality rating of events was 2.61 (SD = .42; range = 2.00 to 3.46).

Therapists initiated 85% (SD = 18%) of the events (ranging from 25% to 100% per case). In terms of types of immediacy events (recall that events could be coded into more than one type), an average of 59% (SD = 26%, range = 0% to 85%) involved an exploration of unexpressed or covert feelings, 26% (SD = 17%, range = 0% to75%) involved negotiation of tasks and goals, 26% (SD = 20%, range = 0% to 75%) involved discussion of parallels to other relationships, and 8% (SD = 13%, range = 0% to 50%) involved discussion of ruptures.

Thus, the typical immediacy event was brief and infrequent. The events were typically initiated by the therapist, and focused on helping clients explore unexpressed or covert feelings about the therapeutic relationship. The rated quality of the event was near the midpoint of our scale, probably signifying a moderately effective immediacy event.

Consequences of Therapeutic Immediacy

Coding consequences of therapeutic immediacy. Table I shows the results of the judges' consequences coding. We report the results both for an event-level analysis (i.e., the number of times each category of consequence was coded for events in each case divided by the total number of immediacy events in the case) and for a case-level analysis (i.e., the consequences that were coded as characteristic of the entire case). Thus, the event-level analysis represents the consequences for events, whereas the case-level

Table I. Consequences of immediacy for the 16 cases based on events and case analysis

Consequence	Current study events-level analysis M (SD)	Current study case-level analysis
Helped to establish relationship	.05 (.08)	.12
Helped to establish or clarify boundaries (negotiated relationship)	.36 (.24)	.44
Repaired ruptures in relationship	.04 (.07)	.12
Clients expressed feelings about therapist or therapy	.50 (.32)	.50
Client expressed interest in making changes in relationships outside of therapy	.01 (.02)	.00
Client had a corrective relational experience	.02 (.03)	.12
Client felt validated, cared for, reassured	.13 (.19)	.12
Client opened up and gained insight	.21 (.21)	.50
Negative effects (felt worse, blamed, attacked, confused, pressured)	.08 (.17)	.00
No effects	.24 (.19)	.19

Note. The events-level analysis was based on judgments about the effects of immediacy within events summarized across all events for each case. The case-level analysis was based on a judgment of the impact of immediacy across the entire case.

analysis represents what the judges viewed as representative of the cases as a whole. Events could have had an immediate effect but not have maintained across that effect time.

The most frequent consequences across both types of analyses (see Table I) were the client expressing feelings about the therapist or therapy, the establishment or clarification of boundaries, the client opening up and gaining insight, no effects, and the client feeling validated and cared for. Using an arbitrary criterion of at least a 5% difference to denote meaningful differences, we can see that the client opening up/gaining insight was identified more often (50% vs. 21%) whereas negative effects were coded less often (0% vs. 8%) in the case-level analysis than in the event analysis. These differences based on level of analysis suggest that insight had a more lasting effect whereas the negative effects were more temporary.

Two examples might help to explain the disparity in results of the event-level and case-level analyses. In one case in which the overall effects of immediacy were judged as very good, there was one session right before termination where both positive and negative effects were noted. More specifically, the client was very upset about terminating and was sobbing. The therapist was able to facilitate the client's expression of feelings, and the client opened up and felt validated, but it was also clear that the therapist was uncomfortable with the depth of the client's emotions. In another case with overall positive effects, a number of sessions had negative effects. The therapist used immediacy during these sessions to process the client's consistent lateness. These events were difficult because the client felt considerable shame and discomfort, and the therapist had difficulties setting boundaries and dealing with the client's ambivalence about therapy. In both cases, the few negative effects were minor in relation to the overall positive effects of immediacy.

Client evaluation of immediacy in post-therapy interviews. Of the 11 clients who were interviewed post-therapy, all remembered discussing the therapeutic relationship with the therapist at some point during the therapy. Eight of the 11 said very positive things about the effects of the immediacy (e.g., "very touched, wasn't expecting it"; "It became more of a basic relationship. She became very significant in my life because I felt like she was the one person who saw who I was, who understood things about me"; "Felt closer"; "Definitely appreciated") Three clients reported neutral or ambivalent reactions (e.g., "I would have to explain things that normally in our culture, because obviously if the culture is different, and, and I expect them because it's, it's you know he was not aware of it so it was not a big deal"; "It felt good that I could tell her that, but I was kind of worried that she'd think that was what I wanted [to get her to give me an answer]"). Thus, most of the clients who provided post-therapy evaluations recalled that immediacy had occurred and was helpful (although the five clients who dropped out and were not interviewed might have had negative things to say about immediacy).

Immediacy in relation to post-session measures. To examine the relationship between immediacy and post-session measures, we first conducted correlations between the average percent of immediacy events in sessions and average client and therapist post-session ratings of process and outcome (recall that these evaluations were of the session in general rather than of immediacy specifically). Because of the small sample, we relied primarily on effect size estimates (where $r = .10$ is a small effect, .30 is a medium effect, and .50 is a large effect). Average percent of immediacy was positively correlated with therapists' ratings of SES, $r(14) = .50$, $p = .05$, RRI, $r(14) = .40$, $p = .12$, and WAI, $r(14) = .24$, $p = .36$. Average percent of immediacy events in sessions was not significantly associated with clients' ratings of SES, $r(14) = -.10$, RRI, $r(14) = .17$, and WAI, $r(14) = .12$. Thus, amount of immediacy events was related to therapists' but not clients' evaluations of session process and outcome.

In addition, no correlations above .30 were found between average ratings of quality or average length of events with therapist- or client-rated post-session measures. Thus, there was a lack of association among these measures.

Immediacy in relation to changes in interpersonal functioning. After all the immediacy coding had been completed, we determined outcome by assessing changes from pre-intake to post-termination on the IIP. Because we had some problems in data collection, we were missing some data. Two cases that were missing intake data completely were dropped from this analysis. For four cases, we substituted post-intake data (completed immediately after the intake) for pre-intake data (completed immediately before the intake); this substitution seemed acceptable given that pre- and post-intake data were not significantly different for cases that had both. Second, we substituted clients' final point of IIP progress data (completed after every eight sessions) for post-therapy data for three clients who did not return for the post-therapy evaluation; this substitution seemed acceptable given that final eighth session and post-therapy data were not significantly different for cases that had data at both time points.

The IIP average for the 14 clients for whom we had data at pre-therapy was 1.16 ($SD = .54$) and at post-therapy was 1.18 ($SD = .58$), indicating no overall change. In comparison, Barkham, Hardy, and Startup (1996) reported that outpatients scored $M = 1.51$, $SD = .68$, and the general population scored $M = .98$, $SD = .52$, indicating that the current sample had low levels of interpersonal distress both initially and at post-therapy.

To obtain an index of change on the IIP, we subtracted the pre-intake scores from the post-therapy scores. This change score was not significantly correlated with the percentage of total immediacy events, $r(12) = .21$, or average quality of events, $r(12) = .16$. Thus, the amount or quality of immediacy was not meaningfully associated with changes in interpersonal functioning as measured by the IIP.

Immediacy Events in Relation to Attachment Style

Pre-therapy attachment. Due to missing pre-intake ECR data for one client, we conducted multiple imputation with SPSS 19. For these analyses, we used baseline data from ECR Avoidance and Anxiety subscales and the CATS Avoidant-Fearful, Preoccupied-Merger, and Secure subscales from sessions 3 and 8. Multiple imputation was justified given the strong correlations in our data between ECR Avoidance and CATS Avoidant-Fearful scales, $r(13) = .54$, $p = .03$, and between ECR Anxiety and CATS Preoccupied-merger, $r(13) = .52$, $p = .04$. Similarly, Mallinckrodt, Porter, and Kivlighan (2005) reported a significant positive correlation between ECR Avoidance and CATS Avoidant-Fearful, $r(36) = .38$, $p < .05$, and a non-significant, positive correlation between the CATS Preoccupied-Merger and ECR Anxiety subscale, $r(36) = .24$, $p > .05$. Thus, after imputing the one missing data point, we had complete data for all clients. A preliminary comparison indicated that our sample was similar to Marmarosh et al.'s (2009) for attachment anxiety ($M = 3.93$, $SD = 1.27$ in our study vs. $M = 3.91$, $SD = 1.32$ in Marmarosh et al., $d = .02$) but was lower on attachment avoidance ($M = 2.89$, $SD = 1.03$ in our study vs. $M = 3.27$ in Marmarosh et al., $SD = 1.37$, $d = -.31$).

Based on suggestions by Fraley and Shaver (1997) and Mohr, Gelso, and Hill (2005) that a fearful attachment pattern can be conceptualized as being high on Anxiety and Avoidance whereas a secure pattern is low on both scales, we summed the scores of the ECR subscales to form a secure–fearful continuum. We then divided scores on the secure–fearful dimension at the median, considering the eight clients above the median to be secure and the eight clients below the median to be fearful. Given that we had imputed one score, we examined each of the five resulting imputations to ensure fair division of the sample. All clients fell into the same category on at least three of the five imputations and thus we were fairly confident of our categorization.

The means and standard deviations for the eight immediacy variables for the two attachment groups can be found in Table II. Given the small sample size, we relied primarily on the results of effect size analyses, using a criterion of at least a medium effect size ($d > .50$) to indicate an important difference.

In the eight analyses comparing the initially fearful with the initially secure clients, fewer immediacy events focused on tasks, $t(14) = -2.04, p < .05, d = -1.03$, more focused on feelings, $t(14) = 1.70, p = .09, d = .91$, fewer focused on ruptures, $t(14) = -1.53, p = .13, d = -.80$), the average quality of immediacy events was higher $t(14) = 1.65, p = .10, d = .82$, therapists initiated more often, $t(14) = 2.21, p < .05, d = 1.10$, and the immediacy events were longer, $t(14) = 1.95, p = .05, d = .99$. Thus, with clients who initially presented as fearful as compared with those who initially presented as secure, immediacy events were focused less on tasks and ruptures and more on feelings. Also, for the more fearful clients, the immediacy events were higher in quality, therapists initiated these events more often, and the average length of immediacy events was longer.

Client attachment to therapist. Scores for all administrations of the CATS-Secure were summed, so the resulting scores represent the average attachment to therapist across the course of therapy. A preliminary comparison indicated that our sample was similar to Mallinckrodt et al.'s (1995) outpatient sample ($M = 71.19$, $SD = 5.99$ in our study vs. $M = 72.86$, $SD = 10.11$ in Mallinckrodt et al., $d = .20$).

We divided the average CATS-Secure scores at the median, with the eight above the median considered more securely attached to their therapists and the eight below the mean considered less securely attached to their therapists. The means and standard deviations for the eight immediacy variables for the two attachment groups can be found in Table II. We report both the t-tests and effect sizes (again requiring at least a medium effect size of $> .50$). With clients who were less securely attached to therapist as compared with more securely attached clients, more events focused on feelings, $t(14) = 1.83, p = .07, d = .91$, fewer addressed ruptures in therapy, $t(7.67) = -2.13, p < .05, d = -1.05$, and therapists initiated more, $t(14) = 2.13, p < .05, d = 1.05$. Thus, therapists focused immediacy events more on feelings and

Table II. Characteristics of immediacy events averaged across cases for the total sample, for secure versus fearful clients on the ECRS, and for more versus less secure clients with their therapists on the CATS

	Total sample (*N* = 16) *M* (*SD*)	ECR fearful cases (*N* = 8) *M* (*SD*)	ECR secure cases (*N* = 8) *M* (*SD*)	*d*	Insecure attachment with therapist (*N* = 8)	Secure attachment with therapist (*N* = 8)	*d*
% total immediacy events	.61 (.31)	.56 (.37)	.66 (.25)	.32	.64 (.34)	.57 (.29)	.22
% task events	.27 (.17)	.19 (.11)	.35 (.19)	1.03	.26 (.19)	.28 (.17)	.11
% feeling events	.59 (.25)	.70 (.20)	.49 (.26)	.91	.70 (.21)	.49 (.25)	.91
% parallel events	.26 (.20)	.30 (.22)	.23 (.19)	.34	.27 (.25)	.26 (.16)	.05
% rupture events	.08 (.13)	.03 (.05)	.13 (.17)	.80	.02 (.04)	.15 (.17)	1.05
Quality	2.61 (.42)	2.78 (.48)	2.45 (.31)	.82	2.69 (.52)	2.54 (.31)	.35
% T initiated	.85 (.18)	.94 (.07)	.76 (.22)	1.10	.94 (.06)	.77 (.22)	1.05
Length in seconds	264.81 (114.25)	315.91 (129.13)	213.53 (69.21)	.99	289.91 (109.62)	239.38 (120.53)	.44

Note. % immediacy events = average number of total immediacy events divided by total number of sessions; % task events = average number of tasks events divided by total number of rated sessions; % feeling events = average number of feeling immediacy events divided by total number of sessions; % parallel events = average number of parallel immediacy events divided by total number of sessions; % rupture events = average number of rupture immediacy events divided by total number of sessions. Quality = average rated quality of immediacy events. % T initiated = average percentage of events initiated by therapists. Length = average duration in seconds of immediacy events. Determination of secure versus fearful was based on a median split on the pre-therapy ECRS scores. Determination of insecure versus secure attachment with therapist was based on a median split of the averaged CATS data across therapy. Effect sizes were considered important if they were at least medium (i.e., >.50).

less on ruptures, and they initiated the immediacy events more often with clients who were less securely attached to them as compared with more securely attached clients.

A comparison of the CATS results with the ECR data indicates that the direction of findings was similar across both sets of analyses with the exception of total percent of immediacy events. Eleven of the 16 cases were coded similarly in the median splits, suggesting that initially fearful clients were likely to form insecure attachments with their therapists whereas initially secure clients were likely to form secure attachments with their therapists.

Case examples. To illustrate the moderating influence of attachment on the use and effects of immediacy, we present examples of two cases with secure attachments to the therapists and positive change in terms of interpersonal functioning. The first client, however, had a secure initial attachment style, whereas the second client had a fearful initial attachment style. Descriptions of the cases are based on an amalgam of input from the therapists, supervisors, and judges who observed the sessions. Clients were given an opportunity to read and comment on the cases. They made no suggestions for changes.

Client with a secure initial attachment. Joe (a pseudonym) was a 52-year-old divorced and remarried man. He had a secure attachment style both on the pre-therapy measure (ECR) as well as a secure attachment to the therapist (CATS). Joe was seen by a 27-year-old European-American female therapist (TB, pseudo initials) for a total of 59 sessions (the therapy ended when the therapist left the clinic for internship). Joe's presenting problem was tension in relationships with his ex-wife and children from his first marriage, and conflicts with his current wife. Joe had a tendency to avoid conflict and experienced substantial ambivalence in many areas of his life. He also exhibited a stringent superego, and thus harshly judged himself and his significant others. In terms of defenses, the client tended to use intellectualization and isolation, with the aim of avoiding strong, anxiety-arousing affects. Joe's case is notable because of the large number of immediacy events (26 in the 35 sessions in the data set) in relation to other cases.

A few examples illustrate the immediacy in this case. Midway through the intake session, TB asked Joe how he felt working with a younger female therapist. Joe responded that it was a little startling, although he knew that younger people had expertise that he did not. He said that he expected TB to guide the process rather than have all the answers. Joe then asked TB how it felt to work with someone older than her. TB responded that it was different but they could work at it together. At the end of the intake session, TB asked how Joe felt talking with her about his issues. Joe responded that it was fine and he felt like he could talk to her. These two events set the stage for future discussions of the relationship and enabled Joe to express his obvious concerns about whether TB could understand him.

In session 38, Joe told a long story but did not express any feelings. When TB asked if he could articulate his emotional reactions, Joe responded that he did not have very good access to his feelings. TB pointed out that Joe's storytelling often involved neglecting his own feelings or reactions. Joe interrupted her and said that he "bristled" because he was in touch with his feelings but just could not express them quickly. TB non-defensively asked if it was okay to ask him about his reactions, and Joe said that it was okay but that he would probably bristle. When TB asked what she should do if Joe bristled, he said to just let it go. When probed further, Joe acknowledged that he did not like to be interrupted when telling a story. TB said she understood that storytelling was comfortable for Joe. After this discussion, Joe asked TB to tell him if his bristling became too much, and they agreed to keep track of it.

These examples show how TB and Joe were able to directly address problems as they arose in the relationship. Although Joe often tried to dominate TB, she was able to maintain confidence and presence and address the interactional dynamics. The immediacy events were relatively long, and Joe seemed to be able to benefit from the immediacy. Given that Joe had an initial secure attachment style (based on self-report, although clinically we would argue that he had more of an avoidant attachment style), a secure attachment to the therapist, and a good outcome, we suggest that TB was being responsive to Joe and encouraging him to work on interpersonal relationships by negotiating and examining their relationship.

Client with an initial fearful attachment style. The client, James (a pseudonym), was a 24-year-old, Reform Orthodox Jewish, White, gay man. He had a fearful attachment style on the pre-therapy measure (ECRS) but he was securely attached to the therapist (on the CATS). James was seen by a 29-year-old, European-American, gay male therapist (KN, pseudo initials) for a total of 28 sessions (the therapy with this therapist ended when the therapist left the clinic for internship). During intake, James reported marked distress in his interactions with his parents and siblings after they discovered through reading his mail that he was gay. James's parents confronted him about his sexuality, sending him to a number of rabbis and therapists for "conversion" or "reparative" psychotherapy to try to become heterosexual. James also discussed turmoil in a number of his peer relationships and an inability to develop meaningful romantic relationships. He seemed to be highly defended, primarily using externalizing defenses, such that outside events and people were seen as the causes of his difficulties. He had great difficulty exploring how his inner experiences played into his relationships and problems.

The four immediacy events in this case were all brief, and all but one event were scored as low in quality. The first event in session 14 was preceded by James describing the frustration and humiliation he experienced as the result of his parents speaking to him as if he were a misguided child. James avoided conflict with his parents and peers by keeping a distance in relationships. KN asked James if he was building walls in *their* relationship to prevent any conflict or confrontation from arising. James responded tersely by stating, "I tend not to do that with psychologists. There's no reason to."

Near the end of session 21, KN acknowledged having seen James on a campus bus and asked whether that was "awkward for you?" James responded, "No, I figured there'd be a professional-personal boundary thing. It's totally fine." KN said, "Maybe I'm saying this . . . just for me, because I feel awkward about it." James responded, "I'm not worried about it." They concluded the event by acknowledging that they might see one another again outside session. KN then noted their upcoming termination and asked, "How are things going for us? I've been thinking about how things are going for us. As we wrap up, I hope that the things we've been doing have been meaningful for you . . . and if there were things that you feel were missing . . ." James answered, "It's been pretty good. It's been pretty thorough." KN commented that perhaps they could continue thinking about their work together; James agreed with a nod.

In this case, KN typically made tentative bids for immediacy, which James deflected by implicitly sending the message that, "Everything's fine. Let's not speak this way. Let's move on." Rather than forcing exploration of the here-and-now, KN let it go. Given that James had a fearful initial attachment style, but a secure attachment to the therapist and a good outcome, we think that KN was responsive to James and did not push him further than he could go.

Conclusions from the examples. These examples illustrate how therapists responded differently to clients based on initial client attachment dynamics, even when therapists were able to forge secure attachments with their clients. With Joe, who had an initial secure attachment style, the therapist was able to productively use immediacy. They talked about their relationship and negotiated misunderstandings. Joe was able to work with the therapist in a collaborative manner. With James, who had an initial fearful attachment style, by contrast, the therapist used immediacy minimally. And when he did try to introduce immediacy, the client clearly indicated that he did not want to talk about the relationship. It is interesting to note that James was able to form a secure relationship with his therapist but the initial fearful attachment perhaps made him reluctant to process the relationship in any way. Interestingly, both therapists were judged as highly competent in using immediacy in general, but clearly modified the way they used immediacy to fit the needs of specific clients.

These examples also clearly indicate how immediacy is not necessarily needed for positive outcome. Rather, the important factor is whether the therapist uses immediacy responsively with the client. Some clients seem not to like or value immediacy and it is important for therapists to recognize this and modulate their use of immediacy accordingly.

Discussion

In these 16 cases of individual psychodynamic psychotherapy conducted by doctoral students with adult clients, the use and consequences of immediacy varied widely across cases, at least partially based on initial attachment dynamics. All therapists used immediacy, but some therapists used immediacy in most sessions, whereas other therapists rarely used immediacy. In some cases, there were positive consequences of immediacy, whereas no effects for immediacy were found in other cases.

Before discussing the results in greater depth, we remind the readers that this study was a naturalistic field study. Thus, rather than being able to make causal inferences, we can only describe what happened in these 16 cases. We also remind readers that these therapists were doctoral students who had been trained in the use of immediacy. They had not, however, been selected on the basis of how much and how well they used immediacy. Finally, clients were not selected as being particularly suitable for relational work. Thus, we would expect results to diverge from those of the three case studies (Hill et al., 2008; Kasper et al., 2008; Mayotte-Blum et al., 2012) in which therapists and clients were specifically chosen to be exemplars for how immediacy could be used in psychotherapy.

Frequency of Immediacy

Immediacy was used relatively infrequently, occurring from 5% to 14% of the total time in the 16 cases of psychodynamic/interpersonal psychotherapy. Immediacy was used less in this sample than in three case studies involving therapists selected because of their interpersonal orientation and frequent use of immediacy (Hill et al., 2008; Kasper et al., 2008; Mayotte-Blum et al., 2012), where the range was from 12% to 38% of therapist speech in sessions. Thus, the psychodynamically oriented therapist-trainees in the present study did not use this intervention as extensively as did therapists who were strongly identified with an interpersonal approach. These therapists may have been less interpersonally oriented or less sure of their ability to use immediacy than were the highly experienced interpersonal therapists in the cases presented by Kasper et al., Hill et al., and Mayotte-Blum et al.

Initiation

Therapists most often initiated the immediacy, although this varied widely across cases. Because immediacy represents a shift from how most people interact in daily life, it appears that it is incumbent upon therapists to be the ones to bring up issues as they arise in therapeutic relationships.

Types

We were able to distinguish different types of immediacy. The most typical type of immediacy was an exploration of unexpressed or covert feelings (e.g., "How are you feeling about the termination?"). Used somewhat often were a negotiation of tasks and goals (e.g., "Would you like to work with me?") and discussion of parallels to other relationships (e.g., "You said that no one understands you lately. I wonder if you feel that I don't understand you?"). Used least often, surprisingly, were discussions of ruptures (e.g., "I wonder if you are angry at me because of having to terminate?"). We suspect that it is easiest to talk about feelings and most difficult to talk about ruptures. Relatedly, we noticed that therapists often asked clients to talk about their feelings about the relationship but were not as forthcoming about their own feelings.

Quality

In terms of quality, the average event was rated a 2.61 on a 5-point scale (5 = high). Judges tended not to use the extremes of the scale, which we expect reflects external judges' often-noted criticalness when watching and evaluating psychotherapy sessions. None of the events were viewed as harmful, whereas most were considered as neutral or mildly helpful, and a few were lengthy and impactful. We suspect that these data reflect the difficulty of implementing high-quality immediacy events.

Consequences of Immediacy

In the two methods that we used to assess the consequences, immediacy appeared to be effective. One way that we examined consequences was by asking clients during post-therapy interviews about their experiences with immediacy. Eight of the 11 interviewed clients said extremely positive things about the effects of the immediacy, indicating that immediacy had a major impact, sometimes facilitating a corrective relational experience. Therefore, for some clients, immediacy had a great impact, perhaps because talking about the immediate relationship can be an intense and beneficial endeavor when done well.

A second method of assessing consequences was through judgments of the events by observers. The most frequent, positive consequences of immediacy as judged by observers were client expression of feelings about the therapist or therapy, client opening up/gaining insight, and the establishment/clarification/negotiation of boundaries, and client feelings of validation and caring.

Some differences were found between the event and case analyses. Specifically, in the case-level analyses as compared with the event-level analyses, immediacy was viewed more often as helping to establish or negotiate boundaries, as leading to a corrective relational experience, and as helping the client open up or gain insight, but less often to negative or no effects. Thus, positive consequences were viewed as having more intense and perhaps lasting effects, whereas negative/no effects were more transient and minor in relation to the overall positive effects of immediacy.

We also compared the consequences found in this study with those found in the three other case studies (Hill et al., 2008; Kasper et al., 2008; Mayotte-Blum et al., 2012). In at least three of the four studies, immediacy helped therapists and clients negotiate the therapeutic relationship, helped clients express feelings about the therapist/therapy, facilitated a corrective relational experience, and helped clients feel validated and cared for. Thus, consistent results for the effectiveness of immediacy were found across the four studies. Importantly, similar consequences were found for the doctoral student therapists as were found for the experienced therapists.

Association of Immediacy with Session Process/Outcome and Treatment Outcome

Although no significant associations were found for amount, quality, and length of immediacy with ratings of session process and outcome for clients, therapists rated session process and outcome higher when more immediacy was used (no association was found for quality or length). It is not surprising that therapists rated sessions as better when immediacy occurred given that they were trained in immediacy and were often excited when they were able to use it. It is more surprising that clients did not evaluate sessions involving immediacy more highly, especially given that they said very positive things about immediacy in the post-therapy interviews. One explanation might be that if therapists were doing what needed to be done in each session (e.g., were responsive to clients' needs, as Stiles, 1988), there is no reason to suggest that sessions involving immediacy should be evaluated any better than sessions involving other interventions. In addition, we suggest that it makes more sense to evaluate the effects of immediacy (or any therapeutic intervention) at the event-level rather than in relation to session or treatment outcome given that so many other variables interfere with the relation to outcome (see also Hill et al., 1988). Thus, using an event analysis and carefully assessing the context is more likely to yield consequences related to immediacy rather than to other interventions.

The Use of Immediacy with Clients of Different Attachment Styles

Immediacy was used differently based on the level of security of the clients' attachment. When examining the results that replicated across the pre-therapy ECR and average of the CATS-Secure across therapy, it appeared that therapists initiated immediacy more often, and focused less on ruptures and more on feelings during immediacy events with fearfully/insecurely attached than with securely attached clients. Thus, it appears that therapists had to take more initiative and work more gently with fearfully attached than with securely attached clients. Perhaps the fearfully attached clients exhibited greater repression of affect, thus requiring therapists to initiate more exploration and ask more about feelings. We also speculate that fearful clients were not as able to tolerate direct discussion of ruptures. In contrast, with securely attached clients, therapists felt more comfortable openly discussing problems in the therapeutic relationships. Therapists clearly were able to distinguish which clients responded well to the immediacy interventions.

Similarly, Woodhouse et al. (2003) noted that attachment security likely enabled clients to explore more deeply and vulnerably with their therapists, and even to share more negative feelings toward their therapists. From the perspective of a relatively novice therapist, it may feel safer and less risky to initiate and sustain an intense immediate discussion with a securely attached client than with a fearfully attached client. It may also be more effective.

Strengths and Limitations

A major strength of this study is that it was conducted within a clinical setting rather than in a laboratory setting or with carefully selected therapists and clients. The results, therefore, may be especially representative of actual therapy conducted by psychodynamically oriented doctoral student therapists with adult clients with a wide range of presenting concerns. An additional strength is the intensive nature of the analyses; at least three judges observed and coded all the sessions involving immediacy in 15 cases, and in 35 of 59 sessions in a longer case.

The sample, however, was relatively small with only 16 clients and nine therapists. There was good representation of both men and women among the therapists and clients, but there was an overrepresentation of European Americans. In addition, potential clients were screened out if they were under 18 years of age, were not experiencing interpersonal problems, reported drug or alcohol abuse, were psychotic, were currently suicidal, were currently in individual therapy elsewhere, and/or were more appropriate for couples or family therapy. Hence, results might not generalize to these other populations and settings.

The CQR-C (Jackson et al., 2012) method, as implemented by the judges (recall that all but two judges were also therapists or supervisors), had both strengths and limitations. One strength of the CQR-C method is that the judges were able to fully immerse themselves in the data by watching sessions and reading progress notes. A possible limitation is that judges may have been biased because of their expectations about immediacy. The judges had all been trained in psychodynamic and interpersonal psychotherapy, and, more specifically, in the use of immediacy, thus they may have been biased towards the positive aspects of immediacy. The judges, however, tried to bracket their biases, watched videos of sessions multiple times to ensure that they had evidence for their conclusions, and had in-depth discussions to ensure that they considered various alternatives regarding the data. In addition, as we have noted, judges did indeed observe negative or no effects of immediacy.

We examined the consequences of immediacy in several different ways (judges' narrative accounts of their perceptions of the outcomes, evaluations of the post-therapy interviews with clients, and associations between the use of immediacy and session process/outcome and treatment outcome). Each of these methods had strengths and limitations. One strength of the use of judges' observations, for example, was that judges were able to carefully observe the session process. A disadvantage, however, was that they could not observe the inner experiences of therapists and clients. The post-therapy interviews provided a perspective on immediacy directly from the clients, but we were not able to conduct interviews with five of the clients, and these clients may have been more negative regarding immediacy since they dropped out of therapy. Examining the use of immediacy in sessions in relation to session and treatment process and outcome uses ratings that come directly from the participants, but these evaluations were not specifically of the immediacy events but were rather of the sessions and treatments as a whole.

We studied only immediacy events, and did not study comparison events (e.g., when therapists gave direct guidance). Hence, we cannot say conclusively that the same consequences would not have occurred with other types of events.

An additional consideration regards the selection of cases. These eight cases were relatively brief in comparison with typical time-unlimited psychodynamic psychotherapy conducted in private practice. Furthermore, we would not consider these cases to be representative of successfully completed psychodynamic psychotherapy. Seven cases ended when the therapists left the clinic (four of these seven clients were transferred to other therapists within the clinic). In addition, three clients ended therapy against the therapists' advice, three clients dropped out with no explanation, two clients terminated because they moved to a different geographical area, and one client transferred to another clinic for couples therapy. We only selected cases that had at least eight sessions so that we could see the range of immediacy across time. Other cases in the clinic involving longer therapy were not included in this sample because they were still ongoing at the time we ended data collection. Hence, these cases were not selected because they were considered completed successful cases (as was the case presented by Mayotte-Blum et al., 2012), but rather they were the first 16 cases with at least eight sessions that had terminated since our clinic opened. We should also note that this is the largest sample of case studies conducted thus far on immediacy.

Implications for Practice and Training

The major implication of the data for practice is that immediacy is not necessarily appropriate or beneficial for every client, and that therapists need to carefully assess client responsiveness to immediacy. It appears that securely and fearfully attached clients react differently to therapist immediacy. With specific clients, therapists might try immediacy early on (e.g., to negotiate the boundaries) and see how clients respond. When particular difficulties (i.e., ruptures) arise, therapists might think through their own reactions first, including sorting through potential countertransference conflicts (Gelso & Hayes, 2007) and determine whether immediacy would be a valuable intervention with the particular client in the particular situation.

Given that immediacy is a difficult skill for most therapists to use effectively, it typically requires a great deal of practice and supervision for most trainees. We suggest that therapists need to be trained to use immediacy and need to work through their own anxieties about using the intervention, particularly in terms of working with ruptures in therapy. A recent study (Spangler et al., under review) assessed the effects of training undergraduate students in helping skills classes about how to use immediacy. Clearly, additional studies need to be conducted with graduate-level trainees and experienced therapists because different issues might arise in training more experienced therapists.

Given the differences found for trainees in this sample compared with the experienced therapists in the three previous cases studies (Hill et al., 2008; Kasper et al., 2008; Mayotte-Blum, 2012), it may well be that immediacy is a skill that takes years to master. It would thus be interesting to more directly compare inexperienced and experienced therapists in their use of immediacy, as well as to follow therapists over several years to watch how they develop in their ability to use immediacy.

It would also be valuable to compare the effects of immediacy with the effects of therapist self-disclosure. Because immediacy has the potential of being so much more intense than disclosures, we would imagine that they would have different consequences. In some of the past literature, these two therapist techniques have been combined (see Hill & Knox, 2009 review), so sorting out the differences could provide beneficial clarification.

In addition, we need evidence about the effects of immediacy used in therapy on relationships outside therapy. In other words, if therapists are able to effectively use immediacy to help clients understand how they come across in the therapeutic relationship, clients should be able to apply what they have learned about the therapeutic relationship to other relationships with other people in their lives. Comments about changes in outside relationships did not come up spontaneously in the sessions we observed or in the post-treatment interviews, however, suggesting that other methods will have to be devised to determine generalizations to outside relationships. Researchers may need to ask clients or significant others more directly about changes in external relationships.

Finally, we suggest that other moderating variables could be investigated. We would guess that the security of the therapist's attachment makes a difference (we did not have enough therapists to test this speculation). Cultural considerations also undoubtedly play a role, given that direct communication about maladaptive behaviors is frowned upon in some cultures. We also suspect that level of awareness on the part of the client and empathic ability on the part of the therapist are moderating factors, but all of these factors need to be examined.

Conclusions

Given the consistent findings across this study and the three previous case studies (Hill et al., 2008; Kasper et al., 2008; Mayotte-Blum et al., 2012), we can be fairly confident about some of the consequences of immediacy. More specifically, immediacy can help therapists and clients negotiate the therapeutic relationship, help clients express feelings about the therapist/therapy, facilitate a corrective relational experience, and help clients feel validated and cared for.

On the basis of the results of the present study, we cannot unequivocally say that immediacy is always good and powerful or even that it has a positive impact most of the time. Clearly, it is helpful some of the time, with some therapists and with some clients (particularly those with a secure attachment); but it may even have a negative effect or no effect at other times. These observations are consistent with Gelso and Palma's (2011) call for increased efforts to study variables that moderate the effects of therapist immediacy and self-disclosure on process and outcome. Thus, rather than asking whether or not to use immediacy, the more appropriate question to ask is with what clients and under what conditions immediacy is helpful, when offered by which therapists, at what point in treatment, and for which outcomes.

References

Barkham, M., Hardy, G. E., & Startup, M. (1996). The IIP-32: A short version of the Inventory of Interpersonal Problems. *British Journal of Clinical Psychology, 35*, 21–35. doi:10.1111/j.2044-8260.1996.tb01159.x

Brennan, K. A., Clark, C. L., & Shaver, P. R. (1998). Self-report measurement of adult attachment: An integrative overview. In J. A. Simpson & W. S. Rholes (Eds.), *Attachment theory and close relationships* (pp. 46–76). New York: Guilford Press.

Cashdan, S. (1988). *Object relations therapy: Using the relationship.* New York: Norton.

Dattilio, F. M., Edwards, D. J. H., & Fishman, D. B. (2010). Case studies within a mixed-method paradigm: Towards a resolution of the alienation between researcher and practitioner in psychotherapy research. *Psychotherapy, 47*, 427–441. doi: 10.1037//a0021181.

Fraley, R. C., & Shaver, P. R. (1997). Adult attachment and the suppression of unwanted thought. *Journal of Personality and Social Psychology, 73*, 1080–1091.

Fuertes, J., Mislowack, A., Brown, S., Shovel, G.-A., Wilkinson, S., & Gelso, C. J. (2007). Correlates of the real relationship in psychotherapy: A study of dyads. *Psychotherapy Research, 17*, 423–430. doi: 10.1080/10503300600789189.

Gelso, C. J., & Bhatia, A. (2012). Crossing theoretical lines: The role and effect of transference in nonanalytic psychotherapies. *Psychotherapy, 49*, 384–390. doi: 10.1037/a0028802.

Gelso, C. J., & Hayes, J. (2007). *Countertransference and the therapist's inner experience: Perils and possibilities*. Mahwah, NJ: Lawrence Erlbaum.

Gelso, C. J., Kelley, F. A., Fuertes, J. N., Marmarosh, C., Holmes, S. E., Costa, C., & Hancock, G. R. (2005). Measuring the real relationship: Initial validation of the therapist form. *Journal of Counseling Psychology, 52*, 640–649. doi: 10.1037/0022-0167.52.4.640.

Gelso, C. J., Kivlighan, D. M., Busa-Knepp, J. Spiegel, E. B., Ain, S., Hummel, A. M., Ma, Y. E., and Markin, R. D. (2012). The unfolding of the real relationship and the outcome of brief psychotherapy. *Journal of Counseling Psychology, 59*. 495–506. doi: 10.1037/a0029838.

Gelso, C. J., & Palma, B. (2011). Directions for research on self-disclosure and immediacy: Moderation, mediation, and the inverted U. *Psychotherapy, 48*, 342–348. doi: 10.1037/a0025909.

Gelso, C. J., & Samstag, L. W. (2008). A tripartite model of the therapeutic relationship. In S. Brown & R. Lent (Eds.), *Handbook of counseling psychology*. (Pp. 267–283). NY: Wiley.

Hatcher, R. L., & Gillaspy, J. A. (2006). Development and validation of a revised short version of the Working Alliance Inventory. *Psychotherapy Research, 16*, 12–25. doi: 10.1080/10503300500352500.

Hill, C. E. (2009). *Helping skills: Facilitating exploration, insight, and action* (3rd ed.). Washington DC: American Psychological Association.

Hill, C. E. (Ed.). (2012). *Consensual qualitative research: A practical resource for investigating social science phenomena*. Washington, DC: American Psychological Association.

Hill, C. E., Helms, J. E., Tichenor, V., Spiegel, S. B., O'Grady, K. E., & Perry, E. S.(1988). The effects of therapist response modes in brief psychotherapy. *Journal of Counseling Psychology, 35*, 222–233.

Hill, C. E., & Kellems, I. S. (2002). Development and use of the Helping Skills Measure to assess client perceptions of the effects of training and of helping skills in sessions. *Journal of Counseling Psychology, 49*, 264–272. doi: 10.1037/0022-0167.49.2.264.

Hill, C. E., & Knox, S. (2009). Processing the therapeutic relationship. *Psychotherapy Research, 19*, 13–29. doi: 10.1080/10503300802621206.

Hill, C. E., Sim, W., Spangler, P. T., Stahl, J., Sullivan, C., & Teyber, E. (2008). Therapist immediacy in brief psychotherapy: Case study II. *Psychotherapy: Theory, Research, Practice, Training, 45*, 298–315. doi: 10.1037/a0013306.

Horowitz, L. M., Rosenberg, S. E., Baer, B. A., Ureno, G., & Villasenor, V. S. (1988). Inventory of Interpersonal Problems: Psychometric properties and clinical applications. *Journal of Consulting and Clinical Psychology, 56*, 885–892. doi: 10.1037/0022-006X.56.6.885.

Horvath, A. O., Del Re, A. C., Fluckiger, C., & Symonds, D. (2011). Alliance in individual psychotherapy. In J. C. Norcross (Ed.), *Psychotherapy relationships that work: Evidence-based responsiveness* (2nd ed., pp. 25–69). New York, NY: Oxford University Press.

Horvath, A. O., & Greenberg, L. S. (1986). The development of the Working Alliance Inventory. In L. S. Greenberg & W. M. Pinsof (Eds.), *The psychotherapeutic process: A research handbook* (pp. 529–556). New York: Guilford Press.

Jackson, J., Chui, H., & Hill, C. E. (2012). The modification of CQR for case study research: An introduction to CQR-C. In C. E. Hill (Ed.), *Consensual qualitative research: A practical resource for investigating social science phenomena*. Washington DC: American Psychological Association.

Janzen, J., Fitzpatrick, M., & Drapeau, M. (2008). Processes involved in client-nominated relationship building incidents: Client attachment, attachment to therapist, and session impact. *Psychotherapy: Theory, Research, Practice, Training, 45*, 377–390.

Kasper, L., Hill, C. E., & Kivlighan, D. M. (2008). Therapist immediacy in brief psychotherapy: Case study I. *Psychotherapy: Theory, Research, Practice, Training, 45*, 281–297. doi: 10.1037/a0013305.

Kelley, F., Gelso, C. J., Fuertes, J., Marmarosh, C., & Lanier, S. (2010). The real relationship: development and psychometric investigation of the Client Form. *Psychotherapy, 47*, 540–553. doi: 10.1037/a0022082.

Kiesler, D. J. (1988). *Therapeutic metacommunication: Therapist impact disclosure as feedback in psychotherapy*. Palo Alto, CA: Consulting Psychologists Press.

Kuutmann, K., & Hilsenroth, M. J. (2011). Exploring in-session focus on the patient-therapist relationship: Patient characteristics, process and outcome. *Clinical Psychology and Psychotherapy, 19*, 187–202. doi: 10.1002/cpp.743.

Lent, R. L., Hoffman, M. A., Hill, C. E., Treistman, D., Mount, M., & Singley, D. (2006). Client-specific counselor self-efficacy in novice counselors: Relation to perceptions of session quality. *Journal of Counseling Psychology, 53*, 453–463. doi: 10.1037/0022-0167.53.4.453.

Levy, K. N., Ellison, W. D., Scott, L. N., & Bernecker, S. L. (2011). Attachment style. In J. C. Norcross (Ed.), *Psychotherapy relationships that work: Evidence-based responsiveness* (2nd ed., pp. 377–401). New York, NY: Oxford University Press.

Lo Coco, G. G., Gullo, S., Prestano, C., & Gelso, C. J. (2011). Relation of the real relationship and the working alliance to the outcome of brief psychotherapy. *Psychotherapy, 48*, 359–367. doi: 10.1037/a0022426.

Mallinckrodt, B. (2010). The psychotherapy relationship as attachment: Evidence and implications. *Journal of Social and Personal Relationships, 27*, 262–270. doi: 10.1177/0265407509360905.

Mallinckrodt, B., Gantt, D. L., & Coble, H. M. (1995). Attachment patterns in the psychotherapy relationship: Development of the Client Attachment to Therapist Scale. *Journal of Counseling Psychology, 42*, 307–317. doi: 10.1037/0022-0167.42.3.307.

Mallinckrodt, B., Porter, M., & Kivlighan, D. M. (2005). Client attachment to therapist, depth of in-session exploration, and object relations in brief psychotherapy. *Psychotherapy: Theory, Research, Practice, Training, 42*, 85–100. doi: 10.1037/0033-3204.42.1.85.

Marmarosh, C., Gelso, C. J., Markin, R., & Majors, R. (2009). The real relationship in psychotherapy: Relationship to adult attachments, working alliance, transference, and therapy outcome. *Journal of Counseling Psychology, 56*, 337–350. doi: 10.1037/a0015169.

Martin, D. J., Garske, J. P., & Davis, M. K. (2000). Relation of therapeutic alliance with outcome and other variables: A meta-analytic review. *Journal of Consulting and Clinical Psychology, 68*, 438–450.

Mayotte-Blum, J., Slavin-Mulford, J., Lehmann, M., Pesale, F., Becker-Matero, N., & Hilsenroth, M. (2012). Therapeutic immediacy across long-term psychodynamic psychotherapy: An evidence-based case study. *Journal of Counseling Psychology*, *59*, 27–40. doi: 10.1037/a0026087.

Mikulincer, M., Shaver, P. R., Cassidy, J., & Berant, E. (2009). Attachment-related defensive processes. In J. H. Obegi & E. Berant (Eds.), *Attachment theory and research in clinical work with adults*. New York: Guilford Press.

Mohr, J. J., Gelso, C. J., & Hill, C. E. (2005). Patient and counselor trainee attachment as predictors of session evaluation and countertransference behavior in first counseling sessions. *Journal of Counseling Psychology*, *52*, 298–309. doi: 10.1037/0022-0167.52.3.298.

Norcross, J. C., & Wampold, B. E. (2011). Evidence-based therapy relationships: Research conclusions and clinical practices. In J. C. Norcross (Ed.), *Psychotherapy relationships that work: Evidence-based responsiveness* (2nd ed., pp. 423–430). New York: Oxford University Press.

Safran, J. D., & Muran, J. C. (2000). *Negotiating the therapeutic alliance: A relational treatment guide*. New York: Guilford.

Spangler, P. T., Hill, C. E., Dunn, M. G., Hummel, A., Liu, J., Walden, T., Jackson, J., Ganginis, H., & Salahuddin, N. (Under review). Helping in the here-and-now: Teaching undergraduates to use immediacy.

Stiles, W. B. (1988). Psychotherapy process-outcome correlations may be misleading. *Psychotherapy*, *25*, 27–35. doi:10.1037/h0085320

Stiles, W. B. (2007). Theory-building case studies of counseling and psychotherapy. *Counselling and Psychotherapy Research*, *7*, 122–127. doi: 10.1080/14733140701356742.

Stiles, W. B. (2009). Logical operations in theory-building case studies. *Pragmatic Case Studies in Psychotherapy*, *5*, 9–22.

Teyber, E. (2006). *Interpersonal process in psychotherapy: A relational approach* (5th ed.). Pacific Grove, CA: Brooks/Cole.

Woodhouse, S. S., Schlosser, L. Z., Crook, R. E., Ligiero, D. P., & Gelso, C. J. (2003). Client attachment to therapist: relations of transference and client recollection of parental caregiving. *Journal of Counseling Psychology*, *50*, 395–408. doi: 10.1037/0022-0167.50.4.395.

The role of empathy in promoting change

JEANNE C. WATSON[1], PATRICIA L. STECKLEY[2], & EVELYN J. McMULLEN[1]

[1]*Applied Psychology and Human Development, OISE/University of Toronto, Toronto, Ontario, Canada &* [2]*Private Practice, Toronto, Ontario, Canada*

Abstract

Since Rogers identified empathy as an important variable in therapy, it has been found to be a consistent predictor of client change; less clear is how this occurs. The objective in this study was to test a mediation model to determine whether clients' self-reported experience of therapists' empathy contributed to changes in their attachment styles and treatment of self, after 16 weeks of psychotherapy for depression. There was a significant direct relationship between therapists' empathy and outcome and a significant indirect effect, showing that clients' perceptions of therapists' empathy was associated with significant improvement in attachment insecurity and significant decreases in negative self-treatment at the end of therapy as well as reductions on BDI, IIP, DAS and SCL-90-R, GSI, and increases on RSE. The findings suggest that clients' perception of their therapists as empathic is an important mechanism of change in psychotherapy that warrants further investigation.

In 1951, Rogers hypothesized that if distressed clients perceived their therapists to be empathic, accepting, prizing, and genuine, then they would be able to effect changes in psychotherapy. Since then, numerous studies have shown that the three conditions posited by Rogers are related to positive outcome across different therapeutic orientations (Beutler & Castonguay, 2006; Bohart, Elliott, Greenberg & Watson, 2002; Bohart & Greenberg, 1997; Castonguay & Beutler, 2006; Duan & Hill, 1996; Elliott, Bohart, Watson, & Greenberg, 2011; Hill, Rochlen, Zack, McCready, & Dematatis, 2003; Lambert & Barley, 2001; Norcross, 2002, 2011; Norcross & Wampold, 2011; Orlinsky, Grawe & Parks, 1994; Truax & Mitchell, 1971; Watson, 2002; Watson & Geller, 2005). It has been shown that therapists' empathy accounts for more of the variance in outcome than specific interventions (Bohart et al., 2002), therapist's psychotherapy orientation, or other therapist qualities such as credibility (Luborsky, McLellan, Woody, O'Brien, & Auerbach, 1985).

Empathy is thought to contribute to positive outcomes in psychotherapy by facilitating the development of a positive therapeutic alliance (Castonguay & Beutler, 2006; Watson & Geller, 2005). Horvath and Greenberg (1989) reported that clients' perceptions of therapists' empathy accounted for a significant amount of the variance in total Working Alliance Inventory scores. Further support for the positive role of empathy in psychotherapy is provided by other studies that have found a positive relationship between the therapeutic alliance and therapists' affiliative behaviours, such as being attuned, supportive, empathic, and sensitive to patient's feelings (Price & Jones, 1998). Similarly, Najavits and Strupp (1994) found that affirming and understanding behaviours in psychodynamic therapy contributed to a positive alliance. While there is much support for the role that empathy plays in establishing and maintaining a positive therapeutic relationship, less attention has been paid to investigating other ways that empathy might facilitate change in psychotherapy.

In addition to promoting the establishment and maintenance of a positive alliance, theorists from diverse therapeutic orientations have argued that therapists' empathy is associated with good outcome in psychotherapy because it facilitates changes in client's internal representations of self (Bohart &

Greenberg, 1997; Kohut, 1984; Rogers, 1963). Rogers (1957) posited that therapists' empathy positively impacts clients' internalized conditions of worth. He suggested that psychological well-being is based on acceptance and openness to one's inner experiencing, and believed that therapists' communication showing understanding and acceptance of their clients' inner experiencing facilitated the latters' awareness and acceptance of their feelings (Rogers, 1963, 1976). According to Rogers, when clients experience their therapists' acceptance and empathy, this helps them to moderate their conditions of worth and value their own internal experience as a guide for their behaviour (Rogers, 1963).

Subsequently Barrett-Lennard (1997) argued that therapists' empathy facilitates the development of self-empathy in clients. Moreover he suggested that as clients become more empathic towards themselves, they become more open and empathic towards others. Experiential theorists have argued that therapists' empathic responses toward clients' inner experiences helps clients to access their emotions, recognize their needs, and develop more effective affect regulation strategies (Paivio & Laurent, 2001; Watson 2002; Watson, Goldman, & Vanaerschot, 1998). Watson (2011), extending Rogers's Process Model, proposed that the manner in which clients' inner experience and perceptions are treated by and responded to by others is internalized and gives rise not only to conditions of worth but to behaviours and ways of treating subjective experience and perceptions in order to regulate and moderate them. It is through interactions with the environment and specifically significant others that individuals learn whether to attend to and accept their inner subjective experience and act in ways that are enhancing, protective and nurturing towards the self; or alternatively, to act in ways that are more negative towards their subjective experience, for example, silencing, neglecting, oppressing, and controlling their inner experience in order to regulate and moderate it. Negative ways of treating the self can contribute to depression and other psychological difficulties.

This view is consistent with theorists from other orientations that have viewed empathy as healing within the therapeutic encounter. Bowlby (1969, 1988) theorized that psychotherapy could facilitate and contribute to changes in clients' adult attachment models consisting of representations of self and others. Kohut (1984) viewed the analyst's empathy as core to the psychoanalytic cure, seeing it as essential to making accurate and timely interpretations, which form the basis for the patient to internalize the analyst as a good self-object. According to Kohut it is the internalization of the empathic analyst that leads to the repair and development of the client's psychic structures. In sum, these theorists argue that therapists' empathic behaviours towards their clients can affect how clients treat themselves and contribute to positive outcomes in psychotherapy.

It has been shown that clients' treatment of self and their attachment styles can change in positive directions over the course of effective psychotherapy, and that changes in client's internal representations of self and others is associated with positive outcome (Harrist, Quintana, Strupp & Henry, 1994; Henry, Schacht & Strupp, 1990; Kalogerakos, 1997; Quintana & Meara, 1990; Travis, Bliwise, Binder, & Horne-Moyer, 2001). Harrist et al. (1994) found that higher levels of internalization of positive therapist behaviours were correlated with decreased levels of anxiety and dysthymia and higher levels of global functioning as assessed by clinicians. The objective in this paper is to determine the direct and indirect effects of therapists' perceived empathy as a mechanism of change in a sample of clients who were treated in a randomized clinical trial (RCT) with cognitive behavioural therapy (CBT) or emotion-focused therapy, the process experiential approach, (EFT-PE) for depression (Watson, Gordon, Stermac, Kalogerakos & Steckley, 2003). Watson et al. (2003) found that comparisons between these two treatment types were generally equivalent for all outcome indices, with the exception of a significantly greater decrease in clients' self-report of their interpersonal problems in EFT-PE than in CBT.

Hypotheses

The primary goal in this study was to test a multivariate model to determine whether clients' ways of treating their inner experience and clients' attachment styles mediated the relationship between therapeutic empathy and outcome. Specifically it was hypothesized that:

1. There would be a significant decrease in clients' levels of insecure attachment and negative self-treatment over the course of psychotherapy.
2. Clients' experience of therapists' empathy would be associated with a decrease in their level of insecure attachment and less negative self-treatment at the end of therapy.
3. A reduction in clients' levels of insecure attachment and negative self-treatment would be associated with fewer depressive symptoms, dysfunctional attitudes, and interpersonal problems, as well as less psychological distress, and higher self-esteem.

4. The relationship between therapists' empathy and clients' outcome indices would be mediated by a decrease in clients' insecure attachment scores and less negative self-treatment at the end of therapy.
5. The relationship between therapists' empathy and clients' outcome indices mediated through changes in clients' self-representations would be significant over and above the working alliance.

Method

Participants

Clients. The data for this research study were drawn from an RCT comparing clients who received 16 sessions of either CBT or EFT-PE once per week for depression (Watson et al., 2003). The initial sample consisted of 66 depressed clients. Using casewise deletion to address missing data, the sample for the current study consisted of 55 clients (26 in CBT and 29 in EFT-PE; 37 females and 18 males). Clients were predominantly of European decent (89%). The age range was 21 to 59 ($M = 37.55$, $SD = 12.09$). All clients met the minimum DSM-IV (American Psychiatric Association, 1994) criteria for a current major depressive episode and scores for Global Assessment Functioning ranged from 51 to 65 ($M = 58.02$, $SD = 4.02$). There were no significant differences between the initial sample and the sample used in this study on any of the demographic variables, or any of the variables used in the analyses for the current study, with one exception. The mean residualized gain score for negative self-treatment for the deleted cases ($M = -4.75$, $SD = 6.94$) was significantly lower than for the current sample ($M = 0.86$, $SD = 9.45$).

Therapists. There were 15 therapists in the study, three males and 12 females, all of whom had previous clinical experience. Two therapists were psychologists, 10 were doctoral students and three were master's students; all of the students were enrolled in counselling or clinical psychology graduate programs. CBT therapists had an average of 5.4 years clinical experience and EFT-PE therapists an average of 5.7 years; experience ranged from 1 to 15 years. Therapists' mean age was 35 for CBT and 33 for EFT-PE. There were no significant differences between groups for therapists' level of experience or age.

Treatments

CBT treatment followed a protocol based on an adaptation of Beck, Rush, Shaw, and Emery's (1979) model of cognitive therapy for depression. Therapists were directed to have an awareness of social and contextual issues and focus on accessing clients' cognitive schemes in order to facilitate client change. The treatment was primarily a cognitive therapy with some behavioural components, such as recording daily activities and behavioral experiments.

EFT-PE treatment followed the manual developed by Greenberg, Rice, and Elliott (1993). EFT-PE combines client-centred conditions with specific treatment tasks such as: systematic evocative unfolding; experiential focusing; empty chair work; and two-chair dialogues. During the first three sessions therapists focused on building the therapeutic alliance and began to formulate therapeutic tasks that were introduced after the third session and were employed with clients' agreement.

Self-Report Measure

Attachment Style Questionnaire (ASQ; Feeney, Noller, & Hanrahan, 1994). The ASQ is a 40-item self-report questionnaire, rated on a Likert scale from 1 to 6, with 1 indicating strong disagreement and 6 indicating strong agreement. It assesses five styles of adult attachment: one securely attached style, *Confidence (in self and others)*, and four insecurely attached styles, *Discomfort with Closeness*, *Need for Approval*, *Preoccupation with Relationships*, and *Relationships as Secondary (to achievement)*. The four insecure subscales were combined for the purpose of this study. Feeney and colleagues (1994) reported high internal consistency across the five styles ($\alpha = .76$ to $.84$), good validity, and acceptable test-retest reliability ($\alpha = .67$ to $.78$). Cronbach's alpha scores for the current study were .84 and .84 for the *Secure* style, and .84 and .91 for the overall *Insecure* style, pre and post treatment respectively.

In-session Process Measure

Structural Analysis of Social Behaviour – introject surface (SASB; Benjamin, 1974). The SASB process measure is based on a circumplex model of social behaviour. The introject surface, used in this study, pertains to behaviours directed towards the self. It is divided into quadrants in a circular matrix along two axes. The horizontal axis represents a continuum of affiliative behaviours towards the self, from hostile disaffiliation (left of the vertical axis) to loving/friendly affiliation (right of the vertical axis). The vertical axis represents interdependence describing behaviours that range from controlling to neglectful and happy go-lucky treatment towards self. The four quadrants are represented by these four categories of behaviour: Accept/Enjoy Self, Manage/Cultivate Self, Oppress Self, and Reject Self. The SASB model has been supported by tests employing techniques of factor analysis, autocorrelational analysis, circumplex analysis, and a dimensional ratings procedure (Benjamin, 1996).

Post-Session Measures

Barrett-Lennard Relationship Inventory – Empathy Subscale (BLRI-E; Barrett-Lennard, 1995). The BLRI is a 40-item client self-report measure. Clients rate their therapists' level of empathy, congruence, prizing, and acceptance on a scale from -3 to $+3$, indicating strong disagreement to strong agreement, about the extent to which they experienced the conditions. The BLRI has been shown to have high overall internal consistency ($\alpha =$ .91), construct and content validity, and reliability ($r = .90$; Barrett-Lennard, 1986). The 10-item Empathy subscale was used in the present study (BLRI-E; $\alpha = .84$, $r = .83$; Barrett-Lennard, 1986). Scores were averaged across two measurement points (sessions 9 and 12). Cronbach's alpha scores for the current study, for sessions 9, 12 and the combination of the two sessions, were .92, .91 and .95, respectively.

Working Alliance Inventory-Short Form (WAI-S). The WAI-S (Tracey & Kokotovic, 1989) is a 12-item self-report questionnaire, rated 1 to 7, derived from Bordin's (1979) conceptualization of the working alliance consisting of agreement on tasks and goals, as well as the therapeutic bond. It is short-form version of the 36-item instrument Horvath & Greenberg (1989) validated using factor analysis (Tracey & Kokotovic, 1989). Higher scores, summing the 12 items, indicate a stronger overall working alliance. In this study the mean scores across the 16 sessions of therapy were used. The WAI-S instrument demonstrates good internal consistency, construct, convergent and predictive validity (Horvath & Greenberg, 1989; Tracey & Kokotovic, 1989) and Tryon and Kane (1993) reported a reliability estimate of $r = .98$. The Cronbach's alpha for the current study was a mean of .89 for across the 16 sessions.

Outcome Measures

Beck Depression Inventory (BDI; Beck, Ward, Mendelson, Mock, & Erbaugh, 1961). The BDI is a 21-item, self-report inventory, rated 0 to 3, assessing severity of depression. Higher scores, summing the 21 items, indicate greater distress. The BDI has demonstrated good internal consistency ($\alpha = .73$ to .93; Beck, Steer, & Garbin, 1988), good construct, convergent, concurrent and divergent validity (Beck et al., 1961, 1988; Gould, 1982), as well as good test-retest reliability ($r = .65$; Ogles, Lambert, & Sawyer, 1995). Scores collected post-therapy were used in this study. The Cronbach's alpha for the current study was .93.

Dysfunctional Attitudes Scale (DAS; Weissman & Beck, 1978). The DAS is a 40-item, self-report inventory, rated 1 to 7, developed to identify pervasive negative attitudes toward self, outside world, and future that may relate to or cause depression. Lower scores, summing the 40 items, represent more adaptive beliefs and fewer cognitive distortions. Psychometric evaluations revealed very good internal consistency ($\alpha = .84$ to .92), excellent concurrent validity (Kuiper & Olinger, 1989), and excellent stability ($r = .80$ to .84). Scores collected post-therapy were used in this study. The Cronbach's alpha for the current study was .94.

Inventory of Interpersonal Problems (IIP; Horowitz, Rosenberg, Baer, Ureno, & Villasenor, 1988). The IIP is a 127-item, self-report inventory, rated 0 to 4, pertaining to behaviours that are associated with interpersonal problems. Lower scores, averaging the 127 items, represent more adaptive beliefs and fewer cognitive distortions. Good internal consistency, validity, and reliability ($r = .90$; Hansen & Lambert, 1996) have been demonstrated (Horowitz et al., 1988). Scores collected post-therapy were used in this study. The Cronbach's alpha for the current study was .98.

Symptom Checklist-90-Revised (SCL-90-R; Derogatis, Lipman, & Covi, 1973; Derogatis, Rickels & Rock, 1976). The SCL-90-R is a 90-item, self-report questionnaire, rated 0 to 4, measuring general psychological distress. Scores for the Global Symptom Index (GSI) were used in this study. Higher scores on the GSI, averaging the 90 items, indicate higher overall distress. Psychometric evaluations for the SCL-90-R have shown good internal consistency ($\alpha = .77$ to .90), good concurrent, construct, and discriminant validity (Derogatis, 1983, 1994; Morgan, Wiederman, & Magnus, 1998), and good test-retest reliability ($r = .80$ and .90; Derogatis, 1983, 1994).

Rosenberg Self-Esteem Inventory (RSE; Rosenberg, 1965). The RSE is a 10-item self-report questionnaire, rated 1–5, employed to measure self-esteem. Higher scores, summing the 10 items, indicate higher self-esteem. This instrument has shown good internal consistency ($\alpha = .89$ to .94), good concurrent, predictive and construct validity, and good test-retest reliability ($r = 80$ to .90; Bachman & O'Malley, 1977; Rosenberg, 1979). Scores collected post-therapy were used in this study. The Cronbach's alpha for the current study was .93.

Procedure

The procedure with respect to participants' consent, assessment and assignment to therapy groups is outlined in Watson et al. (2003). For the purposes of this study clients' self-report data on the BDI, DAS, IIP, GSI, and RSE at post therapy were used. The BLRI.E was administered to clients after the 9th and 12th sessions and the WAI-S was administered after every session. Mean scores across sessions for the BLRI.E and WAI-S were calculated for this study. The adult attachment questionnaire (ASQ) was completed at pre and post therapy. Both the secure attachment style scores and the composite score for insecure attachment were investigated in the current study.

For clients' self-treatment, the middle 15 minutes of session 3 and session 15 were transcribed and then segmented into thought units. Two independent raters, who were doctoral candidates in counselling psychology, were trained according to the SASB coding manual guidelines (Benjamin, Giat, & Estroff, 1981) and rated the transcripts. Transcripts were randomly divided between the two raters with an overlap of one-third. Inter-rater reliability was significant using Cohen's Kappa ($\kappa = .97$, $p < .01$; Cohen, 1960).

Ratings were then categorized as either positive or negative towards the self and the raw sum of statements was computed. Raw scores were used in the analyses rather than calculating derived scores (i.e., proportions), because derived scores are believed to change the meaning of constructs and raw scores are considered to be more stable. Using proportions not only changes the metric of the raw score but also creates a dependent relationship between positive and negative units (Cronbach & Furby, 1970; Golembiewski, Billingsley, & Yeager, 1976). Thus in this study, the total number of positive statements and the total number of negative statements, resulting in two separate variables, for two time points (sessions 3 and 15) were used.

Results

Preliminary Data Analyses

Screening. Prior to analysis, SPSS programs were used to screen the accuracy of data entry, missing values, potential outliers, and to test for univariate normality. Casewise deletion was employed. Post-regression assumptions were checked and concerns addressed. Pearson product-moment correlations among the variables used in the current study are presented in Table I.

Change Over Time by Therapy Group for ASQ and SASB

To determine (a) if clients' *attachment style and treatment of self* changed over the course of psychotherapy, and (b) if there were differences between the two therapy groups, four 2 × 2 analyses of variance (ANOVA) were conducted, with Time (SASB early/late; ASQ pre/post) as the within-subjects repeated measure and Therapy Group (CBT, EFT-PE) as the between-subjects factor.

Table I. Inter-correlations among empathy, alliance, attachment, self-treatment, and outcome ($n = 55$)

Variable	1.	2.	3.	4.	5.	6.	7.	8.	9.	10.
1. BLRI-E	–	–	–	–	–	–	–	–	–	–
2. WAI-S	.80	–	–	–	–	–	–	–	–	–
3. ASQ Secure	.40	.53	–	–	–	–	–	–	–	–
4. ASQ Insecure	−.50	−.46	−.64	–	–	–	–	–	–	–
5. SASB Positive	.07	.02	.10	−.20	–	–	–	–	–	–
6. SASB Negative	−.37	−.33	−.30	.40	−.19	–	–	–	–	–
7. Post BDI	−.32	−.51	−.56	.48	−.13	.33	–	–	–	–
8. Post DAS	−.48	−.48	−.62	.55	−.20	.45	.56	–	–	–
9. Post IIP	−.42	−.41	−.45	.55	−.21	.45	.68	.67	–	–
10. Post GSI	−.32	−.47	−.47	.47	−.07	.41	.86	.50	.62	–
11. Post RSE	.38	.43	.48	−.55	.13	−.47	−.69	−.69	−.60	−.61

Note. BLRI-E = Barrett-Lennard Relationship Inventory: Empathy Subscale. WAI-S = Working Alliance Inventory- Short Form. ASQ = Adult Attachment Questionnaire, Secure and Insecure Styles, residualized gain scores. SASB = Structural Analysis of Social Behaviour, Introject Surface, Positive and Negative residualized gain scores. BDI = Beck Depression Inventory at post therapy. DAS = Dysfunctional Attitudes Scale at post therapy. IIP = Inventory of Interpersonal Problems at post therapy. GSI = Symptom Checklist-90-Revised: Global Symptom Index at post therapy. RSE = Rosenberg Self-esteem Inventory at post therapy.
If $r \leq .24$, p = ns. If $r = .25$ to .32, $p < .05$. If $r = .33$ to .39, $p < .01$. If $r \geq .40$, $p < .001$.

The main effects for Time and the Therapy × Time interaction effects were tested using Wilks's Lambda (Λ). Means and standard deviations for variables used in this study are presented in Tables II and III.

As predicted, main effects for improvements in scores were significant for *secure attachment*, $\Lambda = .68$, $F(1,53) = 25.36$, $p < .001$, $\eta^2 = .33$, observed power .99; *insecure attachment*, $\Lambda = .68$, $F(1,53) = 24.55$, $p < .001$, $\eta^2 = .32$, observed power .99; *positive self-treatment*, $\Lambda = .93$, $F(1,53) = 4.16$, $p = .05$, $\eta^2 = .07$, observed power .52; and *negative self-treatment*, $\Lambda = .83$, $F(1,53) = 10.62$, $p < .01$, $\eta^2 = .17$, observed power .89. The Therapy × Time interaction effects were not significant for any of these analyses.

Mediation Analyses – Direct and Indirect Effects of Therapist Empathy

Due to the small sample size and low power, mediation analyses were conducted with therapy groups combined. No differences were found between therapy groups for any of the variables used in the study, with one exception. The mean score for clients' negative self-treatment was significantly lower in EFT-PE at post therapy than in CBT, $t(53) = 2.74$, $p < .01$. To reduce the number of predictors and address multicollinearity between pre and post scores, residualized gain scores were computed for secure and insecure attachment, and positive and negative self-treatment, first predicting post scores from pre scores and then subtracting predicted scores from actual post therapy scores (MacKinnon, 2008).

To determine the *direct* and *indirect* effects of *therapists' perceived empathy* as a *mechanism of change*, the procedures were followed for mediation analysis as outlined by Baron & Kenny (1986). To establish mediation three pathways must be significant (Baron & Kenny, 1986): the relationship between the independent variable (IV) and the mediator (M), between the IV and the dependent variable (DV), and between the M and the DV. In addition, the strength of the relationship between the IV and the outcome indices must be appreciably smaller when the mediator is included in the model, as compared to when it is not.

First, linear regression analyses were performed to test whether the IV, *therapists' empathy* (BLRI-E), predicted the proposed mediators (M): improvement in *secure* and *insecure attachment* (ASQ) and in *positive* and *negative self-treatment* (SASB) at the end of therapy. The regression analyses were significant with *therapists' empathy* predicting change in secure attachment, $t(53) = -3.14$, $p < .01$, $\beta = .40$, $R^2 = .16$, adjusted $R^2 = .14$; insecure attachment, $t(53) = -4.14$, $p < .001$, $\beta = -.50$, $R^2 = .25$, adjusted $R^2 = .23$; and negative self-treatment, $t(53) = -2.90$, $p < .01$, $\beta = -.37$, $R^2 = .14$, adjusted $R^2 = .12$. However, *therapists' empathy* failed to significantly predict change in positive self-treatment, $t(53) = 0.47$, $p = .64$, $\beta = .01$; therefore, the positive self-treatment variable was dropped from the meditational analyses.

Second, linear regression analyses were performed to test whether the IV, *therapists' empathy* (BLRI-E), predicted the DV, including lower scores on depression (Post BDI), dysfunctional attitudes (Post DAS), interpersonal problems (Post IIP), and global symptom distress (Post GSI) as well as higher self-esteem (Post RSE) at the end of therapy. See equation 1 in Table IV, V and VI. The regression analyses were significant, with *therapists' empathy* predicting Post BDI ($\beta = -.32$), Post DAS ($\beta = -.48$) Post IIP ($\beta = -.42$), Post GSI ($\beta = -.32$) and Post RSE ($\beta = .38$).

Third, hierarchical linear regression analyses were performed to test whether improvement in *attachment* (ASQ secure, ASQ insecure) and improvement in *negative self-treatment* (SASB negative) mediated the relationship between therapists' empathy and outcome. First the BLRI.E was entered into the regression model and then the

Table II. Means and standard deviations for empathy, alliance, attachment, self-treatment, and outcome ($n = 55$)

	ASQ Secure			ASQ Insecure			SASB Positive			SASB Negative		
	Pre	Post	Residual	Pre	Post	Residual	Pre	Post	Residual	Pre	Post	Residual
EFT	3.43[a]	3.99	.06	3.65	3.24	−.06	28.38	34.31	1.84	19.45	10.91	−2.27
$n = 26$	(.93)[b]	(.89)	(.72)	(.61)	(.56)	(.42)	(17.01)	(18.32)	(16.36)	(12.70)	(7.35)	(7.54)
CBT	3.44	3.87	−.06	3.71	3.39	.05	24.58	28.73	−2.06	21.31	17.86	4.36
$n = 29$	(1.03)	(.90)	(.55)	(.61)	(.76)	(.58)	(13.59)	(16.09)	(15.58)	(11.12)	(10.93)	(10.25)
All	3.43	3.93	.00	3.68	3.31	−.01	26.58	31.67	.00	20.33	14.22	.86
clients	(.97)	(.89)	(.64)	(.61)	(.66)	(.51)	(15.46)	(17.37)	(15.97)	(11.90)	(9.78)	(9.45)

Note. EFT = Emotion-Focused Therapy. CBT = Cognitive-Behavioural Therapy. ASQ = Adult Attachment Questionnaire, Secure and Insecure Styles, pre, post treatment and residualized gain scores. SASB = Structural Analysis of Social Behaviour, Introject Surface, Positive and Negative, pre, post treatment and residualized gain scores.

[a] Mean scores; [b] Standard deviation.

Table III. Means and standard deviations for empathy, alliance, attachment, self-treatment, and outcome ($n = 55$)

	Mean BLRI	Mean WAI	Post BDI	Post DAS	Post IIP	Post GSI	Post RSE
EFT	22.50[a]	5.83	8.21	115.28	1.02	.51	38.86
$n = 26$	(4.33)[b]	(.51)	(8.19)	(34.62)	(.50)	(.52)	(6.46)
CBT	20.48	5.65	11.23	124.42	1.19	.71	36.04
$n = 29$	(6.79)	(.94)	(10.44)	(32.62)	(.56)	(.62)	(8.05)
All	21.55	5.75	9.64	119.60	1.10	.61	37.53
Clients	(5.67)	(.74)	(9.36)	(33.69)	(.53)	(.57)	(7.32)

Note. EFT = Emotion-Focused Therapy. CBT = Cognitive-Behavioural Therapy. BLRI = Barrett-Lennard Relationship Inventory: Empathy Subscale. WAI = Working Alliance Inventory – Short Form. BDI = Beck Depression Inventory at post therapy. DAS = Dysfunctional Attitudes Scale at post therapy. IIP = Inventory of Interpersonal Problems at post therapy. GSI = Symptom Checklist-90-Revised: Global Symptom Index at post therapy. RSE = Rosenberg Self-Esteem Inventory at post therapy.
[a] Mean scores; [b] Standard deviation.

residualized gains scores for secure and insecure attachment and negative self-treatment, respectively, were entered in the second step for each of the five outcome variables. Thus, as a final step, to control for the effect of the working alliance mediating the effect between BLRI.E and outcome, the WAI was added to the model. The results for secure attachment are presented in Table IV, for insecure attachment in Table V, and negative self-treatment in Table VI.

Table IV. Empathy effects outcome through greater secure attachment ($n = 55$)

Equation	IV	DV	β	t	p	R^2	$F_{(df)}$	P_M	sr	sr^2
1.1	BLRI-E	Post BDI	−.32	−2.49	.016	.11	$6.20_{(1,53)}$*			
1.2	BLRI-E		−.12	−.96	.341				.11	.01
	ASQ Secure	Post BDI	−.52	−4.19	.000	.33	$12.82_{(2.52)}$***	.63	.48	.23
1.3	BLRI-E		.21	1.17	.249				.13	.02
	ASQ Secure		−.40	−3.11	.003			.49	.34	.11
	WAI-S	Post BDI	−.47	−2.41	.020	.40	$11.27_{(3,51)}$***		.26	.07
2.1	BLRI-E	Post DAS	−.48	−4.02	.000	.23	$16.16_{(1,53)}$***			
2.2	BLRI-E		−.28	−2.52	.015				.26	.07
	ASQ Secure	Post DAS	−.51	−4.58	.000	.45	$21.60_{(2.52)}$***	.42	.47	.22
2.3	BLRI-E		−.32	−1.85	.071				.19	.04
	ASQ Secure		−.52	−4.30	.000			.43	.44	.20
	WAI-S	Post DAS	.05	.29	.777	.46	$14.17_{(3,51)}$***		.03	.00
3.1	BLRI-E	Post IIP	−.42	−3.41	.001	.18	$11.64_{(1.53)}$***			
3.2	BLRI-E		−.29	−2.26	.028				.26	.07
	ASQ Secure	Post IIP	−.34	−2.62	.011	.28	$9.90_{(2.52)}$***	.31	.31	.10
3.3	BLRI-E		−.29	−1.46	.151				.17	.03
	ASQ Secure		−.34	−2.39	.020			.31	.29	.08
	WAI-S	Post IIP	−.01	−.01	.992	.28	$6.48_{(3.51)}$***		.01	.00
4.1	BLRI-E	Post GSI	−.32	−2.44	.018	.10	$5.96_{(1.53)}$*			
4.2	BLRI-E		−.16	−1.20	.236				.15	.02
	ASQ Secure	Post GSI	−.40	−3.06	.004	.24	$8.13_{(2.52)}$***	.50	.37	.14
4.3	BLRI-E		.13	.67	.505				.08	.01
	ASQ Secure		−.30	−2.15	.037			.37	.25	.06
	WAI-S	Post GSI	−.41	−1.95	.057	.29	$6.98_{(3.51)}$***		.23	.05
5.1	BLRI-E	Post RSE	.38	2.94	.005	.14	$8.66_{(1.53)}$**			
5.2	BLRI-E		.22	1.71	.094				.20	.04
	ASQ Secure	Post RSE	.39	3.01	.004	.27	$9.52_{(2.52)}$***	.41	.36	.13
5.3	BLRI-E		.11	.57	.569				.07	.00
	ASQ Secure		.35	2.49	.016			.37	.30	.09
	WAI-S	Post RSE	.15	.71	.482	.28	$6.45_{(3.51)}$***		.09	.01

Note. IV = independent variable; DV = dependent variable. BLRI-E = Barrett-Lennard Relationship Inventory: Empathy subscale. ASQ = Attachment Style Questionnaire: Secure Style. BDI = Beck Depression Inventory. DAS = Dysfunctional Attitudes Scale. IIP = Inventory of Interpersonal Problems. GSI = Symptom Checklist-90-Revised: Global Symptom Index. RSE = Rosenberg Self-Esteem Inventory. WAI = Working Alliance Inventory – Short Form. P_M = the proportion of the variance accounted for by mediation. sr = semi-partial correlation. sr^2 = proportion of variance in outcome uniquely predictable from improvement in secure attachment, and where applicable controlling for WAI.
* $p < .05$. ** $p < .01$. *** $p < .001$.

Table V. Empathy effects outcome through improvments in insecure attachment ($n = 55$)

Equation	IV	DV	β	t	p	R^2	$F_{(df)}$	P_M	sr	sr^2
1.1	BLRI-E	Post BDI	−.32	−2.49	.016	.11	$6.20_{(1,53)}$*			
1.2	BLRI-E		−.11	−.82	.418				.10	.01
	ASQ Insecure	Post BDI	.43	3.06	.004	.24	$8.26_{(2.52)}$***	.65	.37	.14
1.3	BLRI-E		.37	1.95	.057				.21	.05
	ASQ Insecure		.37	2.88	.006			.56	.32	.10
	WAI-S	Post BDI	−.64	−3.45	.001	.39	$10.63_{(3,51)}$***		.38	.14
2.1	BLRI-E	Post DAS	−.48	−4.02	.000	.23	$16.16_{(1,53)}$***			
2.2	BLRI-E		−.28	−2.21	.032				.25	.06
	ASQ Insecure	Post DAS	.41	3.19	.002	.36	$14.55_{(2.52)}$***	.42	.35	.13
2.3	BLRI-E		−.15	−.76	.449				.09	.01
	ASQ Insecure		.39	3.03	.004			.40	.34	.11
	WAI-S	Post DAS	−.18	−.97	.335	.37	$10.01_{(3,51)}$***		.11	.01
3.1	BLRI-E	Post IIP	−.42	−3.41	.001	.18	$11.64_{(1.53)}$***			
3.2	BLRI-E		−.20	−1.55	.127				.18	.03
	ASQ Insecure	Post IIP	.45	3.44	.001	.33	$12.94_{(2.52)}$***	.52	.39	.15
3.3	BLRI-E		−.11	−.58	.562				.07	.00
	ASQ Insecure		.44	3.34	.002			.51	.38	.14
	WAI-S	Post IIP	−.12	−.61	.543	.34	$8.65_{(3.51)}$***		.07	.00
4.1	BLRI-E	Post GSI	−.32	−2.44	.018	.10	$5.96_{(1.53)}$*			
4.2	BLRI-E		−.11	−.80	.430				.10	.01
	ASQ Insecure	Post GSI	.42	2.99	.004	.23	$7.90_{(2.52)}$***	.65	.36	.13
4.3	BLRI-E		.28	1.43	.158				.16	.03
	ASQ Insecure		.37	2.79	.007			.57	.32	.10
	WAI-S	Post GSI	−.52	−2.70	.009	.33	$8.33_{(3.51)}$***		.31	.10
5.1	BLRI-E	Post RSE	.38	2.94	.005	.14	$8.66_{(1.53)}$**			
5.2	BLRI-E		.14	1.03	.309				.12	.01
	ASQ Insecure	Post RSE	−.48	−3.67	.001	.32	$12.07_{(2.52)}$***	.64	.42	.18
5.3	BLRI-E		−.07	−.36	.721				.04	.00
	ASQ Insecure		−.46	−3.49	.001			.60	.40	.16
	WAI-S	Post RSE	.27	1.43	.160	.34	$8.89_{(3.51)}$***		.16	.03

Note. IV = independent variable; DV = dependent variable. BLRI-E = Barrett-Lennard Relationship Inventory: Empathy subscale. ASQ = Attachment Style Questionnaire: Insecure Style. BDI = Beck Depression Inventory. DAS = Dysfunctional Attitudes Scale. IIP = Inventory of Interpersonal Problems. GSI = Symptom Checklist-90-Revised: Global Symptom Index. RSE = Rosenberg Self-Esteem Inventory. WAI = Working Alliance Inventory – Short Form. P_M = the proportion of the variance accounted for by mediation. sr = semi-partial correlation. sr^2 = proportion of variance in outcome uniquely predictable from improvement in secure attachment, and where applicable controlling for WAI.
* $p < .05$. ** $p < .01$. *** $p < .001$.

The models significantly predicted outcome on all five of the outcome measures at the end of therapy. Specifically, clients' improvements in *secure attachment* post-therapy significantly predicted outcome on the BDI, DAS, IIP, GSI, and RSE after controlling for BLRI-E. As predicted, the β weight for *therapists' empathy* dropped from −.32 to −.12 on BDI; −.48 to −.28 on DAS; −.42 to −.29 on IIP; −.32 to −.22 on the GSI; and .38 to .22 on RSE, indicating that improvements in *secure attachment* at the end of therapy mediated the relationship between *therapists' empathy* and outcome for all five outcome indices. Effect sizes were calculated using P_M, the ratio of the indirect effect divided by mediation to the total effect (Preacher & Kelley, 2011). The magnitude of the indirect effect of therapist empathy mediated by improvements in *secure attachment* was .63 for BDI, .42 for DAS, .31 for IIP, .50 for GSI, and .41 for RSE, which uniquely accounted for 23%, 22%, 10%, 14% and 13% of the variance in outcome, respectively. Even after controlling for the WAI, improvements in *secure attachment* uniquely accounted for 11% (BDI), 20% (DAS), 8% (IIP), 6% (GSI) and 9% (RSE) of the variance in outcome across the five models.

Similarly, clients' improvements in *insecure attachment* post-therapy significantly predicted outcome on the BDI, DAS, IIP, GSI, and RSE after controlling for BLRI-E. As predicted, the β weight for *therapists' empathy* dropped from −.32 to −.11 on BDI; −.48 to −.28 on DAS; −.42 to −.20 on IIP; −.32 to −.11 on the GSI; and .38 to .14 on RSE, indicating that improvements in *insecure attachment* at the end of therapy mediated the relationship between *therapists' empathy* and outcome for all five outcome indices. The magnitude of the indirect effect of therapist empathy mediated by improved *insecure attachment* was .65 for BDI, .42 for DAS, .52 for IIP, .65 for GSI, and .64 for RSE, which uniquely accounted for 14%, 13%, 15%, 13%

Table VI. Empathy effects outcome through improvements in negative self-treatment ($n = 55$)

Equation	IV	DV	β	t	p	R^2	$F_{(df)}$	P_M	Sr	sr^2
1.1	BLRI-E	Post BDI	−.32	−2.49	.016	.11	$6.20_{(1,53)}$*			
1.2	BLRI-E		−.23	−1.70	.096				.22	.05
	SASB Negative	Post BDI	.25	1.79	.079	.16	$4.84_{(2.52)}$**	.28	.23	.05
1.3	BLRI-E		.31	1.59	.119				.18	.03
	SASB Negative		.22	1.80	.077			.26	.21	.04
	WAI-S	Post BDI	−.69	−3.60	.001	.33	$8.28_{(3,51)}$***		.41	.17
2.1	BLRI-E	Post DAS	−.48	−4.02	.000	.23	$16.16_{(1,53)}$***			
2.2	BLRI-E		−.37	−2.98	.004				.34	.12
	SASB Negative	Post DAS	.31	2.54	.014	.32	$12.15_{(2.52)}$***	.24	.29	.08
2.3	BLRI-E		−.19	−.96	.343				.11	.01
	SASB Negative		.31	2.49	.016			.23	.28	.08
	WAI-S	Post DAS	−.23	−1.22	.229	.34	$8.67_{(3,51)}$***		.14	.02
3.1	BLRI-E	Post IIP	−.42	−3.41	.001	.18	$11.64_{(1.53)}$***			
3.2	BLRI-E		−.30	−2.36	.022				.28	.08
	SASB Negative	Post IIP	.34	2.65	.011	.28	$10.01_{(2.52)}$***	.29	.31	.10
3.3	BLRI-E		−.16	−.81	.421				.10	.01
	SASB Negative		.33	2.60	.012			.29	.31	.09
	WAI-S	Post IIP	−.17	−.89	.381	.29	$6.90_{(3.51)}$***		.10	.01
4.1	BLRI-E	Post GSI	−.32	−2.44	.018	.10	$5.96_{(1.53)}$*			
4.2	BLRI-E		−.19	−1.45	.153				.18	.03
	SASB Negative	Post GSI	.33	2.50	.016	.20	$6.40_{(2.52)}$**	.39	.31	.10
4.3	BLRI-E		.25	1.28	.208				.15	.02
	SASB Negative		.32	2.52	.015			.37	.29	.09
	WAI-S	Post GSI	−.57	−2.92	.005	.31	$7.73_{(3.51)}$***		.34	.11
5.1	BLRI-E	Post RSE	.38	2.94	.005	.14	$8.66_{(1.53)}$**			
5.2	BLRI-E		.24	1.83	.073				.22	.05
	SASB Negative	Post RSE	−.38	−2.95	.005	.26	$9.32_{(2.52)}$***	.37	.35	.12
5.3	BLRI-E		−.03	−.13	.900				.02	.00
	SASB Negative		−.37	−2.92	.005			.36	.34	.12
	WAI-S	Post RSE	.33	1.69	.097	.30	$7.39_{(3.51)}$***		.20	.04

Note. IV = independent variable; DV = dependent variable. BLRI-E = Barrett-Lennard Relationship Inventory: Empathy subscale. SASB = Structural Analysis of Social Behaviour, Negative Introject Surface, residualized gain scores. BDI = Beck Depression Inventory. DAS = Dysfunctional Attitudes Scale. IIP = Inventory of Interpersonal Problems. GSI = Symptom Checklist-90-Revised: Global Symptom Index. RSE = Rosenberg Self-Esteem Inventory. WAI = Working Alliance Inventory – Short Form. P_M = the proportion of the variance accounted for by mediation. sr = semi-partial correlation. sr^2 = proportion of variance in outcome uniquely predictable from improvement in negative self-treatment, and where applicable controlling for WAI.
* $p < .05$. ** $p < .01$. *** $p < .001$.

and 18% of the variance in outcome respectively. Even after controlling for the WAI, improvements in *insecure attachment* uniquely accounted for 10% (BDI), 11% (DAS), 14% (IIP), 10% (GSI) and 16% (RSE) of the variance in outcome across the five models.

In addition, clients' improvements in *negative self-treatment* post-therapy significantly predicted outcome on the DAS, IIP, GSI, and RSE, and approached significance for BDI, after controlling for BLRI-E. As predicted, the β weight for *therapists' empathy* dropped from −.32 to −.23 on BDI; −.48 to −.37 on DAS; −.42 to −.30 on IIP; −.32 to −.19 on the GSI; and .38 to .24 on RSE, indicating that improvements in *negative self-treatment* at the end of therapy mediated the relationship between *therapists' empathy* and outcome for all five outcome indices. The magnitude of the indirect effect of therapist empathy mediated by improved *negative self-treatment* was .28 for BDI, .24 for DAS, .29 for IIP, .39 for GSI, and .37 for RSE, which uniquely accounted for 5%, 8%, 10%, 10% and 12% of the variance in outcome respectively. Even after controlling for the WAI, improvements in *negative self-treatment* uniquely accounted for 4% (BDI), 8% (DAS), 9% (IIP), 9% (GSI) and 12% (RSE) of the variance in outcome across the five models.

To see whether clients' pre-treatment level of attachment and negative treatment of self differentially predicted the relationship between empathy and outcome, post hoc linear regression analyses were performed to test for differences in the effect of perceived empathy on outcome for *high* versus *low insecure attachment* groups, and *high* versus *low negative self-treatment* groups based on a median split of pre-treatment scores. The results for the group comparisons are presented in Table VII. The relationship between perceived empathy and outcome indices was stronger for clients who were more insecurely attached than those less so, particularly

Table VII. Effects of empathy on post-therapy scores by subgroups ($n = 55$)

	Attachment insecurity					Negative self-treatment				
DV	Group	β	p	R^2	$F_{(df)}$	Group	β	p	R^2	$F_{(df)}$
BDI	L	−.18	.383	.03	$.79_{(1,25)}$	L	−.42	.029	.18	$5.36_{(1,25)}$
	H	−.44	.019	.19	$6.22_{(1,26)}$	H	−.24	.221	.06	$1.58_{(1,26)}$
DAS	L	−.37	.057	.14	$3.98_{(1,25)}$	L	−.49	.010	.24	$7.84_{(1,25)}$
	H	−.64	.000	.41	$17.70_{(1,26)}$	H	−.53	.004	.28	$10.09_{(1,26)}$
IIP	L	−.42	.030	.18	$5.31_{(1,25)}$	L	−.39	.044	.15	$4.48_{(1,25)}$
	H	−.54	.003	.29	$10.76_{(1,26)}$	H	−.45	.017	.20	$6.46_{(1,26)}$
GSI	L	−.07	.742	.01	$.11_{(1,25)}$	L	−.31	.122	.09	$2.57_{(1,25)}$
	H	−.48	.011	.23	$7.59_{(1,26)}$	H	−.30	.128	.09	$2.47_{(1,26)}$
RSE	L	.22	.275	.05	$1.25_{(1,25)}$	L	.56	.002	.32	$11.58_{(1,25)}$
	H	.50	.007	.25	$8.50_{(1,26)}$	H	.18	.349	.03	$.91_{(1,26)}$

Note. DV = dependent variable; L = low-scoring group; H = high-scoring group. Attachment insecurity = Attachment Style Questionnaire: Insecure Style. Negative self-treatment = Structural Analysis of Social Behaviour: Negative Introject Surface. BDI = Beck Depression Inventory. DAS = Dysfunctional Attitudes Scale. IIP = Inventory of Interpersonal Problems. GSI = Symptom Checklist-90-Revised: Global Symptom Index. RSE = Rosenberg Self-Esteem Inventory.

for BDI, GSI and RSE. The relationship between perceived empathy and outcome indices was stronger for clients who displayed less negative self-treatment than those who displayed higher negative self-treatment, but only for BDI and RSE.

Discussion

The findings support the view that client perceived therapist empathy contributes to changes in clients' negative treatment of self (Rogers, 1951, 1957; Barrett-Lennard, 1997; Bohart et al., 2002; Watson, 2002) and to their level of security in close interpersonal relationships. The mediation model showing that changes in clients' attachment style mediated the role of therapists' empathy on outcome accounted for moderate to large amounts of variance (6–20%), while that showing changes in clients' negative treatment of self accounted for a smaller proportion of the variance (4–12%), even controlling for the therapeutic alliance. A significant direct relationship between therapists' empathy and outcome as well as a significant indirect effect was found at the end of therapy, indicating that therapists' empathy was associated with significant improvement in clients' reports of secure attachment in close interpersonal relationships and significant decreases in negative ways of treating themselves and their experience. The results support the view that clients' perception and experience of therapists' empathy contribute to changes in the ways that clients treat themselves and their experience, and that these changes facilitate improvements in clients' self-reported functioning, including their dysfunctional attitudes, self-esteem, interpersonal difficulties, symptoms of distress and levels of depression at the end of therapy.

Interestingly the effect of therapist empathy on all outcome indices was stronger for clients who reported that they were more insecure in their attachment relationships, suggesting that these clients may need therapists to be more empathic if they are to engage in therapy and effect the changes that are necessary. Conversely therapist empathy was more effective in terms of levels of depression and self-esteem with those clients who showed lower levels of negative self-treatment than those who showed higher levels at the beginning of therapy. This result supports the findings of Zuroff et al. (2000), who found that perfectionism was negatively associated with outcome and the observation that clients with harsh negative introjects do not do as well in short-term therapy as those with less punitive introjects (Watson, Goldman, & Greenberg, 2007).

The findings from the current study are consistent with previous research that has shown a relationship between therapists' empathy and outcome (Beutler & Castonguay, 2006; Bohart et al., 2002; Bohart & Greenberg, 1997; Castonguay & Beutler, 2006; Duan & Hill, 1996; Hill et al., 2003; Lambert & Barley, 2001; Norcross, 2002, 2011; Norcross & Wampold, 2011; Orlinsky et al., 1994; Truax & Mitchell, 1971; Watson, 2002; Watson & Geller, 2005). However, the findings of the current study go further in so far as they suggest how empathy might work as an active ingredient of change. The findings support the view that empathy helps clients feel more secure in close interpersonal relationships and decreases the negative ways in which they treat their experience in short-term CBT and EFT-PE.

Clients who perceived their therapists as empathic reported less avoidance and anxiety in their relationships with significant others. They were less mistrustful about others' care and support, felt less worried about others' approval, experienced less discomfort with closeness, and felt more worthy. In terms of negative self-treatment, the SASB ratings suggest that clients who perceived their therapists as empathic were less controlling, rejecting, neglectful, critical, blaming or oppressive of themselves and their experience at the end of therapy. This supports the view that therapist empathy is multifunctional in psychotherapy in so far as it not only contributes to the development and maintenance of a positive working alliance (Castonguay & Beutler, 2006; Lambert & Barley, 2001; Watson & Geller, 2005) but over and above this contribution it also facilitates changes in clients' interpersonal and intrapersonal functioning.

The finding that clients' attachment styles or experience in interpersonal relationships can change over the course of therapy supports that of other studies (Travis et al., 2001), and provides some support for Rogers's (1951) hypothesis that experiencing a responsive and accepting therapist enables clients to revise conditions of worth such that they are able to change ways of treating themselves and have a different experience of themselves in relationship with others (Barrett-Lennard, 1997; Watson, 2011).

Strengths of this study include the use of both an observer measure and a self-report measure to assess changes over the course of treatment. Second, the data were taken from an RCT, which increased the internal validity of the findings. However, there are limitations with the current study. First, the findings are based on a small sample size. It will be important to replicate the results with larger samples and other client populations. Second, only 15 minutes of the session was rated on SASB, thus the changes on the circumplex may have been under-reported. This could be tested in future studies by rating more of the session. Third, it is possible that other variables might explain clients' self-reported changes at the end of therapy, including interventions specific to different treatments, clients' levels of depression, and their levels of attachment security at the beginning of treatment. Fourth, we did not distinguish between anxious and avoidant styles of insecure attachment. It will be important in future studies to see whether therapist empathy differentially predicts outcome for these two groups. Finally, there was insufficient power to conduct analyses by therapy group. Given EFT-PE places a stronger emphasis on empathic attunement in comparison to CBT, differences might be expected.

Future research should investigate additional factors that contribute to changes in clients' adult attachment styles and negative ways of treating the self in psychotherapy and examine whether changes in clients' treatment of self is related to the maintenance of therapeutic gains at follow-up. It would be important to measure therapist empathy earlier in treatment to see if less symptomatic clients perceive their therapists as more empathic from the beginning. More research is needed to investigate the role of the therapeutic relationship conditions and specifically empathy as a mechanism of change to achieve a better understanding of the relationship between empathy and the development of affect regulation strategies and the relationship of both these variables to depression.

Acknowledgments

This research was supported by research grant # 410-97-0525 from the Social Sciences and Humanities Research Council of Canada to the first and third authors. The authors wish to thank the reviewers for their thoughtful reading of earlier versions of this manuscript.

References

American Psychiatric Association. (1994). *Diagnostic and statistical manual of mental disorders* (4th ed.). Washington DC: Author. Retrieved from http://search.proquest.com/docview/618779365?accountid=14771.

Bachman, J., & O'Malley, P. (1977). Self-esteem in young men: A longitudinal analysis of the impact of educational and occupational attainment. *Journal of Personality and Social Psychology, 35*, 365–380. doi:10.1037/0022-3514.35.6.365

Baron, R. M., & Kenny, D. A. (1986). The moderator–mediator variable distinction in social psychological research: Conceptual, strategic, and statistical considerations. *Journal of Personality and Social Psychology, 51*(6), 1173–1182. doi:10.1037/0022-3514.51.6.1173

Barrett-Lennard, G. T. (1986). The Relationships Inventory now: Issues and advances in theory, method and use. In L. S. Greenberg & W. M. Pinsof (Eds.), *The psychotherapeutic process: A research handbook* (pp. 439–476). New York: Guilford Press. Retrieved from http://search.proquest.com/docview/617344012?accountid=14771.

Barrett-Lennard, G. T. (1995). Barrett-Lennard Relationship Inventory: Form OS-40 and MO-40. Author published research questionnaire (revised from RI forms OS-64 and MO-64).

Barrett-Lennard, G. T. (1997). The recovery of empathy - toward others and self. In A. C. Bohart, & L. S. Greenberg (Eds.), *Empathy reconsidered* (pp. 103–121). doi:10.1037/10226-000

Beck, A. T., Rush, A. J., Shaw, B. F., & Emery, G. (1979). *Cognitive therapy of depression: A treatment manual.* New York: Guilford Press.

Beck, A. T., Steer, R. A., & Garbin, M. G. (1988). Psychometric properties of the Beck Depression Inventory: Twenty-five years of evaluation. *Clinical Psychology Review, 8*(1), 77–100. doi:10.1016/0272-7358(88)90050-5

Beck, A. T., Ward, C. H., Medelson, M., Mock, J., & Erbaugh, J. (1961). An inventory for measuring depression. *Archives of General Psychiatry, 4*, 561–571. doi:10.1001/archpsyc.1961.01710120031004

Benjamin, L. S. (1974). Structural analysis of social behaviour. *Psychological Review, 81*, 392–425. doi:10.1037/h0037024

Benjamin, L. S. (1996). An interpersonal theory of personality disorders. In J. F. Clarkin (Ed.), *Major theories of personality disorder* (pp. 141–220). New York: Guilford Press. Retrieved from http://search.proquest.com/docview/619020260?accountid=14771.

Benjamin, L. S., Giat, L., & Estroff, S. (1981). *Coding manual for structural analysis of social behaviour (SASB)*. Unpublished manuscript.

Beutler, L. E., & Castonguay, L. G. (2006). The task force on Empirically Based Principles of Therapeutic Change. In L. G. Castonguay, & L. E. Beutler (Eds.), *Principles of therapeutic change that work* (pp. 3–12). New York: Oxford University Press.

Bohart, A. C., Elliott, R., Greenberg, L. S., & Watson, J. C. (2002). Empathy. In J. Norcross (Ed.), *Psychotherapy relationships that work* (pp. 89–108). New York: Oxford University Press. Retrieved from http://search.proquest.com/docview/620036842?accountid=14771.

Bohart, A. C., & Greenberg, L. S. (1997). Empathy and psychotherapy: An introductory overview. In A. Bohart, & L. S. Greenberg (Eds.), *Empathy reconsidered*. doi:10.1037/10226-000

Bordin, E. S. (1979). The generalizability of the psychoanalytic concept of the working alliance. *Psychotherapy: Theory, Research & Practice, 16*(3), 252–260. doi:10.1037/h0085885

Bowlby, J. (1969). *Attachment and loss: Vol. 1 Attachment*. New York: Basic Books.

Bowlby, J. (1988). *A secure base: Clinical applications of attachment theory*. London: Routledge.

Castonguay, L. G., & Beutler, L. E. (2006). Principles of therapeutic change: A task-force on participants, relationships, and techniques factors. *Journal of Clinical Psychology, 62*, 631–638. doi:10.1002/jclp.20256

Cohen, J. (1960). A coefficient of agreement for nominal scales. *Educational and Psychological Measurement, 20*, 37–46. doi:10.1177/001316446002000104

Cronbach, L. J., & Furby, L. (1970). How we should measure "change"—or should we? *Psychological Bulletin, 74*, 68–80. doi:10.1037/h0029382

Derogatis, L. R. (1983). *SCL–90–R: Administration, scoring, and procedures manual II*. Baltimore: Clinical Psychometric Research.

Derogatis, L. R. (1994). *Symptom Checklist 90–R: Administration, scoring, and procedures manual* (3rd ed.). Minneapolis, MN: National Computer Systems.

Derogatis, L. R., Lipman, R. S., & Covi, L. (1973). The SCL–90: An outpatient psychiatric rating scale—Preliminary report. *Psychopharmacology Bulletin, 9*, 13–28.

Derogatis, L. R., Rickels, K., & Rock, A. (1976). The SCL–90 and the MMPI: A step in the validation of a new self-report scale. *British Journal of Psychiatry, 128*, 280–289. doi:10.1192/bjp.128.3.280

Duan, C., & Hill, C. E. (1996). The current state of empathy research. *Journal of Counseling Psychology, 43*(3), 261–274. doi:10.1037/0022-0167.43.3.261

Elliott, R., Bohart, A. C., Watson, J. C., & Greenberg, L. S. (2011). Empathy. *Psychotherapy, 48*(1), 43–49. doi:10.1037/a0022187

Feeney, J. A., Noller, P., & Hanrahan, M. (1994). Assessing adult attachment: Developments in the conceptualization of security and insecurity. In M. B. Sperling, & W. H. Berman (Eds.), *Attachment in adults: Clinical and developmental perspectives* (pp. 128–152). New York: Guildford Press. Retrieved from http://search.proquest.com/docview/618574950?accountid=14771.

Golembiewski, R. T., Billingsley, K., & Yeager, S. (1976). Measuring change and persistence in human affairs: Types of change generated by OD designs. *Journal of Applied Behavioural Science, 12*, 133–157. doi:10.1177/002188637601200201

Gould, J. (1982). A psychometric investigation of the standard and short form Beck Depression Inventory. *Psychological Reports, 51*, 1167–1170. doi: 10.2466/pr0.1982.51.3f.1167

Greenberg, L. S., Rice, L. N., & Elliot, R. (1993). *Facilitating emotional change: The moment by moment process*. New York: Guilford Press. Retrieved from http://search.proquest.com/docview/618551874?accountid=14771.

Hansen, N. B., & Lambert, M. J. (1996). Brief report: Assessing clinical significance using the Inventory of Interpersonal Problems. *Assessment, 3*, 133–136. Retrieved from http://search.proquest.com/docview/618849347?accountid=14771.

Harrist, R. S., Quintana, S. M., Strupp, H. H., & Henry, W. (1994). Internalization of interpersonal process in time-limited dynamic psychotherapy. *Psychotherapy, 31*(1), 49–57. doi:10.1037/0033-3204.31.1.49

Hill, C. E., Rochlen, A. B., Zack, J. S., McCready, T., & Dematatis, A. (2003). Working with dreams using the hill cognitive-experimental model: A comparison of computer-assisted, therapist empathy, and therapist empathy and input conditions. *Journal of Counseling Psychology, 50*(2), 211–220. doi:10.1037/0022-0167.50.2.211

Henry, W. P., Schacht, T. E., & Strupp, H. H. (1990). Patient and therapist introject, interpersonal process, and differential psychotherapy outcome. *Journal of Consulting and Clinical Psychology, 58*(6), 768–774. doi:10.1037/0022-006X.58.6.768

Horowitz, L. M., Rosenberg, S. E., Baer, B. A., Ureno, G., & Villasenor, V. S. (1988). Inventory of Interpersonal Problems: Psychometric properties and clinical applications. *Journal of Consulting and Clinical Psychology, 56*, 885–892. doi:10.1037/0022-006X.56.6.885

Horvath, A. O., & Greenberg, L. S. (1989). Development and validation of the Working Alliance Inventory. *Journal of Counseling Psychology, 36*, 223–233. doi:10.1037/0022-0167.36.2.223

Kalogerakos, F. (1997). *Therapist and client variables related to therapeutic alliance and outcome in process-experiential therapy*. Unpublished master's thesis, Ontario Institute for Studies in Education/University of Toronto, Toronto, Ontario, Canada.

Kohut, H. (1984). *How does analysis cure?* Chicago: University of Chicago Press.

Kuiper, N. A., & Olinger, L. J. (1989). Stress and cognitive vulnerability for depression: A self-worth contingency model. In R.W.J. Neufeld (Ed.), *Advances in the investigation of psychological stress* (pp. 367–391). New York: Wiley. Retrieved from http://search.proquest.com/docview/617675520?accountid=14771.

Lambert, M. J., & Barley, D. E. (2001). Research summary on the therapeutic relationship and psychotherapy outcome. *Psychotherapy, 38*(4), 357–361. doi:10.1037/0033-3204.38.4.357

Luborsky, L., McLellan, A. T., Wopody, G. E., O'Brien, C. P., & Auerbach, A. (1985). Therapist success and its determinants. *Archives of General Psychiatry, 42*, 602–611. doi:10.1001/archpsyc.1985.01790290084010

MacKinnon, D. P. (2008). *Introduction to statistical mediation analyses*. New York: Erlbaum.

Morgan, C. D., Wiederman, M. W., & Magnus, R. D. (1998). Discriminant validity of the SCL–90 dimensions of anxiety and depression. *Assessment, 5*, 197–201. doi:10.1177/107319119800500210

Najavits, L. M., & Strupp, H. H. (1994). Differences in the effectiveness of psychodynamic therapists: A process-outcome study. *Psychotherapy, 31*, 114–123. doi:10.1037/0033-3204.31.1.114

Norcross, J. C. (Ed.), (2002). *Psychotherapy relationships that work*. New York: Oxford University Press. Retrieved from http://search.proquest.com/docview/620036842?accountid=14771.

Norcross, J. C. (Ed.), (2011). *Psychotherapy relationships that work* (2nd ed.). New York: Oxford University Press. Retrieved from http://search.proquest.com/docview/897336217?accountid=14771.

Norcross, J. C., & Wampold, B. E. (2011). Evidence-based therapy relationships: Research conclusions and clinical practices. *Psychotherapy, 48*(1), 98–102. doi:10.1037/a0022161

Ogles, B. M., Lambert, M. J., & Sawyer, J. D. (1995). Clinical significance of the national institute of mental health treatment of depression collaborative research program data. *Journal of Consulting and Clinical Psychology, 63*(2), 321–326. doi:10.1037/0022-006X.63.2.321

Orlinsky, D. E., Grawe, K., & Parks, B. K. (1994). Process and outcome in psychotherapy—noch einmal. In A. E. Bergin, & S. L. Garfield (Eds.), *Handbook of psychotherapy and behavior change* (4th ed., pp. 270–376). New York: Wiley. Retrieved from http://search.proquest.com/docview/618552384?accountid=14771.

Paivio, S. C., & Laurent, C. (2001). Empathy and emotion regulation: Reprocessing memories of childhood abuse. *Journal of Clinical Psychology/In Session: Psychotherapy in Practice, 57*(2), 213–226. doi:10.1002/1097-4679(200102)57:2<213::AID-JCLP7>3.0.CO;2-B

Preacher, K. J., & Kelley, K. (2011). Effect size measures for mediation models: Quantitative strategies for communicating indirect effects. *Psychological Methods, 16*(2), 93–115. doi:10.1037/a0022658

Price, P. B., & Jones, E. E. (1998). Examining the alliance using the Psychotherapy Process Q-Set. *Psychotherapy: Theory, Research, Practice, Training, 35*(3), 392–404. doi:10.1037/h0087654

Quintana, S. M., & Meara, N. M. (1990). Internalization of therapeutic relationships in short-term psychotherapy. *Journal of Counseling Psychology, 37*(2), 123–130. doi:10.1037/0022-0167.37.2.123

Rogers, C. R. (1951). *Client-centered therapy*. Boston: Houghton Mifflin.

Rogers, C. R. (1957). The necessary and sufficient conditions of therapeutic personality change. *Journal of Consulting Psychology, 21*, 95–103. doi:10.1037/0022-006X.60.6.827

Rogers, C. R. (1963). The actualizing tendency in relation to 'motives' and to consciousness. In M. R. Jones (Ed.), *Nebraska Symposium on motivation: Current theory and research in motivation, Vol. 11* (pp. 1–24). Lincoln: University of Nebraska Press.

Rogers, C. R. (1976). Toward a modern approach to values: The valuing process in the mature person. In C. R. Rogers, & B. Stevens (Eds.), *Person to person: The problem of being human* (pp. 4–21). New York: Pocket Books. (Reprinted from *Journal of Abnormal and Social Psychology*, Vol. 68, No. 2, 1964, 160–176.)

Rosenberg, M. (1965). *Society and the adolescent self image*. Princeton, NJ: Princeton University Press. Retrieved from http://search.proquest.com/docview/617871219?accountid=1477.

Rosenberg, M. (1979). *Conceiving the self*. New York: Basic Books.

Simpson, J. A., & Rholes, W. S. (2004). Anxious attachment and depressive symptoms: An interpersonal perspective. In W. S. Rholes, & J. A. Simpson (Eds.), *Adult attachment: Theory, research and clinical implications* (pp. 408–437). New York: Guildford Press. Retrieved from http://search.proquest.com/docview/620640825?accountid=14771.

Tracey, T. J., & Kokotovic, A. M. (1989). Factor structure of the working alliance inventory. *Psychological Assessment: A Journal of Consulting and Clinical Psychology, 1*(3), 207–210. doi:10.1037/1040-3590.1.3.207

Travis, L. A., Bliwise, N. G., Binder, J. L., & Horne-Moyer, H. L. (2001). Changes in clients' attachment styles over the course of time-limited dynamic psychotherapy. *Psychotherapy, 38*(2), 149–159. doi:10.1037/0033-3204.38.2.14

Truax, C. B., & Mitchell, K. M. (1971). Research on certain therapist interpersonal skills in relation to process and outcome. In A. E. Bergin, & S. L. Garfield (Eds.), *Handbook of psychotherapy and behavior change* (pp. 299–344). New York: Wiley. Retrieved from http://search.proquest.com/docview/615778858?accountid=14771.

Tryon, G. S., & Kane, A. S. (1993). Relationship of working alliance to mutual and unilateral termination. *Journal of Counseling Psychology, 40*(1), 33–36. doi:10.1037/0022-0167.40.1.33

Watson, J. C. (2002). Re-visioning empathy. In D. Cain, & J. Seeman (Eds.), *Handbook of research in humanistic therapies* (pp. 445–471). doi:10.1037/10439-014

Watson, J. C. (2011). The Process of growth and transformation: Extending the process model. *Person Centered and Experiential Psychotherapy, 10*(1), 11–27. doi: 10.1080/14779757.2011.564760

Watson, J. C., & Geller, S. M. (2005). The relation among the relationship conditions, working alliance, and outcome in both process-experiential and cognitive-behavioral psychotherapy. *Psychotherapy Research, 15*(1–2), 25–33. doi:10.1080/10503300512331327010

Watson, J. C., Goldman, R. N., & Greenberg, L. S. (2007). *Case-studies in the experiential treatment of depression: A comparison of good and bad outcome*. Washington, DC: APA Press.

Watson, J. C., Goldman, R., & Vanaerschot, G. (1998). In L. S. Greenberg,, J. C. Watson, and G. Lietaer (Eds.), *Empathic: A postmodern way of being?* New York: Guilford Press. Retrieved from http://search.proquest.com/docview/619394299?accountid=14771.

Watson, J. C., Gordon, L. B., Stermac, L., Kalogerakos, F., & Steckley, P. (2003). Comparing the effectiveness of process-experiential with cognitive-behavioural psychotherapy in the treatment of depression. *Journal of Consulting and Clinical Psychology, 71*, 773–781. doi:10.1037/0022-006X.71.4.773

Weissman, A. N., & Beck, A. T. (1978, August). *Development and validation of the Dysfunctional Attitudes Scale: A preliminary investigation*. Paper presented at the 86th Annual Convention of the American Psychological Association, Toronto, Ontario, Canada.

Zuroff, D. C., Blatt, S. J., Sotsky, S. M., Krupnick, J. L., Martin, D. J., Sanislow, C. A., & Simmens, S. (2000). Relation of therapeutic alliance and perfectionism to outcome in brief outpatient treatment of depression. *Journal of Consulting and Clinical Psychology, 68*(1), 114–124. doi: 10.1037/0022-006X.68.1.114

Client attachment, attachment to the therapist and client-therapist attachment match: How do they relate to change in psychodynamic psychotherapy?

HADAS WISEMAN[1] & ORYA TISHBY[2]

[1]*Counseling and Human Development, University of Haifa, Haifa, Israel &* [2]*Psychology, Hebrew University, Jerusalem, Israel*

Abstract
Objective: We examined the associations between client attachment, client attachment to the therapist, and symptom change, as well as the effects of client-therapist attachment match on outcome. Clients (n = 67) and their therapists (n = 27) completed the ECR to assess attachment. **Method:** Clients completed also the Client Attachment to Therapist scale three times (early, middle, and late sessions) and the OQ-45 at intake and four times over the course of a year of psychodynamic psychotherapy. **Results:** Clients characterized by avoidant attachment and by avoidant attachment to their therapist showed the least improvement. A low-avoidant client-therapist attachment match led to a greater decrease in symptom distress than when a low-avoidant therapist treated a high-avoidant client. **Conclusions:** These findings suggest the importance of considering client-therapist attachment matching and the need to pay attention to the special challenges involved in treating avoidant clients in order to facilitate progress in psychotherapy.

Attachment theory constitutes a promising framework for studying the contributions of the client, the therapist, and the relationship bond to psychotherapy process and outcome. Bowlby (1962/1982) posited that individuals form internal working models of the self and others in close relationships based on their experiences with childhood caregivers. The therapeutic relationship is likely to reactivate the client's long-standing expectations about the availability and responsiveness of others (Bowlby, 1988; Farber & Metzger, 2009). Of the vast number of client variables that have been studied in relation to the process and outcome of psychotherapy (Bohart & Wade, 2013; Clarkin & Levy, 2004), a growing body of research suggests that clients' attachment styles may have an important influence on the relationship clients develop with their therapist (e.g., Diener & Monroe, 2011; Eames & Roth, 2000; Mallinckrodt, 2000, 2010) and on the final outcome (Fonagy et al., 1996; Levy, Ellison, Scott, & Bernecker, 2011; Meyer & Pilkonis, 2002).

Attachment styles in adulthood have been depicted as reflecting the intersection of two dimensions: A positive versus negative model of self and a positive versus negative model of other (Bartholomew & Horowitz, 1991). These dimensions yield a four-style typology: Securely attached individuals have positive models of the self and others; preoccupied individuals have a positive model of others but a negative model of the self; dismissing types have a negative model of others, but a positive self-model; and the fearful have negative models of the self and others.

Studies on attachment and the therapeutic alliance suggest that securely attached clients obtain higher alliance scores (Satterfield & Lyddon, 1998).

A recent meta-analysis of 17 studies linking client attachment style and alliance found a significant overall effect size (r = .17) indicating that more securely attached clients have stronger alliances, whereas more insecurely attached clients have weaker alliances (Diener & Monroe, 2011).

The findings regarding the various insecure styles have been diverse, probably due to the reliance on different attachment assessment methods such as the interview-based AAI (Dozier, Cue, & Barnett, 1994; Fonagy et al., 1996) and self-report typological or dimensional attachment measures (Eames & Roth, 2000; Mallinckrodt, Porter, & Kivlighan, 2005), as well as due to the different time points of alliance assessment over the course of therapy. Client fearful attachment was found to be related to lower client-rated early working alliance (Eames & Roth, 2000). Findings on the preoccupied and dismissing attachment styles are less clear and may partly depend on the interaction between client and therapist attachment styles (Roth & Fonagy, 2005; Rubino Barker, Roth, & Fearson, 2000) and on early versus late assessments of the alliance.

Client Attachment and Psychotherapy Outcome

The association between adult attachment and psychotherapy outcome was examined in a recent meta-analytic review (Levy et al., 2011). This meta-analyses included 14 studies (containing 19 separate samples) that measured client attachment style and treatment outcome, with a combined N of 1467 patients. To overcome the problem of the use of 11 different attachment measures in these studies (e.g., Adult Attachment Prototype Rating, Adult Attachment Interview, and Adult Attachment Scale), Levy et al. focused the analysis on the two attachment dimensions: Anxiety and avoidance. These two dimensions have been found to underlie most measures of adult attachment style (Brennan, Clark, & Shaver, 1998; Mikulincer & Shaver, 2007), with attachment security conceptualized as a blend of anxiety and avoidance dimensions (individuals low on both are securely attached whereas individuals high on both or only on one dimension are insecurely attached). The meta-analytic findings showed that higher attachment anxiety predicted worse outcomes after therapy, whereas higher attachment security predicted more favorable outcomes. Attachment avoidance had a negligible overall effect on outcomes in psychotherapy. The authors concluded that the effect sizes of the associations of both attachment anxiety (r = −.22) and attachment security (r = .18) with treatment outcomes were "in the small but moderate range, but just below those found for the association of therapeutic alliance with outcomes" (Levy et al., 2011, p. 201).

One of the limitations of this recent meta-analytic review is the absence of baseline levels which would make it possible to assess actual change in symptoms. Post-treatment symptoms were considered to be the outcome; hence, the associations may to some extent reflect the relation between attachment and psychopathology (Levy et al., 2011). Taking this point into consideration, the present study includes a baseline assessment of symptoms at intake and at different time points throughout psychotherapy. Client attachment to the therapist and symptom change over the course of psychotherapy were also assessed at several points in time.

Client Attachment to the Therapist

Conceptualizing the therapeutic relationship from an attachment perspective, Mallinckrodt, Gantt, and Coble (1995) developed the Client Attachment to Therapist Scale (CATS). This led to the identification of three patterns of client attachment to the therapist that reflect patterns of adult attachment. Secure clients perceive their therapist as emotionally responsive, accepting, and promoting a "secure base" (Bowlby, 1988) for the exploration of threatening emotional experiences. Avoidant-Fearful clients tend to distrust their therapists and fear rejection, and are reluctant to cooperate in the self-disclosure tasks of therapy and feel threatened or humiliated during sessions. Preoccupied-Merger clients desire more intense contact and to be "at one" with their therapists. They aim for a dissolution of boundaries because they are preoccupied with the therapist and want to be their therapist's "favorite" client (Mallinckrodt et al., 1995, 2005). Mallinckrodt (2010) suggests that although not specifically intended to assess the essential elements of attachment bonds, the CATS items appear to tap the five essential elements identified by Mikulincer and Shaver (2007): (1) therapist as stronger and wiser, (2) proximity seeking, (3) safe haven, (4) secure base, and (5) separation anxiety in anticipation of loss of the therapist. He argued that this correspondence "provides some evidence that the psychotherapy relationship can serve the functions of an attachment bond" (Mallinckrodt, 2010; p. 263).

The secure base element of the psychotherapy relationship was supported in two studies that employed the CATS to test the hypothesis that secure client attachment to the therapist would be associated with deeper exploration (Mallinckrodt et al., 2005; Romano, Fitzpatrick, & Janzen, 2008). Clients who reported a secure attachment in their relationship with their therapist described their sessions on the Session Evaluation Questionnaire (SEQ; Stiles & Snow, 1984) as characterized by greater depth.

Considering the conceptual triangle of adult attachment, client attachment to the therapist, and alliance suggests that these constructs, although related, do not overlap (Mallinckrodt et al., 2005). Diener and Monroe's (2011) meta-analytic review showed that client attachment style was linked to alliance in individual therapy. However, they noted that "much of the variance in alliance remains to be accounted for even after taking into consideration patients' attachment styles" (p. 244). In Mallinckrodt et al.'s (2005) study, the association between clients' attachment to significant others and the CATS showed that avoidant adult attachment (assessed on the Experiences in Close Relationships Scale; Brennan et al., 1998) was positively correlated with avoidant-fearful attachment to the therapist. Regarding the association between the CATS and the alliance, as assessed on the Working Alliance Inventory (WAI; Horvath & Greenberg, 1989), it was found that secure attachment to the therapist was strongly associated with positive alliance, whereas avoidant-fearful CATS was strongly associated with a negative alliance. No associations were found between preoccupied-merger CATS and WAI. Addressing a concern regarding the discriminant validity of the CATS (Meyer & Pilkonis, 2002), Mallinckrodt et al. (2005) showed that the CATS scales account for unique variance over and above the WAI in session depth and smoothness, as well as in object relations deficits.

Studies utilizing the CATS have mostly measured client attachment to the therapist in the early sessions of therapy (e.g., Janzen, Fitzpatrick, & Drapeau, 2008), middle sessions (e.g., sessions 5 to 9 in Romano et al., 2008), or administered it only once in later sessions (Woodhouse, Schlosser, Crook, Ligiero, & Gelso, 2003). The present study was designed to examine the association between ECR attachment avoidance and attachment anxiety and the client's attachment to the therapist over the course of psychotherapy at three time points: Early, middle, and late sessions.

Previous research has examined the link between client attachment to the therapist and psychotherapy process variables such as the working alliance and session depth and smoothness (Mallinckrodt et al., 2005; Romano et al., 2008). Researchers have only recently begun to test the relationship between the CATS and psychotherapy outcome (Mallinckrodt, 2011). Sauer, Anderson, Gormley, Richmond, and Preacco (2010) examined the association between client attachment to the therapist on the CATS (assessed in the third session) and progress in therapy on the Outcome Questionnaire (OQ-45) and found that secure attachment to the therapist was associated with greater reduction in client distress over time.

Client-Therapist Match versus Mismatch in Attachment

The client-therapist match has long been suggested as accounting for outcome beyond any single client or therapist variable (Bernier & Dozier, 2002; Berzins, 1977; Beutler, et al., 2004; Taber, Leibert, & Agaskar, 2011; Talley, Strupp, & Morey, 1990). Research on matching involves studies on similarities and dissimilarities between client and therapist on demographic variables (e.g., gender, ethnicity), attitudes, beliefs and values, and personality variables (e.g., self-concept, personality types) and interpersonal styles. Attachment theory and research on individual differences in attachment (Mikulincer & Shaver, 2007) provide a solid framework to examine the benefit of client-therapist match versus mismatch in attachment styles.

In a study of case managers working with severely impaired psychiatric patients, therapists were most effective with patients showing attachment states of mind (on the AAI) different from their own (i.e., dissimilar attachment tendencies on the dismissing-preoccupied dimension). Case managers in dissimilar dyads rated the patients as higher in global functioning and the patients reported better life satisfaction and stronger working alliances than dyads with similar attachment states of mind (Tyrrell, Dozier, Teague, & Fallot, 1999). This finding on the benefits of dissimilar attachment was attributed to the case managers' ability to challenge the clients' rigid and maladaptive interpersonal strategies and refrain from colluding with them (see Eagle & Wolitzky, 2009).

In a study with college students and volunteer professors providing academic counseling, the students' attachment was measured on the AAI and the professors' relational style was measured on a self-report questionnaire (Bernier, Larose, & Soucy, 2001; reported in Bernier & Dozier, 2002). It was found that students with dismissing attachment tendencies worked better with counselors who reported valuing interdependence and relationships, whereas students with preoccupied attachment tendencies had better relationships with professors valuing independence and achievement. Thus, based on these two studies, Bernier and Dozier (2002) suggested that contrasting (mismatch) relational styles are optimal for treatment, though they caution that these results need to be replicated with trained therapists in psychotherapy dyads.

The combination of client attachment and therapist attachment (interaction effects) was studied using the ECR in two studies with volunteer clients and counselor trainees. Mohr, Gelso and Hill (2005) found that counselor attachment moderated the association between client attachment and negative counselor countertransference reactions. In dyads composed of a high attachment anxiety (preoccupied) client and a high attachment avoidance (fearful or dismissing) counselor, the supervisor rated the counselors as higher in distancing and hostile countertransference behavior. In Romano et al.'s (2008) study, this combination of client high attachment anxiety with counselor high to moderate attachment avoidance predicted lower levels of client perceived session depth.

Thus although in some studies dissimilarity in reliance on attachment strategies, hyperactivation or deactivation was advantageous, in other studies this dissimilarity was related to negative aspects of the counseling process. In their meta-analytic review on attachment style and outcome, Levy et al. (2011) indicated that there were not enough studies to address the issue of matching patients to treatment or therapists based on attachment patterns. In the present study we examine the effects of match and mismatch in client-therapist attachment in predicting client progress from intake to outcome.

The Present Study

The aims of the present study were to test the associations between client attachment characteristics, client attachment to the therapist, and symptoms over the course of psychodynamic psychotherapy, and between therapist attachment characteristics and client attachment to the therapist. We also examined the effects of client attachment to the therapist on change in symptoms. Finally, we explored the effects of the configuration of client-therapist attachment match versus mismatch on change in symptoms. The following hypotheses were tested:

1. Clients' insecure attachment (attachment avoidance and attachment anxiety) will be associated with higher symptom distress at each time point (intake, early, middle, and later stages of therapy).
2. Client global attachment will be associated with client attachment to the therapist at the beginning, middle, and later stages of therapy. Specifically, secure attachment (low on both avoidance and anxiety) will be associated with client secure attachment to therapist, avoidant attachment with avoidant-fearful attachment to therapist, and anxious attachment with preoccupied-merger attachment to therapist. In addition, therapist global attachment will be associated with client attachment to the therapist at the different stages of therapy.
3. CATS scores will be associated with OQ at each time point over the course of psychotherapy, and client's early CATS scores will predict changes in OQ from intake to the last OQ assessment point (session 32).
4. Therapist attachment will moderate the relationship between client attachment and change in OQ (i.e., therapist attachment by client attachment interaction). Given previous contradictory findings, we did not hypothesize the specific configuration of client-therapist attachment that would be most beneficial to outcome.

Method

Participants

Clients. At the outset, the sample of the study consisted of 67 clients at a university counseling center. Two-thirds were female (46 females and 21 males), which is a common ratio in university psychological services. They were mostly young adults with a mean age of 24.89 (range 20 to 32) and the majority were undergraduate students (76.6%). These students are somewhat older than the usual sample in the USA as in Israel most students begin university after their compulsory army service (3 years for men and 2 for women and many only begin university after another year of travel abroad). They were single (95.5%), the majority were Israeli-born (82.4%), and 78.5% came from intact families. Most of the clients were diagnosed either with mild depression and/or anxiety, presenting with difficulties in relationships, in their academic studies, or issues pertaining to identity formation. Of these 67 clients, 54 remained in psychotherapy and 13 dropped out. No significant differences were found on the variables of the study at the fifth session between clients who remained in therapy and those who dropout out.

Therapists. The therapists were 22 females and five males, with a mean age of 36 (range 23–57), 63% were married, and 59% had at least one child. The therapists were mostly Israeli-born (85%) and came from intact families (81.5%). The majority held MA degrees (70.4%) in clinical psychology (63%) or social work (26%). In terms of their experience level, 63% were interns and 18.5% were licensed therapists (with 5 to 15 years of experience). Due to the training program structure in Israel, the number of years of experience of the interns ranged from 3 to 5 years. All therapists (except one) were receiving supervision at the time of the study. The number of clients per therapist ranged from 1 to 6 clients, with a mean of 2.41, $SD = 1.18$.

Therapy. The therapy was conducted at a large university counseling center. Clients were seen once a week for 50 minutes in a year-long psychodynamic psychotherapy. The model of psychotherapy in our naturalistic study can be described as based mainly on principles of contemporary psychodynamic psychotherapy (e.g., Summers & Barber, 2010) and on object relations (Winnicott, 1971) and relational psychotherapy (Aron, 1996; Mitchell, 1993).

Measures

Outcome Questionnaire (OQ-45; Lambert et al., 1996). This a 45-item self-report instrument designed for repeated measurement of client changes throughout the course of mental health treatments. Clients are asked to rate their functioning in the past week on a 5-point Likert scale from 0 (*never*) to 4 (*almost always*). The OQ-45 is composed of three subscales, Symptom Distress, Interpersonal Problems, and Social Role, which are summed to provide a total score. The total score ranges from 0 to 180, with high scores indicating greater overall levels of symptom severity. Research has shown that the OQ-45 has adequate test-retest reliability (.84) and high internal consistency (.93). Concurrent validity has been demonstrated with a wide variety of self-report scales (e.g., Beck Depression Inventory, State-Trait Anxiety Inventory) (Lambert et al., 1996). The OQ-45 is widely used in university counseling centers and mental health centers. The total distress score has been found to be sensitive to change in counseling center clients (Vermeersch et al., 2004). The OQ-45 has been translated into several languages, including Hebrew (Gross et al., in press). In the present study, the alpha coefficient of the total Hebrew version was .91. Using formulas developed by Jacobson and Truax (1991), the reliable change index of the OQ was estimated to be 14 points and the clinical range cutoff was 63 (Lambert et al., 1996, 2001).

Experiences in Close Relationships Scale (ERC; Brennan et al., 1998). The ERC is a widely used 36-item self-report measure of adult attachment. The ERC employs a 7-point Likert-type response scale ranging from 1 (*not at all*) to 7 (*very much*). Eighteen items assess attachment anxiety (e.g. "I worry about being abandoned") and 18 assess avoidance (e.g., "I prefer not to show a partner how I feel deep down"). These yield two highly consistent dimensions: Anxiety and Avoidance (alpha coefficients of .91 and .94, respectively). The Hebrew version of the ERC has also demonstrated high internal reliabilities (Mikulincer & Florian, 2000). Evidence of validity has been widely established (see Mikulincer & Shaver, 2007, for a review). In the present study, Cronbach's alpha was .92 and .91 for the anxiety scale and .92 and .82 for the avoidance scale, for clients and therapists, respectively.

Client Attachment to Therapist Scale (CATS; Mallinckrodt et al., 1995). The CATS was developed to measure the psychotherapy relationship from the perspective of attachment theory. This 36-item self-report questionnaire consists of three subscales: Secure, Avoidant-Fearful, and Preoccupied-Merger. Clients respond using a 6-point scale ranging from strongly agree (1) to strongly disagree (6). In the study that reported the construction and psychometric properties of the scale (Mallinckrodt et al., 1995), clients had to complete at least five sessions with a median of 10 sessions (range 5–62). Test-retest reliability, which was obtained on average after a 3-week interval, was moderate to high for the three dimensions (.84, .86, and .72). In a study on brief psychotherapy, clients completed the CATS once after the fourth or eighth sessions (Mallinckrodt et al., 2005). With permission received from the author of the CATS, the scale was translated into Hebrew. In the present study, Cronbach's alphas (fifth session) were .84 for secure, .77 for avoidant, and .68 for preoccupied.

Procedure

Therapists at a large university counseling center were asked to give their initial consent to participate in the study and to indicate that they agreed in principle that their clients could be invited to participate in the study. Clients were recruited through the reception office upon seeking counselling and a research assistant contacted only those clients whose therapists agreed to participate. Clients received information about the study and were assured that their participation was voluntary, and that they could choose to terminate their participation in the study at any time. Clients signed a consent form in which it was stated that the data would not be transferred to their therapist, and that their anonymity would be preserved. The clients and therapists in this study took part in a research project that included also undergoing RAP (Relationship Anecdote Paradigm; Luborsky & Crits-Christoph, 1998) interviews three times during psychotherapy and completing post-session questionnaires (Wiseman & Tishby, 2011; Wiseman, Tishby, & Barber, 2012). Clients were paid 50 NIS ($12) after completing the questionnaires and taking part in the RAP interviews at the three time points.

Clients completed the OQ-45 at five time points: At intake, after session 5, session 15, session 28, and session 32. They completed the CATS at three time points: after sessions 5, 15, and 28. Due to technical problems, some clients completed the ECR at intake and also after session 28 and most clients completed the ECR only at session 28. No differences were found in the ECR scores of these two groups, and no differences in the ECR scores at intake and session 28 for those clients who completed the ECR at both times. Hence, we only used the ECR scores for session 28. Therapists completed the ECR when their first client joined the study. The study was approved by the Helsinki Ethics Committee.

Data Analysis

Due to the assumed dependency of the scores on each variable per therapist, and the fact that the variables were measured at both the client and the therapist levels, the data were analyzed in a hierarchical three-level model (mixed models): Time (within the individual), client level, and therapist level. Individual level variables included: Client attachment, Client CATS, and Client OQ, and therapist level variables included Therapist attachment. OQ was measured five times, and CATS was measured three times. All temporal differences and predictions were analyzed via mixed hierarchical models. Post hoc tests that were used were paired comparisons. In cases in which the independent variables did not temporally precede the dependent variables the results are described in terms of relationships rather than predictions. In the mixed models analysis that tested the client-therapist attachment match, significant interactions were plotted according to the simple slopes procedure (Aiken & West, 1991; Preacher, Curran, & Bauer; 2006) and the significance of the slopes was assessed.

Results

Descriptive Statistics

The means and standard deviations of all the study variables are presented in Table I. For the OQ there were five time points (from intake through sessions 5, 15, 28, and 32) and for the CATS there were three time points (sessions 5, 15, and 28). The ECR of the clients and of the therapists were measured once.

The OQ and CATS scores of clients who dropped out after the fifth session were compared to those who completed session 28. No significant differences were found on the fifth session between completers and dropouts on the OQ [$F(1,63.76) = 2.50$, $p = .119$, $\eta^2 = .029$] (completers $M = 67.29$, $SD = 19.61$, $n = 54$; dropouts $M = 77.50$; $SD = 18.14$, $n = 13$). Similarly, there were no differences on the CATS between the two groups for the three scales: CATS secure $F(1,61.31) = 1.83$, $p = .181$, $\eta^2 = .050$ (completers $M = 4.65$, $SD = .74$; dropouts $M = 4.14$, $SD = .78$); CATS avoidance $F(1,62.14) = .05$, $p = .828$, $\eta^2 = .005$ (completers $M = 1.93$, $SD = .64$; dropouts $M = 2.06$, $SD = .57$); and CATS preoccupied $F(1,62.15) = 2.68$, $p = .107$, $\eta^2 = .031$ (completers $M = 2.33$, $SD = .79$; dropouts $M = 2.75$, $SD = .81$).

Change over Time in Outcome (OQ). The results of a repeated measures ANOVA that tested client change on OQ over the five time points showed that the total difference was significant, $F(4,209.63) = 12.79$, $p < .001$, $\eta^2 = .206$. Post hoc paired comparisons of the time differences indicated that compared to OQ at intake ($M = 75.57$, $SD = 22.76$), OQ decreased significantly ($p = .003$, $\eta^2 = .027$) on the fifth session ($M = 68.51$, $SD = 19.60$) and was significantly lower on the 15th ($M = 64.41$, $SD = 22.00$, $p < .001$, $\eta^2 = .059$), 28th ($M = 60.54$, $SD = 25.52$, $p < .001$, $\eta^2 = .090$), and 32nd sessions ($M = 55.69$, $SD = 23.41$, $p < .001$, $\eta^2 = .155$). Compared to the OQ at session 5, OQ was significantly lower on the 28th session ($p = .004$, $\eta^2 = .031$) and significantly lower on the 32nd session ($p < .001$, $\eta^2 = .081$). Compared to the 15th session OQ was significantly lower on the 32nd session ($p = .011$, $\eta^2 = .035$). However, no significant change was found between sessions 28 and 32 ($p = .221$, $\eta^2 = .010$, see Table I). In terms of the reliable change index of the OQ, which is estimated to be 14 points (Lambert et al., 2001), on average, clients made reliable change on the OQ from the assessment at intake to session 28. In terms of the OQ clinical range cutoff of 63 (Lambert et al., 2001), 63% of the clients had OQ scores in the nonclinical range on session 28, and 70% of the clients were in the nonclinical range on the last assessment point (session 32), thus demonstrating clinically reliable improvement.

Client Global Attachment and OQ

The findings on global attachment and OQ at each of the five time points indicated that higher client avoidant attachment was related to higher OQ at the 5th [$B = 8.69$, $Se = 3.59$; $t(29.41) = 2.42$, $p < .05$]

Table I. Means and standard deviations for the OQ-45, CATS and client and therapist ECR

	Intake	5th session	15th session	28th session	32nd session
OQ-45	75.57 (22.76) (*n* = 58) Range 23–138	68.51 (19.60) (*n* = 67) Range 25–118	64.41 (22.00) (*n* = 61) Range 18–102	60.54 (25.52) (*n* = 54) Range 15–120	55.69 (23.41) (*n* = 39) Range 15–98
CATS - Secure		4.59 (.76) (*n* = 66)	4.79 (.79) (*n* = 61)	4.98 (.66) (*n* = 54)	
CATS - Avoidance		1.94 (.63) (*n* = 66)	1.86 (.70) (*n* = 61)	1.84 (.72) (*n* = 54)	
CATS - Preoccupied		2.38 (.80) (*n* = 66)	2.34 (.85) (*n* = 61)	2.35 (.96) (*n* = 54)	
		Clients (*n* = 55)		Therapists (*n* = 27)	
ECR - Avoidance		3.63 (1.16)		2.31 (.58)	
ECR - Anxiety		3.88 (1.19)		3.53 (1.03)	

and 32nd [$B = 10.53$, $Se = 3.90$; $t(15.90) = 2.70$, $p < .05$] sessions. Interestingly, in the middle phase of therapy it was found that higher client anxious attachment was related to higher OQ at 15th [$B = 7.34$, $Se = 3.53$; $t(26.10) = 2.08$, $p < .05$] and 28th sessions [$B = 9.80$, $Se = 3.85$; $t(25.95) = 2.54$, $p < .05$].

Client and Therapist Global Attachment and Client Attachment to the Therapist

Client ECR and CATS. The results of the mixed models for the relationship between clients' global attachment on ECR and their attachment to their therapist on the CATS at the three time points showed that client ECR avoidance was significantly and positively associated with CATS avoidant attachment to therapist at both the 5th [$B = .23$, $Se = .11$; $t(23.79) = 2.09$, $p = .047$] and the 15th [$B = .31$, $Se = .11$; $t(21.24) = 2.82$, $p = .01$] sessions. By contrast, client ECR avoidance was associated negatively with CATS secure attachment to therapist [$B = -.30$, $Se = .14$; $t(33.44) = -2.07$, $p = .046$] at the 15th session. Client ECR anxiety was associated positively with CATS avoidant attachment to therapist [$B = .32$, $Se = .13$; $t(13.21) = 2.44$, $p = .029$] on the 28th session. Finally, client ECR on both avoidance and anxiety was unrelated to CATS preoccupied attachment to therapist.

Therapist ECR and CATS. An analysis (mixed models) of the relationship between therapists' global attachment on the ECR and the client attachment to the therapist on the CATS at each of the three time points revealed only one significant association. Namely, therapist ECR anxious attachment was significantly related to lower client secure attachment to therapist on the CATS on the 5th session [$B = -.23$, $Se = .11$; $t(23.09) = -2.06$, $p = .050$]. No other relationships were found between therapist ECR and client attachment to therapist.

Client Attachment to Therapist, OQ and Change in OQ

The findings on CATS and OQ-45 at the same time points (see Table II) indicated that higher OQ on the 5th session was significantly related to higher client preoccupied attachment to therapist [$B = 7.72$, $Se = 2.76$; $t(35.22) = 2.80$, $p = .008$]. Higher OQ at the 15th session was significantly related to both higher client avoidant [$B = 7.96$, $Se = 3.58$; $t(32.36) = 2.22$, $p = .033$], as well as higher client preoccupied attachment to therapist [$B = 7.66$, $Se = 3.39$; $t(31.90) = 2.26$, $p = .031$].

We also examined the prediction of change in OQ from intake to session 32 by the client's CATS on the fifth session. The mixed models analysis showed no significant relationships of CATS secure and of CATS preoccupied with the change in OQ; however, higher CATS avoidance was significantly related to an increase in symptoms from intake to the 32nd session [$B = .45$, $SE = .19$; $t(20.48) = 2.36$, $p = .028$]. That is, lower CATS avoidance was associated with a decrease in OQ from intake to the 32nd session; i.e., greater improvement. In line with the literature on the alliance-outcome correlation that tests whether change in symptoms before the

Table II. Mixed models for the relationship between client attachment to therapist and OQ-45

OQ - 5th session			OQ - 15th session			OQ - 28th session		
CATS - Secure	CATS - Avoidance	CATS - Preoccupied	CATS - Secure	CATS - Avoidance	CATS - Preoccupied	CATS - Secure	CATS - Avoidance	CATS - Preoccupied
$B = -2.11$	$B = 4.30$	$B = 7.72$	$B = -2.30$	$B = 7.96$	$B = 7.66$	$B = 4.21$	$B = 4.59$	$B = -3.56$
$SE = 2.85$	$SE = 2.82$	$SE = 2.76$	$SE = 3.76$	$SE = 3.58$	$SE = 3.39$	$SE = 5.51$	$SE = 4.95$	$SE = 4.58$
$t(34.24) = -.74$	$t(34.08) = 1.52$	$t(35.22) = 2.80$**	$t(31.22) = -.61$	$t(32.36) = 2.22$*	$t(31.90) = 2.26$*	$t(25.61) = .76$	$t(25.61) = .93$	$t(25.61) = -.78$

*$p < .05$, **$p < .01$, ***$p < .001$; ($N = 54$–66).

measurement of the alliance causes subsequent change in symptoms or is it the alliance (Barber, Muran, McCarthy, & Keefe, 2013; Crits-Christoph, Connolly Gibson, & Mukherjee, 2013), we also examined the prediction of subsequent change in OQ (from session 5 to 32) by the client's CATS on session 5, while controlling for prior change from intake to session 5. The results of this mixed models analysis for subsequent change in OQ showed no significant effects for either client CATS avoidance in session 5 [$B = .36$, $SE = .23$; $t(20.89) = 1.49$, $p = .151$] or early change in OQ from intake to session 5 [$B = -.33$, $SE = .19$; $t(25.22) = -1.70$, $p = .101$].

Predicting Symptom Change from Client and Therapist Global Attachment: Client-Therapist Attachment Match

To test the prediction of change in OQ from clients' and therapists' global attachment since several clients were treated by each therapist, a hierarchical linear method was used (Mixed Models) to predict change in OQ from client attachment and therapist attachment. In these models change in OQ was defined as residual gains from intake to session 32, while controlling for the OQ intake score. Global attachment of the client and of the therapist consisted of the ECR avoidance and anxiety scores. To examine the extent to which therapist attachment moderated the relationship between client attachment and change in OQ, the independent and moderator variables were standardized. The model tested the prediction of change in OQ in terms of client attachment, therapist attachment, and their two-way interactions (four combinations of client attachment by therapist attachment).

The findings of the mixed models analysis showed a significant main effect for client attachment on the avoidance scale, $t(13.98) = 2.20$, $p = .045$. This suggests that regardless of the therapist's attachment, higher-avoidant clients had a greater increase in symptoms from intake to the 32nd session. Moreover, consistent with the hypothesis that change in OQ would be predicted by the configuration of client-therapist attachment, the interactions of therapist avoidance by client avoidance was found to be statistically significant, $t(13.02) = -3.09$, $p = .009$ (See Table III). This interaction was plotted according to the simple slopes procedure (Aiken & West, 1991; Preacher, Curran, & Bauer; 2006). An examination of the significance of the slopes showed that when treated by low-avoidant therapists, low-avoidant clients were likely to decrease to a greater extent in OQ than high avoidant clients ($B = 1.80$, $t = 3.33$, $p = .003$). However, when treated by high-

Table III. Mixed models predicting change in OQ-45 from intake to session 32 with client and therapist global attachment

	B	*SE*	*t*
Client - Anxiety	.22	.20	$t(10.01) = 1.13$
Client - Avoidance	.56	.26	$t(13.98) = 2.20^{*}$
Therapist - Anxiety	.12	.22	$t(18.14) = .53$
Therapist - Avoidance	−.07	.31	$t(17.31) = -.24$
Anxiety - Therapist * Anxiety - Client	.35	.65	$t(20.79) = .54$
Anxiety - Therapist * Avoidance - Client	−.40	.52	$t(20.34) = -.76$
Avoidance - Therapist * Anxiety - Client	−.31	.46	$t(13.87) = -.68$
Avoidance - Therapist * Avoidance - Client	−1.24	.40	$t(13.02) = -3.09^{**}$

$N = 31$. $^{*}p < .05$, $^{**}p < .01$.

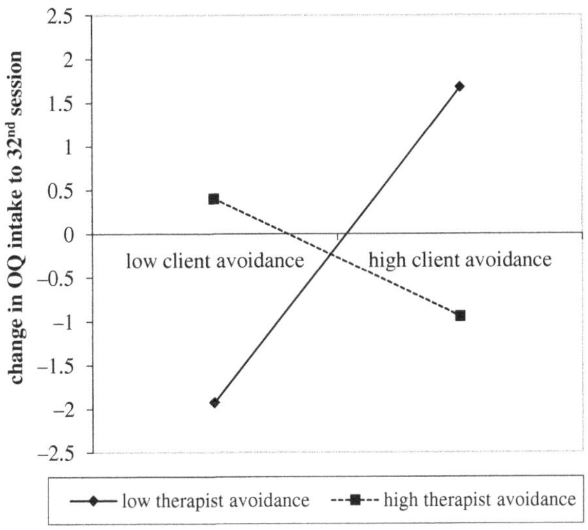

Figure 1. Interaction of client avoidant attachment by therapist avoidant attachment in predicting change in OQ-45 from intake to session 32.

avoidant therapists, the change in OQ of low-avoidant clients in comparison to high-avoidant clients did not differ significantly ($B = -.67$, $t = -1.69$, $p = .104$) (see Figure 1).

In summary, the results of the model examining change in OQ from intake to session 32 as a function of client attachment, therapist attachment, and their combination indicated: (1) Overall, regardless of therapist attachment, avoidant clients showed the least change from intake to the 32nd session; and (2) when treated by low-avoidant therapists, low-avoidant clients were likely to decrease to a greater extent in OQ than high-avoidant clients treated by low-avoidant therapists.

Discussion

In the last decade, Bowlby's attachment theory has received growing attention as a theoretical framework for studying psychotherapy process and outcome (Mikuklincer & Shaver, 2007; Obegi & Berant, 2009). Through the lenses of attachment theory and research, in this study we examined client attachment characteristics as a personality factor that the client brings to psychotherapy and the specific attachment the client forms with the therapist as an element of the therapy relationship. The association between client attachment and client attachment to the therapist was tested, as well as the association of each to symptom distress over the course of psychodynamic psychotherapy. Furthermore, we extend previous research on the effects of client attachment on post-treatment symptoms by exploring the moderating effect of therapist attachment on the relationship between client attachment and change in symptom distress.

Overall, the symptom distress of the clients in the study, as measured on the OQ-45 at five time points, decreased throughout psychotherapy. On average, in terms of the reliable change index (Lambert et al., 2001), clients made reliable change (14 points) from the intake to session 28. In terms of the clinical range cutoff (OQ below 63), 63% of the clients (on session 28) and 70% (on session 32) showed clinically reliable improvement. Our sample presented initially with higher distress levels ($M = 75.57$, $SD = 22.76$) than that reported (OQ intake: $M = 66.43$, $SD = 28.69$) in a recent study that used the OQ in a sample of clients from two psychology Midwestern US university-based training clinics (Sauer et al., 2010, p. 706). Hence, the distress levels of the clients in our sample are more similar to those reported in community outpatient clinics. Our major focus in this paper was on client attachment characteristics, the relationship between these characteristics and the attachment bond that develops with the therapist during psychotherapy, and the relationship of each to symptom distress; as well as on how client-therapist attachment match versus mismatch relate to client change in symptom distress over the course of psychodynamic psychotherapy.

Client Attachment and Symptom Distress

The hypothesized relationship between client attachment and symptom distress was supported for the different time points (early, middle, and later) during psychotherapy. Although none of the client attachment dimensions significantly related to distress at intake, attachment avoidance predicted distress in the early (session 5) and last (session 32) measurement points, whereas attachment anxiety predicted distress in mid (session 15) and late (session 28) psychotherapy. In a meta-analytic review, Levy et al. (2011) reported that higher attachment anxiety predicted the worst outcome, but that attachment avoidance did not have an overall effect on outcome after therapy. Our findings suggest that the effects of the avoidance and anxiety dimensions may differ at different stages of therapy. This may depend on the way clients begin and end psychotherapy and on the way they experience the working phase of psychotherapy. Specifically, clients' strategies of deactivating (high avoidance) or hyperactivating (high anxiety) the attachment system (Mikulincer& Shaver, 2007) may impact their symptom distress differently at different stages of psychotherapy. Deactivating clients may experience more symptom distress during the engagement phase and termination phase, whereas hyperactivating clients may feel intensified distress during the working phase of psychotherapy. Overall, regardless of phase of psychotherapy, secure clients (low on both avoidance and anxiety) reported lower distress. This is in keeping with the meta-analytic findings that showed that higher attachment security predicted more favorable outcomes (Levy et al., 2011).

Client Attachment to Therapist, Symptom Distress and Change

The associations between client global attachment and client attachment to the therapist at the different time points confirmed the hypothesis that clients who are high on avoidance in their close relationships (global attachment) form avoidant attachment to their therapist in the early- and mid-points of psychotherapy. This finding replicates earlier findings with the CATS in American university counseling samples (Mallinkrodt et al., 2005). Studies that employed the CATS with volunteer clients (Romano et al., 2008) or assessed the CATS on the third counseling session (Sauer et al., 2010) did not find such a relationship. In addition, we found that greater client global avoidance was associated with less security with the therapist in mid-therapy (session 15). This may suggest that avoidant clients are less able to use the therapist as a secure base (Mallinckdrodt, 2010) during the working phase of therapy. Contrary to our hypothesis, clients high in global attachment anxiety, rather than being preoccupied about their attachment to the therapist, report higher avoidant-fearful attachment to the therapist at the later stage of therapy (session 28). Thus, as termination approaches, the fear of rejection and abandonment (anxiety) is associated with resentment and the feeling that the therapist is rejecting (avoidant-fearful attachment to the therapist) to a greater extent than the fear of intimacy (avoidance), which is less at the forefront toward the end of therapy (Joyce, Piper, Ogrodniczuk, & Klein, 2007). The variability that we found in the associations between clients' global attachment and the attachment that clients developed with their therapist over time may be understood as due to differences in the therapeutic tasks that require different levels of closeness in the relationship at different phases in psychodynamic psychotherapy.

Regarding the impact of the therapist's global attachment on the client's attachment to his or her therapist, higher therapist anxiety attachment was related to lower client secure attachment to the therapist on the fifth session. Hence, the therapist's anxious attachment may interfere with helping the client to feel that the therapist is a comforting presence. The therapist may be too caught up in his or her own insecurity and consequently the client may perceive the therapist as less responsive, sensitive, or emotionally available. The therapist's anxiety attachment may be particularly detrimental given that this occurs during the alliance-building stage of the therapy relationship (Horvath, 2006).

The relationship between client attachment to the therapist and symptom distress at each time point showed that avoidant CATS was related to greater distress in mid-therapy (session 15). This is unlike avoidance ECR attachment, which was not related to distress in mid-therapy, but rather at the early (session 5) and late (session 32) time points. Preoccupied attachment to the therapist was associated with greater distress in early and mid-therapy. Although no significant associations were found between distress and secure attachment to the therapist, the findings clearly show that insecure attachment to the therapist characterized by greater avoidance and preoccupation in the therapy relationship is associated with higher distress levels in mid-therapy. During this working stage of therapy, the relationship tends to be vulnerable to cycles of rupture and repair (Eubanks-Carter, Muran, & Safran, 2010; Horvath, 2006; Safran & Muran, 2000; Safran, Muran, & Eubanks-Carter, 2011).

Finally, we also tested the prediction of change in symptoms from intake to session 32 by the three

CATS scales. The results showed that the lower the avoidant attachment to the therapist during early therapy, the greater the improvement was (decrease in OQ from intake to late therapy). It should be noted that our exploratory examination of the issue of the temporal sequence of attachment to the therapist and symptom distress, which has received much attention in alliance-outcome research (see Barber et al., 2013; Crits-Christoph et al, 2013), did not show that avoidant attachment to the therapist predicted subsequent change in OQ; nor did it show that in our sample initial symptom reduction predicted subsequent change. The only study that we are aware of that examined the CATS and change in OQ over time (Sauer et al., 2010) found that secure attachment to the therapist was related to reduction in client distress over time, paralleling that of the working alliance that was tested separately, whereas we found that avoidant-fearful attachment to therapist, rather than security in clients' attachment to the therapist, was predictive of change. It is possible that, the time at which the CATS was collected (third session) and the length of therapy (four to 11 sessions for clients contributing a termination OQ) may partially account for the differences between Sauer et al.'s study and our findings.

Client-Therapist Attachment Match

The findings on the contribution to symptom change of client attachment, therapist attachment, and their combination showed a significant main effect for client avoidant attachment. These findings on change in OQ from intake to session 32, while taking into account the client's baseline at intake, suggest that clients characterized by higher attachment avoidance not only may not improve, but their OQ may increase after 32 sessions of psychodynamic psychotherapy. In a study of a 16-session supportive-expressive (S-E) dynamic psychotherapy for depression with an outpatient Australian university sample, Reis and Grenyer (2004) found that clients reporting high levels of fearful attachment (as assessed using the Relationship Questionnaire, RQ; Bartholomew & Horowitz, 1991) showed significantly less improvement (as assessed on the Hamilton Rating Scale for Depression, HRSD).

Going beyond previous studies on client attachment and outcome, our study suggests that therapist avoidant attachment moderates the association between client avoidant attachment and outcome. This moderating therapist effect on change in symptom distress is germane to the issue of client-therapist matching in attachment (Eagle & Wolitzky, 2009), addressing the question of whether similarity or dissimilarity in client-therapist attachment results in better outcome. It has been suggested from the perspective of both interpersonal theory and attachment theory that "contrasting" (dissimilar) interpersonal orientations of the client and therapist are optimal for the process and outcome of psychotherapy (Bernier & Dozier, 2002). Our findings on the impact of client-therapist attachment match and mismatch suggest the benefits of similarity in attachment, but only in the case when therapists and their clients are both low in avoidance. This was not the case when therapists low in avoidance treated clients high in avoidance or when both therapist and client were high in avoidance. Hence, therapist attachment moderates the impact of client attachment on client change, such that low-avoidant clients improve significantly more than high-avoidant clients only when treated by a low-avoidant therapist. That is, although overall low-avoidant clients improved more than high-avoidant clients, when the therapist of low-avoidant clients himself or herself was high in avoidance the difference in the change in symptoms between low- and high-avoidant clients was not apparent. Moreover, the findings suggest that high-avoidant therapists do not fare significantly better either with low-avoidant clients or with high-avoidant clients who are similar to them.

Taken together, our findings on change in symptom distress suggest that avoidant clients not only appear to improve the least, but they also do not enjoy the benefits that low-avoidant clients experience when treated by a low-avoidant therapist. Mallinckrodt (2010) emphasized the need to consider the fluid nature of the attachment relationship. As he put it: "A corrective emotional experience is fostered *not* by one attachment relationship offered by the therapist, but rather by many relationships tailored to meet the client's needs through the changing phases of therapy" (p. 266, authors' emphasis). Based on interviews with experienced therapists who were given vignettes of hypothetical clients described as having high attachment avoidance or anxiety, Daly and Mallinkrodt (2009) suggested that these therapists sought to establish the optimal therapeutic distance from each client as a function of the client's attachment style as well as the phase of treatment. They distinguished between clients that hyperactivate (anxious) and those that deactivate (avoidant) the attachment system in terms of the optimal therapeutic distance in each of three phases of therapy: Engagement, working, and termination. Our findings on client-therapist attachment matching suggest that therapists face the challenge of finding the optimal therapeutic distance, especially with avoidant clients. Even therapists who are themselves characterized by low avoidant attachment tendencies need training and supervision (e.g., alliance-focused training, Muran, Safran, & Eubanks-Carter, 2010; alliance-fostering techniques, Crits-Christoph, Crits-Christoph, & Gibbons, 2010) on how to face these challenges in treating avoidant clients at the different phases of therapy.

Limitations and Future Directions

Our study contributes to the growing interest in client-therapist match versus mismatch in attachment style (Eagle & Wolitzky, 2009). However, the client-therapist match in attachment may depend on the specific outcome under study (Bernier & Dozier, 2002). Previous studies on the effects of client-therapist attachment matching on the session level, such as client depth ratings on the SEQ (Romano et al., 2008) and supervisor's ratings of countertransference behavior in first sessions (Mohr et al., 2005), have reported significant findings for the combination of high-anxiety clients and high-avoidance therapists. We obtained significant findings that included the combination of therapist avoidance and client avoidance, but not the combination of client anxiety and therapist avoidance. Our focus on change in symptom distress on the OQ-45 from intake to a later stage in psychodynamic therapy may have highlighted the difference in avoidance but was less sensitive to the combination of client anxiety and therapist avoidance.

It should be noted that overall the therapists in this study had much lower anxiety and avoidance scores than their clients. Thus, higher-avoidant therapists in our study were still not as high in avoidance as their clients. This contrasts with previous research on therapist attachment that employed the ECR with trainee counselors (Mohr et al., 2005; Romano et al., 2008) who appeared to be less secure (higher scores on both avoidance and attachment) than the relatively more experienced therapists in our study (3 years and up). In conducting our study in a naturalistic manner, we faced difficulties in administering the ECR at intake for all clients. The associations we found between the ECR and the CATS and between the CATS and the OQ strengthen our claim that the ECR indeed captured attachment as a personality characteristic. However, there is a need to replicate our findings with the client ECR taken at intake and also at later phases of therapy, possibly also as an outcome (Levy et al., 2011).

Another limitation is that due to the sample size we were unable to test the effects on symptom change of attachment characteristics and attachment to the therapist in the same model. We showed that client attachment characteristics impact the attachment to the therapist developed by the client at different stages. Our findings suggest that avoidant clients appear to develop an avoidant attachment to the therapist and this difficulty in the attachment bond with their therapist at the engagement stage (session 5) was found to be related to significantly less improvement from intake to session 32. Nevertheless, client avoidant attachment to the therapist did not predict subsequent change when controlling for early symptom change, but neither did early symptom change predict subsequent change. Future research with larger numbers of clients and therapists is needed to further explore the interplay of attachment characteristics of the partners and the therapeutic relationship that evolves over time and client change and to address the temporal sequence of client attachment to therapist and symptom change. Overall, in our study the level of probability was controlled for in each set of analyses (HLM, MANOVAs); however, the overall probability of getting a significant result by chance alone experiment-wise may be elevated. The results of this study should thus be interpreted with caution, and further study with larger samples is required which will also address various client diagnostic categories and client problems.

In addition, given that the meeting of the client and therapist interpersonal patterns is dynamic rather than static (Mallinkrodt, 2010), more sensitive measures of attachment are needed to capture these dynamics, such as the AAI (e.g., Levy et al., 2006) or the Adult Attachment Prototype Rating (e.g., Strauss et al., 2006). Using the AAI and the CATS in a large sample of inpatients, Petrowski, Pokorny, Nowacki, and Buchheim (2013) recently found that rather than the general security/insecurity of the therapist's attachment representation the type of insecurity (preoccupied or dismissing) was associated with the patient's attachment to the therapist.

The conceptualization and measurement of client attachment to the therapist requires further development and empirical evidence taking the issue of sensitivity to change over time into account as well as the temporal sequence of the association between CATS and outcome (i.e., prior symptom change). In our naturalistic study there were three assessment points for the CATS throughout treatment (sessions 5, 15, and 28) and the OQ was also assessed at session 32. While session 32 was the most advanced assessment point of the OQ in our design, it was not the post-treatment point for all patients. Future research on attachment and outcome is needed that will take into account the setting (e.g., inpatient, university clinic), the timing of measurements during psychotherapy, and length of treatment.

Bowlby (1988) posited that the therapist's role is to provide patients with the conditions in which they can explore their representational models of self and of attachment figures with a view to reappraising and restructuring them in light of new understanding and new experiences in the therapeutic relationship. Our findings on the associations with the attachment elements need to be understood in the specific context of psychodynamic therapy in which the hallmark of this type of treatment is that it focuses on the therapist-patient relationship over time to achieve therapeutic goals (Messer & Wolitzky, 2010). In fact, Barber (2009) asserted that the prediction of outcome by alliance beyond initial symptom improvement is more evident in psychodynamic models that focus on interpersonal patterns. Nevertheless our findings may be applicable to CBT approaches that include relational features (Castonguy, 2011; Muran et al., 2009). Future research would need to explore the generalizability of our findings to other psychotherapy orientations.

In his call for pathways of connections and integration, Castonguay (2011) suggests connecting between research domains, such as developmental studies on attachment, as a promising direction that can "provide us with rich conceptual heuristics in our exploration of individual differences" (p. 133). In pursuing the research recommendations of the second Task Force on Evidence-Based Therapy Relationships to disentangle the patient's contributions and the therapist's contributions to relationship elements and ultimately to outcome (Norcross & Wampold, 2011, p. 425), we explored the usefulness of the attachment framework. However, it should be acknowledged that although promising, attachment elements are only part of the complex picture of the interplay between the client's and the therapist's contributions to the therapeutic relationship and to client change.

Acknowledgments

We express our deep gratitude to our research coordinators: Miri Cardonis, Ayelet Gal-Oz and Miri Frank; Dr. Edna Guttmann for providing invaluable statistical assistance; and the Student Psychological Services at the Hebrew University for their co-operation.

Funding

This research was supported by the Israel Science Foundation (ISF) [grant 178/07] to Hadas Wiseman and Orya Tishby.

References

Aiken, L. S., & West, S. G. (1991). *Multiple regression: Testing an interpreting interactions.* Newbury Park, CA: Sage.

Aron, L. (1996). *A meeting of minds: Mutuality in psychoanalysis.* Hillsdale, N.J: Analytic Press.

Barber, J. P. (2009). Toward a working through of some core conflicts in psychotherapy research. *Psychotherapy Research, 19,* 1–12. doi:10.1080/10503300802609680

Barber, J. P., Muran, C. J., McCarthy, K. S., & Keefe, J. R. (2013). Research on dynamic therapies. In M. J. Lambert (Ed.), *Bergin and Garfield's handbook of psychotherapy and behavior change* (6th ed., pp. 443–494). New York, NY: Wiley.

Bartholomew, K., & Horowitz, L. M. (1991). Attachment styles among young adults: A test of a four-category model. *Journal of Personality and Social Psychology, 61,* 226–244. doi:10.1037/0022-3514.61.2.226

Bernier, A., & Dozier, M. (2002). The client-counselor match and the corrective emotional experience: Evidence from interpersonal and attachment research. *Psychotherapy: Theory/Research/Practice/Training, 39,* 32–43. doi:10.1037//0033-3204.39.1.32

Bernier, A., Larose, S., & Soucy, N. (2001). *Students' attachment state of mind and process and outcomes in academic counseling.* Manuscript submitted for publication.

Beutler, L. E., Malik, M., Alimohamed, S., Harwood, T. M., Talebi, H., Noble, S., & Wong, E. (2004). Therapist variables. In M. Lambert (Ed.), *Bergin & Garfield's handbook of psychotherapy and behavior change* (5th ed. pp. 227–306). NewYork, NY: Wiley.

Bohart, A. C., & Wade, A. G. (2004). The client in psychotherapy. In M. J. Lambert (Ed.), *Bergin & Garfield's handbook of psychotherapy and behavior change* (6th ed., pp. 219–257). New York, NY: Wiley.

Bowlby, J. (1969/1982). *Attachment and loss: Vol 1. Attachment.* London: Hogarth Press and the Institute of Psycho-Analysis.

Bowlby, J. (1988). *A secure base.* London: Tavistock Routledge.

Berzins, J. I. (1977). Therapist-patient matching. In A. S. Gurman & A. M. Razin (Eds.), *Effective psychotherapy: A handbook of research* (pp. 222–251). New York, NY: Pergamon.

Brennan, K. A., Clark, C. L., & Shaver, P. R. (1998). Self-report measurement of adult attachment: An integrative overview. In J. A. Simpson & W. S. Rholes (Eds.), *Attachment theory and close relationships* (pp. 46–76). New York, NY: Guilford Press.

Castonguay, L. G. (2011). Psychotherapy, psychopathology, research and practice: Pathways of connections and integration. *Psychotherapy Research, 21,* 125–140. doi:10.1080/10503307.2011.563250

Clarkin, J. F., & Levy, K. N. (2004). The influence of client variables on psychotherapy. In M. Lambert (Ed.), *Bergin & Garfield's handbook of psychotherapy and behavior change* (5th ed., pp. 194–226). New York, NY: Wiley.

Crits-Christoph, P., Connolly Gibson, M. B., & Mukherjee, D. (2013). Psychotherapy process-outcome research. In M. J. Lambert (Ed.). *Bergin and Garfield's handbook of psychotherapy and behavior change* (6th ed., pp. 298–340). New York, NY: Wiley.

Crits-Christoph, P., Crits-Christoph, K., & Connolly Gibbons, M. B. (2010). Training in alliance-fostering techniques. In J. C. Muran & J. P. Barber (Eds.), *The therapeutic alliance: An evidence-based guide to practice* (pp. 304–319). New York, NY: Guilford Press.

Daly, K. D., & Mallinkrodt, B. (2009). Experienced therapists' approach to psychotherapy for adults with attachment avoidance or attachment anxiety. *Journal of Counseling Psychology, 56,* 549–563. doi:10.1037/a0016695

Diener, M. J., & Monroe, J. M. (2011). The relationship between adult attachment style and therapeutic alliance in individual psychotherapy: A meta-analytic review. *Psychotherapy, 48,* 237–248. doi:10.1037/a0022425

Dozier, M., Cue, K., & Barnett, L. (1994). Clinicians as caregivers: Role of attachment organization in treatment. *Journal of Consulting and Clinical Psychology, 62,* 793–800. doi:10.1037/0022-006X.62.4.793

Eagle, M., & Wolitzky, D. L. (2009). Adult psychotherapy from the perspective of attachment theory and psychoanalysis. In J. Obegi & E. Berant (Eds.), *Attachment theory and research in clinical work with adults* (pp. 352–378). New York, NY: Guilford Press.

Eames, V., & Roth, A. (2000). Patient attachment orientation and the early working alliance: A study of patient and therapist reports of alliance quality and ruptures. *Psychotherapy Research, 10*, 421–434. doi: 10.1093/ptr/10.4.421

Eubanks-Carter, C., Muran, J. C., & Safran., J. (2010). Alliance ruptures and resolution. In J. C. Muran & J. P. Barber (Eds.), *The therapeutic alliance: An evidence-based guide to practice* (pp. 74–94). New York, NY: Guilford Press.

Farber, B. A., & Metzger, J. A. (2009). The therapist as secure base. In J. H. Obegi & E. Berant (Eds.), *Attachment theory and research in clinical work with adults* (pp. 46–70). New York, NY: Guilford Press.

Fonagy, P., Leigh, T., Steele, M., Steele, H., Kennedy, R., Mattoon, G., Target, M., & Gerber, A. (1996). The relation of attachment status, psychiatric classification, and response to psychotherapy. *Journal of Consulting and Clinical Psychology, 64*, 22–31. doi:10.1037/0022-006X.64.1.22

Gross, R., Glasser, S., Elisha, D., Tishby, O., Jacobson, D., Levitan, G., & Ponizovsky, A. M. (in press). Validation of the Outcome Questionnaire (OQ-45): Hebrew and Arabic versions adapted for use in Israel. *Israel Journal of Psychiatry*.

Horvath, A. O. (2006). The alliance in context: Accomplishments, challenges and future directions. *Psychotherapy: Theory, Research, Practice, Training, 43*(3), 258–263. doi:10.1037/0033-3204.43.3.258

Horvath, A. O., & Greenberg, L. S. (1989). Development and validation of the Working Alliance Inventory. *Journal of Counseling Psychology, 36*, 223–233. doi:10.1037/0022-0167.36.2.223

Jacobson, N. S., & Truax, P. (1991). Clinical significance: A statistical approach to defining meaningful change in psychotherapy research. *Journal of Consulting and Clinical Psychology, 59*, 12–19. doi:10.1037/0022-006X.59.1.12

Janzen, J., Fitzpatrick, M., & Drapeau, M. (2008). Processes involved in client-nominated relationship building incidents: Client attachment, attachment to therapist, and session impact. *Psychotherapy: Theory, Research, Practice, and Training, 45*, 377–390. doi:10.1037/a0013310

Joyce, A. S., Piper, W. E., Ogrodniczuk, J. S., & Klein, R. H. (2007). *Termination in psychotherapy: A psychodynamic model of processes and outcomes*. Washington, DC: American Psychological Association.

Lambert, M. J., Burlingame, G. M., Umphress, V., Hansen, N. B., Vermeersch, D. A., Clouse, G. C., & Yanchar, S. C. (1996). The reliability and validity of the Outcome Questionnaire. *Clinical Psychology and Psychotherapy, 3*, 249–258. doi:10.1002/(SICI)1099-0879(199612)

Lambert, M. J., Whipple, J. L., Smart, D. W., Vermeersch, D. A., Nielsen, S. L., & Hawkins, E. J. (2001). The effects of providing therapists with feedback on patient progress during psychotherapy: Are outcomes enhanced?*Psychotherapy Research, 11*, 49–68. doi:10.1080/713663852

Levy, K. N., Ellison, W. E., Scott, L. N., & Bernecker, S. L. (2011). Attachment style. *Journal of Clinical Psychology, 67*, 193–203. doi:10.1002/jclp.20756

Levy, K. N., Meehan, K. B., Kelly, K. M., Reynoso, J. S., Clarkin, J. F., & Kerenberg, O. F. (2006). Change in attachment patterns and reflective function in a randomized control trial of transference-focused psychotherapy for borderline personality disorder. *Journal of Consulting and Clinical Psychology, 74*, 1027–1040. doi: 10.1037/0022-006X.74.6.1027

Luborsky, L. A., & Crits-Christoph, P. (1998). *Understanding transference: The CCRT method*. Washington, DC: American Psychological Association.

Mallinckrodt, B. (2000). Attachment, social competencies, social support, and interpersonal process in psychotherapy. *Psychotherapy Research, 10*, 239–266. doi:10.1093/ptr/10.3.239

Mallinckrodt, B. (2010). The psychotherapy relationship as attachment: Evidence and implications. *Journal of Social and Personal Relationships, 27*, 262–270. doi:10.1177/0265407509360905

Mallinckrodt, B. (2011). *The psychotherapy relationship as attachment: Evidence and implications*. Paper presented at the 42nd International meeting of the Society for Psychotherapy Research, Berne, Switzerland.

Mallinckrodt, B., Gantt, D. L., & Coble, H. M. (1995). Attachment patterns in the psychotherapy relationship: Development of the Client Attachment to Therapist Scale. *Journal of Counseling Psychology, 42*, 307–317. doi:10.1037/0022-0167.42.3.307

Mallinckrodt, B., Porter, M. J., & Kivlighan Jr., D. M. (2005). Client attachment to therapist, depth of in-session exploration, and object relations in brief psychotherapy. *Psychotherapy: Theory, Research, Practice, Training, 42*, 85–100. doi:10.1037/0033-3204.42.1.85

Messer, S. B., & Wolitzky, D. L. (2010). A psychodynamic perspective on the therapeutic alliance: Theory, research, and practice. In J. C. Muran & J. P. Barber (Eds.), *The therapeutic alliance: An evidence-based guide to practice* (pp. 97–122). New York, NY: Guilford Press.

Meyer, B., & Pilkonis, P. A. (2002). Attachment style. In J. C. Norcross (Ed.), *Psychotherapy relationships that work* (pp. 367–382). New York, NY: Oxford University Press.

Mikulincer, M., & Florian, V. (2000). Exploring individual differences in reactions to mortality salience: Does attachment style regulate terror management mechanisms? *Journal of Personality and Social Psychology, 79*, 260–273. doi:10.1037/0022-3514.79.2.260

Mikulincer, M., & Shaver, P. R. (2007). *Attachment in adulthood: Structure, dynamics, and change*. New York, NY: Guilford Press.

Mitchell, S. A. (1993). *Hope and dread in psychoanalysis*. New York, NY: Basic Books.

Mohr, J. J., Gelso, C. J., & Hill, C. E. (2005). Client and counselor trainee attachment as predictors of session evaluation and countertransference behavior in first counseling sessions. *Journal of Counseling Psychology, 52*, 298–309. doi:10.1037/0022-0167.52.3.298

Muran, J. C., Safran, J. D., & Eubanks-Carter, C. (2010). Developing therapist abilities to negotiate alliance rupture. In J. C. Muran & J. P. Barber (Eds), *The therapeutic alliance: An evidence-based guide to practice* (pp. 320–340). New York, NY: Guilford Press.

Muran, J. C., Safran, J. D., Gorman, B. S., Samstag, L. W., Eubanks-Carter, C., & Winston, A. (2009). The relationship of early alliance ruptures and their resolution to process and outcome in three time-limited psychotherapies for personality disorders. *Psychotherapy: Theory, Research, Practice, Training, 46*, 233–248. doi:10.1037/a0016085

Norcross, J. C., & Wampold, B. E. (2011). Evidence-based therapy relationships: Research conclusions and clinical practices. *Psychotherapy, 48*, 98–102. doi:10.1037/a0022161

Obegi, J. H., & Berant, B. (Eds.). (2009). *Attachment theory and research in clinical work with adults*. New York, NY: Guilford Press.

Petrowski, K., Pokorny, D., Nowacki, K., & Buchheim, A. (2013). The therapist's attachment representation and the patient's attachment to the therapist. *Psychotherapy Research, 23*(1), 25–34. doi:10.1080/10503307.2012.717307

Preacher, K. J., Curran, P. J., & Bauer, D. J. (2006). Computational tools for probing interaction effects in multiple linear regression, multilevel modeling, and latent curve analysis. *Journal of Educational and Behavioral Statistics, 31*, 437–448. doi:10.3102/10769986031004437

Reiss, S., & Grenyer, B. (2004). Fearful attachment, working alliance and treatment response for individuals with major depression. *Clinical Psychology and Psychiatry, 11*, 414–424. doi:10.1002/cpp.428

Romano, V., Fitzpatrick, M., & Janzen, J. (2008). The secure-base hypothesis: Global attachment, attachment to counselor, and session exploration in psychotherapy. *Journal of Counseling Psychology, 55*, 495–504. doi:10.1037/a0013721

Roth, A., & Fonagy, P. (2005). *What works for whom? A critical review of psychotherapy research* (2nd ed.). New York, NY: Guilford Press.

Rubino, G., Barker, C., Roth, T., & Fearson, P. (2000). Therapist empathy and depth of interpretation in response to potential alliance ruptures: The role of therapist and patient attachment styles. *Psychotherapy Research, 10*, 408–420. doi:10.1093/ptr/10.4.408

Safran, J. D., & Muran, J. C. (2000). *Negotiating the therapeutic alliance: A relational treatment guide.* New York, NY: Guilford Press.

Safran, J. D., Muran, J. C., & Eubanks-Carter, C. (2011). Repairing alliance ruptures. *Psychotherapy, 48*, 80–87. doi:10.1037/a0022140.

Satterfield, W. A., & Lyddon, W. J. (1998). Client attachment and the working alliance. *Counseling Psychology Quarterly, 11*, 407–415. doi:10.1080/09515079808254071

Sauer, E. M., Anderson, M. Z., Gormley, G., Richmond, C. J., & Preacco, L. (2010). Client attachment orientations, working alliances, and responses to therapy: A psychology training clinic study. *Psychotherapy Research, 20*, 702–711. doi:10.1080/10503307.2010.518635

Stiles, W. B., & Snow, J. S. (1984). Counseling session impact as viewed by novice counselors and their clients. *Journal of Counseling Psychology, 31*, 3–12. doi:10.1037/0022-0167.31.1.3

Strauss, B. M., Kirchmann, H., Eckert, J., Lobo-Drost, A. J., Marquet, A., Papenhausen, R., & Hoger, D. (2006). Attachment characteristics and treatment outcome following inpatient psychotherapy: Results of a multisite study. *Psychotherapy Research, 16*, 573–586. doi:10.1080/10503300600608322

Summers, R. F., & Barber, J. P. (2010). *Psychodynamic therapy: A guide to evidence-based practice.* New York, NY: Guilford Press.

Taber, B. J., Leibert, T. W., & Agaskar, V. R. (2011). Relationships among client-therapist personality congruence, working alliance and therapeutic outcome. *Psychotherapy, 48*, 376–380. doi:10.1037/a0022066

Talley, P. F., Strupp, H. H., & Morey, L. C. (1990). Matchmaking in psychotherapy: Patient-therapist dimensions and their impact on outcome. *Journal of Consulting and Clinical Psychology, 58*, 182–188. doi:10.1037/0022-006X.58.2.182

Tyrrell, C. L., Dozier, M., Teague, G. B., & Fallot, R. D. (1999). Effective treatment relationships for persons with serious psychiatric disorders: The importance of attachment states of mind. *Journal of Consulting and Clinical Psychology, 67*, 725–733. doi:10.1037/0022-006X.67.5.725

Vermeersch, D. A., Whipple, J. L., Lambert, M. J., Hawkins, E. J., Burchfield, C. M., & Okiishi, J. C. (2004). Outcome Questionnaire: Is it sensitive to changes in counseling center clients?*Journal of Counseling Psychology, 51*, 38–49. doi:10.1037/0022-0167.51.1.38

Winnicott, D. W. (1971). *Playing and reality.* London: Tavistock.

Wiseman, H., & Tishby, O. (2011). The client-therapist 'dance': Interplay of client and therapist interpersonal patterns, working alliance and psychothearpy outcome. *Final Scientific Research Report: Israel Science Foundation (ISF).* [Grant No. 187/07, 2007–2011].

Wiseman, H., Tishby, O., & Barber, J. P. (2012). Collaboration in psychodynamic psychotherapy. *Journal of Clinical Psychology: In Session, 68*(2), 136–145. doi:10.1002/jclp.21834

Woodhouse, S. S., Schlosser, L. Z., Crook, R. E., Ligiero, D. P., & Gelso, C. J. (2003). Client attachment to therapist: Relations to transference and client recollections of parental caregiving. *Journal of Counseling Psychology, 50*, 395–408. doi:10.1037/0022-0167.50.4.395

Types of countertransference dynamics: An exploration of their impact on the client-therapist relationship

ORYA TISHBY[1], & HADAS WISEMAN[2]

[1]*Psychology, Hebrew University, Jerusalem, Israel & [2]Counseling and Human Development, University of Haifa, Haifa, Israel*

Abstract

Objective: The purpose of this study was to develop a typology of countertransference (CT) based on therapists' narratives about their parents and their clients. **Method:** Data are based on interviews conducted in the early, middle and late phases of ongoing psychodynamic psychotherapy with five therapists who treated 12 clients. Narratives were analyzed using the Core Conflictual Relationship Theme Method (CCRT). CT was defined as repetition of CCRT components from therapists' relationship with their parents in their narratives with their clients. **Results:** Raters identified five types of CT in the narratives: Wish from parent transferred to client, Projection of the parent Response from Other (RO) to client, Repetition of the Response of Self (RS), Repeating the negative parent RO, and Repair of the parent RO. **Conclusions:** A preliminary analysis of two psychodynamic therapies, one with good outcome and one with poor outcome, showed that CT types could be reliably rated.

The distinction between "treatment method" and "therapy relationship" is gradually receding, in part because recent studies have pointed to the complex reciprocal relationship between them (Lingiardi, Colli, Gentile, & Tanzilli, 2011; Norcross & Lambert, 2011; Safran & Muran, 2011; Tryon & Winograd, 2011). Whereas in the past the relationship was considered significant mainly in psychodynamic and humanistic-experiential therapies, it is now considered central to the therapeutic process across different types of therapy. One of the conclusions of the second APA task force on evidence-based psychotherapy relationships is that "the therapy relationship acts in concert with treatment methods, client characteristics and practitioner qualities in determining effectiveness" (Norcross & Wampold, 2011). One component of the therapeutic relationship which has been studied extensively is the alliance. A recent meta-analysis has shown that alliance is predictive of outcome regardless of the type of treatment employed (Fluckiger, Del Re, Wampold, Symonds, & Horvath, 2012). The same study suggests that therapists' contributions to the quality of the alliance are critical. This finding is in line with one of the recommendations of the APA task force, that researchers employ methodologies that can be used to disentangle therapist and client contributions to the relationship, and ultimately to outcome. One of these therapist contributions is countertransference management, which the APA task force on Empirically Supported Therapy Relationships judged to be a "promising" element in psychotherapy research although there is currently insufficient research to judge its impact on therapy (Norcross & Wampold, 2011).

Countertransference (CT) has gained prominence in the literature on psychotherapy, and is considered central in the client-therapist relational matrix (Gabbard, 2001). Although it originated in psychoanalysis, CT is currently considered a pantheoretical construct, as "therapists of all persuasions have soft spots that can be and are touched upon in their work" (Gelso & Hayes, 2007, p. 49). However, research on countertransference has lagged behind, due to difficulties both in defining and operationalizing such a complex construct. Various schools of psychoanalytic psychotherapy have defined countertransference somewhat differently, ranging from the narrow classical view of countertransference as an unconscious, conflict-based response to the client's transference, to the totalistic view that includes *all* of the therapist's feelings, thoughts and behaviors towards the client (for a review of the definitions of CT, see Hayes, 2004; Hayes, Gelso & Hummel, 2011). Gelso and Hayes (2007) proposed an integrative conceptualization of CT, defined as therapists' reactions to clients based on their unresolved conflicts. These reactions may be conscious or unconscious, *triggered by client transference* or other phenomena. This definition retains the classical view of therapists' unresolved conflicts as the source of countertransference. However, it also fits with a modern relational view that defines countertransference as a combination of the therapist's own dynamics invoked by the client and the interaction between client and therapist (Mitchell, 1993). In the present study we used the integrative definition described above (Gelso & Hayes, 2007), which has served as the basis for most of the research in this area (Fauth, 2006).

In terms of operationalizing countertransference, we have found Hayes's (2004) operational model of countertransference to be the most useful in delineating the various aspects of countertransference. Hayes breaks it down into five components: *Origins*—those areas of unresolved conflict in the therapist from which countertransference reactions stem; *Triggers*—therapy-related events that touch on these conflicts, such as client transference, certain content areas discussed by the client, or the phase of therapy (e.g., termination); *Manifestations*—affective, cognitive, behavioral and visceral reactions that therapists experience (e.g., avoidance behaviors, over-involvement with clients); *Effects*—consequences of these reactions on the quality of the therapy process and outcome; and *Management*—the ability to deal with and minimize the negative impact of countertransference (e.g., how therapists deal with their anger, or anxiety and the degree of self-awareness in sessions).

Measuring CT Manifestations and Management

Most research to date has focused on identifying and classifying *manifestations of countertransference* and *countertransference management*, and linking them to client outcome. These manifestations include cognitive, affective, and behavioral responses to client material or to the relationship, and can be measured by self-report or observer ratings, in the lab, or in the field. One of the most well-validated measures of *CT manifestations* is the Avoidance Index (Bandura, Lipsher, & Miller, 1960), which is an observer-rated, trans-theoretical scale. The scale categorizes therapists' responses as approach or avoidance, where avoidance is indicative of countertransference. In a study by Hayes and Gelso (1993), therapists' homophobia was directly related to their avoidance behavior in response to a videotaped vignette of gay clients. Although the scale taps into CT reactions, it has several shortcomings. In particular, reports of scale reliability across different studies have been inconsistent (Fauth, 2006), and the scale categories may not identify a wider variety of countertransference manifestations. For instance, there is no way to rate the approach as CT when there is over-involvement.

Several other measures have been developed that assess feelings, thoughts, and behaviors that arise from countertransference. Betan, Heim, Zittel Conklin, and Westen (2005) devised the Countertransference Questionnaire, a self- report measure that can be used by clinicians from different theoretical orientations. The questionnaire consists of 79 items that assess a range of thoughts, feelings, and behaviors expressed by therapists towards their clients. Some items describe specific feelings, such as: "I get bored in the sessions" or complex feelings, such as "I feel like I've been pulled into things that I didn't realize until after the session was over." Items are grouped into eight factors, such as "feeling disengaged," or "feeling/acting parental and protective," or "feeling sexual." Using this questionnaire the authors identified characteristic CT responses to clients with different personality disorders. Another self-report measure, The Feelings Checklist (Holmqvist, 2001), contains 48 feeling words, which therapists rate on a scale of 0 to 3 following each session. Similar to the results reported by Betan et al. (2005), the Feeling Checklist was shown to correspond to different diagnostic groups, thus indicating that different types of clients evoke typical feelings in their therapists. In a study conducted with nine therapists and 28 clients, Holmqvist (2001) found that, overall, different therapists had distinct feeling patterns that were quite consistent over time and across different clients (i.e., therapist-specific countertransference pattern). However, within each therapist's rather stable and unique emotional universe, different clients, some consistently and some occasionally, evoked different patterns of reactions (i.e., client-specific countertransference). These two measures assess totalistic CT, and do not assess CT as an integrative measure.

One of the limitations of the measures described above is their reliance on therapist self-reports to measure CT. In order to assess CT more objectively, additional measures have been developed that also include the supervisor's perspective on CT. Hayes, Riker, and Ingram (1997) developed the CT Index, a single-item Likert-type scale indicating the degree to which supervisors felt that CT influenced therapists' in-session behavior. However, the fact that this is a single-item scale, and global in nature, limits its usage. A more robust supervisor measure of CT is the Inventory of Countertransference Behavior (ICB; Friedman & Gelso, 2000). The scale consists of 21 Likert-type items rated from 1 to 5 and contains two subscales that have a positive or negative valence. An example of a positive item is "enmeshed," "overly supportive," or "dependent therapist behavior." Examples of negative items include "punitive," "avoidant," or "aggressive therapist behaviors." The scale has adequate reliability (alpha = .83 for the total score) and has demonstrated concurrent validity with the CT Index and the Countertransference Factors Inventory (described below). The CT Behavior Measure (CBM; Mohr, Gelso, & Hill, 2005) is another measure that contains items reflecting CT behavior that is dominant, hostile or distant. A more recent measure assesses CT as prototypes (Hofsess & Tracy, 2010), and shows good rater agreement on identifying CT behaviors versus non-CT behaviors in the session.

In terms of *CT management*, the most widely used instrument is the Countertransference Factors Inventory (CFI; Van Wagoner, Gelso, Hayes, & Diemer, 1991), and its revised version, CFI-R (Gelso, Latts, Gomez, & Fassinger, 2002). The CFI contains 50 items tapping therapist characteristics theorized to facilitate CT management in general. It contains five subscales reflecting therapist attributes that are important to successful CT management: self-insight, self-integration, anxiety management, empathy, and conceptualizing ability (Fauth, 2006; Hayes et al., 2011). In a recent meta-analysis based on 10 studies, Hayes et al. (2011) reported a strong and significant relationship ($r = .56$, $p = .000$) between CT *management* and therapy outcome.

Countertransference and outcome. There is a limited amount of research that links CT to therapy outcome. Rosenberger and Hayes (2002), in an analysis of a single therapy dyad, showed that when the client talked about topics related to the therapist's unresolved conflicts (based on a pre-treatment interview), the therapist was less avoidant and the working alliance was stronger. However, the more frequently clients discussed such issues, the more therapists perceived the sessions as shallow, and themselves as less attractive or less expert. In another study, consisting of 50 therapists and their supervisors, both positive and negative CT appeared to be associated with weaker alliances, (Ligiero & Gelso, 2002). In a study of 20 counseling psychology doctoral students (Hayes et al., 1997), supervisors examined 20 cases of brief therapy, rating each session for CT on the Countertransference Index. In the less successful cases there was a strong negative relationship between CT and outcome, whereas for the successful cases no relationship between CT and outcome was found. Hill, Nutt-Williams, Heaton, Thompson, and Rhodes (1996) interviewed 12 therapists about their experiences with impasses that led to termination. Interviews were analyzed using Consensual Qualitative Research Methodology. Among the variables contributing to impasses were possible therapist mistakes and therapists' personal issues.

Using the CCRT Method to Study the Origins of Countertransference

Our review of the measures of CT points to a lacuna in the study of CT, given that the measures described above pertain to *manifestations* of the conflict, but very little research has been conducted on the *origins* of CT, and how they are triggered in psychotherapy. As Hayes (2004) emphasized within the integrative conceptualization of CT: "to study countertransference meaningfully one needs to be confident that therapist reactions stem from areas of personal conflict" (p. 32). Gelso and Hayes (2007) formulated the countertransference interaction hypothesis, which states that countertransference reflects the interaction between Origins and Triggers: "Each therapist needs to reflect upon what client material or attributes trigger his or her own conflicts and vulnerabilities as a basic step in managing countertransference" (p. 44).

The present study focused on developing a method to identify the origins of CT based on applying the Core Conflictual Relationship Theme Method (CCRT; Luborsky & Crits-Christoph, 1998), which was originally developed to study transference. A person's CCRT consists of three basic components: *Wish* (W), the *Response from Other* (RO), and *the Response of Self* (RS). The Wish component refers to a wish, desire, or intention that the person has towards the other (e.g., to be loved, to be assertive); the RO refers to an actual, anticipated, or fantasized response from the other (e.g., supportive, disapproving); and the RS refers to the person's anticipated or fantasized response of the self in the form of thoughts, emotions, behaviors, or symptoms (e.g., feels accepted, depressed). The three components of the CCRT are derived from relationship episodes (REs), which are narratives that subjects tell about specific interactions with significant others. In addition to their specific content, the RO and RS can be rated as negative or positive, and the relationship between the three components is rated as complementary or conflictual. The first study to apply the CCRT method to study countertransference was conducted by Tishby and Vered (2011). The method was tested with 12 therapists treating adolescents. They were asked to relate narratives about their parents, and about two of their clients. The interviews were conducted at one time point, approximately in the middle of treatment. The findings showed that all three components of the therapists' CCRTs with their parents (W, RO, and RS) appeared in their narratives about their two clients. However, the parental themes were expressed somewhat differently with each of their clients; namely, different parent ROs appeared with each of the clients, suggesting that countertransference is created both by therapists' personal issues and client triggers. Based on a content analysis of the types of repetition of the CCRT components in the relational episodes with the therapists' parents in the relational episodes with their clients Tishby and Vered (2011) identified four types of countertransference dynamics. These types appeared to link "origins" and "triggers" with countertransference manifestations. The four types were: Identifying with the client RS; Repeating the parent RO; Repairing the parent RO; and Withdrawing.

The Present Study

Based on the encouraging findings of Tishby and Vered (2011), the goal of this study was twofold: (i) To refine and further develop the classification of CT types using the therapist's CCRT with their parents and with their clients in a systematic manner at three different phases of therapy. (ii) To examine in depth the CT types and how they evolve in relation to self-report alliance, session evaluation, and outcome, during one year of psychodynamic psychotherapy. Towards the first goal we studied the countertransference types in 12 cases, in the course of 1 year of psychodynamic psychotherapy (see Method section). To examine CT types therapists were interviewed at the same three time points (early, middle, and late in therapy), rather than at one random point, as was done in the Tishby and Vered (2011) study. Towards the second goal two cases were chosen for in-depth analysis of the types of CT dynamics. Through these cases we will illustrate the CT dynamics over time and their relation to measures of alliance, and post-session measures from client and therapist perspectives and client outcome.

Method

Participants

Twelve cases were selected from a sample of 67 clients who took part in a study conducted in a large university counseling center (Wiseman & Tishby, 2011, 2014). The 12 clients were treated by five therapists, each treating more than one client (except one therapist who at the time had only one client in the study). These cases were chosen to represent successful and less successful outcomes (on the OQ-45): seven cases showed clinically significant change, whereas five cases showed little improvement that was not clinically significant.

Clients. RAP interviews of 10 female clients and two male clients were selected for this study. The clients were undergraduate students in a large university, ranging in age from 20 to 26. They were diagnosed with either mild depression and/or anxiety, presented with difficulties in relationships, with their academic studies, or in consolidating their identity as young adults.

Therapists. The five therapists were clinical psychology interns with 2–5 years of experience, with an age range of 29–32 (four women, one man). They all received weekly individual supervision and group supervision in psychodynamic psychotherapy. The therapists who agreed to participate in the study were told that this is a study on interpersonal relationships and process in psychodynamic therapy. The terms "transference" and "countertransference" were not mentioned, and the therapists were blind to our research hypotheses and questions.

Therapy. Clients were seen once a week for 50 minutes, in psychodynamic psychotherapy, based mainly on object relations (Winnicott, 1971) and relational psychotherapy (Aron, 1996; Mitchell, 1993). The therapy in the counseling center is usually a year long, but in some cases it is extended. In all the cases in this study data were collected up to session 32.

Measures

Core Conflictual Relationship Theme (CCRT) method. The Relationship Anecdote Paradigm (RAP) interview (Luborsky & Crits-Christoph, 1998) was employed to assess clients' and therapists' interpersonal patterns. The therapists were interviewed about relationships with significant others in which they were asked to describe meaningful interactions (Relationship Episodes = RE) with each of the following significant others: Parents (four REs, two for each parent), romantic partner or close friend (three REs). In addition, the therapists were asked to relate relationship episodes (three REs) about their clients who participated in the study, but were interviewed by a different interviewer (Wiseman & Tishby, 2011). The initial RAP interview with the therapists consisted of 10 Relationship episodes (parents, romantic partner and client) and lasted approximately 45 minutes. It was conducted early in the course of therapy (after session 5). In order to assess the relational dynamics from the therapists' perspective over time, the therapists participated in two additional RAP interviews in which in each they were to relate narratives (three REs) about the interactions with their clients in the middle and later points of therapy (after sessions 15 and 28, respectively). All three RAP interviews were audio-recorded and transcribed verbatim. A group of graduate students in clinical psychology, trained by the second author, rated the therapist episodes on the Hebrew version of the CCRT rating form, which has an adequate reliability coefficient (Wiseman, Metzl, & Barber, 2006).

Self-Report Questionnaires

The self-report questionnaires for the present study included the OQ-45, the Working Alliance Inventory completed by clients and therapists (WAI-C and WAI-T), the Session Evaluation Questionnaire (SEQ), and a Post Session Questionnaire completed by clients and therapists.

Outcome Questionnaire-45 (OQ-45; Lambert et al., 1996). This is a 45-item self-report instrument designed for repeated measurement of client changes occurring throughout the course of mental health treatments. Clients are asked to rate their functioning in the past week on a 5-point Likert scale, from 0 (never) to 4 (almost always). The OQ-45 consists of three subscales: Symptom Distress, Interpersonal Problems, and Social Role. Research has indicated that the OQ-45 has adequate test-retest reliability (.84) and high internal consistency (.93). Concurrent validity has been demonstrated with a wide variety of self-report scales (e.g., Beck Depression Inventory, State-Trait Anxiety Inventory). The OQ-45 is widely used in university counseling centers and mental health centers. The total distress score has been found to be sensitive to change in counselling center clients (Vermeersch et al., 2004). The OQ-45 has been translated into several languages, including Hebrew (Gross et al., in press). In the present study, the alpha coefficient of the total OQ-45 was .91. Clients completed the OQ-45 at intake and after sessions 5, 15, 28, and 32.

Working Alliance Inventory: Client and Therapist versions. The Working Alliance Inventory (WAI; Horvath & Greenberg, 1989) is a widely used 36-item self-report questionnaire that was developed based on Bordin's (1979, 1994) conceptualization of the alliance, and consists of three subscales: Bond, Task, and Goal. Each item is rated on a 7-point Likert scale. The psychometric properties of the WAI are well established (Horvath, 1994). A Hebrew version of the scale yielded high alpha coefficients (Wiseman, Markiewitz, & Berman, 2006). In the present study the WAI alpha coefficients were .87 and .92, for clients and therapists respectively.

Session Evaluation Questionnaire (SEQ; Stiles, 1980). This included the Depth and Smoothness scales of the SEQ. The alpha coefficients for the SEQ were .85 and .75 for depth and .78 and .85 for smoothness for clients and therapists respectively.

Client and Therapist Post-session Questionnaire (PSQ; Muran, Safran, Samstag, & Winston, 1991). The PSQ is a self-report questionnaire that is used to assess post-session outcomes. We used the PSQ rupture and repair items, which were translated into Hebrew for the purpose of this study. For two cases, we report the ratings on the following four items: "Did you experience any problems or tensions in your relationship with the therapist/patient during the session?" (PSQ1); "Please rate the highest degree of tension you felt during the session as result of this problem" (PSQ3): "To what extent was this problem addressed in this session?" (PSQ5); and "To what extent do you feel this problem was resolved by the end of the session?" (PSQ6) (Samstag, Batchelder, Muran, Safran, & Winston, 1998, Appendix A).

Procedure for Identifying the CT Types

Two clinical psychologists (the first author, a senior clinical psychologist and supervisor, and a post-doctoral clinical psychologist) worked independently to identify repetition of parent CCRT components in the narratives of therapists about their relationship with their clients. The raters were provided with two kinds of material: (i) RAP interviews of the 12 therapists, which included relationship episodes about their parents (four REs) and about a specific client at three time points (total of nine REs, three for each time point); (ii) the completed CCRT ratings of these relationship episodes (W, RO, and RS for each RE with parents and with the client). These CCRT ratings were done by a different group of independent raters (four graduate clinical psychology students) at another university. The narratives with romantic partners were not used in this procedure. The process of identification of the CT types consisted of three steps.

Step 1: Each rater worked independently to identify similar CCRT components (Wishes, Responses of Other, and Responses of Self) in the therapists' relational patterns with their parents and with each of their clients. To be considered as similar, the rated W, RO, and RS with the parent and with the client had to belong to the same CCRT cluster standard category (Edition 3; Barber, Crits-Christoph, & Luborsky, 1998). For example, wishes such as to be loved, to be understood, and to be respected are all part of the cluster "to be loved and understood." The responses from other, which include hurt, dependent, anxious and angry, are all part of the cluster "other is hurt and angry." The responses of self, such as feeling comfortable, feeling loved, and feeling happy, are all part of the cluster "Feeling accepted and respected." In order to identify CT types, raters used the four types in the Tishby and Vered (2011) study as a starting point, examining whether or not these types applied to the data, and looking for additional CT types. On the basis of similarities between the CCRT with parents and clients in the first four cases, the two raters identified the following CT types: Transferring the Wish from parent to client, Projecting the parent RO to the client, repetition of the RS, and repetition of the parent RO. The first three types were new, and stemmed from the data. The fourth was found in data, confirming one of the types in Tishby and Vered. A fifth type was also identified, based on Tishby and Vered: When the therapist's Response of Self to the client was the *opposite* of their own parents' negative RO, raters classified this CT type as "Repair of the parent RO." For instance, if the therapist's parent RO was "misunderstanding" or "distant," the "repair" was the therapist's Response of Self to the client as "understanding" or "close." After rating the first four cases, and identifying five CT types, the raters consulted together with an auditor (the second author), and reviewed and consolidated the CT types and their definitions. The CT type "withdrawal" from Tishby and Vered was re-considered and re-defined as a specific case of repetition of RS (i.e., I withdraw), or of the RO (other withdraws), rather than a separate type of CT. The end product of this process was the definition of each of the five CT types. Compared to the CT types initially suggested by Tishby and Vered (2011) two types were retained (Repeating the negative parent RO and Repair of the parent RO) and three new types were identified.

Step 2: The remaining eight cases were analyzed according to the five CT types. Raters met to discuss differences or uncertainties they had about the rating of specific CT types. After completing the ratings of all 12 cases, the types in these cases were reviewed and discussed with the audit. This led to further refinement of the definitions of each of the five types.

Step 3: The final and third step involved counting the recurrence of each CT type in the 12 cases.

Results

Countertransference Types and their Recurrence

The analysis of the 12 cases following the first two steps described above led to the final list of CT types. Each of the five CT types includes a repetition of CCRT components (W or RO or RS) from the therapist's relationship with his or her parents in the CCRT components with his or her client. Table I presents the definitions for each of the five CT types accompanied by an example that illustrates the repetition that corresponds to the type of CT. The recurrence of each CT type in the 12 cases was identified on the basis of the ratings of CT types in the Relationship Episodes of therapists with their clients at the three time points. In order for a CT type to be counted as a recurrence, it had to be identified at two different time points (out of three), and within each time point to be identified in at least two (out of three) relationship episodes. Table II presents the frequency of the five CT types across the 12 cases for the five therapists in relation to each of the clients who were part of the present study. As can be seen in Table II, the most frequent CT types were Transferring the Wish from Parent to Client (in all 12 cases) and Projection of the Parent RO to the client (in 11 out of 12 cases). The CT type with the lowest frequency was Repair of the Parent RO, which appeared in half of the cases (six cases out of 12). In addition, as can be seen in Table II, there was variability in CT types across cases, showing that there were different patterns of CT for different therapists and clients. For example, Therapist 1 and therapist 4 had all five types across their caseloads, and therapist 2 and therapist 5 had three types out of five, and therapist 3 had four types out of five.

In-Depth Analysis of Two Therapist-Client Dyads: CT Types, Alliance, Post-Session and Outcome

To illustrate the five countertransference types and how they can be related to post-session processes and outcomes, we present two different cases selected from the sample of 12 cases. The cases were selected based on the quantitative data, which showed that one

Table I. Countertransference types

CT type	Definition
1) Wish from parent transferred to client	Therapist's wish from his/her parents is repeated in his/her relationship with his clients.
Example*: *The therapist's wish from her parents is* not to hurt them, and to calm their distress. *In an RE about her father, she tells how she called her father every day while she was abroad, so that he would not be anxious. In an RE about the client, she describes the client's concerns about people abandoning her, wondering whether the therapist will also abandon her in a year or two. The therapist says: "I immediately* wanted to calm her *and say that I am not leaving yet .... These are the places that pull me in:* I need to guard her and calm her.*"	
2) Projection of the parent RO on the client	Therapist perceiving the client's response to him/her in a similar way to his perception of the parent RO.
Example*:** *Therapist perceives his father as a reticent man with difficulty expressing his feelings or opening up to others. In his RE about a female client he describes a session which takes place on the day that she moved out of her parent's house to her own apartment. She was confused, was not sure what to talk about, and asked the therapist to be more active. The therapist* ***then perceived her as cold and emotionally distant, *wondering if they were not able to talk anymore.*	
3) Repetition of the RS	The therapist's response to the client (emotional, cognitive or verbal) is similar to his/her characteristic response to his/her parents.
Example*:** *The therapist feels misunderstood by her parents, and feels that they don't really accept her. Her characteristic RS with her parents is "feeling hurt" and "feeling rejected". When she recounts her initial session with a client, she describes the client as looking surprised to see her, and then saying that she is feeling angry. The therapist felt that these words were directed at her. She* ***immediately felt terribly hurt, *without taking the time to explore the reasons for the client's anger. She said: It was very strong, and I immediately projected it on myself, that she is angry to see me. I don't really know what was going on, but I was hurt. I took it personally, even though she was talking about more general things in her life."*	
4) Repeating the (negative) parent RO	The therapist's response to the client (RS) is the same as his parents' negative response to him.
Example*:** *The therapist's father tends to worry a great deal, and the therapist describes how, as a girl, she was overwhelmed by his worries and later learned to sooth his anxieties. In her RE about her client she says: "She told me about some things that she does,* ***which made me very very very worried. *I told her that* ***I worried about her,*** *that is* ***I disclosed my worry.*** *I think she knew that what she was doing would make me worried, but she was not really concerned about it. Perhaps she even wanted me to worry, but maybe I am making an inference here...."*	
5) Repair of the (negative) parent RO	The therapist's response to the client (RS) appears to be an attempt to **correct** his own parents' negative response to him.
Example*:** *The therapist perceived her parents (Parent RO) as controlling and not attuned to her emotional needs. Furthermore, she described them as becoming angry when her emotional needs conflicted with their work schedule. In her RE about the client she described the difficulty in finding a fixed time for therapy sessions with a new client. The client asked to reschedule several times, because she had other activities, and the therapist said: I felt that she needed space in order to enter therapy, and I wanted to give it to her.* ***I didn't feel angry, *as I might have with other clients.*	

client (dyad A1 in Table I) terminated treatment unilaterally after 28 sessions, with her outcome measures still in the clinical range (see Table III). Throughout her treatment this client's alliance ratings were lower than her therapist's ratings of the alliance (dyad A1 in Table IV). The second client (dyad B2 in Table I) made substantial gains in therapy, and had one of the best outcomes in the study. She maintained a strong and steady alliance throughout therapy, exceeding the sample mean from both client and

Table II. Frequency of countertransference types in 12 cases of psychodynamic psychotherapy

Cases	Wish from Parent transferred to client	Projection of Parent RO to client	Repetition of the RS (parent to client)	Repeating the (negative) parent RO	Repair of the (negative) parent RO	Total CT types per case
A1 Case A	V	V	V	—	V	4
A2	V	V	V	—	V	4
B1	V	V	V	V	—	4
B2 Case B	V	V	V	—	V	4
B3	V	V	V	V	V	5
B4	V	V	V	V	—	4
C1	V	V	V	V	—	4
C2	V	V	—	V	V	4
C3	V	V	V	V	—	4
D1	V	V	—	—	—	2
D2	V	V	V	—	—	3
E1	V	—	—	V	V	3
Sum	12	11	9	7	6	

Table III. OQ-45 scores for two cases over time: Intake, early, middle, and late therapy

	Intake	Time 1	Time 2	Time 3	Time 4	Gain for longest time span
Client A1	89	79	75	75	NA	0.347
Client B2	82	52	62	59	35	−1.13

Note. A negative gain value signifies improvement.

therapist perspectives (dyad B2 in Table IV). Relevant ratings of rupture and repair drawn from the PSQ are incorporated in the presentation of each dyad over time (early, middle, and late therapy sessions). In describing each case we present information about the client, including a brief description of the client's CCRT as identified separately as a context for the therapist-client relationship and dynamics that evolved with the client. After presenting the therapist's CCRT with parents we illustrate the CT types with the client over time in the three phases of therapy.

Case Example of a Therapist-Client Dyad with a Weaker Alliance and Outcome

Client (case A1). A 29-year-old female graduate student, whose presenting problems, included a general sense of anxiety and feeling insecure and difficulty forming intimate relationships. Her OQ-45 score at intake was 89 (see A1 in Table III). The client's CCRT with her parents was the following: She wished to have her needs and feelings recognized and validated (W), perceived her parents as rational, not supportive, and at times blaming (RO), and her response of self was feeling angry, hurt and alone (RS).

Therapist A. A 32-year-old married female with 3 years of clinical experience. The analysis of her CCRT with her parents showed that her primary wishes were to be close, not to be abandoned. However, she also wished to oppose the other (let her voice be heard) and at the same time not to hurt the other (W). She perceived her parents as misunderstanding her, angry and controlling and also anxious and helpless (RO). Her response of self with them was to feel helpless, angry, guilty or disappointed (RS). These themes are manifested in the following relationship episode:

> I was 5 years old, and my parents dressed me up as Peter Pan for a costume party in kindergarten. I really didn't want to wear that costume. I objected and I cried. My father took me to preschool with the costume, and he sort of pushed me in forcefully ... and I continued to object. He was probably stressed about getting to work on time. It was unpleasant. He wanted to get it over with, wanted me to stop crying and go inside. I felt angry and helpless. You can't really decide anything when you are 5 years old.

Table IV. Working alliance scores for the two cases over time: Early, middle, and late

Therapist/client	Time 1	Time 2	Time 3	Gain T1–T3
Client A1	4.67	4.78	4.03	−1.96
Therapist A1	5.47	5.22	4.81	−1.08
Client B2	5.81	6.47	6.08	0.32
Therapist B2	4.89	5.53	5.43	0.36

Note. A negative gain value signifies deterioration.

CT Types During Psychotherapy (dyad A1)

Early therapy (session 5). The CT types were: Transfer of the wish from the parent, repetition of the parent RO, and particularly repair of the parent RO, which appeared in all three relationship episodes. *Transfer of Wish*: The wish to be close was predominant in all three REs. The therapist emphasizes this wish to be close to her client over and over again throughout her RAP interview. *Repetition of the Parent RO*: She perceives the client as anxious and vulnerable, similar to the way she perceived her mother. The therapist relates to her client's experiences as extremely painful, even when these events seem no more than ordinary frustrating events. For example, the client tells about her disappointment when she received a grade of 92 on a paper that she worked very hard on. The therapist described the patient as being in acute distress, repeating over and over again how hard this situation was. *Repair of the Parent RO*: The therapist perceived her parents as not supportive and not attuned to her emotional needs. In all three episodes about the client the therapist seems to try and "repair" this pattern, by making great efforts to be attuned and not controlling with the client. For example, the client complained about the inconvenient session time, even though the therapist tried to be flexible and change the hour to suit the client's needs. The therapist said: "I felt that I cannot push her ... It's not easy getting into therapy and she must have had mixed feelings about it. I had to give her some space, leave it open and I did *not* tell her: 'look, this is your hour and you have to make it work.' I felt that she needed the space and I could give it to her, and I wanted to give it to her. I mean, it didn't annoy me." This episode "echoes" the episode with her father described above, where she was pushed into kindergarten and her father was annoyed with her. At this time point the therapist's CT seems to respond to the client's needs to be supported, and the therapist is certainly not blaming, unlike the client's parents.

WAI, PSQ and OQ at session 5. At the end of five sessions, there was a 10-point decrease from the intake in her OQ-45 scores (Table III). The therapist's rating of the WAI was higher than the client's rating (Table IV), which is the reverse pattern of what is usually found (i.e., therapists rate the alliance lower than clients). Both client and therapist rated the session as deep and quite smooth; however, the therapist's ratings of depth were higher (Table V). Neither therapist nor the client indicated any tension in the alliance on the rupture and repair items.

Mid therapy (following session 15). The CT types in this phase were: Transfer of the Wish from parent to client, and Repair of the Parent RO. The transfer of the *wish to be close and connected* continued to appear in all three REs; for example, "I can feel her pain—it's good to be so close," or "she read out loud some poems she had written in adolescence and I was really impressed. There was a moment there—an intimate connection." *Repair of the Parent RO* was apparent, as the therapist repeatedly emphasized her need to "be there" for the client, in ways that her own parents had not been able to "be there" for her. For example, the client related her difficulties with one of her professors, and the therapist, in her RE, said: "She needs an adult who will help her understand what is happening, to help her get a grip on herself. At those times I have a gut feeling that she needs someone to be there, to help her, to guide her how to talk, or how to say what she wants." The therapist is somewhat aware of her CT as she indicates to the interviewer: "How do I differentiate between her subjective reality and my own feelings?" Another example of repair was as follows: The client recalled how her mother did not want her to read detective stories as a child, and preferred that she read classical children's literature. The therapist tried hard to be a different type of parent: "I was really in touch with her pain: The child who is being told she is nagging, that she should just get a hold on herself … I also remember my own difficulties as a child with reading, and those hard feelings towards my parents." In the RAP interview the therapist described the strong maternal feelings that the client evoked in her. She described herself as easily shifting into giving advice, and being calming and soothing. It should be noted that some therapists in our study referred to countertransference spontaneously in their RAP interviews, but this was not presented as a focus of the study.

WAI, PSQ and OQ at session 15. There was no change in the client's OQ-45 scores (Table III); the working alliance ratings showed the same gap as before, in that the therapist rated the alliance somewhat higher than client (Table IV). Both therapist and client rated sessions as deep and smooth, with no tension in the relationship (Table V).

Late therapy (following session 28). Four CT types were identified: Transfer of the wish from parent to therapist, repetition of the negative parent RO, repetition of the RS, and Repair of the Parent RO. *Transfer of the Wish* was similar to what was described in the previous sections. *Repetition of the Parent RO*: The therapist talked about an episode in which she perceived the client not only as anxious, but as clearly negative towards her, similar to her perception of her parents: Out of control, doesn't like me, doesn't accept me, and doesn't trust me. However, the description of the interactions was vague and it was not clear what exactly prompted her conclusions about the client's reactions. In the last RE she related how the client announced that she was terminating unilaterally, and the announcement sounded harsh and final. The client was seen as rejecting her and as very controlling, much like her parents. Her Responses of Self at this point repeated the responses in her CCRT with her parents; namely feeling helpless, ambivalent, unloved, and guilty. The therapist talked about feeling cheated, thinking that they had a close bond and discovering that it was not that strong after all. The therapist's narrative about the interaction, concerning the client's

Table V. Session depth and smoothness scores for the two cases over time: Early, middle, and late

	Time 1		Time 2		Time 3		Gain T1-T3	
Therapist/client	Depth	Smooth	Depth	Smooth	Depth	Smooth	Depth	Smooth
Client A1	5.67	4.17	5.17	5.50	3.67	4.00	−1.16	−0.750
Therapist A1	6.67	6.17	5.67	4.83	6.33	3.17	0.995	−1.50
Client B2	6.67	3.33	6.83	5.17	6.50	4.00	1.12	−0.44
Therapist B2	5.17	4.00	6.00	3.83	5.00	4.00	−0.36	−0.20

Note. A negative gain value signifies deterioration.

decision to terminate, shows that she did not recognize or validate the client's wish to terminate (the client's Wish in her CCRT to have her needs recognized and validated). *Repair of the Parent RO*: The therapist described herself as feeling hurt and angry, but also insisting that she liked the client, and saw the termination as a move toward independence. This latter part does not seem very convincing given how hurt she was. It seems as though she was still trying to be the "good parent," accepting the client's unexpected move (while simultaneously feeling very hurt) without exploring the client's reasons for her decision.

WAI, PSQ and OQ at session 28. The client and therapist ratings of the WAI at this point dropped below the sample mean, and the client's OQ-45 score did not change from the previous time point. The client's ratings of session depth dropped whereas the therapist's ratings of depth increased, creating a gap between their ratings. Both client and therapist ratings of session smoothness dropped below the sample mean. In the PSQ, the rupture and repair items both indicated a high level of tension (PSQ3 = 4 on a 5-point scale) and both stated that the tension was addressed (PSQ5 = 5), but only partially resolved (PSQ6 = 3).

Summary of the case with a weaker alliance and outcome. Two CT types seemed to predominate throughout this therapy: The Transfer of the wish for the parents to the client that entailed a wish for closeness and connection, and a strong emphasis on Repair of the Parent RO, which was concretized by giving the client "space," constantly validating her anguish and pain, even when the events described in the RE did not seem to be very dramatic. In none of the REs did the therapist describe interventions aimed at helping the client explore or deepen her understanding of her conflicts and pain. It seemed that over and over again the therapist was making sure they were close and that she was a "better parent" than her own parents. These CT dynamics may have impeded the process by making it difficult to be attuned to the client's changing needs throughout therapy, including her need to be independent and terminate the therapy with the therapist's validation and mutual agreement.

Case Example of a Therapist-Client Dyad with a Strong Alliance and a Successful Outcome

Client (case B2). A 30-year-old graduate student who presented with mild depression and concerns over intimate relationships. Her OQ-45 score at intake was 82 (see B2 in Table III).The client's CCRT with her parents: She wished for them to be attuned to her needs and to "see her" (W). She perceived her mother as very loving and caring (positive RO), but at times she was also quite intrusive (negative RO), which made her feel angry and impatient (RS). Her father was described as very rigid and controlling (RO). However, she also felt that he loved her deeply and wanted to help and support her (positive RO) and for this she felt very grateful (RS).

Therapist B. A 28-year-old male therapist with 3 years of clinical experience. This therapist's CCRT with his parents: The main wish was to have clear, preferably verbal, proof of emotional closeness (W). The father was perceived as caring but with a limited ability for verbal emotional expression (RO). There was some emotional closeness with his mother, but the support she offered was usually associated with pragmatic tasks. She also tended to exaggerate the positive aspects of stressful situations, which he perceived as signs that she was not attuned, and did not understand (RO). His responses of self with his parents were mixed: Feeling good, self-confident, and liking the other (positive RS), or feeling anxious and misunderstood (negative RS). The following relationship episode with his father demonstrates these themes:

> I called my father because my sister-in-law had just delivered a baby. I had a new niece and my father had a new granddaughter. I was very excited and wanted to share the excitement with him. I called and asked him how he was, and he didn't say anything so I mentioned the baby, and he said "yes, that's great." He sounded happy but said very little. I asked him about the baby and the delivery, and he said that I should ask my mother because he didn't know these things. I wanted to talk, to share the feelings but he was pretty quiet, so in the end I said that we would probably meet at my brother's house and the conversation ended.

CT Types During Psychotherapy (Dyad B2)

Early therapy (session 5). The CT types in the first RAP interview were as follows: Transferring the wish from parent to client, projecting the parent RO, repeating the RS, and repeating the (negative) parent RO. *Transferring the wish from the parent*: The therapist relates that the client arrived a few minutes late, which made him very anxious. The client began to criticize one of the paintings in the room, which was the therapist's favorite painting. She also commented on the dry plants, wondering why nobody took care of them. The therapist felt surprised and uncomfortable. He was expecting something else: A warmer and more positive encounter. The CT dynamic here is of the therapist *transferring the wish for closeness and intimacy* from the relationship with his parents to the client. *Projecting the parent RO*: The therapist described the client as distant and practical, wondering whether she was irritated with him, even though he acknowledged that her tone was not angry. The way in which he perceived her resonated with his mother's RO, which was distant and focused on practicalities. *Repeating the RS*: The therapist described himself as feeling misunderstood and not accepted, as he did with his parents. *Repair of the Parent RO*: The client asked to cancel the session, because she had several papers to write. The therapist accepted her request to skip the session but he had mixed feelings about this. He wanted to make sure that he was attuned to the client's emotional needs: Did she want his "permission" to cancel the session, or did she want to be pursued and offered a session on another day? This type of CT seems like an attempt to repair the parent RO (to be empathic and attuned to her emotional needs and not just to be practical like his own parents). Interestingly in this case, the therapist's dynamic of Repair of the RO also fit the client's main CCRT wish: To be seen and for the other to be attuned to her.

WAI, PSQ and OQ at session 5. The client's OQ-45 score decreased considerably from intake to session 5 (Table III). The working alliance ratings of both therapist and client increased above the sample mean (Table IV). On the SEQ both client and therapist rated session depth as higher than the sample means; however, their ratings of smoothness were lower, indicating that although the sessions were valuable they were not experienced as comfortable (Table V).

Mid therapy (session 15). At this time point, the therapist's Wish from the parents does not appear in any of the narratives about the client. *Projection of the Parent RO* appeared once, when the client arrived a few minutes late with a new, flattering haircut, and immediately left the room to get a drink of water. The therapist described her as distant, and interested mainly in practical issues, such as her haircut or a drink, and and not "caring" enough about the therapy process. This claim echoes his perception of his mother, who focuses on practicalities and not on the emotional process between them. However, the therapist says that he restrained himself, and did not say anything about it until later on in the session when he was able to reflect on her coming late with more empathy. Using his CT reactions as a signal to explore her behavior rather than react to it as directed toward him, he asked her whether arriving late might reflect her feelings that she did not deserve to receive therapy. He said that the client accepted the interpretation, which opened up a fruitful mutual exploration. *Repeating the RS*: In this phase, the RS responses were mostly positive, thus repeating the positive feelings that he had in his relationship with his parents (feeling good about himself and self-confident). *Repair of the parent RO*: This appeared in two episodes. In one episode the client told him that a friend's father died, and then asked him not to discuss this further. The therapist wanted to respect her request, but he also thought that her reluctance to discuss the old man's death was related to her guilt about not visiting him in the hospital. He recognized one of the client's typical conflicts: Caring for others versus caring for herself. He decided to pursue this line of interpretation, despite her request not to discuss the issue. He wanted to be a good therapist and bring up important material, but he also wanted to be sensitive to her needs and her ability to process material. His sensitivity to her needs was a repair of his father's limited ability to open up emotionally or be sensitive to his son's needs.

WAI, PSQ and OQ-45 at session 15. In this phase the client's OQ-45 continued to decrease. The client and therapist working alliance ratings increased above the sample mean and the session depth and smoothness ratings (by client and therapist) increased above the sample mean. Neither therapist nor client reported any tension in the session.

Late therapy (session 28). The CT types were: Wish from parent to client and Repair the negative parent RO. Projection of the negative parent RO appeared in only one episode. The therapist RS was mostly positive, with no Repetition of the negative RS. *Transfer of Wish from parent to client*: The client told him that she had bought a new dress, but she felt uncomfortable wearing it, because it exposed her legs too much. The therapist tried to clarify what she meant, and she burst out crying, and told him that her legs were short and chubby, and that she had always been embarrassed about exposing them. The therapist said he was touched by her expressing such intimate concerns openly with him. *Repair of the Parent RO*: The therapist described a dream that the client told him, about a male friend asking her to lay down beside him. In the dream, the client at first felt comfortable, but then she panicked and ran away. In his narrative about the client, the therapist described how he wanted to quickly connect the dream to her ambivalence about forming a romantic relationship (and also to the transference). However, he spoke of his awareness of his own pressing need to connect deeply very quickly, as opposed to the client's need to regulate closeness and maintain privacy (see the clients' CCRT above). He told himself to slow down, and as the session progressed he gradually interpreted her fear of intimacy in relationships. Although this was painful for her, she continued collaborating with him on this issue. The therapist felt that he succeeded in being emotionally attuned to her, and was able to put his needs aside (unlike his own parents, as well as the client's parents).

WAI, PSQ and OQ-45 scores following session 28. At this time point there was a decrease in the client's OQ-45 score (Table III). There was an increase in the alliance ratings (Table IV) and both client and therapist rated the sessions as quite deep. The client's rating of session smoothness matched the therapist's ratings, which were slightly below the sample mean, which seems to be a product of the deep work (Table V). Both client and therapist reported some tension in the sessions (PSQ3 = 3), but they both indicated that they were able to discuss it and resolve it (PSQ6 = 5).

Summary in the case with a strong alliance and a successful outcome. This therapist had a strong need for emotional closeness and spontaneity; however, it also appeared that he was attuned and sensitive to his client's needs to be recognized, respected, and cared for. At the beginning of therapy, whenever the client needed some distance and privacy the therapist became tense, perceiving her as distant and reticent, thus projecting his parents' RO of distance on her. Later on in therapy this CT type was not present, indicating that perhaps he was able to overcome his anxiety and not allow his CT to influence his perceptions of the client. The narratives told by therapist B2 reflect his tolerance for frustration and his use of self-awareness and empathy. This therapist actually became more flexible throughout therapy, with less projection of the negative parent RO. The therapist's CT of Repairing the parent RO in this particular case seemed to fit the client's needs. Although there are many factors that operated in this treatment, it is possible that the change in CT types and the therapist's ability to manage his CT contributed to the success of this therapy.

Discussion

In this paper we proposed a new method of studying countertransference using relational narratives that therapists tell about their parents and their clients in the course of psychodynamic psychotherapy. These narratives are told during RAP interviews and then coded according to the CCRT method (Luborsky & Crits-Christoph, 1998). By comparing therapists' conflictual relationship patterns expressed in their narratives about their parents to the interpersonal patterns expressed in their narratives about their clients, we can identify therapists' CT dynamics that are *triggered* in their interaction with their clients. These dynamics stem from the therapists' areas of personal conflict; i.e. the "origins" of CT (Hayes, 2004). According to Gelso and Hayes (2007) researchers have long been looking for client characteristics and behaviors that trigger countertransference. However, this body of work has not proven to be very fruitful. Moreover, they point out that countertransference is a mutual process. The specific client behaviors that trigger CT depend on the particular vulnerabilities of the therapist, and not just on client characteristics. Thus, CT is a product of the interaction between client "triggers" and therapist "origins." The CT types identified in our study capture this interaction by providing a link between the client's behavior or speech (perceived by the therapist as the client RO), and the therapist's unresolved conflicts (W, RO, and RS with the parents). It this interaction between the client's responses as perceived by the therapist and the unresolved conflicts which produces CT dynamics that are *unique* to a therapeutic dyad.

Based on the in-depth analysis of the type of repetition of the CCRT components in therapists' relational narratives about parents and about their clients in the present study we defined five types of CT dynamics. Examining these five CT types in 12 cases of psychodynamic therapy showed that some types were prevalent across all therapies (such as Projecting the parent RO), whereas other types appeared only in some of the cases (e.g., Repairing the parent RO). Thus, the number of CT types and the specific types varied from one dyad to another, which supports the "countertransference interaction hypothesis" presented by Gelso and Hayes (2007). These CT types can be hindering or facilitating depending on the therapist's awareness of his or her CT, ability to use it to the client's benefit, or to manage it, as demonstrated by the intensive analysis of the two cases. This analysis constituted a preliminary attempt to identify the five types of CT in a successful case and a less successful one (assessed on the OQ-45), and to explore them in relation to therapist and client self-reports of the alliance (WAI), session depth and smoothness (SEQ), and rupture and repair (PSQ) over time.

In the less successful case (dyad A1), the CT dynamics revealed in the therapist's narratives in early and mid-therapy were: *Transfer of the wish from parent to client*, and *Repair of the parent RO*. The therapist was highly motivated to help the client and felt very connected and close to her. The initial alliance scores were around the sample mean, and both client and therapist perceived the sessions as deep and smooth. Thus it seems that at the beginning of therapy these CT types may have facilitated the therapy process. However, from the beginning of therapy the therapist experienced the alliance as much stronger than her client did, which is the opposite of what is usually found in alliance research (Horvath, Del Re, Flückiger, & Symonds, 2011). Thus, the therapist's strong wish for closeness and the wish (conscious or unconscious) to repair her parents' RO may have colored this therapist's perceptions of the alliance, so that she was not attuned to the client's changing needs for autonomy later on in therapy. As therapy progressed, the process measures took a plunge, as both the working alliance and the client-rated session depth decreased. The PSQ items showed a rupture, in that there was tension in the session which was not resolved. In this phase the CT type *Projection of the Parent RO* appeared in all the therapist's narratives, with the therapist perceiving her client more and more like her distant and preoccupied parents. As her wish "to be close" and "not to be abandoned" transferred from her parents to her client, and as the client's RO was perceived as distant, the therapist became less and less attuned to her client's relational needs (to recognize and validate her need for autonomy). What was facilitative at the initial phase of therapy became hindering at this phase. The rupture in the collaboration was evident by the disparity between the therapist's and client's WAI ratings of the alliance, which was apparent throughout therapy. At the later stage of therapy the therapist was motivated by CT that had not been processed and her lack of awareness of it was expressed in that she was surprised and hurt by her client's announcement of termination. This seems to have interfered with the therapist's ability to explore the client's reasons for wanting to end therapy and to process the termination (Joyce, Piper, Ogrodniczuk, & Klein, 2007).

In the successful case (dyad B2) the CT dynamic of *transferring the wish from the parent* was also predominant, as the therapist wished for immediate intimacy with his client. However, this wish was mostly facilitative as it helped build the client-therapist bond and closeness in the sessions. Moreover, based on the therapist's narratives over time there was a gradual shift in his response to this dynamic, indicating his ability to manage his CT (Gelso & Hayes, 2007). At first the therapist expected the client to initiate intimacy, and withdrew when she seemed too cold (similar to the CCRT pattern with parents: Projecting the parent RO and Repeating the RS). In the course of therapy he became more flexible, and suppressed his natural tendency to withdraw. Instead, he invited the client in a sensitive manner to explore her feelings, as seen in the "new dress episode." Thus, the therapist was capable of using the CT in a way that was facilitative to the process, by working collaboratively with the client. The CT type *repairing the parent RO* was prevalent, but not as dominant as in the less successful case. In addition, when this therapist tried to "repair" he was cautious, and careful not to force his needs for closeness on the client and to be attuned to what she needed from him at this time. This therapist, unlike the therapist in dyad A1, was able to contain his CT and to withhold or delay responses based on his CT, until the timing seemed right. As a result, he may actually have been able to "repair" both for himself (being more spontaneous and intimate) and for the client (she was seen and heard). The therapist's growth and change over the course of therapy is an important aspect of the collaborative process (Wiseman, Tishby, & Barber, 2012), and has been described by several writers in the relational analytic literature (Maroda, 1991; Muran, 2002).

Our initial conclusion from the exploration of these five types of CT dynamics and the ways in which they facilitated or hindered processes over the course of psychodynamic psychotherapy suggests that CT types are not hindering or facilitating in and of themselves. The interpersonal context and the therapist's management of the CT dynamics play an important role in the impact of CT on process and outcome. The CT dynamics that constitute repetition of a conflictual negative pattern (*transferring the wish*, *projection of parent RO*, *therapist as parent RO*, and *Repeating the RS*) may have a potential for hindering, if not processed and held in check. However, with careful attention, as was the case for the therapist in the successful outcome, these CT dynamics can also provide important clues about the client's emotional states, and lead to useful interventions. This therapist's sensitivity to ambivalence around issues of closeness in relationships (depicted in his "origins"—projection of the distant parent RO) alerted him to his client's ambivalence and guilt about receiving therapy in the middle phase of her treatment. This type of relational process fits with the modern relational view of enactment in therapy, and the role of the therapist's CT in those enactments (Safran, 2002).

The CT dynamic *Repair of the parent RO*, if it does not predominate, as in the less successful case (dyad A1), can be facilitative to the process. This seems to be the case especially if the therapist's need to "repair" resonates with the kind of repair that a particular client needs. When "repair" was successful, it seemed to contribute to a "corrective emotional experience" (Castonguay & Hill, 2012) for both participants. Such potentially corrective processes were illustrated in both cases, for example, when therapist A provided "space" for her client at the beginning of psychotherapy (dyad A1), or therapist B's work with his client's dream about intimacy. However, when the "pull" to repair appeared to operate at the expense of attunement to client needs, as in the case of the therapist in dyad A1 during the late phase of therapy, it hindered progress and possibly contributed to the client's initiated termination.

Limitations of the Study and Recommendations for Future Research

The analyses presented in this paper constitute a first step towards developing a typology of CT. Our initial experience in classifying these types seems promising, as they are relatively easy to identify and appear to provide useful clinical information. Because the systematic identification of CT dynamics was based on 12 cases, and complements a previous study of CT with adolescents (Tishby & Vered, 2011), we believe that analyzing additional cases might lead to refining the CT types and perhaps identifying additional types. Our study was a preliminary one, and a larger body of cases needs to be examined to further prove the usefulness of our typology with other client samples.

The next step in this research project is to create a manual for identifying these CT types in CCRT narratives, and to test the reliability of the ratings. In addition to creating the manual, we plan to continue to examine links between CT types, processes, and outcomes in a larger sample of clients and therapists. CT types can then be linked to manifestations, using scales such as CFI or ICB, and other measures of CT. In addition, the relationship between CT dynamics, the alliance, and rupture and repair is a promising direction for future investigation. For example, CT dynamics can be investigated in instances where therapists report strong negative or positive emotions that may indicate over-involvement, and when the client or an outside observer (e.g., supervisor) report a rupture. The CT categorization can be used to study processes in conjunction with the observation of videotaped therapy sessions, so that judges can assess what actually went on in the session. Of course judges will need to have access to therapists' CCRTs or other sources of information on personal conflicts. In addition, interviews with therapists on the extent and nature of their awareness of CT can add important information.

Finally, we note that analyzing therapists' narratives without taking into account the clients' narratives presents a limited perspective on the therapy process. Clients' relational narratives about the therapist are a source of information not only on their transference, but also on therapists' countertransference. We are currently developing guidelines to further study client narratives, and the ways in which to describe dyadic processes. In future studies a combination of therapists' and clients' narratives, along with videotapes of therapy sessions, would provide a rich source of data for studying how the interpersonal process unfolds, and how transference and countertransference dynamics (Safran, 2002) develop in the client-therapist encounter.

Our preliminary conclusions and recommendations are in line with those made by Hill and Knox (2009) on studying the therapeutic relationship. These authors advocate the use of qualitative approaches to study the relationship and recommend combining methods that examine events as they occur overtly by interviewing clients and therapists about their inner experiences in the sessions.

Recommendation for Clinical Practice

Therapists' CCRTs may prove to be a useful tool for supervision. Though it may not be suitable for novice therapists, advanced trainees who are ready to examine and process their CT can use it for their personal and professional growth. The modern relational conceptualization of psychotherapy is "an ongoing cycle of therapeutic enactment, disembedding and understanding, enactment and disembedding" (Safran, 2002, p. 171). Within this framework, identifying one's CT pattern is an important supervisory tool. Monitoring one's countertransference can assist in building a positive alliance. In addition, understanding and managing countertransference can help therapists to repair an alliance rupture, which is central to good process and outcome (Safran & Muran, 2011). Monitoring countertransference also provides therapists with clues as to subtle or unconscious communications from clients about their relational needs. Finally, although countertransference was originally defined in psychoanalytic theory, we believe that it is a useful construct for other orientations as well, since all types of therapy are carried out in the context of a relationship in which there is an encounter between the therapist and client's interpersonal patterns.

Acknowledgments

Thanks to Edna Guttman for statistical consultation, and Miri Vered our research assistant and doctoral student.

References

Aron, L. (1996). *A meeting of minds: Mutuality in psychoanalysis.* Hillsdale, NJ: The Analytic Press.

Bandura, A., Lipsher, D., & Miller, P. (1960). Psychotherapists' approach–avoidance reactions to clients' expressions of hostility. *Journal of Consulting Psychology, 24,* 1–8. doi:10.1037/h0043403

Barber, J. P., Crits-Christoph, P., & Luborsky, L. (1998). A guide to the CCRT standard cateeories and their classification. In: L. Luborsky & P. Crits-Christoph (Eds.), *Understanding transference: The CCRT method* (pp. 43–54). Washington, DC: American Psychological Association.

Betan, E., Heim, A. K., Zittel Conklin, C., & Westen, D. (2005). Countertransference phenomena and personality pathology in clinical practice: An empirical investigation. *American Journal of Psychiatry, 162,* 890–898. doi:10.1176/appi.ajp.162.5.890

Bordin, E. S. (1979). The generalizability of the psychoanalytic concept of the working alliance. *Psychotherapy: Theory, Research, and Practice, 16,* 252–260. doi:10.1037/h0085885

Bordin. E. S. (1994). Theory and research on the therapeutic working alliance. In: A. O. Horvath & L. S. Greenberg (Eds.), *The working alliance: Theory, research and Practice* (pp. 13–37). New York: Wiley. doi:10.1037/h0085885

Castonguay, L. G., & Hill, C. E. (Ed.). (2012). *Transformation in psychotherapy: Corrective experiences across cognitive behavioral, humanistic and psychodynamic approaches.* Washington, DC: APA Books.

Fauth, J. (2006). Towards more and better countertransference research. *Psychotherapy: Theory, Research, Practice, Training, 43,* 16–31. doi:10.1037/0033-3204.43.1.16

Fluckiger, C., Del Re, A. C., Wampold, B., Symonds, D., & Horvath, A. (2012). How central is the alliance in psychotherapy?*Journal of Counseling Psychology, 59,* 10–17. doi:10.1037/a0025749

Friedman, S. M., & Gelso, C. J. (2000). The development of the inventory of countertransference behavior. *Journal of Clinical Psychology, 56,* 1221–1235. doi:10.1002/1097-4679(200009)56:9<1221::AID-JCLP8>3.0.CO;2-W

Gabbard, G. O. (2001). A contemporary model of countertransference. *Journal of Clinical Psychology, 58,* 861–867. doi:10.1002/jclp.1065

Gelso, C. J., & Hayes, J. A. (2007). *Countertransference and the therapist's inner experience: Perils and possibilities.* Mahwah, NJ: Lawrence Erlbaum.

Gelso, C., Latts, M., Gomez, M., & Fassinger, R. (2002). Countertransference management and therapy outcome: An initial evaluation. *Journal of Clinical Psychology, 58*(7), 861–867. doi:10.1002/jclp.2010

Gross, R., Glasser, S., Elisha, D., Tishby, O., Jacobson, D., Levinson, G., & Ponizovsky, A. M. (in press). Validation of the Outcome Questionnaire (OQ-45): Hebrew and Arabic versions adapted for use in Israel. *Israel Journal of Psychiatry.*

Hayes, J. A. (2004). The inner world of the psychotherapist: a program of research on countertransference. *Psychotherapy Research, 14*(1), 21–36. doi:10.1093/ptr/kph002

Hayes, J. A., & Gelso, C. G. (1993). Counselors' discomfort with gay and HIV infected clients. *Journal of Counseling Psychology, 40,* 86–93. doi:10.1037/0022-0167.40.1.86

Hayes, J. A., Gelso, C. G., & Hummel, A. M. (2011). Managing countertransference. *Psychotherapy, 48*(1), 88–97. doi:10.1037/a0022182

Hayes, J. A., Riker, J. R., & Ingram, K. M. (1997). Countertransference behavior and management in brief counseling: A field study. *Psychotherapy Research, 7,* 145–153. doi:10.1080/10503309712331331933

Hill, C. E., & Knox, S. (2009). Processing the therapeutic relationship. *Psychotherapy Research, 19,* 13–29. doi:10.1080/10503300802621206

Hill, C. E., Nutt-Williams, E., Heaton, K. J., Thompson, B. J., & Rhodes, R. H. (1996). Therapist retrospective recall of impasses in long-term psychotherapy: A qualitative analysis. *Journal of Counseling Psychology, 43,* 207–217. doi:10.1037/0022-0167.43.2.207

Hofsess, C. D., & Tracy, T. G. J. (2010). Countertransference as prototype: The development of a measure. *Journal of Counseling Psychology, 57,* 52–67, doi:10.1037/a0018111

Holmqvist, R. (2001). Patterns of consistency and deviation in therapists' countertransference feelings. *Journal of Psychotherapy Practice and Research, 10,* 104–116.

Horvath, A. O., & Greenberg, L. S. (1989). Development and validation of the Working Alliance Inventory. *Journal of Counseling Psychology, 36,* 223–233. doi:10.1037/0022-0167.36.2.223

Horvath, A. O., Del Re, A. C., Flückiger, C., & Symonds, D. (2011). Alliance in individual psychotherapy. *Psychotherapy, 48* (1), 9–16. doi:10.1037/a0022186

Joyce, A. S., Piper, W. E., Ogrodniczuk, J. S., & Klein, R. H. (2007). *Termination in psychotherapy: A psychodynamic model of processes and outcomes.* Washington, DC: American Psychological Association.

Lambert, M. J., Burlingame, G. M., Umphress, V., Hansen, N. B., Vermeersch, D. A., Clouse, G. C., & Yanchar, S. C. (1996). The reliability and validity of the Outcome Questionnaire. *Clinical Psychology and Psychotherapy, 3,* 249–258. doi:10.1002/(SICI)1099-0879(199612)

Ligiero, D. P., & Gelso, C. J. (2002). Countertransference, attachment, and the working alliance: The therapist's contributions. *Psychotherapy, 39,* 3–11. doi:10.1037/0033-3204.39.1.3

Lingiardi, V., Colli, A., Gentile, D., & Tanzilli, A. (2011). Exploration of session process: relationship to depth and alliance. *Psychotherapy, 48,* 391–400. doi:10.1037/a0025248

Luborsky, L., & Crits-Christoph, P. (1998). *Understanding transference: The CCRT method.* Washington, DC: American Psychological Association.

Maroda, K. J. (1991). *The power of countertransference.* New York, NY: Jason Aronson.

Mitchell, S. A. (1993). *Hope and dread in psychoanalysis.* New York, NY: Basic Books.

Mohr, J. J., Gelso, C. J., & Hill, C. E. (2005). Client and counselor trainee attachment as predictors of session evaluation and countertransference behavior in first counseling sessions. *Journal of Counseling Psychology, 53,* 298–300. doi:10.1037/0022-0167.52.3.298

Muran, J. C. (2002). A relational approach to understanding change: Plurality and contextualism in a psychotherapy research program. *Psychotherapy Research, 12,* 113–138. doi:10.1080/713664276

Muran, J. C., Safran, J. D., Samstag, L. W., & Winston, A. (1991). *Client and therapist post-session questionnaires.* Unpublished instruments, Beth Israel Medical Center, New York.

Norcross, J. C., & Lambert, M. J. (2011). Psychotherapy relationships that work II. *Psychotherapy, 48,* 4–8. doi:10.1037/a0022180

Norcross, J. C., & Wampold, B. E. (2011). Evidence based therapy relationships: Research conclusions and clinical practices. *Psychotherapy, 48,* 98–102. doi:10.1037/a0022161

Rosenberg, E. W., & Hayes, J. A. (2002). Origins, consequences, and management of countertransference: A case study. *Journal of Counseling Psychology*, *49*, 221–232. doi:10.1037/0022-0167.49.2.221

Safran, J. D. (2002). Brief relational treatment. *Psychoanalytic Dialogues*, *12*, 171–195. doi:10.1080/10481881209348661

Safran, J. D., & Muran, J. C. (2011). Repairing alliance ruptures. *Psychotherapy*, *48*, 80–87. doi:10.1037/a0022140

Samstag, L. W., Batchelder, S., Muran, J. C., Safran, J. D., & Winston, A. (1998). Predicting treatment failure from in-session interpersonal variables. *Journal of Psychotherapy Practice and Research*, *7*, 126–143.

Stiles, W. B. (1980). Measurement of the impact of psychotherapy sessions. *Journal of Consulting and Clinical Psychology*, *48*, 178–185. doi:10.1037/0022-006X.48.2.176

Tishby, O., & Vered, M. (2011). Countertransference in the treatment of adolescents and its manifestation in the therapist-client relationship. *Psychotherapy Research*, *21*, 621–630. doi:10.1080/10503307.2011.598579

Tryon, G. S., & Winograd, G. (2011). Goal consensus and collaboration. *Psychotherapy*, *48*, 50–57. doi:10.1037/a0022061

Van Wagoner, S. L., Gelso, C. J., Hayes, J. A., & Diemer, R. A. (1991). Countertransference and the reputedly excellent therapist. *Psychotherapy: Theory, Research, Practice, Training*, *28*, 411–421. doi:10.1037/0033-3204.28.3.411

Vermeersch, D. A., Whipple, J. L., Lambert, M. J., Hawkins, E. J., Burchfield, C. M., & Okiishi, J. C. (2004). Outcome Questionnaire: Is it sensitive to changes in counseling center clients? *Journal of Counseling Psychology*, *51*, 38–49. doi:10.1037/0022-0167.51.1.38

Winnicott, D. W. (1971). *Playing and reality*. London: Tavistock.

Wiseman, H., Markiewitz, M., & Berman, E. (2006, June). *Working alliance and CCRT in the narratives about the therapist in different stages of psychotherapy*. Paper presented at the 37th Annual Meeting of the Society for Psychotherapy Research, Edinburgh, Scotland.

Wiseman, H., Metzl, E., & Barber, J. P. (2006). Anger, guilt, and intergenerational communication of trauma in the interpersonal narratives of second generation Holocaust survivors. *American Journal of Orthopsychiatry*, *76*, 176–184. doi:10.1037/0002-9432.76.2.176

Wiseman, H., & Tishby, O. (2011). The Client-therapist 'dance': Interplay of client and therapist interpersonal patterns, working alliance and psychotherapy outcome. *Final Scientific Research Report: Israel Science Foundation (ISF)*[Grant No. 187/07, 2007–2011].

Wiseman, H., & Tishby, O. (2014). Client attachment, attachment to the therapist and client-therapist attachment match: How do they relate to change in psychodynamic psychotherapy? *Psychotherapy Research*, *24*.

Wiseman, H., Tishby, O., & Barber, J. P. (2012). Collaboration in psychodynamic therapy. *Journal of Clinical Psychology: In Session*, *68*(2), 136–145. doi:10.1002/jclp.21834

Client disclosure and therapist response in psychotherapy with women with a history of childhood sexual abuse

BARRY A. FARBER[1], SARAH FELDMAN[1], & A. JORDAN WRIGHT[2]

[1]*Department of Counseling & Clinical Psychology, Teachers College, Columbia University, New York, NY, USA &* [2]*Empire State College, Psychology, New York, NY, USA*

Abstract

This study investigated the perceptions of adult clients ($N = 98$; M age $= 32$) with a history of childhood sexual abuse (CSA) of the costs and benefits of disclosure of this material. Significant benefits of disclosing included a sense of relief from sharing bottled-up emotions, and feeling more accepted and understood by one's therapist; significant negative consequences included feeling emotionally overwhelmed, and feeling uncomfortably vulnerable and exposed. Linear regressions indicated that CSA patients who generally disclose more have a greater tendency to experience both positive and negative effects of disclosure about abuse. In addition, a hierarchical regression analysis indicated that higher levels of symptomatology were predictive of higher levels of anxiety related to disclosure in therapy, suggesting that clinicians need to be cautious in encouraging disclosure about CSA with patients with severe pathology.

> [There was] a barber named Abraham Bomba, who went about clicking his scissors at a barbershop in Tel Aviv as he recounted his wartime experienced in Treblinka, Poland. The SS wanted to transport bags of human hair to Germany and, with this object in mind, assigned the barber to cut off the hair of already naked women in the moments before they were ushered into the chamber, or when they were already inside . . . Lanzmann reminds us, that, as the interview proceeded, the barber, pressed almost cruelly by Lanzmann to go on speaking, began to lose control over his emotions . . . it is a relief to learn that, after the interview had drawn to a close, the barber and Lanzmann embraced. (Berman, 2012, p. 21)

> "You know too much, now I will have to kill you." (A client of a doctoral student)

Although client disclosure has often been considered the foundation of psychotherapy (Stiles, 1995), providing the primary material with which therapists work, questions abound as to whether and how therapists should encourage disclosure and whether and how they should respond. Whereas the usual and perhaps appropriate answer to either of these questions is "it depends"—on, among factors, the client's needs, the nature of the disclosure, the intensity or depth of the disclosure, the circumstances of the disclosure, the theoretical orientation of the therapist, the strength of the alliance, and the function(s) served by the disclosure (Farber, 2006; Knox & Hill, 2003; Stiles, 1995)—the dictates of science propel us to find at least some empirically based rules or principles that might guide these decisions. Indeed, the nature of our responses to clients' disclosures, especially those disclosures that are shameful or otherwise distressing, is likely to affect the outcome of clinical work as well as the therapist-client relationship that in itself contributes to therapeutic success.

The primary aim of the research described in this paper was to investigate the perceptions of adult clients with a history of childhood sexual abuse (CSA) of the costs and benefits of disclosure of this material in psychotherapy. Our clinical assumption, one that guided the methodology of this project, is that a knowledge of the benefits and costs of disclosure among CSA clients can help therapists better formulate appropriate responses to difficult material, thus facilitating further disclosure while strengthening the alliance.

Saeed (2000) observed that "the relationship part [of psychotherapy] is hard to define, even harder to grasp clinically, and difficult to study empirically" (p. 106). Each element of this statement is certainly true of research in the area of patient disclosure. It has been difficult to define, as clinicians and researchers have struggled with questions regarding the appropriate unit of analysis: Should everything said by a patient in session be considered a disclosure, or should only relevant or distressing disclosures "count"? Should non-verbal behavior (e.g., body language) be considered disclosures? It is also clinically difficult to determine whether and when to encourage disclosure of distressing material and when to respect defenses against such disclosure. Lastly, it is difficult to study disclosure, in part because determining an appropriate unit or focus of measurement has been so elusive: Should we focus on type (topic) of disclosure? Amount of disclosure? Amount or type of nondisclosure? Depth of disclosure? Relevance of disclosure? Discrepancy between what is disclosed and what clients consider relevant?

For all these reasons, we still do not have definitive answers regarding the relationship between patient disclosure and therapeutic outcome (see Farber, 2006; Kahn, Achter, & Shambaugh, 2001; Stiles, 1995; Stiles & Shapiro, 1994). Nevertheless, the consensus view, one backed by considerable research, is that disclosure, when it occurs in a safe environment, is essentially therapeutic, exerting significant effects on emotional and physical health (e.g., Farber, 2006; Lepore & Smyth, 2002; Pennebaker, 1995).

The question, however, is whether the positive consequences of patient disclosure still hold in cases where the client has been abused. There is evidence to support both positions. One the one hand, as one group of researchers has noted, "an impressive body of data indicates that even simple acts of disclosing past traumatic experiences to others can exert a salubrious effect on subsequent health and well-being" (Bonanno, Noll, Putnam, O'Neill, & Trickett, 2003, p. 302). These positive effects have typically been attributed to the extinction of clients' maladaptive thoughts, feelings, and behaviors (e.g., Foa, Keane, & Friedman, 2000), their replacement by more adaptive thoughts, feelings, and behaviors (e.g., Davies & Frawley, 1994; Resick & Calhoun, 2001), or the establishment of "a new interpersonal experience that helps the client to contain overwhelming emotions and to maintain a sense of connection to the therapist" (Bradley & Follingstad, 2001, p. 10). Martsolf and Draucker's (2005) review of the empirical literature on psychotherapy treatment of CSA also resulted in a positive perspective on disclosure. These authors concluded that while no one particular therapeutic approach (including cognitive-behavioral, eye movement desensitization and reprocessing, feminist empowerment group therapy, and emotion-focused individual therapy) was more effective than another, psychotherapy that focused on the abuse, no matter the modality, was a promising treatment for adult CSA survivors. On the other hand, for women with a history of CSA, disclosure of abuse-related material in psychotherapy is typically fraught with a great deal of anxiety, including the possibility of re-traumatization (Depue, Curran, & Banich, 2006; Herman & Harvey, 1997; Seery, Silver, Holman, Ence, & Chu, 2008). Harber and Pennebaker (1992) have pointed out the "cruel paradox" of disclosure of traumatic material, wherein the benefits of disclosure are so often balanced by shame and by apprehensions regarding how others will view this material.

Further complicating the cost-benefit analysis of disclosure of traumatic material are the emerging findings that some individuals tend to benefit from such disclosure whereas others do not. For example, Bonanno et al. (2003) found that CSA survivors who did not disclose an abuse experience (repressors) when provided a laboratory opportunity to do so were more likely to show nonverbal expressions of shame and non-genuine (i.e., non-Duchenne) smiling, whereas CSA individuals who did disclose an abuse experience showed greater facial expressions of anger and disgust. Moreover, they found that repressive copers were relatively healthy. Based on their findings, they concluded that "Repressive copers may not require a detailed review of their traumatic experiences to benefit from treatment... CSA survivors who are not particularly focused on the trauma of sexual abuse or who consistently appear to shift their attention away from the affective tone of the abuse when asked about such events may be exhibiting adaptive forms of affective-autonomic response discrepancy" (p. 315). In a similar vein, Elliot and Briere (1994) found that among a sample of 248 children, all victims of CSA, the group that immediately disclosed their abuse (to a forensic evaluator at a crisis center) had higher levels of PTSD than those who had never disclosed or denied victimization. These results of these studies may well be clinically informative but it also bears keeping in mind that those CSA survivors who come to therapy may be those for whom repression hasn't been effective. It is also important to consider that these results are consistent with the hypothesis that for many with a history of CSA, the consequences of disclosure may be complex, encompassing a wide variety of positive and negative aspects.

Thus, despite the number of women affected by CSA— in clinical settings, about 40% of women report a history of abuse (Cloitre, Cohen, & Koenen, 2006)—and the seriousness of its effects—clinical problems include depression, anxiety, post-traumatic stress disorder, sexual difficulties, and borderline personality disorder (Beitchman et al., & Cassavia, 1992; Dube et al., 2005)—there are still significant questions regarding effective treatment, many of which focus on the appropriate stance therapists should take in regard to client disclosure. Whereas multiple reports suggest that therapists working with CSA clients need to be sensitive, compassionate, empathic, patient, and need to avoid expressing anger or criticism in response to disclosures or lack of disclosures (e.g., Farber, Khurgin-Botts, & Feldman, 2009), these recommendations, while seemingly clinically appropriate, tend to be lacking in empirical support. In fact, while Bradley and Follingstad (2001) contend that "it is incumbent upon psychologists to be able to explicitly lay out [for CSA clients] the expected benefits of disclosure in psychotherapy and to explain both when and why it should be used in treatment" (p. 2), there are few, if any, empirical bases for such actions or explanations.

Thus, there is a need to establish an empirical basis for helping therapists negotiate the complex nature of client disclosure of abusive experiences in a way that honors and respects CSA clients' needs, strengthens the therapeutic relationship, and maximizes the potential for therapeutic benefit. As one means toward this end, we have pursued what we believe is a new line of inquiry: Investigating the perceptions CSA clients have of the benefits and costs of disclosing their abusive experiences to their therapist. In addition, this study examines the potential associations of these benefits and costs to clients' demographics (e.g., age) and to their present level of symptomatology, time in therapy, overall extent of disclosure in therapy, and overall severity of sexual abuse.

This study is based on previous work of Farber et al. (2009) that hypothesized various ways in which the benefits and costs of disclosure manifest in the therapy of CSA patients. In that clinical paper, based on reviewing the professional and popular literature on the treatment of women with a history of CSA, the authors proposed that disclosure of trauma-related material within psychotherapy was a complex phenomenon that encompassed multiple, often concomitantly experienced positive and negative effects (e.g., greater self-awareness and a closer connection to one's therapist, as well as greater uncertainty about oneself and greater mistrust of others).

Method

Participants

The sample consisted of 98 female self-reported survivors of sexual abuse who were currently in psychotherapy. The decision to focus on women was predicated on the fact that women have been shown to be at 2.5–3 times the risk of being abused sexually during childhood compared to men (Finkelhor & Dziuba-Leatherman, 1994; Putnam, 2003) and that the great majority of the literature in this field, both professional and popular, has focused on women CSA survivors.

Participants' ages ranged from 18 to 62, with a mean age of 32.4 ($SD = 10.4$). The sample was predominantly Caucasian (87.8%). Among the non-white participants, 4.1% self-identified as Asian, 3.1% as "Other," 2% as African-American, 2% as Native-American/Alaskan Native, and 1.0% as Latina. The sample was collected from a number of countries (Australia, China, India, Canada, and the UK), though the great majority of participants (71.5%) were from the USA. The total time in therapy of all participants ranged from 1 month to 30 years, with a mean of 3.5 years ($SD = 3.4$); mean time in participants' current therapy was 1.9 years ($SD = 3.0$). The sample was highly educated: 2% of the sample had less than a high school education, 48.9% completed high school or a vocational equivalent, 30.6% had a Bachelor's degree, and 18.4% a graduate degree. Most of the sample was currently single—56.1% were either never married, widowed, separated, or divorced; 43.9% were currently either married or in a significant relationship.

Participants' therapists were predominantly female (76.5%) and Caucasian (85.7%). Among the non-white therapists, 6.1% were Asian, 3.1% Latino/a, 3.1% "Other," and 1% African-American. The majority of therapists were between the ages of 41 and 60 (64.3%). The professional status of therapists in this study included social worker (20.4%), psychologist (39.8%), psychiatrist (10.2%), counselor (22.4%), unknown (4.1%), and "Other" (3.1%).

Measures

Demographic questionnaire. Participants were given a demographic questionnaire that requested information about their age, race, education, parents' education, marital status, therapy, and therapist.

Childhood Sexual Abuse Assessment (CSAA). This nine-item self-report questionnaire is an adaptation of two measures assessing childhood trauma and experiences, The Childhood Trauma Questionnaire (CTQ; Bernstein et al., 1994) and the Sexual

Experiences Questionnaire (Farber & Sacco, 1999), a questionnaire that itself was expanded from the Sexual Experiences Survey (DiTomasso & Routh, 1993). Subjects were asked to rate the frequency of several types of abuse from when they were "growing up (before the age of 18)." Subjects could select responses on a frequency scale ranging from 0 (never) to 6 (more than 20 times).

Brief Symptom Inventory (BSI; Derogatis & Spencer, 1982). This self-report measure consists of 53 items that assess subjects' level of psychological functioning over the past 7 days on a Likert scale ranging from 0 (not at all) to 4 (extremely). It measures current distress on nine primary symptom dimensions (e.g., anxiety and depression) and also on three global indices. For the current study, only the Global Severity Index (GSI) was used, a measure derived from the average rating given to all 53 items.

Dimensions of Self-Disclosure for adult survivors of childhood sexual abuse (DSD). This 23-item measure, based on Farber et al.'s (2009) categorization of the benefits and costs of self-disclosure among adult survivors of CSA, uses a Likert-scale (0 = not at all; 1–2 = minimally; 3–5 = moderately; 6–7 = greatly) to assess CSA patients' perceptions of the extent to which they disclose in psychotherapy (in general and about abuse, specifically), and their perceptions of the positive and negative aspects of their abuse-related disclosures. This measure was developed by the authors and an eight-person team of psychology graduate students who devised questions to reflect the six different dimensions of disclosure proposed by Farber and colleagues (Farber, 2006; Farber et al., 2009). Originally, 39 questions were developed. Following feedback from a 10-person pilot study (a part of which requested participants to provide their thoughts about the appropriateness and clarity of these questions), the measure was revised and shortened to 23 items.

Three general questions about disclosure in therapy were retained, as well as 20 questions about specific positive and negative consequences that might follow disclosure about abuse. The three general questions included the following items: Overall, how self-disclosing (i.e., revealing of personal information about yourself) have you been to your most recent therapist? Overall, how self-disclosing have you been to your therapist regarding your history of abuse? Overall, how self-disclosing have you been to your therapist regarding how past abuse continues to affect your life? The remaining 20 questions encompass the following six dimensions of disclosure of abuse; note that within each dimension there are items that reflect both positive and negative consequences:

Self-awareness and identity formation (3 items). One potential benefit of self-disclosure in therapy is that it contributes to a patient's understanding and awareness of who she is, helping her to have a more clearly defined sense of self. However, the potential risk with this newfound identity is that it may disrupt a patient's tenuous sense of herself. In this regard, several authors (e.g., Duval & Wicklund, 1972; Farber, 1989) have shown that focused attention on the self may cause a decline in self-esteem; through self-examination, one becomes aware of what qualities and accomplishments one lacks. Thus, the positive item for this dimension was "To what extent has self-disclosure to your therapist about the abuse you experienced led to a deeper/better understanding of who you are?" One of the negatively-valenced items was: "To what extent has self-disclosure in therapy led you to feel less sure of who you are?"

Intimacy (4 items). Genuine and meaningful disclosure often leads patients to feel a sense of closeness and connectedness to their therapists. In addition, disclosing CSA experiences to an empathic, nonjudgmental, and believing listener is often thought of as the first step in a "process of healing that can reopen channels of intimate relatedness to self and other" (Frawley, 1990, p. 251). On the other hand, in the abused patient's past, being close to another has meant being taken advantage of. For a CSA patient to put herself in the position of becoming close to another is to open up the potential of feeling betrayed by her therapist, a potentially terrifying prospect. Thus, a positive item for this dimension was: "To what extent has self-disclosure in therapy about the abuse you experienced led to a greater feeling of emotional closeness or connection to your therapist?" A complementary (negatively valenced) question was "To what extent has self-disclosure to your therapist about the abuse you experienced led you to feel mistrustful or fearful of your therapist?"

Validation and affirmation (being known and affirmed by another) (4 items). It is human to want to be validated and accepted by others (Kohut, 1977; Rogers, 1961). Being affirmed and validated by a therapist, especially when one is beset with shameful experiences, can lead to powerful feelings of being understood, cared for, and valued. One positively phrased item in this category was stated as follows: "To what extent has self-disclosure in therapy about the abuse you experienced helped you to feel more accepted and understood by your therapist?" On the other hand, even if the CSA patient accepts the therapist's affirmation and validation, she may experience new unsettling feelings. For example, she may perceive her therapist's affirming sentiments as a prelude to re-victimization, a scenario she may have experienced in childhood. Thus, one of the negatively valenced item for this dimension was: "To what extent has self-disclosure in therapy about the abuse you experienced led you to fear that your therapist may use this information to hurt you?"

Differentiation of self: (4 items). Disclosure in therapy, aided by the therapist's questions, empathic statements, and encouragement, can allow a patient to experience a more complex sense of self, including a greater awareness of her positive qualities. The patient begins to realize that her abuse experience is not synonymous with her identity, and that she is a multi-faceted person who unfortunately experienced abuse. Stated somewhat differently, the patient begins to feel that the abuse she experienced is a part of who she is, but not the only part of who she is. However, there are risks that come with a more differentiated sense of self. As the therapist encourages a more nuanced self-image, the patient may feel that the therapist is minimizing the centrality of her abuse. Moreover, experiencing new positive aspects of self may feel strange to the patient; she may feel out of control or uncertain as to what do with these perceptions. Thus, one of the positive items for this dimension was: "To what extent has self-disclosure in therapy about the abuse you experienced helped you to view yourself as a more 'complex person,' someone who has a variety of attributes and is more than just a survivor of abuse?" One complementary (negatively valenced) item: "To what extent has self-disclosure to your therapist about the abuse you experienced made you feel anxious as you began to think about new ways of being in the world and new possibilities for your future?"

Authenticity (3 items). Feeling more authentic through honest disclosure can lessen feelings of shame of having to hide one's true self (Jourard, 1968). CSA survivors may feel revitalized by presenting the full and honest picture of past abuse, events that previously were shrouded in forced secrets, lies, and deceit. However, authenticity comes with risks, especially perhaps for a CSA survivor. She may be beset by self-doubt, worrying (based on her history) that her honesty is merely an attempt to receive her therapist's empathy or validation, which may actually lead her to feel inauthentic. Or, her inability to remember all details may lead to self-doubt and feelings of inauthenticity. The positive item for this dimension: "To what extent has self-disclosure in therapy about the abuse you experienced helped you to feel more authentic and genuine (i.e. make you feel as though you are being your true self)?" One of the negatively toned items: "To what extent has self-disclosure in therapy about the abuse you experienced led you to feel inauthentic because you've realized you haven't been able to accurately or completely remember all the details of what happened?"

Catharsis (relieving the physiological and psychological pressures of painful and/or shameful experiences) (2 items). The experience of abuse is often shrouded in secrecy as survivors are warned not to speak of it and demoralized by being told that it is their fault. Survivors may experience these "bottled up" feelings as too confusing or overwhelming to express. Thus, it is not surprising that when patients unburden themselves by disclosing these details they experience a sense of cathartic release. The psychodynamic theory underlying this experience of relief is that the survivor is using great emotional energies to keep the secrets and feelings in and that once these feelings are released, she is able to think and feel more freely. There is, however, evidence that catharsis may not always provide relief and instead may do harm. For example, Tavris (1984) has demonstrated that, at least in the short term, releasing anger may actually increase tension rather than provide relief. Indeed, patients may feel frustration that after a "breakthrough" moment there are still unanswered questions; in addition, cathartic release may lead to the patient becoming overcome with emotions that feel impossible to control and thus quite frightening. The positive item for this dimension: "To what extent has self-disclosure in therapy helped you to feel a sense of relief from sharing some of the bottled up emotions connected to the abuse you experienced?" The negative item: "To what extent has self-disclosure in therapy about the abuse you experienced led you to feel overwhelmed by your own emotions?"

In this initial administration of this measure, we have examined the scores on each of these 20 questions and have also subjected the entire measure to a principal components analysis (see in Results).

Procedure

Participants were recruited from several sources. Some were recruited through flyers posted or emailed to several New York City universities mental health clinics, and hospitals. However, the great majority (93.59% out of the 78 participants who reported the source of the link) responded to postings advertised on abuse and trauma survivor websites. In all cases, individuals were told that they were invited to participate in an online survey that explored the benefits and costs of discussing childhood sexual abuse in therapy. They were also told that if they were interested they could be entered into a lottery for a chance to win $100.

Participants were given a web address and a password to type in at the website in order to be connected to the survey. They were then led to a page that stated that continuing the survey was equivalent to giving informed consent to participate in the study. They were told that their responses would be kept confidential and would not be linked to their names. In addition, they were told that they could terminate their participation at any point. They were alerted to the fact that the questionnaire would ask some questions about past sexual abuse that could be upsetting, and were given several phone numbers for counseling services in the area should they need to speak to someone. Subjects were also given an email address and phone number to contact the senior author should they have any concerns or questions about the study.

Results

As an initial step in the data analysis, means and standard deviations on participants' abuse history, current level of symptomatology, and disclosure patterns in therapy were calculated. An overall severity of abuse score was calculated by aggregating participants' ratings on each of the questions on the CSAA. Thus, this severity score incorporates both the different types of sexual abuse experienced as well as the frequency of abuse. Of a possible severity score of 48, the sample's mean was 35.9 ($SD=11.3$), equivalent to a significant degree of abuse. The average amount of distress experienced in the last 7 days (as measured by the Global BSI score) by these participants was 2.6 ($SD=.80$), a score that falls between the designations "a little bit" and "moderately." Using an 8-point scale to assess disclosure (where 0 = not at all; 6–7 = greatly), the perceived amount of general self-disclosure in therapy for these participants was 6.0 ($SD=2.0$); the perceived amount of disclosure in therapy about abuse per se was 5.5 ($SD=2.3$), and the perceived amount of disclosure regarding how one's past experiences of abuse affect current functioning was 5.7 ($SD=2.3$). In addition, an aggregate of these variables, overall disclosure, was computed, $M=5.7$ ($SD=2.1$).

The means and standard deviations for each of the 20 items on the DSD scale were also calculated. As Table I indicates, the most positive consequences of disclosing experiences of abuse in therapy were a sense of relief from sharing bottled up emotions ($M=5.6$), gaining a better sense of "who you are" ($M=5.4$), and feeling "more accepted and understood by my therapist" ($M=5.3$). Other strong positive consequences (i.e., items with mean scores over 5 on the 8-point scale) included "viewing myself as a more complex person, someone with a variety of attributes" ($M=5.2$; $SD=2.4$), "feeling more authentic and genuine" ($M=5.0$; $SD=2.5$), and "feeling more emotionally close and connected to my therapist" ($M=5.0$; $SD=2.4$). The strongest perceived negative consequences included feeling overwhelmed by my own emotions ($M=5.56$), feeling more uncomfortably vulnerable and exposed ($M=5.5$), and feeling anxious about new ways of being in the world ($M=5.0$). The fear most often cited in the literature as an iatrogenic effect of disclosure among CSA clients, "feeling worse about yourself," translated into mid-range ratings among this sample, $M=3.7$ ($SD=2.2$), equivalent to a "moderate" effect.

Principal Components Analysis of the DSD

As a further step in the data analyses, we conducted a principal component analysis (PCA) of the 20 items of the DSD that assessed positive and negative consequences of disclosing abuse experiences. Three significant components emerged with eigenvalues of over 1. Because the third component was composed of a single item, which also loaded significantly onto Component 1, the third component was not used in subsequent analyses. Component 1 (13 items;

Table I. Most highly rated positive and negative aspects of CSA-related disclosure ($N=98$)

Positive consequences	M (SD)	Negative consequences	M (SD)
1. Relief from sharing bottled up emotions	5.6 (2.6)	1. Feeling overwhelmed by my emotions	5.6 (2.1)
2. Understanding more who I am	5.4 (2.4)	2. Feeling uncomfortably vulnerable and exposed	5.5 (2.3)
3. Feeling more accepted and understood by my therapist	5.3 (2.4)	3. Feeling anxious about new ways of being in the world	5.0 (2.2)

Note. Based on an 8-point scale (0 = not at all; 1–2 = minimally; 3–5 = moderately; 6–7 = greatly).

alpha = .80), with an eigenvalue of 7.8, accounted for 38.3% of the total variance; Component 2 (seven items; alpha = .81), with an eigenvalue of 3.9, accounted for 19.4% of the total variance. An examination of the items within each of these two components indicated that the first component represented positive feelings around disclosure (e.g., "To what extent has self-disclosure to your therapist about the abuse you experienced led to a deeper/better understanding of who you are?"), whereas the items within the second component reflected negative or anxious feelings around disclosure (e.g. "To what extent has self-disclosure to your therapist about the abuse you experienced led you to feel mistrustful of others in your life?").

Pearson product correlations between these two components (positive and anxious consequences of disclosure) and several other variables of interest were calculated: Neither positive nor negative consequences of disclosure were found to be significantly associated with either time in therapy ($r = .01$ and $r = .14$, respectively) or severity of abuse ($r = .05$ and $r = .11$, respectively), but both dimensions were significantly associated with overall disclosure in therapy ($r = .59$, $p < .001$, and $r = .29$, $p < .01$, respectively) and with BSI scores ($r = -.49$, $p < .001$. and $r = .29$, $p < .01$, respectively).

Regression Analyses

Single block, multiple linear regressions were conducted to ascertain the relationship between demographic and other predictor variables and these two overall disclosure variables (components). The demographic predictor variables were subject's race, age, marital status, education level, and mother's education level, and the other predictors of interest were time in therapy, overall disclosure, global BSI score, and overall severity of sexual abuse. Single block linear regressions were used because the purpose of these analyses was to discover each demographic and predictor variable's independent relationship to the disclosure variables. Table II indicates age and mother's level of education predicted positive disclosure (i.e., the extent to which disclosure related to abuse was perceived as beneficial), as did both mental health symptom level and overall amount of disclosure. Those higher in age and maternal education (a proxy for socio-economic status) had a lower level of perceived positive consequences of disclosing their abuse experiences ($\beta = -.16$, t $(90) = -2.10$, $p < .05$; $\beta = -.13$, t $(90) = -2.22$, $p < .05$, respectively). In addition to these demographic predictors, holding demographic characteristics constant, a higher level of mental health symptomotology predicted lower positive experiences CSA clients have as a result of abuse-related disclosure ($\beta = -.33$, t $(90) = -4.57$, $p < .01$). Additionally, the greater the overall amount of disclosure these CSA clients reported, the greater the positive experience and feelings they had about abuse-related disclosure ($\beta = .69$, t $(90) = 9.46$, $p < .01$).

A second linear regression analysis (see Table III) indicated that among the demographic variables only marital status significantly predicted disclosure-related anxiety ($\beta = -.26$, t $(90) = -2.86$, $p < .01$), such that single CSA clients experienced more anxiety related to abuse-related disclosure in therapy than their non-single counterparts. Again, overall level of disclosure in therapy and level of mental health symptomatology significantly predicted clients' experience of abuse-related disclosure in therapy, this time in terms of anxiety (i.e., dysfunctional consequences). Specifically, a higher overall level of disclosure significantly predicted more anxiety following abuse-related disclosure ($\beta = .33$, t $(90) = 9.46$, $p < .01$). Additionally, the greater the mental health symptom level, the more anxious feelings CSA clients experience as a consequence

Table II. Linear regression analysis for subject variables predicting a positive CSA-related disclosure experience

Variable	*B*	*SE B*	β	*t*	*p*
Race	.02	.20	.01	.10	.92
Age	−.02	.01	−.16	−2.10	.04
Marital status	.04	.13	.02	.33	.75
Education	−.02	.06	−.03	−.35	.73
Mother's education	−.13	.06	−.16	−2.22	.03
Time in therapy	−.01	.02	−.02	−.22	.83
Overall disclosure	.33	.04	.69	9.46	.00
BSI	−.42	.09	−.33	−4.57	.00
CSAA	.00	.01	.04	.55	.58

Note. $R^2 = .65$ ($N = 98$, $p < .001$); BSI = Brief Symptom Inventory Global Severity Index; CSAA = Childhood Sexual Abuse Assessment.

Table III. Linear regression analysis for subject variables predicting an anxious CSA-related disclosure experience

Variable	*B*	*SE B*	β	*t*	*p*
Race	−.09	.27	−.03	−.34	.73
Age	−.01	.01	−.08	−.79	.43
Marital status	−.52	.18	−.26	−2.86	.005
Education	.12	.09	.14	1.44	.15
Mother's education	−.15	.08	−.18	−1.85	.07
Time in therapy	.01	.03	.05	.47	.64
Overall disclosure	.23	.05	.47	4.76	.00
BSI	.56	.12	.44	4.48	.00
CSAA	−.00	.01	−.05	−.51	.61

Note. $R^2 = .35$ ($N = 98$, $p < .001$); BSI = Brief Symptom Inventory Global Severity Index; CSAA = Childhood Sexual Abuse Assessment.

of their abuse-related disclosures in therapy (β =.56, t (90) =4.48, p <.01).

As all the data are correlational and no firm claims can be made regarding directionality of effects, we also conducted two separate hierarchical regression analyses to assess whether positive and anxious disclosure experiences predict mental health symptoms above and beyond demographic variables. For each, the dependent variable was the global severity index from the BSI, which assesses overall mental health symptom level. The predictor variables were entered into the regressions in two blocks. Block 1 included demographic variables and other covariates, including age, relationship status, overall level of disclosure in therapy, and total time in therapy. As shown in Tables IV and V, age, overall disclosure in therapy, and the amount of time in therapy each significantly predicted level of mental health symptomatology. Older CSA clients had lower levels of mental health symptoms (β = −.25, t (90) = −2.30, p <.05); a higher level of overall disclosure in therapy significantly predicted lower levels of mental health symptoms (β = −.28, t (90) = −2.83, p <.05); and greater time in therapy predicted more symptoms (β =.22, t (90) =2.07, p <.05). Block 2 then included the predictor variables of interest, positive disclosure and anxious disclosure.

As shown in Table IV, controlling for demographic and other variables, higher levels of positive experiences about disclosing material in therapy significantly predicted lower levels of mental health symptomatology (β = −.58, t (90) = −4.55, p < .01). The R^2-change from Block 1 to Block 2 was .16, indicating that positive disclosure experiences in therapy accounted for 16% of the variance in symptomotology, controlling for age, relationship status, overall disclosure, and time in therapy. Table V shows that, holding demographic and other variables constant, higher levels of anxiety related to disclosure in therapy significantly predicted more mental health symptoms (β = −42, t (90) =4.29, p <.01). The R^2-change for this model was .15, indicating that anxious experiences of disclosure accounted for 15% of the variance in symptoms, controlling for the demographic and other variables.

Table IV. Hierarchical linear regression analysis summary for positive disclosure predicting mental health symptoms

Variable	*B*	*SE B*	β	*t*	*p*
Block 1					
Age	−.02	.01	−.25	−2.30	.02
Relationship status	−.00	.16	−.00	−.03	.98
Overall disclosure	−.11	.04	−.28	−2.83	.01
Time in therapy	.05	.03	.22	2.07	.04
Block 2					
Positive disclosure	−.46	.10	−.58	−4.55	.00

Note. Block 1: R^2 =.15 (N = 98, p < .001); Block 2: R^2(total) = .31 (N = 98, p < .001).

Table V. Hierarchical linear regression analysis summary for anxious disclosure predicting mental health symptoms

Variable	*B*	*SE B*	β	*t*	*p*
Block 1					
Age	−.02	.01	−.25	−2.30	.02
Relationship status	−.00	.16	−.00	−.03	.98
Overall disclosure	−.11	.04	−.28	−2.83	.01
Time in therapy	.05	.03	.22	2.07	.04
Block 2					
Anxious disclosure	.33	.08	.42	4.29	.00

Note. Block 1: R^2 =.15 (N =98, p <.001); Block 2: R^2(total) =.30 (N =98, p <.001).

Discussion

The purpose of this exploratory study was to better understand the experience of CSA therapy clients. More specifically, our intent was to determine which aspects of disclosure about abuse are perceived as beneficial and which dysfunctional and what factors influence these patterns. These aims were in the ultimate service of beginning to determine when and how therapists might best respond to client disclosures about sexual abuse.

How does disclosure about their abuse experiences help clients? Our results suggest a wide range of benefits, including, most saliently, a true cathartic effect ("sense of relief from sharing some bottled up emotions") and a gain in self-awareness ("better understanding" of self). These positive effects are entirely consonant with the goals of contemporary forms of emotion-focused therapy; in fact, Greenberg (2002) suggested that emotional arousal, in concert with the need to recognize and make sense of one's emotions and in the context of a supportive emotional relationship, is what leads to positive therapeutic change. Consistent too with Greenberg, two other highly rated items reflect significant relational benefits of abuse-related disclosure: the sense of being better understood and accepted by one's therapist, and "feeling more emotionally close and connected to my therapist." A fifth highly rated positive consequence was more intrapsychic than interpersonal, and seemingly related to the above-mentioned increase in self-awareness: A greater ability to view oneself as a complex person, one with a variety of characteristics.

What cannot be determined from this methodology is whether certain types of abuse-related disclosures (e.g., those that focus on the original circumstances of the abuse) are most associated with specific benefits or costs. Similarly, we cannot determine whether these benefits overlap or whether they tend to be experienced as discrete events. Furthermore, it's not clear whether certain individuals are more prone to experience specific benefits from their disclosures, nor whether certain types of therapies (or therapists) are more likely to facilitate specific forms of positive abuse disclosure experiences. Nevertheless, these data do provide some measure of support for the idea that the benefits of abuse-related disclosures are substantial and varied, and include some elements that attest to the importance of the therapeutic relationship for clients with a history of CSA. Moreover, these data are also suggestive of the hypothesis that a therapeutic connection to the therapist in which the CSA client feels close, validated, and understood—mediated by the client's ability and willingness to disclose difficult information—is not only the basis of subsequent therapeutic work but is of itself a positive outcome of therapy. This, of course, is quite consistent with clinical lore that has emphasized the overarching importance of CSA clients' achieving a sense of trusting connection with her therapist, the experience of which may begin to combat long-held feelings of interpersonal fear and mistrust as well as chronic feelings of personal inadequacy.

But the data also suggest that, consistent with multiple clinical reports, abuse-related disclosures come with potential costs and risks, chief among them the related problems of feeling emotionally overwhelmed, and feeling uncomfortably vulnerable and exposed. The therapist's task, it seems, is to titrate abuse-related disclosures. Checking in with one's client frequently during (and/or immediately after) difficult disclosures may reduce the potential for feeling overwhelmed and vulnerable while increasing the potential for the client's experience of feeling understood and accepted. "How are you right now?" "I'm listening as best I can." "That sounds so incredibly difficult." What are you feeling right now?" "Can you go on, or would you like to stop this for now?" "I'm so moved by your willingness to trust me enough to hear this." These data also support the idea that therapists working with this population should be their most empathic, supportive, available selves to their clients prior to the end of a disclosure-intense session. In fact, a critical aspect of Foa's exposure treatment for PTSD is debriefing at the end of a session; the therapist asks the client what it was like to share traumatic memories and what he or she noticed in the re-telling (Foa, Hembree, & Rothbaum, 2007). Thus, even though this treatment encourages client disclosure, it also emphasizes the value of "processing" the expressed feelings and thoughts in order to retain the benefits of focusing on difficult material.

The findings of the present study also indicated that, in addition to age and mother's education level, overall client disclosure in therapy (i.e., including but not limited to disclosures about abuse) and level of distress were significantly related to clients' positive experiences of abuse-related disclosure. That older clients' perceptions of the benefits of abuse-related disclosures tended to be lower than the rest of the sample may reflect the fact that these individuals are further away from their original abusive experience and that they have either learned to cope in alternative (i.e., "non-disclosing") ways or that the beneficial effect of such disclosure has begun to lessen in intensity. That mother's education level is also negatively related to the perceived positive effects of abuse-related disclosure seems consistent with research indicating that in some cases (e.g., with depressed clients) therapy may be less effective with lower SES patients (e.g., Falconnier, 2009). Perhaps most significantly, though, these results indicate that perceptions of the positive consequences of abuse-related disclosures are positively associated with an overall tendency to disclose in therapy and with lower BSI scores (i.e., less symptomatology). In contrast to Bonanno et al. (2003), who found that sensitizers pay a heavy price for their wish and need to disclose, our data suggest that those who experience a greater level of positive consequences of abuse-related disclosures tend to be more generally disclosing and have *lower* levels of distress. While more research is necessary, our hypothesis is that in therapy, as opposed to a laboratory setting, clients have the opportunity to experience the beneficial effects of profound disclosures and that these effects may, over time, be sufficient to tip the scales to the point where the positive effects outweigh (though never quite eliminate) the negative consequences of speaking about traumatic events.

Alternatively, the connection between positive effects of abuse-related disclosure and lower levels of distress may be understood in terms of the well-documented finding that those who are psychologically healthier tend to benefit more from therapy (e.g., Clarkin & Levy, 2004). Severe symptomotology may hamper the capacity of individuals to titrate their "optimal" amounts of disclosure; that is, these individuals may tend to either under- or over-disclose, unable to determine at any moment which or how much disclosure will be beneficial. Because CSA clients in great psychological distress may not know how (or be too overwhelmed) to disclose in a way that is most helpful, it may be particularly important for therapists working with them to gauge the immediate and delayed effects of their disclosures. In fact, if clinicians are faced with a CSA client who is grappling with severe psychopathology, they may need to be far more cautious in encouraging even minimal disclosure about CSA until her symptoms are more under control. Again, in these situations, the alliance is crucial: Empathic statements regarding the difficulty of such disclosure, discussions of the client's readiness to engage in this material, and the client's ability to trust the clinician to help guide her toward or away from abuse-related disclosures are all facilitated by a strong, trusting therapeutic relationship.

More generally, our sense is that the clinician must be an empathic, involved, and caring participant in the therapeutic process, one who can express a deep compassion for the client's most difficult and painful experiences. At the same time, he or she must maintain an unmistakable professional demeanor that bespeaks clear boundaries in order to mitigate the potential negative consequences of hard disclosures. Arguably, even more than is the case with non-abused clients, the therapist must constantly monitor the effects of his or her own interventions (including disclosures) on the therapeutic process, acknowledging occasional but inevitable errors (Safran & Muran, 2000). Based on our findings—specifically, that greater disclosure related to abuse is associated with greater degrees of both positive and negative consequences—we also suggest that therapists engage in a form of role induction for their new CSA clients, introducing the idea that while disclosure of abuse-related material may well be helpful in various ways, it is also likely to evoke at least some painful consequences, including those that may affect the therapeutic relationship.

What of therapist disclosure? While some (e.g., Caudill, 2012) have contended that therapists who themselves have histories of childhood abuse might well share this information with CSA clients as a means of facilitating an empathic bond, our sense is that therapists must proceed with particular caution around personal disclosures in working with CSA survivors. They are a group who have been hurt by far too much familiarity and inappropriate intimacy and are likely to be vigilant, even hyper-vigilant, to information that they have not requested and which might seem puzzling or even frightening in its perceived closeness ("why are you telling me this?"). Indeed, the results of the present study suggest that one of the most anxiety-related consequences of client disclosures is "feeling overwhelmed by my emotions," an experience that might be exacerbated by therapist disclosures that, while well-intentioned, may be misconstrued.

There are several limitations to the present study. The sample is not representative as there are few minority participants; generalization therefore is problematic. In addition, the sample suffers from selection bias as these participants are, de facto, at least somewhat comfortable with disclosure about CSA; they have shown their willingness to fill out a survey for this study and most have participated in "survivor websites." Another major limitation is that the CSA scale and the DSD (disclosure) scales have not been assessed sufficiently regarding their psychometric properties (e.g., validity and reliability). In addition, all scales were self-report and participants' ratings of their own behaviors (including disclosure tendencies and symptoms) could not be corroborated by others. Similarly, because there were no operational definitions of minimal or moderate or great degrees of disclosure, variability in individual assessment of these positions could not be accounted for.

In addition to further psychometric testing and refinement of our instruments, our next step in this line of inquiry is to determine what kinds of therapist responses might best be made to functionally different client disclosures. For example, are disclosures that seem to be in the service of cathartic relief best met by simple therapist acceptance or some other type of response (e.g., affirmation)? What responses might best be used when a client's abuse-related disclosures appear to have primarily dysfunctional consequences? Is empathy the best therapeutic response to the near inevitability of multiple, nearly simultaneous, seemingly opposite consequences to disclosures about abuse? Or is it perhaps, cognitive restructuring (Greenberg, 2002) or maybe repeated psychoeducation—reviewing and normalizing the typical consequences of abuse-related dislcosures? To do this work, we intend to interview therapists and CSA clients, as well as code segments of therapy sessions of women with an identifiable history of CSA. Other potential lines of research in this area include investigating the relationship of client and therapist attachment variables to client disclosure patterns, the relationship of the therapeutic alliance to patient and therapist disclosures, and the nature of the rupture-repair cycle on disclosure patterns of patients with a history of CSA.

Acknowledgment

Portions of this article are based on a paper presented at the North American Society for Psychotherapy Research (NASPR) regional conference (September, 2011, Banff, Canada).

References

Beitchman, J., Zucker, K., Hood, J., DaCosta, G., Akman, D., & Cassavia, E. (1992). A review of the long-term effects of child sexual abuse. *Child Abuse & Neglect*, *16*, 101–118.

Berman, P. (2012, August 12). The Witness. *The New York Times Book Review*, pp. A.21–22.

Bernstein, D. P., Fink, L., Handelsman, L., Foote, J., Lovejoy, M., Wenzel, K., Sapareto, E., & Ruggiero, J. (1994). Initial reliability and validity of a new retrospective measure of child abuse and neglect. *American Journal of Psychiatry, 151*, 1132–1336.

Bonanno, G. A., Noll, J. G., Putnam, F. W., O'Neill, M., & Trickett, P. K., (2003). Predicting the willingness to disclose childhood sexual abuse from questionnaire measures of repressive coping and dissociative tendencies. *Child Maltreatment, 8*, 302–318. doi:10.1177/1077559503257066

Bradley, R. G., & Follingstad, D. R. (2001). Utilizing disclosure in the treatment of the sequelae of childhood sexual abuse: a theoretical and empirical review. *Clinical Psychology Review, 21*, 1–32. doi:10.1016/S0272-7358(00)00077-5

Caudill Jr., B. (2012). Malpractice and licensing pitfalls for therapists: A defense attorney's list. Retrieved from http://kspope.com/ethics/malpractice.php.

Clarkin, J. F., & Levy, K. N. (2004). The Influence of client variables on psychotherapy. In M. J. Lambert (Ed.), *Bergin and Garfield's handbook of psychotherapy and behavior change* (5th ed.) (pp. 194–226). New York: John Wiley & Sons.

Cloitre, M., Cohen, L. R., & Koenen, K. C. (2006). *Treating survivors of childhood abuse: Psychotherapy for the interrupted life.* New York: Guilford Press.

Davies, J. M., & Frawley, M. G. (1994). *Treating the adult survivor of childhood sexual abuse: A Psychoanalytic perspective.* New York, NY: Basic Books.

Depue, B. E., Curran, T., & Banich, M. T. (2006). Suppression of emotional and non-emotional content in memory: Effects of repetition on cognitive control. *Psychological Science, 17*, 441–447. doi:10.1111/j.1467-9280.2006.01725.x

Derogatis, L. R., & Spencer, P. M. (1982). *The Brief Symptom Inventory (BSI): Administration, and procedures manual-I.* Baltimore, MD: Clinical Psychometric Research.

DiTomasso, M., & Routh, D. (1993). Recall of abuse in childhood and three measures of dissociation. *Child Abuse & Neglect, 17*, 477–485. doi:10.1016/0145-2134(93)90022-W

Dube, S. R., Anda, R. F., Whitfield, C. L., Brown, D. W., Felitti, V. J., Dong, M, & Giles, W. H. (2005). Long-term consequences of childhood sexual abuse by gender of victim. *American Journal of Preventive Medicine, 28*, 430–438. doi:10.1016/j.amepre.2005.01.015

Duval, S., & Wicklund, R. A. (1972). *A theory of objective self-awareness.* New York: Academic Press.

Elliott, D. M., & Briere, J. (1994). Forensic sexual abuse evaluations of older children: Disclosures and symptomatology. *Behavioral Sciences & the Law, 12*, 261–277. doi:10.1002/bsl.2370120306

Falconnier, J. (2009). Socioeconomic status in the treatment of depression. *American Journal of Orthopsychiatry, 79*, 148–158. doi:10.1037/a0015469

Farber, B. A. (1989). Psychological-mindedness: Can there be too much of a good thing? *Psychotherapy, 26*, 210–217. doi:10.1037/h0085421

Farber, B. A. (2006). *Self-disclosure in psychotherapy.* New York: Guilford Press.

Farber, B. A., Khurgin-Botts, R., & Feldman, S. (2009). The benefits and risks of patient self-disclosure in the psychotherapy of women with a history of childhood sexual abuse. *Psychotherapy, 46*, 52–67. doi:10.1037/a0015136

Farber, B. A., & Sacco, M. (1999). The relationship of repression to reality testing in adult women who report childhood sexual and physical abuse. *Journal of the American Academy of Psychoanalysis, 27*, 205–220.

Finkelhor, D., & Dziuba-Leatherman, J. (1994). Children as victims of violence: A national survey. *Pediatrics, 94*, 413–420.

Foa, E. B., Hembree, E. A., & Rothbaum, B. O. (2007). *Prolonged exposure therapy for PTSD: Emotional processing of traumatic experiences.* New York: Oxford University Press.

Foa, E. B., Keane, T. M., & Friedman, M. J. (Eds.). (2000). *Effective treatments for PTSD: Practice guidelines from the International Society for Traumatic Stress Studies.* New York: Guilford Press.

Frawley, M. G. (1990). From secrecy to self-disclosure: Healing the scars of incest. In G. Stricker and M. Fischer (Eds.), *Self-disclosure in the therapeutic relationship* (pp. 247–259). New York: Plenum.

Greenberg, L. S. (2002). *Emotion-focused therapy.* Washington DC: American Psychological Association.

Harber, K. D., & Pennebaker, J. W. (1992). Overcoming traumatic memories. In S. A. Christianson (Ed.), *The handbook of emotion and memory: Research and theory* (pp. 359–387). Hillsdale, NJ: Erlbaum.

Herman, J. L., & Harvey, M. R. (1997). Adult memories of childhood trauma: A naturalistic clinical study. *Journal of Traumatic Stress, 10*, 557–571.

Jourard, S. M. (1968). *Disclosing man to himself.* New York: D. Van Norstrand.

Kahn, J. H., Achter, J. A., & Shambaugh, E. J. (2001). Client distress, disclosure, characteristics at intake, and outcome in brief counseling. *Journal of Counseling Psychology, 48*, 203–211. doi:10.1037/0022-0167.48.2.203

Knox, S., & Hill, C. E. (2003). Therapist self-disclosure: Research-based suggestions for practitioners. *Journal of Clinical Psychology, 59*, 229–540.

Kohut, H. (1977). *The restoration of the self.* New York: International Universities Press.

Lepore, S. J., & Smyth, J. M. (2002). *The writing cure; How expressive writing promotes health and emotional well-being.* Washington, DC: American Psychological Association.

Martsolf, D. S., & Draucker, C. B. (2005). Psychotherapy approaches for adult survivors of childhood sexual abuse: An integrative review of outcome research. *Issues in Mental Health Nursing, 26*, 801–825. doi:10.1080/01612840500184012

Pennebaker, J. W. (Ed.). (1995). *Emotion, disclosure and health.* Washington DC: American Psychological Association.

Resick, P. A., & Calhoun, K. S. (2001). Posttraumatic stress disorder. In D. H. Barlow (Ed.), *Clinical handbook of psychological disorders* (pp. 60–113). New York: Guilford Press.

Rogers, C. R. (1961). *On becoming a person.* Boston, MA: Houghton Mifflin.

Saeed, S. A. (2000). Review: The psychotherapy relationship: Theory, research, and practice (by C. J. Gelso & J. A. Hayes). *Journal of Psychotherapy Practice and Research, 9*, 106–107.

Safran, J., & Muran, J. C. (2000). *Negotiating the therapeutic alliance: A relational treatment guide.* New York: Guilford Press.

Seery, M., Silver, R. C., Holman, E. A., Ence, W. A., & Chu, T. Q. (2008). Expressing thoughts and feelings following a collective trauma: Immediate responses to 9/11 predict negative outcomes in a national sample. *Journal of Consulting and Clinical Psychology, 76*, 657–667. doi:10.1037/0022-006X.76.4.657

Stiles, W. B. (1995). Disclosure as a speech act; Is it psychotherapeutic to disclose? In J. W. Pennebaker (Ed.), *Emotion, disclosure, and health* (pp. 71–91). Washington DC: American Psychological Association.

Stiles, W. B., & Shapiro, D. A. (1994). Disabuse of the drug metaphor: Psychotherapy process outcome correlations. *Journal of Consulting and Clinical Psychology, 62*, 942–948.

Tavris, C. (1984). On the wisdom of counting to 10: Personal and social dangers of anger expression. In P. Shaver (Ed.), *Review of personality & social psychology* (pp. 170–191). Thousand Oaks, CA: Sage.

Good versus poor therapeutic alliances with non-accepting parents of same-sex oriented adolescents and young adults: A qualitative study

MAYA S. SHPIGEL & GARY M. DIAMOND

Department of Psychology, Ben-Gurion University of the Negev, Beer-Sheva, Israel

Abstract

Objective: Therapeutic themes and processes associated with five good versus five poor parent-therapist alliances among a sample of non-accepting parents of sexual minority youth/young adults participating in family therapy were examined. **Method:** The Consensual Qualitative Research approach was used to analyse of therapy notes and follow-up interviewsfrom good and poor alliances. **Results:** In good alliances, parents adopted relationship building as a goal, considered essentialist causal attributions of same-sex orientation, acknowledged positive aspects of their child, and perceived the therapist as empathic and accepting. Parents with poor alliances rejected relationship building as a goal, rebuffed essentialist causal attributions, dismissed the possibility of their own coming out, nullified positive aspects of their child, sought to change their child's sexual orientation, blamed therapists for validating their child's same-sex orientation, and pressured therapists for information about their child. **Conclusions:** Clinical implications are discussed.

More and more frequently, adolescents and young adults disclose their same-sex orientation to their parents. While some parents react to their child's coming out with acceptance, understanding, love and support, most parents initially respond with some degree of shock, disbelief, fear, guilt, anger, shame and or grief, with a small minority exhibiting severe forms of rejection and coercive attempts to convert their child to heterosexuality, including verbal threats and, in extreme cases, physical violence and/or ejection from the home (D'Augelli, Grossman, & Starks, 2005; Heatherington & Lavner, 2008; Robinson, Walters, & Skeen, 1989; Saltzburg, 2004; Samarova, Shilo, & Diamond, 2013; Savin-Williams, 2001; Savin-Williams & Dubee, 1998; Savin-Williams & Ream, 2003).

Fortunately, many if not most parents who initially respond negatively become more accepting over time. For example, studies of parents participating in gay affirmative support groups (e.g., Parents and Friends of Lesbians and Gays) found that the great majority reported decreases in internalized homophobia (Holtzen & Agresti, 1990) and increases in acceptance (Ben-Ari, 1995; Robinson et al., 1989). Among lesbian, gay and bisexual (LGB) young adult children themselves, between 25% and 40% report having experienced improvements in their relationships with their parents over time, though a smaller subgroup (6%–25%) reported experiencing a deterioration in their relationships with parents over the same timeframe (Beals & Peplau, 2006; Savin-Williams & Reams, 2003). A recent study of Israeli sexual minority adolescents and young adults found that between 30% and 45% reported that parents who were initially fully rejecting became somewhat more accepting over time, although 15% of parents who were initially fully or moderately accepting actually showed a decrease in acceptance over time. Of particular concern is that 18% of mothers and 26% of fathers remained fully or mostly rejecting a year and half post-disclosure (Samarova et al., 2013). Similarly, Ben- Ari (1995) found that 16%

of mothers and 36% of fathers were non-accepting 11 years after their child's disclosure. So, while most parents eventually come to terms with their child's same-sex orientation, a minority maintain a consistently non-accepting, rejecting posture.

Ongoing parental non-acceptance can negatively impact the welfare of the child, as well as undermine the parent-child relationship. As Goldfried and Goldfried (2001) poignantly noted, "one does not have to be a mental health professional to recognize the devastating effect that parental non-acceptance or outright rejection can have on the psychological well-being of individuals. In a society that continues to stigmatize people for not being heterosexual, those who are LGB emotionally need all the support they can get" (p. 682). Indeed, a substantial body of research has linked parental criticism, invalidation, rejection and abuse to internalized homophobia, expectations for future gay-related rejection by others (Pachankis, Goldfried, & Ramratten, 2008) and increased risk of depression and suicidal ideation (D'Augelli et al., 2005; Remafedi, Farrow, & Deisher, 1991; Ryan, Huebner, Diaz, & Sanchez, 2009). In contrast, parental support of LGB youth has been associated with greater self-esteem and greater perceived social support, and has been found to buffer against psychopathology (D'Augelli, 2002; Eisenberg & Resnick, 2006; Evans, Hawton, & Rodham, 2004; Floyd, Stein, Harter, Allison, & Ney, 1999; Hershberger & D'Augelli, 1995: Needham & Austin, 2010; Ryan, Russell, Huebner, Diaz, & Sanchez, 2010; Savin-Williams, 1989). Not surprisingly, findings from a number of studies suggest that LGB individuals long for greater parental acceptance and closeness (Diamond et al., 2011; Savin-Williams, 2001).

In an effort to decrease criticism and rejection on the part of non-accepting parents, and improve the quality of their relationship with their LGB children, we established the Family Connection project at Ben-Gurion University. As part of the project, we provide a variation of attachment-based family therapy (ABFT; Diamond, Siqueland, & Diamond, 2003) adapted specifically for working with LGB individuals and their non-accepting parents (Diamond et al., 2012; Diamond & Shpigel, in press). ABFT is a manualized, family-based treatment originally developed for depressed and suicidal adolescents. The model is rooted in the structural tradition (Minuchin, 1977), and influenced by multidimensional family therapy (Liddle, 1999) and emotion focused therapy (Johnson & Greenberg, 1995). The theoretical foundation for the treatment is based on attachment theory and current research on adolescent/young adult development and parenting. Secure adolescent/young adult-parent attachment relationships are understood as providing the optimal context for individual development and as protecting against psychopathology (Sheeber, Davis, Leve, Hops, & Tildesley, 2007). Therefore, treatment focuses on improving trust, safety, and communication in the adolescent/young adult-parent relationship.

To accomplish this, therapists work to reduce parental criticism and psychological control and to increase parental care. First, however, parents are helped to work through their own pain, fear, shame, and unmet attachment needs during individual sessions in order to become more available to serve as an attachment figure for their adolescent or young adult. Once parents are less reactive and more committed to their role as parent, they are taught to use emotion coaching skills to elicit and validate their child's experience and unmet attachment needs. Concomitantly, the therapist works individually with the adolescent or young adult to help her or him to articulate his or her pain and relational needs in a more direct, regulated manner. After parents and their children are sufficiently prepared, conjoint, in-session enactments (i.e., attachment episodes) are conducted to allow family members to practice/implement these new postures/behaviors. When parents remain engaged, curious and non-defensive, the adolescent or young adult begins to feel validated and safe. Consequently, a relationship develops which allows family members to remain connected without feeling invalidated or overly vulnerable. ABFT has been found to be efficacious in a number of studies on depressed and suicidal adolescents (Diamond, Reis, Diamond, Siqueland, & Isaacs, 2002, Diamond et al., 2010), including depressed and suicidal sexual minority adolescents (Diamond et al., 2012).

A first and particularly challenging task when working with non-accepting parents is to develop a strong therapeutic alliance. The therapeutic alliance, or the degree to which the client has a positive affective bond with the therapist, and agrees with the therapist on the goals and tasks of treatment (Bordin, 1979), is one of the most robust predictors of treatment outcome across a wide range of treatment approaches (Horvath, 1994, 2000; Horvath, Del Re, Fluckiger, & Symonds, 2011; Horvath & Luborsky, 1993; Horvath & Symonds, 1991; Martin, Garske, & Davis, 2000), including family therapy (Friedlander, Escuerdo, Heatherington, & Diamond, 2011). In our clinical experience, however, developing strong alliances with non-accepting parents in the context of a family-based treatment can be difficult for a number of reasons. First, non-accepting parents do not typically initiate therapy, nor do they necessarily see the need for them to come to therapy.

They generally believe that it is their child, not them or the relationship, who needs to change. Second, such parents typically prefer to avoid any discussion of same-sex orientation because it is just too painful: Acknowledging their child's sexuality means that they have to face their own shame, loss, guilt, etc. Third, such parents often fear that therapists will be allied with their adolescent or young adult and that they (the parents) will be blamed and pressured to accept their child on his/her terms. Finally, many therapists find it difficult to remain empathic towards parents who are hypercritical, invalidating or otherwise behave hurtfully toward their child. For all of these reasons and more, engaging non-accepting parents in therapy, and developing a strong working alliance with them, is a tremendous challenge.

The purpose of this study was to identify therapeutic themes and processes associated with five good versus five poor therapeutic alliances with non-accepting parents in ABFT. Toward this end, one group of coders used the CQR method to qualitatively analyze the session notes from the first three therapy sessions of each case, and another independent group of coders used the same method to analyze the transcripts of post-treatment follow-up interviews. The goal of analyzing both session notes and transcripts from follow-up interviews was to gain multiple perspectives: The impression of objective raters and the client's own, explicit report of their experience. Information derived from diverse, multiple perspectives potentially adds to the depth and breadth of findings (Fielding & Fielding, 1986).

Identifying the themes and processes associated with strong versus poor alliances is meant to be a first step in developing effective alliance-building intervention strategies for this population. Because there has been no research on therapeutic alliances with non-accepting parents of sexual minority offspring, our scientific approach was hypothesis generating rather than hypothesis testing.

Method

Participants

Participants included five sets of parents (10 parents in all). In all five families, the sexual minority adolescent or young adult reported ongoing (lasting at least 1 year) moderate to high levels of parental non-acceptance of their same-sex orientation. In order to be included, the adolescent or young adult had to have reported an average score of 3 or greater on the *family non-acceptance of LGB identity scale* (Semple, Strathdee, Zians, & Patterson, 2009) in relation to each parent.

All five sets of parents were married and they ranged in age from 46 to 68 years old. The first couple was composed of two pensioners who had immigrated to Israel from an Arab country 25 years ago, when they were in their early thirties. They had six children and their youngest child, now a young man studying at the university, came out of the closet 2 years before treatment. The second couple had immigrated to Israel from Russia 20 years prior to treatment. Both worked as computer engineers. Their middle son, now an adolescent, disclosed his same-sex orientation to them a year before treatment. Both members of the third couple were born in Arab countries yet were raised in Israel and were practicing, non-orthodox religious Jews. The father worked in the military and the wife stayed at home. While their adolescent son only explicitly disclosed his sexual orientation to them shortly before the beginning of therapy, both parents suspected that he was gay for over a year prior to treatment based on his peer relationships and gender atypical behavior. The fourth couple was composed of a wife, who emigrated from an Arab country in her adolescence and now worked as a teacher in Israel, and her husband, who was born in Eastern Europe to parents who were holocaust survivors and, after immigrating to Israel as a teenager, found work as a clerk. They started treatment a year after their younger daughter, a graphic designer, disclosed her sexual orientation. The fifth couple included two Israeli born, non-orthodox religious, retired professionals. They discovered that their son was homosexual a year and a half prior to treatment.

Recruitment

Two general strategies were employed to recruit participants. The first strategy was to recruit families via the adolescent/young adult. We reached sexual minority youth via key members in the LGB community, local gay-oriented social and support groups, university bulletin boards, relevant electronic listserves, and through the media. We presented the project as an opportunity for same-sex oriented youths/young adults to work with their parents to repair the relationship and gain increased acceptance. The second recruitment strategy involved contacting and building relationships with parent support groups, such as PFLAG, and inviting them to refer parents who were having a particularly hard time accepting their child's sexual orientation. However, in the end, all participants were recruited via the sexual minority child (none came via outreach attempts aimed directly toward non-accepting parents). Three couples came at the invitation of their child. One mother came alone after being invited by her son, and later in the therapy recruited her husband to join her, and one couple came at the request of their son and the mother's brother. There was no payment or other compensation for participating in the project and the study was approved by the university's human subjects review board. Participants signed necessary consent forms.

Treatment

The treatment delivered was an adaptation of ABFT. The primary goal of ABFT is to help the adolescent or young adult and parent identify, discuss and work through past and current family traumas and conflicts that have strained the attachment bond and damaged trust. To accomplish this goal, there are five ABFT treatment tasks introduced in sequence. Each task may take one or several sessions. The first task, the Relational Reframe Task (Diamond & Siqueland, 1998), aims to shift the focus of therapy from the symptoms (e.g., depression) or point of conflict (e.g., sexual orientation) onto the rupture in the child-parent attachment relationship (e.g., detachment, loss, longing). The second task, the Alliance Building Task with the adolescent or young adult, focuses on engaging the adolescent or young adult in treatment and generating hope for change. Core relational themes and family dynamics that fuel the conflict are articulated, and the adolescent or young adult is prepared to discuss these issues with her or his parents during future conjoint, in-session enactments (i.e., attachment episodes). The third task, the Alliance Building Task with the parent, focuses on reducing parental distress and improving parental responsiveness. The task begins with a supportive exploration of parents' strengths and competencies, and then parlays into an exploration of the stressors affecting the parent and his/her parenting behaviors. The therapist then explores the parents' own attachment experiences in childhood and links their experience to that of their child's attachment experience in an effort to generate empathy on the part of the parent toward their child. Finally, parents are prepared to respond in an empathic, attuned manner to their adolescent/young adult in subsequent conjoint, in-session enactments. The fourth task, the Attachment Task, is the culmination of the work completed in the first three tasks. The attachment task is designed to help adolescents/young adults and their parents, together, work through the pain, disappointment, and longing associated with past relational ruptures and current unmet attachment needs. Once parents and their children have worked through these feelings and needs and have improved the attachment bond, they embark on the final task of constructing a new relationship characterized by both closeness and acceptance of differences: Care and autonomy.

Previous work with sexual minority adolescents has demonstrated that some modifications to the treatment's structure and content are required to best serve this population (Diamond et al., 2012). For example, substantially more time is needed for working in sessions alone with parents in an effort to help them come to terms with their own shame, guilt, anger, loss, and fear before initiating conjoint attachment sessions with the adolescent present. In the context of this study, therapists made further adaptations. First, because of the incendiary nature of the interactions and parents' extreme degree of invalidation, the treatment began with individual alliance building sessions with the sexual minority child alone and parents alone, instead of the typical initial conjoint reframing session used with other, less reactive populations. Indeed, the majority of time in the therapy was spent working with parents alone and the adolescent/young adult alone in separate, parallel sessions, and therapists waited much longer than in previous clinical trials before initiating attachment enactments. The need to work with family subsystems separately with this population has been recognized by others (LaSala, 2000). In this study, the course of treatment lasted between 5 and 14 months, with the number of sessions per case ranging from 10 to 50 ($X = 35.2$, $SD = 17.18$).

Measures

Parental non-acceptance of LGB identity. This was measured using the Family Conflict Scale (Semple et al., 2009). This self-report measure includes five items reflecting individuals' experience of parental non-acceptance over the past year. Items included: "They don't accept you for who you are"; "They are critical of your lifestyle"; "They think that you can change the way you are"; "They seem to avoid you"; and "They don't approve of your partner." In this study, participants were asked to answer these questions in relation their sexual orientation. Items were measured on a 4-point scale ranging from 1 (no disagreement) to 4 (quite a bit of disagreement). In prior research, the Chronbach alpha for the scale was .86. To qualify for this study, participants needed to score an average of 3 or more across the five items.

Vanderbilt Therapeutic Alliance Scale – Revised – Short Form (VTAS-R-SF). The strength of the therapist-parent alliance was measured using the short form (Shelef & Diamond, 2008) of the revised Vanderbilt Therapeutic Alliance Scales (VTAS; Hartley & Strupp, 1983). The VTAS-R-SF is an observer-rated instrument composed of five items rated on a Likert-type scale ranging from 0 (not at all) to 5 (a great deal). The five items include: (1) *Therapist empathy*—client indicates that s/he experiences the therapist as supporting and understanding; (2) *Active participation*—client seems to identify with the therapist's method of working, so that s/he sees himself as an active participant in therapy; (3) *Non-trust*—client acts in a mistrustful or defensive manner toward the therapist; (4) *Agreement on problems*—client and therapist share a common view about the definition, possible causes, and potential alleviation of the client's problems; and (5) *Agreement on goals and/or tasks*—client and therapist agree upon the goals and/or tasks of the session. In this study, the fifth item was divided into two separate items—agreement on goals and agreement on tasks—in order to improve interrater reliability. Previous studies using the VTAS-R and VTAS-R-SF have demonstrated that the scale has acceptable interrater reliability and internal consistency (Diamond, Liddle, Hogue, & Dakof, 1999; Shelef, Diamond, Diamond, & Liddle, 2005; Shelef & Diamond, 2008).

Parent Interview

The interview with parents included a number of open-ended questions meant to capture parents' experience of the therapeutic process in general, and the therapeutic alliance in particular. The interview began with the question, "What was the therapy like for you?" Next, parents were asked about their initial expectations and motivations for coming to therapy. Then, they were asked a number of questions about the therapeutic alliance: Their experience of the therapist, understanding of the therapists' goals and methods, and the degree to which they agreed with the therapists' goals and methods, including whether they felt pressured to agree to specific goals and tasks, or any discomfort with the goals and tasks. They were also asked how they feel now, in retrospect, regarding their decision to participate in the therapy.

Procedure

Therapy. After agreeing to participate, parents and their sexual minority children completed consent forms and treatment began. The treatment was administered by two co-therapists: The second author, a male clinical psychologist and family therapist and one of the developers of ABFT, and the first author, a female licensed psychologist who had been trained by the senior therapist. Sessions were not electronically recorded due to parents' high level of suspiciousness and fear of disclosure. Instead, one of the therapists (the first author) completed detailed post-session notes immediately after each session. The notes included not only content, but also references to the therapy process, including the client's affect, tone, and behavior. The notes from each session were approximately four pages in length and provided more than enough material to reliably rate the alliance (see reliability estimates in the Results section). Because the notes were based on memory and not actual recordings, the potential for omissions and interpretive bias was present.

Training and reliability of alliance coders and coding procedure. Three undergraduate psychology students were trained to use the VTAS-R- SF to code the parent-therapist alliance based on the session notes from the third therapy session (session alone with parents) of each case. The third session was chosen because past research has demonstrated that early alliance, typically measured in session 3, is the most predictive of outcome (Horvath, 2000). One coder was male and the other two were female. They ranged in age from 24 to 27 years old. Training consisted of weekly, 2-hour sessions continuing over the course of 3 months and included reading the VTAS-R-SF manual, practice scoring of verbatim notes from non-study sessions, and discussions of scoring discrepancies. Training continued until coders reached sufficient inter-rater reliability (i.e., interclass correlation coefficients > .80). Two coders rated each set of session notes. Coders were assigned session notes in a random, rotating pair procedure and scored the alliance for each parent separately. Average alliance scores were used in subsequent analyses. We used a median split to distinguish between good and poor alliances so that alliances scores lower than 3.4 on the VTAS-R-SF were characterized as poor alliances and scores above this criterion were considered good alliances.

Conducting of interviews. Qualitative interviews were conducted approximately 7–10 months following the end of treatment. Interviews were conducted with each parent individually and lasted, on average, 50 minutes. All interviews (except for one) were conducted face-to-face by one of the therapists. One interview was conducted by phone. The choice to have therapists conduct the interviews was based on the fact that, even by treatment's end, all 10 parents still voiced concerns about disclosure and were more comfortable speaking with the therapist than with an anonymous interviewer. In order to reduce demand characteristics and help parents feel as comfortable as possible sharing any dissatisfaction and disappointment they may have felt with the therapist or therapy goals, therapists emphasized that they were specifically interested in what parents didn't like about the their behavior, therapy, and the therapeutic relationship and that such information was important to help improve the therapy and therapy process for future clients. Interviews were recorded and transcribed verbatim.

Analytic Strategy

Session notes and interview transcripts were analyzed separately by two different, independent coding groups using the Consensual Qualitative Research method (CQR; Hill, Thompson, & Williams, 1997). CQR is a method for organizing and making meaning of qualitative data. Typically, qualitative studies examine a small number of cases in order to afford an in-depth understanding of each case. The method "incorporates elements from phenomenological (Giorgi, 1985), grounded theory (Strauss & Corbin, 1998), and comprehensive process analysis (Elliott, 1989)" (Hill et al., 2005, p. 196). Described as predominantly constructivist or interpretive in nature, with some postpositivist elements, CQR involves having judges identify core domains and specific ideas manifested in each participant's responses to open-ended questions, and then develop categories to describe consistencies in core ideas across cases. Throughout this process, emphasis is placed on having judges reach consensus through discussion and reflection on the data. Such consensus contributes to the trustworthiness or validity of the data (Hill et al., 1997, 2005).

Developing of domains. The first step in the method is to develop domains. Domains are overarching clusters which provide a conceptual framework for organizing the large amount of narrative data. Judges independently read through all of the interviews or session notes and generate a tentative list of domains. They then assigned relevant segments of the session—be it a phrase, sentence or paragraph—to their respective domain. Subsequently, the judges met as a group to compare their list of preliminary domains and coding. In those cases in which data did not fit into one of the a priori domains, the judge proposed additional domains to reflect the emerging data. Once a final and exhaustive list of domains was agreed upon through consensus, judges then went back and individually recoded the data accordingly. Afterwards, they met yet again as a group and resolved discrepancies through consensus.

Constructing core ideas. Each judge independently read all of the data within each domain for each individual session note/interview separately, and identified what he or she considered as being the core idea associated with each unit of meaning (i.e., word, phrase, sentence or paragraph).

Cross analysis (generating categories). Cross analysis involves looking across cases to determine whether there were core ideas which seemed to cluster into categories. Each judge independently examined all of the core ideas within a given domain across cases and organized the data into categories. The team then met to compare categories and reach agreement through consensus regarding which categories made the most sense and how to name them.

Determining the frequency (or representativeness) of each category in good versus poor alliance cases. In order to compare how representative each category was of good versus poor alliance cases, we examined how frequently that category appeared in each alliance group (i.e., good versus poor). In accordance with CQR convention (Hill et al., 1997), categories that appeared in all cases of a given group (i.e., five) were considered "General". Those appearing in more than half but not all of the cases in a given group (i.e., three or four) were considered "Typical". Those appearing in only two cases in a given group were considered "Variant" and those appearing only once or not all were considered not representative or "NR". A category that was at least typical in one group, and was not representative of the other group, was considered as distinguishing between the two groups.

Demographics and Training of CQR Coders

The group of coders who analyzed the session notes was composed of three female undergraduate psychology students. The second group of coders, who analyzed the follow-up interviews, was also composed of three undergraduate psychology students, two male and one female. Each group participated in separate biweekly training meetings of 2 hours each over the course of 6 months, during which time they practiced, along with the trainer (the first author), conducting CQR analyses on session notes from cases not included in this study. All coders were naïve to the alliance scores of parents, whose notes/transcripts they were analyzing, and the purpose of the study.

Table I. Intraclass correlation coefficient

Item	$ICC_{(1,2)}$ average measures	*F*-value	*P*
Therapist's empathy	.92	12.64	.00
Active participation	.88	8.44	.00
Non-trust	.95	21.04	.00
Agreement of problems	.92	12.93	.00
Agreement on goals	.98	36.16	.00
Agreement on tasks	.88	8.25	.00

Results

Preliminary Results

Reliability. In order to estimate the reliability of the alliance coders, intraclass correlation coefficients (ICCs) were calculated for each item of the VTAS. ICCs are calculated using an ANOVA-based procedure that examines the relationship between interrater agreement within target (i.e., parent) and the degree of variance between targets for each alliance item. As each target was coded by different raters, a one-way model ICC (1,2) was used. One-way models of ICC are, in essence, a measure of agreement. Each target is rated by a different set of judges, and judges are randomly paired with targets. In this case, the effects attributable to judge, target, and judge × target (interaction) are inseparable in the analyses. The ICC estimates for each item appear in Table I.

Alliance scores. Scores for each alliance component (i.e., Bond, Task and Goal), as well as overall alliance scores, appear in Table II. The average alliance score of the good alliance group was 4.49 (*SD* =.19) and that of the poor alliance groups was 2.33 (*SD* = .77).

Primary Results

Final list of domains. Coders agreed upon four domains, which provided the conceptual framework for organizing the narrative data. These domains were: Goal of treatment; Therapist-parent dynamic; Parents' understanding and experience of homosexuality; and Parents' ability to see positive aspects of their child.

Categories distinguishing between good and poor alliances based on the analyses of session notes. The first category distinguishing between good and poor alliances was *parents' willingness to define improving the parent-child relationship as a goal of therapy*. In all five good alliances, parents endorsed relationship building as a primary goal of the treatment. For example, one set of parents emphasized their wish to improve communication with their son.

> Father (to therapists): It seems like since telling us, he (their son) has been more removed. He comes home less on weekend, tells us less about what is going on with his life—it is like he has separated from us. We want him to come home for the weekends.

Another father reflected on his negative reaction to his son's same-sex orientation, acknowledging how his behavior likely hurt his son and pushed him away, and voiced a desire to repair the relationship.

> Father (to therapists): I would like to find a way to fix the relationship. I know that my anger has led to me pushing him away. It is hard for me—I don't know how to be around him. But I regret that—I wish our relationship was better.

In contrast, the five parents with poor alliances strongly resisted defining relationship building as a goal of therapy. In fact, four of these parents described how relationship building would actually undermine the likelihood of their child eventually adopting a heterosexual orientation.

> Father: When he decides to go back to being normal, that is what will improve the relationship. In the meantime, we aren't interested in helping him to feel like things are alright or comfortable. We don't want him to think that we see this as being O.K.

Table II. Demographic information and alliance scores for each parent

Couple	Parent	Age	Sex	Age of child	Bond	Goal	Task	Alliance
1	1	52	Male	16	2.75	1.5	1.25	1.83
	2	47	Female	16	1.25	1.25	1.25	1.25
2	3	51	Male	17	4.5	5	3.75	4.42
	4	47	Female	17	4	2.88	2.88	3.25
3	5	67	Male	37	4.75	5	4.25	4.67
	6	65	Female	37	5	4.75	4.25	4.67
4	7	62	Female	25	4.5	4.25	3.75	4.17
	8	64	Male	25	4.25	5	4.25	4.5
5	9	65	Male	22	4.5	1.63	3.38	3.17
	10	63	Female	22	4.25	0.75	1.5	2.17

A second and related category distinguishing good from poor alliance cases was parents' willingness (or lack thereof) to consider biological, essentialist, non-blaming causal explanations regarding their child's same-sex orientation. In our sample, four of the five parents with good alliances were able to discuss and remain open to the possible role of biology in the development of sexual orientation, and tended to view their child as essentially gay. For example, in one of the good alliances, the father disclosed that he had become depressed after his wife suggested that their daughter's lesbian orientation was the result of their (the parents') fighting—that they hadn't provided a good role model. In this instance, the therapists were able to engage the parents in a conversation about causality and offer relevant empirical findings.

> Father (to the therapists): What do you think about that? Do you think it is possible that our fighting led her to be a lesbian?
>
> Therapist: There is no evidence that parental fighting leads to children becoming gay. Moreover, common sense suggests otherwise. Look at how many couples have conflictual relationships and their children are heterosexual, and look at how many couples have seemingly harmonious relationships and their children are gay.

At this point, father showed a look of surprised.

> Therapist (to mother): I was wondering what was going through your mind as I said that.
>
> Mother (to father and therapist): The truth is, I don't really believe that it was our relationship either. I thought that way in the beginning, when she first told us, but now … I don't really believe that any more. I think she was born that way.
>
> Therapist: (to both parents) I would say that most professionals would agree that biology plays some role in our sexual orientation, and there is some research supporting that idea we can offer you if you are interested.

In another good alliance, the father expressed feeling guilty about how he raised his son. He lamented that if had, perhaps, spent more time with him doing more typically male type activities, things may have turned out differently. Again, the therapists used the opportunity to discuss the likely role of genetics/biology to help alleviate the father's unwarranted guilt.

> Father: It is really, really hard for me to accept that my son is a homosexual. I know in my head that he probably will never change—that the chances are 99% that that is who he is. Even though I can't stop wondering if there is something I could do to change it.
>
> Therapist: It is so hard sometimes. You have talked about how worried you are about his welfare and how his being gay has made you feel less like getting closer to him. I worry that you are also unnecessarily adding to that a feeling of guilt. It is important for us that you know that there is no evidence whatsoever that parents' relationships with their children influence their sexual orientation. The only credible research suggests a possible link between biology and sexual orientation.
>
> Father: I think over time I have begun to feel less and less guilty. But hearing it again from you is comforting.

In contrast, four of the five parents with poor alliances categorically dismissed the possibility that their child was essentially gay: That their child may have been born homosexual, lesbian or bisexual. For example, one parent claimed that his son was gay because he had had an unsuccessful sexual encounter with a woman. He cited the fact that his son had dated many girls during high school, before the encounter.

> Father (to therapist): Let me ask you this. How do you explain the fact that on one hand he says he is in love with another boy—that from the age 10 he has only been interested in looking at other boys—while on the other hand, I saw how many girls he went out with, bought them presents, how many girlfriends he has today? How do you explain it that he has even more girlfriends than my older son? That just last year he spent almost all of his time with the girl next door, an older girl, and that they were inseparable and seemed to always have a great time together? Explain it to me how somebody can suddenly change, from end to end … just like that. Explain it to me!
>
> Therapist: I see how upsetting and confusing this is for you. It is not like some instances in which parents notice that their child is different from early on and somewhere in their minds they expect someday to hear the words "I'm gay". I don't know if you have had a chance to talk to your son about this, ask him these exact questions and really be open to listening to his answers. I think it would be important if we could eventually find a way to help you ask him some of these very questions, here in the sessions, in a curious, non-accusatory manner. I will say, however, that some boys who are homosexual actually feel more comfortable having girls as friends. Just like heterosexual boys may feel more comfortable with other boys. Their interests may be more similar and there isn't the sexual tension—things are easier. It would be interesting to hear exactly what the nature of his relationship with these women was.
>
> Father: I don't believe it. Not because I don't want to believe, simply because I know him.

A third category distinguishing good from poor alliances was *parents' unwillingness to consider coming out of the closet as the parent of a sexual minority child.* In all five poor alliances, parents emphasized the importance of keeping their child's sexual orientation a secret. For example, one mother spoke about the importance of her extended family never finding out.

> Mother: I don't talk about it with anybody. Not my sister, who I am very close with, not my parents, nobody. They must never know since it would devastate them. In the Russian community homosexuality is unacceptable and pathological.

As another couple put it:

> We can't tell anybody. There are no such things among our circle of friends, in our culture. If somebody finds out, they will think we are terrible parents. They will be disgusted by him (our son) and stop inviting us to social and family gatherings.

In contrast, none of parents with good alliances mentioned the importance of keeping their child's sexual orientation secret.

Two of the five good alliance parents spoke about wishing that they had the courage to share with others the fact that their child was gay or lesbian, or reported instances in which they did share with others, despite their trepidation and shame. For example, in one case the father spoke about the parents of one of his daughter's lesbian friends.

> Father: You know, my daughter has a friend who is also lesbian. She and her partner are getting married and her parents are so excited. I don't know how they cope with it ... what, are they less ashamed then we are? I want to know how they got up the courage to tell others, what they said and how they started the conversation.

In contrast, none of the parents with poor alliances were able to consider the possibility of coming out of the closet, though the category of "*expressing a willingness to come out as parents of a same-sex oriented child*" did not formally meet criteria for distinguishing between the two alliance groups.

A fourth category distinguishing good from poor alliances was the *parent's ability to simultaneously reflect upon the positive qualities of their child while, at the same time, acknowledge their disappointment, shame and anger associated with their child's homosexuality*. In three of the five good alliances, parents were able to distinguish between their positive feelings about their child and their difficulty accepting their child's sexuality. For example:

> Mother (to therapist): I am angry at him for not trying harder, giving it one more chance with women. But he is a good kid. He cares about us, worries about how hard this is for us.

In another case, the father expressed his complex feelings in the following manner:

> Father: I am very disappointed that he is a homosexual. I feel angry about it, disgusted. On the other hand, he works hard, takes things seriously. He is very smart, and has good grades.

In four of the five poor alliances, however, parents' negative reaction to their child's same-sex orientation clouded their ability to maintain sight of their child's positive attributes. For example:

> Mother (to therapists): Clearly, he doesn't care about his family. All of his visits home for the weekend, his statements about wanting to maintain a good relationship, succeed in life—it doesn't mean anything if he is going to continue this way [identify as homosexual].

A fifth category distinguishing good from poor alliances was *parents' attempts to coercively influence/change their child's sexual orientation, and therapists' confrontations regarding such behavior*. In four of the five poor alliances, parent's described how they attempted to coercively change their child's sexual orientation. For example, one set of parents described how they had hired a private investigator to follow their son around and report back to them if their son had met with other gay men. That same mother described how she also used guilt induction and invalidation to try to influence her son.

> Mother: I tell him, "think about your mother, your family, your future. Do you want a family? Do you think that if you are going to walk down the aisle with some man I am going to come to your wedding? No. I am going to die of heart attack, that is what I am going to do." It is not about using force. Instead, I just tell him "you don't really know who you are—you are confused."

In another case, the therapists confronted the mother about not protecting her son from his older brother, who had physically threatened and injured him. The mother had refrained from getting involved with the hope that perhaps her older son would help her gay son "get his head on straight."

> Therapist: Neither your son nor we are going to be able to work things out with you if he is not safe. That has to stop and it is your responsibility to stop it. We can understand your desperation and feelings of helplessness but your son's safety is the first priority.

In these two cases, the ruptures were not successfully repaired and the therapy shifted to individual sessions with the young adult and to a focus on separation and grieving rather than reconciliation and reconnection. In none of the five good alliances did parents attempt to coercively change their child's sexual orientation.

Another category differentiating between good and poor alliances was *parents blaming the therapist for validating, and thus reinforcing, the child's same-sex orientation.* In four of the five poor alliances, parents blamed the therapist for supporting and reinforcing the child's same-sex orientation. For example, one mother, who preferred that her son not attend the local LGB youth center for fear that it would increase the likelihood of his maintaining a gay identity, reprimanded the therapist:

> Mother (to therapists): I understand from your conversation with him (son) last week that you talked about his going to the youth center: What made him feel comfortable there and why he so much wanted to go. I don't want him going there—I don't want him to receive support from you in regards to looking in that direction.

Another mother reprimanded the therapists for not showing more support for her efforts to change her son's sexual orientation:

> Mother: If you want to help me, help us, then tell him (her son) to come with us to the Rabbi. Support us when we tell him that we don't want him living with this other boy.

In none of the good alliances did parents blame the therapist.

In four of the five poor alliances, *parents pressured the therapists to gather and reveal information about their child.* More specifically, these parents asked therapists to obtain information about their child's sexuality and day to day behaviors. When therapists responded by attempting to leverage parents' anxiety and desire for more information to promote the goal of direct conversation with their child—conversations in which they could ask such questions directly and receive answers—parents refused, citing their disbelief that their child would answer honestly.

> Father (to therapists): What does he tell you in sessions alone? Which way is he leaning?
>
> Therapist: One thing he has said was that he wishes he could feel more comfortable talking to you both. I want to help you all build a sense of trust and safety so that you can talk about this directly, not through me.
>
> Mother: But he isn't honest with us. You have a better reading of it, what do you think?
>
> Therapist: Why do you think he doesn't feel comfortable being honest with you? What gets in the way? Let's talk about that. I want to help you to help him to feel more comfortable being honest with you two.

None of the five good alliances involved parents' requests for personal information about their child.

Categories distinguishing between good and poor alliances based on the analyses of follow-up interviews. One category distinguishing good from poor alliances was *whether parents defined the goal of therapy in external or internal terms.* In all five good alliances, parents defined the goal of therapy as working either on themselves or on their interactions with their same-sex child. For example, as one father reported:

> Father: The whole point of coming here (to the therapy) was to find a way to get along better—to open the line of communication. Before he came to tell us he was gay, our family talked about everything. Now, it is like he has slipped away.

Another father talked about the therapy as a place that he and his wife could get support in order to cope better:

> Father: We came here because it has been so hard for us. We haven't talked to anybody about this and don't know what to do. We came because this is so difficult and we are so alone with it.

In contrast, four of the parents with poor alliances defined their goal of therapy as external—as changing their child's identity. For example,

> Mother: First of all, it was my daughter's initiative that we come here. She came to me and asked me to come to this project because she thought it would help me to understand her ... and I played along with it. She said that it was very important to her, I don't know, I wanted to help her, because she probably needed it. My hope was that she would take a serious look at herself and her life and realize that she was making a bad choice.

Another distinguishing category was the degree to which *parents experienced the therapists as empathic, attuned, non-judgmental and as creating a safe environment.* Parents in four of the five good alliances explicitly described the therapists as such. For example, one mother stated:

> Mother: I felt like you really understood, felt my pain. That gave me the desire to continue with the sessions.

Another parent reported:

> Father: During the therapy, you gave me the sense that everything was OK—very much OK. You knew how to create a safe environment"

Yet another parent related:

> Mother: You brought a sense of serenity, peacefulness ... you invested in us .... It felt like you listened, like you heard us.

None of the parents with poor alliances made similar statements.

The final category distinguishing good from poor alliances was the *degree to which parents felt like they could speak about their shame and pain without being judged*. This occurred in four of the five good alliances. As one father put it:

> Father: What helped us was that we could finally speak about it (i.e., the disgust and shame) … it was helpful to unburden these things that bothered me.

As another mother put it:

> Mother: It was helpful that if we had something to say, we could simply say it without feeling judged or guilty. I could say that I wished he wasn't gay and that was alright. I could say that I didn't want my parents to know and that it was hard for me to think about her bringing a girlfriend home to our house.

None of the parents with poor alliances made such mention. Frequencies of each domain and category appear in Table III.

Discussion

The purpose of this study was to identify therapeutic processes and themes associated with good versus poor alliances in attachment-based family therapy with non-accepting parents of sexual minority offspring. Analyses of the first three individual therapy sessions alone with parents revealed that, in good alliances, parents evidenced a willingness to define improving the parent-child relationship as a goal of therapy, a willingness to consider biological, essentialist, non-blaming causal explanations regarding their child's same-sex orientation, and an ability to reflect upon the positive qualities of their child, even in the context of their disappointment, shame, and anger associated with their child's homosexuality. In addition, analyses of follow-up interviews revealed that parents with good alliances defined the goals of therapy as internal or relational (e.g., working on their own pain or on their relationship with their child) rather than external (e.g., changing their child), perceived the therapist as empathic, attuned, and as creating a safe environment, and felt like they could express their shame and pain without being judged.

In contrast, in poor alliances, parents rejected relationship building as a goal for therapy, rebuffed the possibility of essentialist (e.g., biological) causal attributions, dismissed the possibility of coming out as parents of a gay child, remained singularly focused on their child's sexual orientation, nullifying any

Table III. Comparison between poor parent-therapist alliances versus good parent-therapist alliances

Domain	Category	Good parent-therapist alliances	Representativeness	Poor parent-therapist alliances	Representativeness
Goal of treatment	*Parents showed willingness to define improving the parent-child relationship as goal of therapy*	5	General	0	NR
	Parents defined the goal of therapy in internal terms	5	General	0	NR
	Parents defined the goal of therapy in external terms	0	NR	4	Typical
Therapist-parent dynamics	*Parents endorsed coercively changing their child's sexual orientation and therapists confronted parents regarding such behavior*	0	NR	4	Typical
	Parents blamed therapist for validating child's same-sex orientation	0	NR	4	Typical
	Parents pressured therapists to gather and reveal information about their child	0	NR	4	Typical
	Parents experienced therapists as empathic, attuned, non-judgmental and as creating a safe environment	4	Typical	0	NR
	Parents could speak about their shame and pain without being judged	4	Typical	0	NR
Parents' understanding and experience of homosexuality	*Parents expressed a willingness to consider essentialist, non-blaming causal explanations regarding their child's same-sex orientation*	4	Typical	1	NR
	Parents considered disclosing their child's sexual orientation to others	2	Variant	0	NR
	Parents emphasized keeping child's sexual orientation secret	0	NR	5	General
Parents see positive aspects of their child	*Parents were able to simultaneously reflect upon the positive qualities of their child while at the same time acknowledging their disappointment, shame and anger*	3	Typical	1	NR

Note: NR = not representative.

positive aspects of the child, defined the goal of therapy in external terms (i.e., to change their child's sexual orientation), blamed therapists for validating and reinforcing their child's same-sex orientation, and pressured therapists to give them information about their child. Also in poor alliances, therapists confronted parents about their use of coercion to influence or try to change their child's sexual orientation.

The finding that in good alliances parents endorsed relationship building as a primary goal of therapy is consistent with the principles and tasks of ABFT. In the early stage of ABFT, therapists work to shift the focus of the therapy away from the presenting problem per se (e.g., my son is gay) and onto the rupture in the attachment relationship (e.g., we don't talk any more—he has drifted away and when we meet it is always a fight) and associated underlying, primary emotions such as loss, sadness, and longing for reconnection (Diamond, Diamond, & Liddle, 2000). Once such a shift, or what has been termed the "relational reframe" (Diamond & Siqueland, 1998; Moran & Diamond, 2008), has been successfully facilitated, parents are motivated and then prepared for subsequent conjoint in-session enactments (i.e., attachment episodes) designed to help them and their child access primary adaptive emotions and reach out to one another in a manner that is validating and increases closeness. Consequently, parents who were able to shift their attention away from their anger, guilt, and shame regarding their child's sexual orientation and onto the loss and longing to reconnect with their child developed stronger alliances with the therapist.

As would be expected, parents who held, or who were at least willing to consider, biological, essentialist causal attributions regarding the origins of their child's same-sex orientation evidenced better alliances. Instead of blaming their children, these parents were able to empathize with them. This finding echoes those from a number of studies which have found that essentialist attributions were associated with more tolerance of, and positive feelings towards, same-sex oriented individuals among the general population (Armesto & Weisman, 2001; Haider-Markel & Joslyn, 2008; Haslam & Levy, 2006) and, recently, among a sample of parents of sexual minority youth and young adults (Belsky & Diamond, under review). For such parents, their child's sexual orientation was not something that could be or needed to be changed but, instead, something that they, as parents, felt they needed to learn how to cope with in the context of their relationship with their child. Consequently, therapists were able to build an alliance with these parents around the goal of processing their sense of loss, shame, anger, disgust, and fear so that they could become more available to love and support their same-sex oriented child.

Relatedly, parents with good alliances explicitly stated that the therapy was a place where they could express previously unspoken, and perhaps difficult to acknowledge, emotions without feeling judged. They described the therapists as empathic, attuned and as creating a safe environment for working through such feelings. These findings are in line with prior research suggesting that working through shame, guilt, and anger is a common, and perhaps necessary, step in the process of acceptance for parents with sexual minority children (Bernstein, 1990; Phillips & Ancis, 2008; Saltzburg, 2004; Samarova et al., 2013). Indeed, the emotional processing of primary emotions has been linked to successful outcome in a number of experiential therapies similar to ABFT (Carryer & Greenberg, 2010; Pascuale-Leon & Greenberg, 2007). Our findings also echo previous research emphasizing the importance of therapist empathy and safety in the development of the therapeutic relationship (Friedlander et al., 2011; Norcross & Wampold, 2011). Creating a space where parents could speak the unspeakable, and work through their most reviled and scary feelings, may have also been what led these parents to be able to more easily imagine coming out to people in their extended family, to friends, and to colleagues at work.

Finally, parents with positive alliances showed an ability to reflect upon the positive qualities of their child, even in the context of their disappointment, shame, and anger. Such ability is not trivial. It reflects the capacity to differentiate between aspects of the other, mentalize, and regulate emotions—all skills associated with development and maintenance of healthy interpersonal relations. The ability to remain cognizant of the fact that one's child is more than his/her sexual orientation, and that one's child is still the same person, even after coming out as gay, lesbian or bisexual, has been noted by some parents as one of the critical elements in their acceptance process (Bernstein, 1990; Fields, 2001).

In contrast to parents with good alliances, four of the five parents with poor alliances tenaciously maintained that their child could and should change his/her sexual orientation. These parents were less empathic and supportive of their child, and less likely to agree to adopt relationship building as the goal for therapy. In fact, many of these parents described using rejection, criticism, and ostracism instrumentally: As leverage for trying to coerce their child into changing his/her sexual orientation. They perceived relationship building as tantamount to granting their child approval or permission to be gay and, consequently, as undermining their ultimate goal—to change their child.

In these cases, therapists typically scaled back (e.g., retreated from focusing on the quality of the attachment relationship) and returned to a supportive, empathic posture, refocusing on how painful and difficult it was for the parent to cope with having a sexual-minority child. Periodically, the therapists gently and cautiously challenged parents' singularly constructivist causal attributions and beliefs that sexual orientation is a choice and malleable, through the use of Socratic questioning and reference to research findings suggesting a biological contribution to sexual orientation and showing the lack of efficacy of sex orientation change efforts (Shpigel, Belsky, & Diamond, 2013). However, in the poor alliances in this study, such interventions resulted in what Safran and Muran (1996) have described as confrontation ruptures: Parents' expression of hostile anger and attempts to pressure the therapists into adopting their goal of changing their child. As one parent put it, "you are not helping me by talking about how hard it is for me, if you want to help, tell him to stop meeting with that boy!" These parents accused the therapists of reinforcing their child's sexual orientation and pressed them for personal information about their child's behavior and thinking process. Such alliance failures were likely the result of the interaction between parents' personalities, the goals of ABFT (i.e., focus on relationship building) and perhaps clinical mistakes by the therapists (Eubanks-Carter, Muran, Safran, & Hayes, 2011). In such cases, therapists ended up recommending limiting contact between the adolescent/young adult and his/her non-accepting parents and worked individually with the same-sex oriented child to help them grieve their loss.

A number of methodological strengths of this study increase our confidence in the validity of the findings. For example, the inclusion criteria were well defined (e.g., degree and length of time of non-acceptance). Also, the use of independent, objective ratings to score the strength of the alliance contributed to the internal validity of the study (i.e., the degree to which the specific phenomenon of interest was captured). In addition, the independent analyses of session notes and post-therapy follow-up interviews allowed for multiple sources of information regarding parents' experience and behavior. Finally, our emphasis on rater training, consensus and monitoring during the data analytic process contributed to the trustworthiness or convergent validity (i.e., reliability) of the qualitative findings.

Alongside these methodological strengths, however, were some methodological limitations. First and foremost was the size of the sample. We did not imagine before embarking on this study how difficult it would be to recruit non-accepting parents. In fact, it required over a year and half to recruit the 10 parents who participated in the study, despite tremendous efforts and the use of multiple recruitment strategies. Indeed, this is an important finding in and of itself: Non-accepting parents are reluctant to come to therapy and, when they do come, it is likely to be at the request of the child, not on their own initiative. In that sense, it is impossible to know how representative our findings are of non-accepting parents. While a sample size of 10 is considered reasonable in the context of such labor-intensive work (Hill et al., 1997), additional participants would have increased our confidence in the stability of the findings. Consequently, our findings should be considered preliminary. Also, the session notes were based on the therapist's recollection and not on audio transcripts. Consequently, a potential for omissions and interpretive bias was present. It is worth noting, however, that session notes were completed immediately after the session and were comprehensive and detailed. They included the therapist's recollection of actual parent statements as well the therapist's remarks about the process (e.g., tone, non-verbal behaviors). Another limitation is that the therapists conducted the post-therapy interviews. The decisions to have therapists interview was because some of the parents, particularly those with poor alliances, remained suspicious even after the end of therapy, and they were not willing to expose themselves to unfamiliar interviewers. The disadvantage, of course, was the potential demand characteristics of the situation. However, it is worth noting that despite any demand characteristics, non-accepting parents presented a litany of complaints and accusations such that it is hard to imagine that there were many feelings of discontent that these parents hid. Another limitation is, of course, the correlational, non-experimental nature of the data. Though we were able to distinguish themes and processes uniquely associated with good versus poor alliance sessions and interviews, it is impossible to know if they contributed to alliance quality. In addition, there were likely to be personality characteristics (e.g., defensiveness, rigidity) and perhaps other unexplored variables (e.g., past experiences with therapy, culture) that contributed directly to both the content and process of the therapy and to the development of good versus poor alliances. Yet another limitation is the amount of time that passed from end of therapy until post-treatment interview. This substantial lag in time may have impacted upon some participants' ability to accurately remember certain details. Finally, our findings are limited to alliances that developed in the context of a relational, family-based model which emphasizes promoting parent-child connection and the importance of age-appropriate attachment. The development of good and poor alliances with this population may look very different in the context of other treatment approaches.

Despite these limitations, this study provides the first empirical data on the therapeutic themes and processes associated with good versus poor alliances with non-accepting parents of sexual minority adolescents and young adults. Such data are exceptionally important in light of the fact that the therapeutic alliance is a robust predictor of both treatment retention and outcome, and that such parents are particularly difficult to recruit and engage in therapy. These findings are a first step in better understanding the challenges of relationship building with this population and can potentially help guide clinical researchers in the development of specific alliance building intervention strategies for these parents. For example, our clinical experience with parents in this sample suggests that introducing the possibility that their child may be essentially gay or lesbian (rather than by choice) and empathically validating and supporting the parent's own feelings of anger, loss, fears, and disappointment in response to their child's sexual orientation was a necessary first step before introducing a relational frame and working on increasing closeness and acceptance. Indeed, working to transform causal attributions, supporting parents' sense of loss and pain, and focusing on the importance of the relationship may be relevant to other hard to engage clinical populations characterized by parental blame and interpersonal conflict (e.g., behavior-disordered children and adolescents). In light of the known negative impact of ongoing parental rejection and criticism of sexual minority children, and the buffering effects of parental warmth and acceptance, the importance of developing, testing, and improving family-based treatments for LGB individuals and their non-accepting parents is self-evident.

References

Armesto, J. C., & Weisman, A. G. (2001). Attribution and emotional reactions to the identity disclosure ("coming-out") of a homosexual child. *Family Process, 40,* 145–161. doi:10.1111/j.1545-5300.2001.4020100145.x

Beals, K. P., & Peplau, L. A. (2006). Disclosure patterns within social networks of gay men and lesbians. *Journal of Homosexuality, 51,* 101–120. doi:10.1300/J082v51n02_06

Belsky, Y., & Diamond, G. M. (under review). Causal attributions and parents' acceptance of their homosexual sons.

Ben-Ari, A. (Ed.). (1995). The discovery that an offspring is gay: Parents', gay men's, and lesbians' perspectives. *Journal of Homosexuality, 30,* 89–112.

Bernstein, B. E. (1990). Attitudes and issues of parents of gay men and lesbians and implications for therapy. *Journal of Gay & Lesbian Psychotherapy, 1,* 37–53. doi:10.1300/J236v01n03_03

Bordin, E. S. (1979). The generalizability of the psychoanalytic concept of the working alliance. *Psychotherapy: Theory, Research & Practice, 16,* 252–260. doi:10.1037/h0085885

Carryer, J. R., & Greenberg, L. S. (2010). Optimal levels of emotional arousal in experiential therapy of depression. *Journal of Consulting and Clinical Psychology, 78,* 190–199. doi:10.1037/a0018401

D'Augelli, A. R. (2002). Mental health problems among lesbian, gay, and bisexual youths ages 14 to 21. *Clinical Child Psychology and Psychiatry, 7,* 433–456.

D'Augelli, A. R., Grossman, A. H., & Starks, M. T. (2005). Parents' awareness of lesbian, gay, and bisexual youths' sexual orientation. *Journal of Marriage and Family, 67,* 474–482. doi:10.1111/j.0022-2445.2005.00129.x

Diamond, G. M., Diamond, G. S., Levy, S., Closs, C., Ladipo, T., & Siqueland, L. (2012). Attachment-based family therapy for suicidal lesbian, gay, and bisexual adolescents: A treatment development study and open trial with preliminary findings. *Psychotherapy, 49,* 62–71. doi:10.1037/a0026247

Diamond, G. M., Diamond, G. S., & Liddle, H. A. (2000). The therapist–parent alliance in family-based therapy for adolescents. *Journal of Clinical Psychology, 56,* 1037–1050. doi:10.1002/1097-4679(200008)56:8%3C1037::AID-JCLP4%3E3.0.CO;2-4

Diamond, G. M., Liddle, H. A., Hogue, A., & Dakof, G. A. (1999). Alliance-building interventions with adolescents in family therapy: A process study. *Psychotherapy: Theory, Research, Practice, Training, 36,* 355–368. doi:10.1037/h0087729

Diamond, G. S., Reis, B., Diamond, G. M., Siqueland, L., & Isaacs, L. (2002). Attachment-based family therapy for depressed adolescents: A treatment development study. *Journal of the American Academy of Child & Adolescent Psychiatry, 41,* 1190–1196. doi:10.1097/00004583-200210000-00008

Diamond, G. M., Shilo, G., Jurgensen, E., D'Augelli, A., Samarova, V., & White, K. (2011). How depressed and suicidal sexual minority adolescents understand the causes of their distress. *Journal of Gay & Lesbian Mental Health, 15,* 130–151. doi:10.1080/19359705.2010.532668

Diamond, G. M., & Shpigel, M. (in press). Attachment-based family therapy for lesbian and gay adults and their persistently non-accepting parents. *Professional Psychology: Research and Practice.*

Diamond, G., & Siqueland, L. (1998). Emotions, attachment and the relational reframe: The first session. *Journal of Systemic Therapies, 17,* 36–50.

Diamond, G. S., Siqueland, L., & Diamond, G. M. (2003). Attachment-based family therapy: a program of treatment development research. *Clinical Child and Family Psychology Review, 6,* 107–128. doi:10.1023/A:1023782510786

Diamond, G. S., Wintersteen, M. B., Brown, G. K., Diamond, G. M., Gallop, R., Shelef, K., & Levy, S. (2010). Attachment-based family therapy for adolescents with suicidal ideation: A randomized controlled trial. *Journal of the American Academy of Child & Adolescent Psychiatry, 49,* 122–131.

Eisenberg, M. E., & Resnick, M. D. (2006). Suicidality among Gay, Lesbian and Bisexual Youth: The Role of Protective Factors. *Journal of Adolescent Health, 39,* 662–668. doi:10.1016/j.jadohealth.2006.04.024

Elliott, R. (1989). Comprehensive process analysis: Understanding the change process in significant therapy events. In M. J. Packer & R. B. Addison (Eds.), *Entering the circle: Hermeneutic investigation in psychology* (pp. 165–184). Albany: State University of New York Press.

Eubanks-Carter, C., Muran, J. C., Safran, J. D., & Hayes, J. A. (2011). Interpersonal interventions for maintaining an alliance. In L. M. Horowitz, & S. T. Strack (Eds.), *Handbook of interpersonal psychology: Theory, research, assessment, and therapeutic interventions* (pp. 519–531). Hoboken, NJ: John Wiley & Sons.

Evans, E., Hawton, K., & Rodham, K. (2004). Factors associated with suicidal phenomena in adolescents: A systematic review of population-based studies. *Clinical Psychology Review, 24*, 957–979. doi:10.1016/j.cpr.2004.04.005

Fielding, N. G., & Fielding, J. L. (1986). *Linking data*. Beverley Hills, CA: Sage.

Fields, J. (2001). Normal queers: Straight parents respond to their children's "coming out". *Symbolic Interaction, 24*, 165–187. doi:10.1525/si.2001.24.2.165

Floyd, F. J., Stein, T. S., Harter, K. S. M., Allison, A., & Nye, C. L. (1999). Gay, lesbian, and bisexual youths: Separation-individuation, parental attitudes, identity consolidation, and well-being. *Journal of Youth and Adolescence, 28*, 719–739. doi:10.1023/A:1021691601737

Friedlander, M. L., Escudero, V., Heatherington, L., & Diamond, G. M. (2011). Alliance in couple and family therapy. *Psychotherapy, 48*, 25–33. doi:10.1037/a0022060

Giorgi, A. (1985). Sketch of a psychological phenomenological method. In A. Giorgi (Ed.), *Phenomenology and psychological research* (pp. 8–22). Pittsburgh, PA: Duquesne University Press.

Goldfried, M. R., & Goldfried, A. P. (2001). The importance of parental support in the lives of gay, lesbian, and bisexual individuals. *Journal of Clinical Psychology, 57*, 681–693. doi:10.1002/jclp.1037

Haider-Markel, D. P., & Joslyn, M. R. (2008). Beliefs about the origins of homosexuality and support for gay rights: An empirical test of attribution theory. *Public Opinion Quarterly, 72*, 291–310. doi:10.1093/poq/nfn015

Hartley, D. E., & Strupp, H. H. (1983). The therapeutic alliance: Its relationship to outcome in brief psychotherapy. In J. Masling (Ed.), *Empirical studies of psychoanalytic theories* (Vol. 1). Hillsdale, NJ: Analytical Press.

Haslam, N., & Levy, S. R. (2006). Essentialist beliefs about homosexuality: Structure and implications for prejudice. *Personality and Social Psychology Bulletin, 32*, 471–485. doi:10.1177/0146167205276516

Heatherington, L., & Lavner, J. A. (2008). Coming to terms with coming out: Review and recommendations for family systems-focused research. *Journal of Family Psychology, 22*, 329–343. doi:10.1037/0893-3200.22.3.329

Hershberger, S. L., & D'Augelli, A. R. (1995). The impact of victimization on the mental health and suicidality of lesbian, gay, and bisexual youths. *Developmental Psychology, 31*, 65–74. doi:10.1037/0012-1649.31.1.65

Hill, C. E., Knox, S., Thompson, B. J., Williams, E. N., Hess, S. A., & Ladany, N. (2005). Consensual qualitative research: An update. *Journal of Counseling Psychology, 52*, 196–205. doi:10.1037/0022-0167.52.2.196

Hill, C. E., Thompson, B. J., & Williams, E. N. (1997). A guide to conducting consensual qualitative research. *The Counseling Psychologist, 25*, 517–572. doi:10.1177/0011000097254001

Holtzen, D. W., & Agresti, A. A. (1990). Parental responses to gay and lesbian children: Differences in homophobia, self-esteem, and sex-role stereotyping. *Journal of Social and Clinical Psychology, 9*, 390–399. doi:10.1521/jscp.1990.9.3.390

Horvath, A. O. (1994). Research on the alliance. In A. O. Horvath & L. S. Greenberg (Eds.), *The working alliance: Theory, research, and practice* (pp. 259–286). Oxford: John Wiley & Sons.

Horvath, A. O. (2000). The therapeutic relationship: From transference to alliance. *Journal of Clinical Psychology, 56*, 163–173. doi:10.1002/(SICI)1097-4679(200002)56:2%3C163::AID-JCLP3%3E3.0.CO;2-D

Horvath, A. O., Del Re, A., Flückiger, C., & Symonds, D. (2011). Alliance in individual psychotherapy. In J. C. Norcross (Ed.), *Psychotherapy relationships that work: Evidence-based responsiveness* (2nd ed., pp. 25–69). New York, NY: Oxford University Press.

Horvath, A. O., & Greenberg, L. S. (Eds.). (1994). *The working alliance: Theory, research, and practice.* Wiley series on personality processes (p. 304). Oxford: John Wiley & Sons.

Horvath, A. O., & Luborsky, L. (1993). The role of the therapeutic alliance in psychotherapy. *Journal of Consulting and Clinical Psychology, 61*, 561–573. doi:10.1037/0022-006X.61.4.561

Horvath, A. O., & Symonds, B. D. (1991). Relation between working alliance and outcome in psychotherapy: A meta-analysis. *Journal of Counseling Psychology, 38*, 139–149. doi:10.1037/0022-0167.38.2.139

Johnson, S. M., & Greenberg, L. S. (1995). The emotionally focused approach to problems in adult attachment. In N. S. Jacobson & A. S. Gurman (Eds.), *Clinical handbook of couple therapy* (pp. 121–141). New York, NY: Guilford Press.

LaSala, M. C. (2000). Lesbians, gay men, and their parents: Family therapy for the coming-out crisis. *Family Process, 39*, 67–81. doi:10.1111/j.1545-5300.2000.39108.x

Liddle, H. A. (1999). Theory development in a family-based therapy for adolescent drug abuse. *Journal of Clinical Child Psychology, 28*, 521–532. doi:10.1207/S15374424JCCP2804_12

Martin, D. J., Garske, J. P., & Davis, M. K. (2000). Relation of the therapeutic alliance with outcome and other variables: A meta-analytic review. *Journal of Consulting and Clinical Psychology, 68*, 438–450. doi:10.1037/0022-006X.68.3.438

Minuchin, S. (1977). *Families and family therapy.* London: Routledge.

Moran, G., & Diamond, G. M. (2008). Generating non-negative attitudes among parents of depressed adolescents: the power of empathy, concern and positive regard. *Psychotherapy Research, 18*, 97–107. doi:10.1080/10503300701408325

Needham, B. L., & Austin, E. L. (2010). Sexual orientation, parental support, and health during the transition to young adulthood. *Journal of Youth and Adolescence, 39*, 1189–1198. doi:10.1007/s10964-010-9533-6

Norcross, J. C., & Wampold, B. E. (2011). Evidence-based therapy relationships: Research conclusions and clinical practices. *Psychotherapy, 48*, 98–102. doi:10.1037/a0022161

Pachankis, J. E., Goldfried, M. R., & Ramrattan, M. E. (2008). Extension of the rejection sensitivity construct to the interpersonal functioning of gay men. *Journal of Consulting and Clinical Psychology, 76*, 306–317. doi:10.1037/0022-006X.76.2.306

Pascual-Leone, A., & Greenberg, L. S. (2007). Emotional processing in experiential therapy: Why "the only way out is through." *Journal of Consulting and Clinical Psychology, 75*, 875–887. doi:10.1037/0022-006X.75.6.875

Phillips, M. J., & Ancis, J. R. (2008). The process of identity development as the parent of a lesbian or gay male. *Journal of LGBT Issues in Counseling, 2*, 126–158. doi:10.1080/15538600802125605

Remafedi, G., Farrow, J. A., & Deisher, R. W. (1993). Risk factors for attempted suicide in gay and bisexual youth. In L. D. Garnets & D. C. Kimmel (Eds.), *Psychological perspectives on lesbian and gay male experiences. Between men—between women: Lesbian and gay studies* (pp. 486–499). New York, NY: Columbia University Press.

Robinson, B. E., Walters, L. H., & Skeen, P. (1989). Response of parents to learning that their child is homosexual and concern over AIDS: A national study. *Journal of Homosexuality, 18*, 59–80. doi:10.1300/J082v18n01_03

Ryan, C., Huebner, D., Diaz, R. M., & Sanchez, J. (2009). Family rejection as a predictor of negative health outcomes in White and Latino lesbian, gay, and bisexual young adults. *Pediatrics*, *123*, 346–352. doi:10.1542/peds.2007-3524

Ryan, C., Russell, S. T., Huebner, D., Diaz, R., & Sanchez, J. (2010). Family acceptance in adolescence and the health of LGBT young adults. *Journal of Child and Adolescent Psychiatric Nursing*, *23*, 205–213. doi:10.1111/j.1744-6171.2010.00246.x

Safran, J. D., & Muran, J. C. (1996). The resolution of ruptures in the therapeutic alliance. *Journal of Consulting and Clinical Psychology*, *64*, 447–458. doi:10.1037/0022-006X.64.3.447

Saltzburg, S. (2004). Learning that an adolescent child is gay or lesbian: The parent experience. *Social Work*, *49*, 109–118. doi:10.1093/sw/49.1.109

Samarova, V., Shilo, G., & Diamond, G. M. (2013, August). Changes over time in parents' acceptance of their Israeli sexual minority adolescents. Advance online publication. doi:10.1111/jora.12071

Savin-Williams, R. C. (1989). Coming out to parents and self-esteem among gay and lesbian youths. *Journal of Homosexuality*, *18*, 1–35 doi:10.1300/J082v18n01_01

Savin-Williams, R. C. (2001). *"Mom, Dad. I'm gay." How families negotiate coming out*. Washington, DC: American Psychological Association.

Savin-Williams, R. C., & Dubé, E. M. (1998). Parental reactions to their child's disclosure of a gay/lesbian identity. *Family Relations: An Interdisciplinary Journal of Applied Family Studies*, *47*, 7–13. doi:10.2307/584845

Savin-Williams, R. C., & Ream, G. L. (2003). Sex variations in the disclosure to parents of same-sex attractions. *Journal of Family Psychology*, *17*, 429–438. doi:10.1037/0893-3200.17.3.429

Semple, S. J., Strathdee, S. A., Zians, J., & Patterson, T. L. (2009). Family conflict and depression in HIV-negative heterosexuals: The role of methamphetamine use. *Psychology of Addictive Behaviors*, *23*, 341–347. doi:10.1037/a0015260

Sheeber, L. B., Davis, B., Leve, C., Hops, H., & Tildesley, E. (2007). Adolescents' relationships with their mothers and fathers: Associations with depressive disorder and subdiagnostic symptomatology. *Journal of Abnormal Psychology*, *116*, 144–154. doi:10.1037/0021-843X.116.1.144

Shelef, K., & Diamond, G. M. (2008). Short form of the revised Vanderbilt Therapeutic Alliance Scale: Development, reliability, and validity. *Psychotherapy Research*, *18*, 433–443. doi:10.1080/10503300701810801

Shelef, K., Diamond, G. M., Diamond, G. S., & Liddle, H. A. (2005). Adolescent and parent alliance and treatment outcome in multidimensional family therapy. *Journal of Consulting and Clinical Psychology*, *73*, 689–698. doi:10.1037/0022-006X.73.4.689

Shpigel, M. S., Belsky, Y., & Diamond, G. M. (2013, March 11). Clinical work with non-accepting parents of sexual minority children: Addressing causal and controllability attributions. *Professional Psychology: Research and Practice*. Advance online publication. doi:10.1037/a0031824

Strauss, A., & Corbin, J. (1998). *Basics of qualitative research: Techniques and procedures for developing grounded theory* (2nd ed.). Thousand Oaks, CA: Sage.

Index

For Product Safety Concerns and Information please contact our EU
representative GPSR@taylorandfrancis.com
Taylor & Francis Verlag GmbH, Kaufingerstraße 24, 80331 München, Germany

www.ingramcontent.com/pod-product-compliance
Ingram Content Group UK Ltd.
Pitfield, Milton Keynes, MK11 3LW, UK
UKHW050059200926
475702UK00019B/2925
* 9 7 8 1 1 3 8 0 6 0 4 4 9 *